STREET SMARTS

Linking Professional
Conduct with
Shareholder Value
in the
Securities Industry

■

ROY C. SMITH AND INGO WALTER

■

Harvard Business School Press / Boston, Massachusetts

Library of Congress Cataloging-in-Publication Data

Smith, Roy C., 1938-
Street smarts : linking professional conduct with shareholder value in the securities
industry / Roy C. Smith and Ingo Walter.
p. cm.
Includes bibliographical references and index.
ISBN 0-87584-653-X (alk. paper)
1. Securities industry—United States. I. Walter, Ingo. II. Title.
HG4910.S564 1997
332.63'2--dc21   96-48383
CIP

Contents

∎

Preface   vii

Acknowledgments   xv

1   A Walk on the Dark Side   1

2   Regulation, Competition, and Market Conduct   29

3   Caveat Emptor and the Retail Investor   59

4   Playing with the Big Boys—Wholesale Transactions   102

5   Market Rigging   121

6   Trading on the Inside   149

7   Conflicts of Interest   169

8   Kickbacks, Payoffs, and Bribes   194

9   Financial Secrecy and Money Laundering   223

10   Whistleblowing   255

11   Zookeeping   284

Notes   319

Index   335

About the Authors   351

133399

Preface

■

Probably no industry in the world has changed as much over the past twenty years as the financial-services industry. During this relatively short period, financial markets have expanded, globalized, integrated, disintermediated, and innovated at a breathtaking pace. These changes have forced strategic reorganizations, acquisitions, alliances, reengineering, and refocusing to a degree never before experienced. Profits have soared and crashed with a volatility unknown in the staid and plodding world of finance only a generation ago. Rivalry among firms and types of firms has reached all-time highs as commissions, fees, and special privileges have been competed and deregulated away. The new market conditions have insured that only the fittest will survive. But they have also given rise to a darker side, conditions under which some firms and individuals have escaped the bounds of control and appropriate conduct traditionally set by government officials and regulators as well as by the well-intentioned efforts of their own senior management.

Enormous volumes of financial transactions occur daily—foreign exchange trading, for example, currently runs at well over $1.5 trillion a *day*—sloshing money at great speed from place to place, and from instrument to instrument, introducing a sense of instability to markets everywhere. World stock markets, bond markets, and markets in financial futures, options, and other derivatives combine to generate volumes measured in the tens of trillions of dollars annually. Financial products have expanded exponentially in number and complexity to meet the demands of issuers and investors from all over the world. Newly energized pension funds, for example, are seeking globally diversified portfolios of investments that outperform local markets in both returns and exposure to risk. And these pension funds are increasingly looking for investments not only in traditionally accepted markets like the United States and Europe, but in emerging markets as well. The juxtaposition of new clients, products, and geographic arenas has created a complex, globally interconnected, but unevenly regulated financial marketplace in which individual financial firms must compete effectively or die.

Market forces and the people who interact with them now seem to rule the global financial economy, and the energy they release is phenomenal. Some critics think the conditions are potentially dangerous, and have talked increasingly about a "fear of finance." Any such dangers are at their greatest when financial power falls into the hands of rogue operators, whether individuals or entire firms.

An Industrial Revolution

A business that thirty years ago was the domain of grey, middle-aged, cautious, local, and relationship-oriented bankers has been mutated by expanding horizons, vast transaction volumes, and unprecedented opportunities for profits (and losses) into one in which only extremely bright, opportunistic, and aggressive young risk takers need apply. These people know that they will be required to perform, first and foremost by making money for their firms—if not for their clients—if they are to have any sort of future at all.

The new breed of high-performance bankers knows that the business today is much tougher than it was before. Competition is totally fierce. Your new idea will probably be copied and discounted before the week is out. Others are standing by to profit from your mistakes and do their best to lure you into making them. Advancing technology encourages ever newer things to be tried, and places a growing premium on being up to date and avoiding obsolescence. Clients are relatively easy to get to, but they have less and less loyalty to their traditional bankers. They have been taught by experience to shop around for the best deal, and that's exactly what they do.

While economists shake their heads in wonder how so many smart people think they can continually make abnormally high returns in near-perfect markets—apparently ignoring the laws of competition—smart people using smart technologies very often do find anomalies and arbitrage opportunities. Product innovation and penetration of new markets explain some of this success. But there has also been a visible shift to trading activities in an effort to find profits that can replace earnings lost to shrinking commissions, narrowing spreads, and client promiscuity. And increased volatility created marvelous trading opportunities in the 1980s and early 1990s, often thanks to government policies, even though the growing horde of competent players flattened out the basic sources of earnings and large trading spreads.

Trading conditions and shifting volatility patterns in some areas have forced firms to make larger and riskier bets with their own money. Market makers can no longer afford to be fully hedged, so they have to rely increasingly on their ability to "read" the market. Those betting heavily and making mistakes can find themselves suddenly wiped out. Those who are too cautious can be eaten up by overhead costs, a malevolent profit killer covering technology, risk management and compliance systems, and other defensive outlays that don't contribute directly to revenues.

Hot new areas like mortgage-backed securities, European equities, Chinese privatizations, and emerging-market mutual funds constantly appear and set off a competitive chase. Firms have to be in these businesses when the spreads are wide and money is being made; such bonanzas usually don't last more than a year or two before severe profit erosion begins to occur. Then the firm finds itself carrying the cost of newly hired specialists and the requisite support systems without the necessary revenues. In such situations, securities firms may be forced to lay off large numbers of personnel, sometimes as much as 15 or 20 percent of the professional work force, often concentrating on older, more experienced people who possess much of the firm's vital institutional memory. Perhaps predictably, after a series of major layoffs, firms repeat the mistakes of the past. Memories are short in times of rapid turnover. "Who remembers the last time this happened?" Hardly anyone. "Anyway, things are different now. . . ."

Falling Standards

A quick flip through today's newspapers is likely to lead even the most ardent advocates of free markets to acknowledge the public perception that professional standards in the banking and securities industry have eroded considerably over the past decade or so. This perception, however, may not in fact be true. The securities industry was plagued by notoriously low standards in the 1920s. In the 1950s and 1960s there were many transactions that might well have run afoul of today's insider-trading laws or notions of fiduciary conduct. By the end of the 1980s, the securities business had been through a period of intense scrutiny and prosecution, and the result was an industry operating under much higher worldwide standards of disclosure, customer protection, and fair trading practices than at any other time in history. In reality, the standards were rising at the same time as the competition was becoming more intense, and it was harder and harder to make a buck the old-fashioned way (by trading in markets with lower standards and larger spreads). As the markets were becoming more efficient, many firms stuck their necks out a bit further and took more risk. Among the risks they took was to focus more on incentive compensation in return for delivered profits, and sometimes to tolerate profits from transactions that might be questionable, or worse.

But in the early 1990s, following an array of financial scandals, the public perception of the securities industry was near its low again. Professional standards, which incorporate the industry's reputation for integrity, service quality, and expertise, had been seriously tarnished by criminal proceedings, regulatory complaints, customer litigation, and all the publicity that attended them. Trust and confidence in the banking and securities industry may have once again reached levels not seen since the "orgy of corporate larceny" of the 1920s. No industry can thrive and prosper for long with such a reputation. Public distrust and increased scrutiny and regulation produce a deadening brew of more competition, greater risks, more litigation, and increased costs of compliance. In such circumstances investors may very well shift to new, alternative markets that are able to sustain higher levels of efficiency, stability, transparency, and honest dealing. And if the industry doesn't clean up its own act, others will take on that job, too.

One of the great challenges to the banking and securities industry is the restoration of its reputation for high professional standards of conduct while coping with the sea changes that have engulfed its underlying economic base over the past twenty years. Surely such a challenge is formidable. But unless it is effectively met, the industry as we know it today may, before too long, be overtaken by new players or by electronic-delivery capabilities that are only just beginning to take hold.

In this book we try to offer some advice to those struggling with the problem of raising the professional standards of market conduct. Rather than preaching a gospel of how things ought to be, we suggest ways to think through the issues, define what needs to be done, and teach others to understand and live with new, higher, and better-communicated norms of professional conduct. The risks of failing to reset and maintain these norms at an acceptable level can have massive adverse effects on the value and the survivability both of individual firms and of the industry as a whole. After all, we teach students of corporate finance to assess firms by estimating the long-term risk-adjusted expected value of their business franchises. Properly done, such a calculation will account for the business risks that each firm faces. In the banking and securities industry today, business risks are indeed considerable. Perhaps because of the ability of the market, regulators, and courts to impose severe penalties for misconduct, these risks are arguably greater than ever before. Maximizing the long-term franchise value of firms in the banking and securities industry therefore presupposes substantial effort to minimize the risks and penalties associated with individual and corporate misconduct.

The securities industry has always prided itself on its "street smarts," its intuitive alertness, native cunning, opportunism, and risk awareness. No one survives very long without street smarts, many experienced players believe. To be street smart today, however, means something different than what it has meant before. It means being aware of the dangers to the firm from poorly managed, highly incentivized risk takers who see themselves as the all-important offensive players on a team that needs no defense. Street-smart executives know better and try to act accordingly. The issue is setting and maintaining "street values" that affect the way that business is conducted. In today's legal and regulatory environment, these values are essential to the preservation of shareholder value in street firms, whether these are owned by the public or by their principal managers.

Our experience in communicating this message has not always been encouraging. Even as senior managers and regulators in the banking and securities industries fear customer and public perceptions of declining standards—and often say they intend to do something about it—little of real consequence seems to happen. All too few "walk the talk." A firm gets into trouble. There is a great flurry of activity and expression of concern, maybe a couple of seminars on ethics. Then it's business as usual. There is a great deal of denial.

> "It doesn't happen here. We have clear policies of putting the client's interests first, and our people know what's expected of them."

> "Those were just mistakes by people no longer representing the firm. They do not reflect our culture at all."

> "We don't do anything other firms don't do. It's a competitive market out there, and we've got to go with the flow. The regulators have got to understand this."

"Our outside board members have been very vocal about this problem and have insisted that we formalize our principles of conduct. We have done so and have circulated them widely. Our employees know that the top people around here really care."

To be effective, our approach requires that we first get past these kinds of thoughts. It *does* happen here. It happens everywhere. Just look at the (hardly comprehensive) record of charges, accusations, and penalties recounted in our first chapter. And when it does happen, the consequences can be truly devastating, way beyond what top management might have expected.

Often the mistakes *do* reflect the culture of the firm. Top management's tolerance (however distantly or implicitly) of low standards of conduct will almost certainly become a self-fulfilling prophecy, sometimes at great cost to the firm and its shareholders. Little is more enduring in a firm's culture than its own standards of behavior. Over the years, those with cultures that reflect high standards develop professional practices that help business and command client respect—a reputation that can be lost all too quickly if practices turn shoddy.

Doing what others do is *not* enough. Going with the flow promises only a trip over the falls. Firms have to set their own courses and recognize that without meaningful effort and often substantial expense, little of value will result. Measures intended to achieve this goal are almost always controversial and subject management to considerable criticism and internal revolt. But the task of management is to do just this sort of thing from time to time—to raise professional standards, recalibrate the incentives, and reduce exposure to the potential consequences of inappropriate conduct. Naturally, management can't get everything right, but firms that try seem to do much better over the years than those that just go with the flow. But trying means more than lip service.

Setting and maintaining standards is not something that should be left to random development. Standards of conduct need to be shaped, taught, and upheld over the long haul. Top management needs to be committed and consistent, and it must resist returning to business as usual once the heat's off. Developing such cultures is indeed expensive (in terms of business forgone and the cost of an internal infrastructure that is often resisted by the troops), but we think such efforts are invaluable investments in problem anticipation and effective damage control, ones that will help assure higher net, risk-adjusted returns for the future.

What This Book Is About

We believe that a firm seeking to enhance its standards of conduct in this industry needs to consider the kind of client relationships it wants (and doesn't want); the changing nature of the fiduciary duties of bankers, brokers, and dealers; the nature of self-regulation; the effect of competitive pressures, stressful environments, and unbalanced compensation systems; and the necessity of communicating the right messages by regular instruction and daily example. Few managers find time in their busy and stressful days to discuss such matters or to work out firmwide positions. But those at the great firms do.

Most of this book focuses on thinking through problems and issues that affect professional standards in this industry. There is a methodology that we try to apply routinely in addressing them, and we believe that using our approach makes the problems easier to analyze and address. Perhaps most important, managers will also learn how to avoid mistakes involving standards that get set but are ultimately ignored with disastrous results. If we succeed in getting this message across, that alone will be worth the effort.

New York   Roy C. Smith
April 1997   Ingo Walter

Acknowledgments

■

Writing this book took well over two years, during which time we were involved in teaching a course at the Stern School entitled Markets, Ethics, and Law. The idea came from observing the severe punishment the markets and the legal system extracted from otherwise respectable and capable individuals and firms active in our financial markets that deviated from accepted professional norms. From a shareholder perspective, it seemed to us, good conduct is good business in this very sensitive industry and is a virtual requirement for achieving and maintaining high shareholder value. As we finished the manuscript, we sent it out for comment by those on the firing line. We benefited from many suggestions and criticisms. Among those who supplied us with detailed and insightful critiques of the entire book or specific sections were Larry Bear, David Bodner, Rob Brokaw, Bruce Buchanan, Rod Chamberlain, Bob Friedman, Bill Gruver, Ken Marshall, Geoff Miller, Bill Nighgreen, Michael Patterson, Dick Scribner, and Hans Vontobel. Patrizia Porrini and Ann Rusolo were invaluable in conducting some of the background research and preparing the manuscript for publication. In the end, of course, we alone are responsible for the results.

A Walk
on the
Dark Side

■

Over the last twenty years or so, the worldwide securities industry has been totally transformed. It has changed perhaps more than any other industry during this comparatively short period as a result of huge doses of deregulation, improved technology, and powerful new global market linkages. In combination, these have caused transaction volumes and price levels to soar, and continue to soar for nearly two decades.

At first, fortunes were made by those with the new products and ideas. But soon, competitors offered the same thing for less and pressures on margins increased. So did the pressures on clients to shop around more actively for the best financial ideas and the lowest prices. The pendulum began to swing the other way, to where the bulk of the advantages in financial services went to their users, not their suppliers. To keep up, firms had to be tougher and more competitive than ever. They had to become smarter, quicker, and more aggressive in pursuing every possible opportunity. On the one hand, their clients wanted better and cheaper services. On the other hand, they couldn't think only about the clients, who were nowhere near as loyal to them as they had been. There was a lot of money to be made in the new, much invigorated markets but most of it now would be from trading with clients, not from advising them. Increasingly the firms had to function more as risk-taking counterparties than as agents. And counterparties first and foremost had to look after themselves.

Many observers wonder now if the industry has become too tough, too competitive. They look at the insider-trading scandals of the eighties, when a few dozen individuals ignored the rules and got themselves into serious trouble. Most were punished, and some served time in jail. This period was bad enough, but, observers wonder, has it got worse in the nineties? Firms too often have appeared to squeeze or manipulate their own clients just to complete a trade. Or failed to supervise overly aggressive employees who were offered disproportionate incentives to *perform,* sometimes even at the expense of the firm itself. There have been many such scandals since 1990 involving major, industry-leading firms such as Bankers Trust, Baring Brothers, Deutsche Morgan Grenfell, Goldman Sachs, Prudential Securities, and Salomon Brothers, among others, which have paid dearly for serious failings of professional conduct while in the hot pursuit of profitable business. But this time around, the ones to suffer most have been the owners of the firms involved who, because of uncontrolled "rogue" activity, have paid *billions* of dollars in damages, settlements, fines, and losses of market value and professional reputation.

Because of such developments—heavily reported in the media—many representatives of corporate America worry about the changes they see in the ways that Wall Street firms do business. From their perspective, securities firms have become perhaps too aggressive, more interested in their own results than in those of their clients. As broker-dealers and market-makers, firms make every effort to get their clients to trade with them—at their prices—whether the trade is good for them or not. As "merchant bankers" and principal investors, they are increasingly showing up as tough-talking bruisers across the table.[1] As counterparties in swaps and other longer-term contracts, they are arguably less than ideal business partners— will they be there at the end of the contract period, or try to weasel out of their obligations? Some well-known houses have gone under, or nearly so, or have been forced to be sold because they worked too close to the edge.

Many Wall Streeters, on the other hand, argue that most of the changes that have pushed some of them to competitive excess have been forced upon them by the incredible economic, regulatory, and technological changes that have enveloped the industry. Now the focus is heavily on trading. Most of the major wholesale investment banks earn over half of their net revenues (after interest) from daily trading activities, and so their profits are increasingly exposed to the volatility of the market. This emphasis on trading has made the industry extremely capital intensive, and major firms have had to grow enormously in size to remain competitive. Increasingly, transactions have become more dependent on price rather than on relationships with clients. These changes have been felt throughout the firms, and they have profoundly altered the way business is done.

Money flows have increased enormously around the world. For those with the capital, the know-how, and the stomach for significant position risks, the profit opportunities are fantastic. Goldman Sachs astonished the financial world in 1993 with a pretax profit of $2.7 billion on capital of less than $5 billion. As the markets become more efficient and more transparent, however, they react more quickly and can be dangerous for those trying to function as market makers. There are fewer easy arbitrages and many more players to trade them away when they do appear. Clients, too, have become much tougher to deal with. They want service, service, and more service. Relationships have to be earned every day. And when it comes time to do a deal, clients always seem to have some other firm ready to do it at a better price. Sometimes *much* better. Profit margins in the bread-and-butter underwriting, brokerage, and trading businesses are being eaten away by this intense competition. Returns on equity capital, much of it now provided by investors in public markets, have also been declining.

To counter the profit erosion, firms have to be quicker, braver, and more innovative than the other guy. Large firms have to be market makers in everything—stocks, bonds, companies for sale, real estate, commodities, foreign exchange, and emerging-market securities. These firms have had to set up trading and sales operations all over the world. They have to use their capital to take on securities positions their clients no longer want, and to seize quickly changing market opportunities. They have to make the investments necessary to have good products and research and to execute deals and transactions effectively. They invest their own money in high-risk private deals and proprietary trading. To do all of this, they have to have highly talented people and pay them for the results they produce. These developments have, not surprisingly, driven many smaller firms into mergers or into niche markets.

With profits increasingly dependent on market conditions, they are subject to much greater risk than before. In 1990, reflecting dreadful conditions in the bond and stock markets, Wall Street firms (as a group) lost money for the first time since the Great Depression. Most firms reacted by cutting back people and budgets quickly and ruthlessly. Layoffs of 10 percent of a firm's total staff were not remarkable. During the following three years, however, conditions were much better (with 1993 a record year for the industry). Firms quickly reversed course and began hiring again. This time the hiring resembled a binge, as firms rushed into new markets and activities to keep up with their competitors. But 1994 was another bad year, and drastic layoffs were again the order of the day. It was getting especially difficult to manage securities firms. Profits were vital to employee retention and loyalty, but profits were themselves highly variable. The greater the turnover, and accompanying employee cynicism, the harder it was to set and maintain high professional standards, especially when those very standards might get in the way of profitable trades. The only mitigating factor was that a few areas of large profits, though perhaps ephemeral, could compensate for thin profits elsewhere in the firm. The balance between high standards and professional reputation and the pursuit of profitable opportunities in competitive markets—always difficult to maintain—was especially so in the turbulent early years of the 1990s.

Maintaining the balance between profits and professional standards has been further complicated by shifts in regulatory practices and legal constraints that govern and punish inappropriate behavior. Dangers loom not only from fines and penalties imposed by regulators, but also from settlements and penalties from civil litigation and criminal charges. Especially ominous is the fact that no securities firm subjected to a criminal indictment in the United States has survived for very long afterwards. Firms have therefore developed risk-control systems to monitor and manage both the activities of employees and the firm's exposure on its positions. Such systems are expensive, however, and, being dependent on human beings to operate them, don't always work well. They may lag behind product developments or have inadequate financial or human resources. Funding these risk-control systems is always problematic because they produce no revenues and no profits in a world where little else counts. But without good systems supporting their riskier and more complex activities, the firms may be risking their own lives as never before.

Legacies of the 1980s

In the 1980s Michael Milken, Ivan Boesky, Dennis Levine, Martin Siegel, Robert Freeman, and various other Wall Streeters who were less senior and less well known went to jail, generally for illegal activities related to insider trading and market manipulation. One could say they took calculated risks based on their perception that such illegalities were hard to define, detect, or prove in court. In any case, the chance of going to jail appeared to be minimal. No one from a prominent Wall Street firm had been to jail for crimes committed on the street since Richard Whitney— head of Richard Whitney & Co., a principal broker to J.P. Morgan & Co. and acting president of the New York Stock Exchange—went to Sing-Sing Prison in 1938 for embezzlement. The economic incentives to cheat and abuse the system were heavily weighted in the 1980s, some may have thought, in favor of the cheaters and abusers.

The general perception in Wall Street and other financial centers was that in increasingly competitive markets, only the aggressive and the risk takers would survive. Being aggressive meant challenging the ambiguities and imperfections of the system whenever one could, and being willing to stick one's neck out and occasionally get into trouble with the regulators. Nothing ventured, nothing gained, even when it meant sailing pretty close to the wind. And to a few of the most successful, the industry's rules and regulations applied only to the "little people."

M&A Jungle of Opportunity . . .

In the 1980s, the most publicized domain of Wall Street activity was mergers and acquisitions, and the various forms of deals and trading opportunities they generated. The decade's burst of merger activity was one of five such booms in the twentieth century. Many of the deals were hostile takeover efforts resisted by both the management and employees of well-known corporations. Many of these deals also involved leveraged-buyout transactions in which the acquiring company would borrow as much as 90 percent of the purchase price, thereby exposing those with a long-term interest in the corporation to a substantial risk of bankruptcy. Some of these transactions were financed with "junk bonds," high-yield corporate bonds of exceptionally low credit standing.

Michael Milken, a Wharton MBA who had joined Drexel Burnham Lambert in 1970, was the genius behind the development of the junk-bond market. Drexel's strategy was to use a dominant position in this market to pull itself into other investment-banking activities, and the firm hired merger star Martin Siegel from Kidder Peabody to put Drexel on the M&A map. Most merger transactions attracted "arbitrageurs," or traders who acquired large holdings in the shares of a takeover target and voted them in favor of a merger or sale, hostile or otherwise, in order to make a short-term trading profit. Many arbitrageurs were individuals like Ivan Boesky, who ran a small firm of his own and managed some money for others. But Goldman Sachs, Morgan Stanley, Bear Stearns, Kidder Peabody, and many other major houses were also active in arbitrage trading.

Most members of the financial community (and many business executives) believed that the aggressive roles played by investment bankers, commercial lenders, takeover lawyers, arbitrageurs, and junk-bond experts were appropriate and healthy. This competitive environment subjected all participants to the discipline of market forces. But many representatives of the besieged and often underperforming companies, as well as sympathizers in the media and in state and national politics, saw the 1980s as a time of lawlessness and greed that was ruining American industry, vastly overrewarding financial deal makers, and corrupting the values of the young in the process.

. . . and Its "Den of Thieves"

Before long these critics were able to point to something concrete. Flagrant violations of the securities laws began to surface. These violations involved some of the industry's most important arbitrage traders and junk-bond specialists, several of whom colluded with each other, supremely confident that no one from the regulatory world could catch up with them.

They may have been right. The regulators were understaffed, underpaid, and nowhere near as sophisticated about financial market activities as the offenders. During the 1980s, regulators observed countless cases where stock prices of target companies rose before bids were actually announced. But apart from some well-known peripheral court cases brought against small-fry financial analysts, journalists, and printers (many of which did not survive appeal), regulators were not very successful at tracking down big time insider traders.

The leading players were not caught until an informer stepped in to tell about the case of Dennis Levine, a Drexel Burnham executive who had engaged in insider trading for twelve years through a Swiss bank in the Bahamas. Levine had organized a ring of low-level Wall Street friends to help collect information, which he then furnished to arbitrageur Ivan Boesky. Following his arrest, and under pressure from the federal government, Levine quickly gave them the yuppies and their first big catch, Boesky himself. To soften his own sentence, Boesky gave evidence against Drexel Burnham, Michael Milken, and some of the latter's associates. Boesky also gave them Martin Siegel, the emerging superstar who had headed mergers and acquisitions at Kidder Peabody before decamping for Drexel Burnham in 1986. Siegel had provided inside information to Boesky in exchange for suitcases stuffed with cash. Siegel implicated Robert Freeman of Goldman Sachs, a Columbia MBA, and two former colleagues at Kidder Peabody, all of whom were arrested publicly and with great fanfare by Rudolf Giuliani, the U.S. Attorney for the Southern District of New

York, who later became mayor of New York City. The chain reaction continued, finally involving dozens of other individuals, most of whom admitted charges against them rather than face trial. All were severely punished with jail terms, fines, or suspension from the industry.

James Stewart's best-selling book *Den of Thieves* recounts these among more than a dozen cases of criminal activity by financial professionals. Stewart concludes this graphic and sweeping book:

> Financial markets have shown remarkable resilience and an ability to curb their own excesses. Yet they are surprisingly vulnerable to corruption from within. If nothing else, the scandals of the 1980s underscore the importance of the securities laws and their vigorous enforcement. The Wall Street criminals were consummate evaluators of risk, and the equation as they saw it suggested little likelihood of getting caught.[2]

The equation was rewritten, however, after Drexel Burnham pleaded guilty to several criminal violations and was fined $630 million, triggering its subsequent bankruptcy and liquidation in 1990. Michael Milken pleaded guilty to six offenses (out of the ninety-eight on which he had been indicted) after a long, vigorous, and expensive effort to escape conviction. He paid over $1 billion in fines and legal settlements, and in 1990 was sentenced to ten years in jail, which was later reduced to three years because of his subsequent cooperation with the government. Boesky paid over $100 million and spent two years in jail. Levine paid $12 million and served two years. Siegel, who had cooperated extensively with the government, was fined $1 million and required to disgorge illegal profits, but sentenced to only two months in prison. Freeman, who did not cooperate with the government at all, was also fined $1 million and served four months. Many others received similar punishments.

This drama provides some new and useful lessons:

- *Insider trading, stock parking, market manipulation, and other violations of securities laws* really are *illegal.*

  For years, partly because of the difficulty in detecting offenses and the absence of case law to support prosecution efforts, not many cases were brought to trial. Flagrant cases involving corporate insiders (or related peripheral players) acting on price-sensitive information were the exception. The more sophisticated forms of insider trading were much more complex, and there was often an open question whether these were actually illegal at all under strict interpretations of the rules. Arbitrage and other trading practices routinely involved the exchange of information on the basis of cryptic expressions, grunts, gestures, and body language. No one ever got in trouble, and a small number of well-connected people made fortunes. "Everybody did it," some Wall Streeters would say, "so it must be OK. They can't arrest everyone." But Giuliani appeared to be prepared to do so.

- *Those involved in illegal acts quickly realized that, once targeted by the authorities, a successful defense is extremely difficult and expensive.*

  One could not walk away unharmed, even if technically innocent of the charges. Giuliani's prosecutors, taking advantage of public sentiment, were patient, ruthless, and well equipped with legal tools and levers (such as the RICO antiracketeering laws) to break down their suspects. They had all the records and documents they needed from employers, and relentlessly encouraged frightened co-workers and others to testify against their targets. Two of the Kidder Peabody men implicated by Siegel were publicly arrested and charged with insider trading. Months later, however, the charges were dropped. Both were fired by Kidder and nearly bankrupted by their legal costs. One retired. The other (much younger) man, a former Rhodes Scholar, had a very tough time finding suitable new employment. People did not want to be anywhere near the prosecutors' list of suspects, even if they were innocent.

- *One cannot engage in illegal securities activities by oneself. Technically, the process requires two or more people to pass along information; to enter and conceal brokerage orders; or to park securities, manipulate markets, or otherwise trade illegally.*

  However difficult it may have been for the regulators to detect illegal trading on their own, the important lesson was that once someone in the know was apprehended (through whatever investigative process, fluke, or otherwise), the imminent threat of jail time was generally enough to eliminate any resistance to interrogation. In order to obtain a reduced sentence, the person apprehended would almost certainly inform on the others. The most likely source of detection was therefore one's own colleagues or partners in crime.

- *The penalties for securities-law violations have risen. In order to discourage misconduct, these penalties now routinely include time in jail.*

  The courts, perhaps reflecting public sympathies, came down hard on such offenses, and sentencing guidelines were tightened.

The crimes themselves may in the past have seemed victimless to some, but the balance was tipped by public resentment of greedy Wall Street wheeler-dealers who were immorally exploiting their advantages in intelligence, education, and connections.

- *Employers and investors learned that serious misbehavior by the officers of a financial firm represents a major risk to its survival.*
  Firms undertook efforts to control information, to ensure compliance with regulations, and to restrict both their own transactions and those of their employees that might involve inside information. These efforts were expensive, however, and they added to overhead at a time when the industry could ill afford it. As noted, the year after the insider-trading scandals broke, 1990, was the worst year for profits on Wall Street since the 1930s.

Things Are Different Now, or Are They?

Insider trading and related offenses more or less disappeared by the end of 1989, when the merger boom subsided. Much of the merger activity then moved to Europe. Activity in the United States recovered in the mid-1990s, however, exceeding the peak levels of the 1980s. But absent now were the hostile LBOs financed by junk bonds. The market had been substantially cleaned up by the vigorous prosecutions and severe penalties of the 1980s.

The insider trading and other cases of the previous decade generally involved so-called rogue financiers, who had managed to get away with significant wrongdoing until they were caught. (Rogues are individuals working within a firm who, without the firm's knowledge or approval, conduct unauthorized or illegal transactions.) Of the many cases brought against rogues, only one involved charges against a major securities firm or bank, Drexel Burnham—where Milken's activities permeated the entire firm. After the blizzard of new regulations and enforcement efforts during the 1980s, firms began to get the upper hand and brought insider trading and related activities under control. To do this, many Wall Street firms eliminated or sharply curtailed their risk-arbitrage businesses, imposed strict internal-trading restrictions, and beefed up their compliance and surveillance programs.

The 1990s began, however, with the Salomon Brothers Treasury-bond auction scandal (see Chapter 5). Serious violations of law and appropriate professional conduct had surfaced in the firm's supposedly well-managed core business, and top managers did nothing about it. Paul Mozer, the individual involved in the misconduct, was in a senior position at the firm; he had influence over the internal controls of his department as well as being responsible for its revenue generation. Mozer submitted billions of dollars of winning bids for Treasury notes at extremely aggressive prices without attracting questions from senior managers as to how he intended to make money from such large and risky positions. (This strategy of taking such large risks to make small amounts of money would hardly be one that others would likely approve.) Any kind of close attention to Mozer's activities might have revealed his passionate and reckless desire to teach the Treasury a lesson about the power of Salomon Brothers and its superior knowledge of the market. Here was a case not just of a rogue trader, but of a senior investment banker—a "Master of the Universe"—run amok in a system without adequate internal controls. But what really makes the case unique is that the firm, when it learned of Mozer's misconduct after the fact, neither reported the infractions nor made any effort to restrain or control him. It did not even attempt to understand why he had done what he did. Instead, the firm gave tacit consent to illegal practices simply in order to maintain its ferocious reputation and to flaunt its power in the marketplace.

Salomon's board of directors did not, of course, directly consent to this sort of behavior. When fully apprised of the facts, the board thoroughly investigated the firm's activities, cooperated with authorities, and took steps to prevent such offenses from recurring. Had the board, led by its new chairman, investor Warren Buffett, not persuaded U.S. attorneys that it was prepared to take Draconian steps to make things right, it seems highly likely that the firm would have been indicted and followed Drexel to investment banking's burial ground. The involvement of Buffett in the management of Salomon had many long-lasting effects on the firm. He appointed new management that, though much criticized, is still in place. He attempted to influence the ethical practices and trading policies of the firm. And he unsuccessfully sought a radical change in the firm's compensation practices. While highly respected by the investment community for his business savvy and common sense, Buffett is nonetheless seen as being out of his depth in attempting to restore the firm's former glory by imposing "outsider" ways. Buffett may have thought so, too. In late 1995 he exercised his option to redeem part of his convertible preferred stock.

Rogues, Rogues, and More Rogues

In the first few years of the 1990s several important securities firms failed, were forced into mergers, or otherwise suffered substantial losses and embarrassments due to the rogue actions of employees and ineffective or acquiescent management.

Trading Rogues

Kidder Peabody. A distinguished American investment bank with roots going back to 1865, Kidder Peabody was embarrassed by having to restate its earnings for 1993, removing $130 million of trading profits that were never earned. Kidder's head government trader, Joseph Jett, was fired. A Harvard Business School graduate and star of the firm who had received a $9 million bonus the year before, Jett was accused of having exploited a loophole in Kidder's accounting system to create an illusion of profits from stripped treasury securities, when the firm was actually accumulating about $350 million of losses. He was fired and sued by the firm for misrepresenting trades in billions of dollars of government bonds. Unaccountably, due to computer misprogramming, Kidder counted as profits trades that were in fact only "wash" transactions. Jett denied all of the claims against him, saying that Kidder had made him a scapegoat. Criminal charges were never filed, although the SEC has been considering an administrative complaint. In November 1996 Jett won an arbitration decision allowing him the right to reclaim $5.3 million in bonuses and other pay that had been frozen by the firm.

Kidder's management, knowing of the huge volume of bonds involved, were unable to explain why they had not investigated the underlying economics behind such a major commitment of the firm's capital and risk-bearing capacity. Nor did they discover the irregularity. Larger problems in the mortgage-backed securities market, which the firm had attempted to dominate through exceedingly aggressive trading under declining market conditions, subsequently emerged and forced Kidder Peabody to report large real losses. These problems resulted from an ambitious business plan to build market share by offering generous incentives for success, but risking all of the firm's capital in the process.

These losses and the apparent inability to control the firm caused great embarrassment and loss of confidence in Kidder's parent firm, the General

Electric Company. Soon after the disclosure of the Jett trades, GE's common stock lost several billion dollars of market value. Unwilling to endure any longer the difficulties that Kidder had imposed on the company since its acquisition in 1986 (for example, the effects of Marty Siegel's shenanigans at Kidder during the 1980s), GE decided to sell the firm. Kidder was merged into Paine Webber in January 1995, with GE receiving a 25 percent interest in Paine Webber.

Baring Brothers. Soon after the debacle at Kidder Peabody, the elegant and aristocratic British merchant bank of Baring Brothers, the bank that financed Thomas Jefferson's Louisiana Purchase, found itself horribly overexposed and unhedged in the Japanese equities market. Despite the Bank of England's effort to organize a rescue, Baring failed in February 1995 and was sold to a Dutch financial conglomerate, Internationale Nederlanden Groep (ING), for the derisive sum of £1. The 233-year-old firm had lost control of a rogue trader in its small Singapore office. The trader, Nicholas Leeson, had single-handedly cost the firm nearly £1 billion.

Leeson had joined Baring's Singapore office in 1992. Soon thereafter, he set up a hidden "error" account that he managed. Modestly at first, then more boldly, Leeson arranged supposedly risk-free trades for the firm's own book through the hidden account. The result was an apparently sweet flow of profits for Baring that were financed entirely by losses in the hidden account. By the end of 1994, the cumulative hidden losses were £200 million. Then Leeson got ambitious. He decided to place a large directional bet that the Japanese stock market would rise and that, correspondingly, Japanese bond prices and the yen would fall. In early January 1995 he bought futures on the Nikkei stock market index and shorted government bond futures. But on 17 January the strategy was shattered by the Kobe earthquake. Anticipating that the Japanese recession would worsen, stock prices plummeted. Anticipating that interest rates would fall, bond prices rose. Leeson's position was disastrous, but he bravely doubled his stake. The markets continued to go against him, however. By the end of February it was all over.

Leeson, who was responsible both for trading and for the activities of the back office in Singapore, had been fiddling accounts undetected for at least a year before the curtain came down. He was able to disguise transactions and misreport them to the head office. His unauthorized trading was difficult for that office to detect—even though Baring's positions had become enormous and were widely known to dominate the Singapore International Monetary Exchange (SIMEX) futures market on the Nikkei index. When ING ultimately stepped in to take over Baring's business, it immediately fired the firm's top twenty-three officers. The Dutch firm believed that these officers either had known about the situation and not done anything about it, or should have known about it but did not. Reports to and by the Bank of England and the British Treasury were extremely critical of management's poor control of Baring's operations, having ignored or otherwise failed to act despite numerous warnings of potential trouble as early as six months before the firm's failure.[3] It took ING only a year or so to stabilize the business and get the otherwise fine firm back on course.

Daiwa Bank. Daiwa Bank was the tenth largest commercial bank in Japan and the nineteenth largest bank in the world at the end of 1995, with 243 branches worldwide and assets of over $211 billion. Its principal activities included pension-trust management and small business loans. In 1956 it opened its New York office and in 1986 was one of the first foreign firms designated as a primary dealer in U.S. Treasury securities. The bank has developed a reputation as one of the most innovative and consistently successful participants in both the primary and secondary Treasury markets. (Daiwa Bank is not related to Daiwa Securities, one of Japan's Big Four securities firms.)

On 24 July 1995 Toshihide Iguchi, head of Daiwa Bank's Treasury-bond trading department in New York, sent a "letter of confession" to Akira Fujita, president of Daiwa Bank in Japan. In his letter, Iguchi outlined how over the previous eleven years he had accumulated and concealed an astonishing $1.1 billion in losses from trading U.S. Treasury bonds. "For the last 10 years, I have been alone in the darkness, shivering with fear," he wrote.[4]

In 1984, Iguchi was made responsible for setting up Daiwa's trading operation in Treasury securities. Since he was hired locally in the United States, he was not rotated to other positions, contrary to the usual practice with Japanese expatriates. He became very active in the markets, regularly trading up to $250 million at once, which was several times the volume of typical government trades. Over the years his total trades grew even bigger, often topping $1 billion a day. His trades were not all profitable, however, so he engaged in bigger and riskier ones in order to cover previous losses.

By 1988, those losses had ballooned to about $200 million. Over the next six years they would increase to over $1 billion.

As head of Daiwa's trading operation in New York, Iguchi had not only trading responsibilities, but also control (similar to Leeson) over much of the bookkeeping. Whenever he lost money on trades, he covered his losses by selling Treasury securities owned by the bank. He would then falsify documents to overstate Daiwa's securities deposits held by the Bank of New York. Because he never took more than a week's vacation at a time, he was never out of the office long enough for his scheme to be detected.

Prior to 1992 U.S. regulators did not perform periodic inspections of foreign banks. But after the scandal involving the Bank of Credit and Commerce International (BCCI), the Federal Reserve began tightening supervision of foreign banks' U.S. branches. After a few Daiwa inspections, regulators charged the bank with poor internal controls, complaining specifically about the dual responsibilities held by Iguchi. In response, Daiwa assured federal officials in 1993 that Iguchi was no longer in charge of both trading and settlement functions. In reality, not only did he retain responsibility for both functions, but he later admitted concealing a downtown New York trading room. He sent its traders to the bank's midtown offices and made the room look like a storage room to fool U.S. regulators making inspections.

Two weeks after receiving Iguchi's letter of confession, Daiwa officials informed Yoshimasa Nishimura, director of Japan's Ministry of Finance. U.S. officials were not notified, however, until six more weeks had passed. Daiwa admitted that it had told Iguchi to continue hiding his losses after his confession to give bank officials time to investigate the matter internally. Ministry of Finance officials claimed that the delay in informing U.S. regulators was merely an attempt to give the bank time to complete its internal investigation.

After being informed of the situation by Daiwa's New York office, U.S. regulators swung into action. Iguchi was almost immediately arrested at his home in New Jersey. He pleaded guilty to charges of fraud, money laundering, falsifying bank documents, embezzling $500,000 for personal use, and misappropriating $1.1 billion of bank funds. He then implicated senior managers in a coverup, which they denied. Daiwa's president and two top executives soon resigned, however, as the scandal unfolded to include Japanese government officials. Japanese investors then began unprecedented proceedings to sue Daiwa, accusing the bank of inadequate risk management.

Daiwa's license to conduct banking operations in the United States was withdrawn by the Federal Reserve. The bank was also assessed a fine of $340 million, a record. The Federal Reserve and various state banking agencies cited false record keeping and reporting, failure to notify regulatory officials as required by law, and deceptions by senior officers. In early 1996, Daiwa Bank announced the sale of its commercial bank branches and most of Daiwa Bank Trust to Sumitomo Bank for $3.37 billion. Daiwa Bank closed its remaining U.S. banking operations. In December 1996 a U.S. federal judge sentenced Iguchi to four years in prison and $2.7 million in fines. A year later, amid concerns about the management of Japanese banking activities in the United States, the Long-Term Credit Bank of Japan was fined $1 million in a similar but much smaller case.

The Daiwa case is similar to those of Salomon Brothers, Kidder Peabody, and Baring Brothers. Rogue trading occurred, but it should have been detected by independent internal controls and then stopped by responsible superiors. In addition, a variety of signals and revelations made top management aware of serious irregularities, but management did not correct or disclose them until it was too late. In each of these four cases the consequences for the firm were catastrophic.

Morgan Grenfell Asset Management. In September 1996 the Deutsche Bank, Germany's largest bank, which had acquired U.K. merchant bank Morgan Grenfell for nearly $1.5 billion in 1989, announced that it would reimburse one of Morgan Grenfell's investment trusts (a public mutual fund) for $280 million in losses inappropriately incurred by its fund manager, Peter Young, a high-strung Oxford graduate. The investment trust had specialized in risky, high-growth technology companies, but Young had evaded U.K. rules by accumulating large investments in untraded stocks that were hidden in Luxembourg holding companies, and whose values were misrepresented. In the end, Deutsche Bank paid out $600 million to make the trust whole, and Morgan Grenfell Asset Management paid about $330 million more in direct compensation to some 90,000 investors and was fined about $1.5 million by the British investment management regulators. In December 1996 the chief executive of Morgan Grenfell Asset Management and four senior colleagues were fired by Deutsche Bank for failing to control Young. When asked what he had learned from the episode, Rolf-Ernst Breuer, then head of Deutsche Bank's global securities activities, and subsequently CEO of the bank, said *"Disziplin!* What should be at the heart of a good business is discipline, not performance for its own sake."[5]

Broker Rogues

Broker rogues, like their dealer cousins, were on the rampage in the early 1990s. They misrepresented investments they were selling to customers and acted on behalf of unscrupulous characters engaged in all sorts of improper transactions.

Complaints of improper conduct by brokers are, of course, nothing new. When brokerage accounts are opened in the United States, customers agree to settle complaints against their brokers through a binding arbitration process run by the National Association of Securities Dealers (NASD), a process that some observers believe is weighted in favor of the brokers. Thousands of cases are processed each year, and millions of dollars are paid to plaintiffs. Many cases are appropriately resolved in the brokers' favor, however. At no time was the intention of the NASD arbitration process to protect customers from losing money invested in securities. The process exists only to protect customers against losses resulting from brokers' abusive and exploitive behavior.

Some cases, by virtue of their size and the damage allegedly done to innocent parties, have risen above the arbitration level to involve major lawsuits involving class actions for fraud and Securities Act violations.

Prudential Securities. When Robert C. Winters, the former chairman of the Prudential Insurance Company of America, the largest insurance organization in the United States, called 1993 a "very tough year," he could have been accused of understatement. In that year, its subsidiary, Prudential Securities, concluded a landmark settlement with the Securities and Exchange Commission: more than $1.6 billion in penalties and restitution, the admission of criminal wrongdoing, and three years' probation. The scandal involved the sale during the 1980s and 1990s of approximately $8 billion of limited partnerships in real estate and in oil and gas. Over 340,000 retail investors lost more than $1 billion in these partnerships, which were often sold with no concern for whether the investment was suitable for the customers. Prudential and its brokers shared up-front commissions and fees of 20 to 30 percent of the money raised by the partnerships, the marketing of which, the SEC said, involved outright lies and deception. The settlement, the industry's first major "product liability" case, was the largest ever. No other Wall Street scandal (including Drexel Burnham) had involved fines and penalties of even half as much.[6]

Prudential Insurance was forced to write off nearly $3 billion against its investment in Prudential Securities, which it had acquired in 1981. The targeting of inappropriate retail customers for sales of limited partnerships was held to result not just from the random action of willing and overeager brokers. Instead, it was deemed to be the product of sales practices tolerated and encouraged by the firm's senior management, contrary to clearly defined "know-your-customer" rules set by securities regulators.[7] George Ball (who had been president of E.F. Hutton before a fatal check-kiting scandal in 1985) was the chief executive of Prudential Securities from 1982 to 1991, when he and other senior managers were dismissed.

The Prudential Securities case was yet another failure of top management that produced disastrous consequences for the firm. In Prudential's case, the rot had spread to other areas of its business. In 1994 Prudential paid millions of dollars to settle lawsuits related to fraudulent valuations of real estate holdings of Prisa, Prudential's prestigious real estate investment fund for pension funds. And in February 1996 its insurance group announced that it was prepared to pay as much as $1 billion to settle allegations of abusive sales practices by its insurance agents. Besides the financial losses and a subsequent change of top management, Prudential's reputation as one of the nation's most solid and trusted financial institutions—"solid as the Rock of Gibraltar"—must have suffered immensely. How much we'll never know, because Prudential is a mutual company, owned by its policyholders, with no common stock traded in the market to signal the damage to the firm's reputation.

The Prudential Securities case prompted the SEC to look into the activities of other retail brokers selling limited partnership investments in the 1980s. The result of such scrutiny at Paine Webber, for example, resulted in the firm's agreement to pay a total of $330 million to settle charges of fraud arising from sales of limited partnerships over a six-year period.[8]

Bankers Trust. In the early 1990s Bankers Trust was a star among American banks. It had gained this reputation because of its successful transition from a fifth-ranking, New York retail bank into a powerful trading and wholesale finance operation with commendable margins and high risk-adjusted returns on assets. Under Charles Sanford, the banking industry's first trading executive to become a CEO, the bank announced and implemented ambitious plans for repositioning the bank in the investment banking industry and for specializing in risk-management services. In its heyday in mid-1991, Bankers Trust stock was trading at approximately twice book value. Frequently referred to as America's best-managed bank, it was a favorite of many banking-industry analysts.

By the end of 1994, Bankers Trust found itself in the midst of several highly visible lawsuits involving the sale of derivative securities to supposedly unsuspecting customers, including Procter & Gamble (P&G), which the bank allegedly had misled and subsequently fleeced by misvaluing the complex, custom-designed, structured derivative products it sold to them. In late 1993, P&G had accepted Bankers Trust proposals for two interest-rate swaps involving five-year Treasury notes and Deutsche Marks. By April 1994, after a substantial rise in U.S. interest rates, the swaps were in trouble. P&G took a $157 million pretax charge and fired its treasurer, who had been responsible for the swaps. Six months later, an angry P&G sued Bankers Trust for fraud and deceptive sales practices, subsequently seeking to have penalties applied under the federal Racketeer Influenced and Corrupt Organizations Act (RICO). Bankers Trust was soon embroiled in several such lawsuits filed by other clients who had also lost money on their swaps in the face of rising interest rates. The losses allegedly caused by such fraudulent trading practices by the bank amounted to about $500 million.

As part of the disclosure efforts undertaken in relation to the law suits, Bankers Trust discovered a number of compromising tape recordings of conversations involving its traders. On one such tape, a trader was recorded telling another that the real job of a derivatives trader was to "lure the clients into the calm, then really fuck them." Such tapes and others indicating an effort to mislead their clients on valuations raised an uproar.[9] The bank's stock dropped like a stone, losing more than $2 billion in market value. The stock's price was the same as the bank's book value in December 1994. Insiders reported that the bank was in major internal turmoil as it began the search for those responsible for the apparently predatory exploitation of the bank's customers. In a 1994 survey, Bankers Trust was ranked dead last among twenty-five investment banks in terms of client relationships, a substantial deterioration from only a few years before.[10]

After reporting a first-quarter loss of $157 million and a plan to slash 1,400 jobs to cut costs, Charles Sanford unexpectedly announced his retirement, as did several other senior executives. Frank Newman, former Deputy Secretary of the Treasury and ex-CFO of Bank of America, was appointed to replace Sanford, bypassing the bank's president and heir apparent, Eugene Shanks. Despite these moves, the high-flying bank of a year or two earlier had become, many believed, a takeover candidate.

Seeking to put the matter behind both himself and the bank, Newman negotiated a deal with P&G just days before the suit was scheduled to go to trial. The bank had resisted settling before on the grounds that the trading losses under the swap contract were not properly its responsibility. P&G was a large and sophisticated counterparty that should have been able to look out for itself. But the tapes of Bankers Trust's traders were sensational and colored the picture irreparably. Newman therefore settled. Bankers Trust would absorb approximately $150 million, about 80 percent of P&G's losses. The bank's costs in settling its suits would approach $300 million, plus the considerable damage to its reputation and stock price.[11]

Rogue Clients

Sometimes it is the customer, not the firm, who is the rogue. But this hardly immunizes brokers against contamination and being held responsible for customers' losses. After all, when losses are large, it is virtually certain that injured parties will sue others involved in the transactions who continue to have money.

The Maxwell Pension Funds. Robert Maxwell was a highly controversial figure in British financial circles when he drowned at sea in November 1991, presumably committing suicide to avoid the consequences of fraudulent behavior on an amazing scale. Maxwell, a Czech immigrant to Britain before World War II, was an entrepreneur who built up a large, highly leveraged media empire in the swashbuckling 1980s. During the recession of 1990–1991, his companies (part publicly owned, part private) fell on hard times. Maxwell intervened, shifting funds from company to company to keep them at least temporarily solvent. When his stock, used as collateral for bank loans, started to fall in value, he intervened in the market to buy it back. Running out of money, he turned to his companies' pension funds and withdrew huge sums without authorization. In the end, his time and credit ran out. The margin loans were called, ultimately with massive losses to the lending banks.

The extent of the fraud and the hopeless condition in which it left the companies and the pension funds were soon revealed. His two sons and some of his other business associates were arrested and tried, although at their first trial they were acquitted as mere dupes of the father. New trustees for the raided pension funds, which had lost approximately $600 million due to Maxwell's maneuvers, were then appointed. They proceeded to sue the brokers—principally the U.S. firms Goldman Sachs and Lehman Brothers—and the accountants who had represented Maxwell. British authorities duly investigated the securities firms involved and, while finding them to have committed no criminal acts, fined the firms $430 million in claims, interest, and penalties. This amount represented more than two-thirds of the total that was allegedly lost, none of which the firms had received themselves; all of the funds had been misappropriated by Maxwell. Goldman Sachs was required to pay $250 million of the total award.[12] Although many prominent British, European, and other U.S. banks and securities firms had had extensive dealings with Maxwell, Goldman Sachs was singled out in London for having such poor judgment as to keep Maxwell as a client.

The Maxwell settlement was a record for firms acting as brokers, that is, as agents in transactions between principals. It was surely the largest financial settlement ever recorded in Europe, once again demonstrating how legal and regulatory actions in the financial sectors abroad are rapidly catching up with those in the United States.

West Virginia CIF. In the 1980s the West Virginia Consolidated Investment Fund (CIF) invested commingled municipal pension and other funds to profit from higher returns available from capital-market investments (versus, for example, bank certificates of deposit). The investment officers in West Virginia were neither experienced nor sophisticated, however, nor did they have outside advisers. After losing $280 million in 1987 by making incorrect bets on interest rates—and being forced to raise taxes to cover the loss—they claimed they had been pressured and lured into inappropriate high-risk investments by irresponsible securities salesmen. Seven Wall Street firms, including Salomon Brothers, County NatWest, and Goldman Sachs, settled with the State of West Virginia for $28 million. One firm, Morgan Stanley, did not settle, claiming that it gave West Virginia no advice and only executed trades that the client ordered. The CIF had been one of Morgan Stanley's biggest accounts, with trading volume reaching $20 billion in one three-month period alone. West Virginia, it said, was responsible for looking after itself and did not have the right to have losses reimbursed by its trading counterparties. Morgan Stanley lost its suit, was barred from doing business with the state, and was held liable for $58 million in damages and penalties. On appeal to the state's highest court, however, the decision of the lower court was reversed. In his opinion, West Virginia Supreme Court Senior Justice Richard Neely said he was disturbed by the investment fund's attempt to recoup losses from "a deep-pocket defendant in an entrepreneurial lawsuit in a jurisdiction where the plaintiffs are the home team."[13] The case was sent back to the lower court for retrial. The parties subsequently settled for $20 million.

Orange County. In early 1995, Orange County, California, lost $1.2 billion as a result of trading losses in the county's commingled investment account that was operated for the benefit of various municipalities and agencies. For several years the county's treasurer, Robert Citron, had invested the county's funds very successfully, always achieving impressive above-market returns. In 1994, however, Citron misjudged the market and lost most of his earlier winnings. This loss created a cash-flow crisis, and the county was forced to declare bankruptcy. Its trustees subsequently sued the county's financial advisor, Merrill Lynch, for $2 billion, claiming that in addition to dispensing bad advice Merrill had sold Citron three-fourths of the instruments in his highly leveraged portfolio.

Citron was a well-informed, high-risk trader, whose losses were the result of borrowing large amounts to finance his positions. In particular, as the market was falling he issued Orange County municipal securities in order to invest in unhedged long positions in fixed income bonds. He dealt with many brokers but was partial to Merrill Lynch, which was appointed advisor. Merrill claims, however, that it attempted to talk Citron out of his risky exposures. The advice was ignored.

The lawsuits initiated a series of complicated maneuvers that turned on whether the actions taken by the responsible county officials were legal. If they were, as Merrill Lynch claimed, then the county itself was fully responsible for the losses. The county, of course, argued the reverse. In early 1996 a federal bankruptcy judge ruled that Merrill would be allowed to demonstrate that the actions of the county's officials were within their legal powers. At about the same time, the SEC weighed into the case by instituting an administrative proceeding against the Board of Supervisors of Orange County on the grounds that the county had violated antifraud provisions of the securities laws. The SEC claimed that the county had failed, in its offering documents for the public sale of bonds (underwritten by Merrill, among others), to disclose its investment strategy and the risks associated with it. Later the SEC made the same claims against officials at CS-First Boston and Merrill Lynch responsible for underwriting the bonds. On November 19, 1996, seventy-one-year-old Robert Citron was sentenced to one year in jail and a fine of $100,000 for his part in the county's bankruptcy and fraud.

Dramshop Liabilities

Although some of the legal issues involving claims for recovery of losses due to broker-dealer misbehavior remain unresolved, clients have come to believe that courts will entertain suits alleging fraud or a breach of fiduciary duty by brokers. These "dramshop" cases are rooted in state laws that require bartenders and proprietors of bars (dramshops) to stop serving patrons who drink too much so they will not injure themselves. Likewise, brokers have a duty to protect clients from investments they should not make. From 1992 to 1994 more than $10 million in damages was awarded in arbitration to plaintiffs, often wealthy investors, in securities-industry dramshop cases. Recent cases involved payments of $3 million by Bear Stearns to a British Virgin Islands investment firm and $2 million by Paine Webber to an executive of a financial firm.[14]

Boards of directors and trustees of offended institutional clients thus had an avenue along which to pursue their claims, and they would use it whenever they could. The business of supplying financial services to certain types of customers was therefore much more dangerous to the broker than it had been before. Broker-dealers would have to think twice about how to work with these customers, especially unsophisticated municipal bodies with substantial sums at their disposal. The threat of litigation introduced another "market force" that had to be reflected in the way in which firms governed their businesses.

Another market force is public opinion in general, which is reflected by juries, arbitration panels, and regulators and prosecutors. The events of the last several years have had their effect on the view that the public holds of Wall Street, always a target of criticism for its supposedly greedy ways. In a Louis Harris and Associates poll released in October 1996, a significant majority of respondents indicated that they believed that most people on Wall Street "would be willing to break the law if they believed they could make a lot of money and get away with it," and that they "only care about making money and nothing else."[15]

Lessons of the 1990s

The lessons learned in the 1980s concerned the realities of high-powered deal making and risk arbitrage. Another set of lessons, this time concerning trading and risk management, had to be learned in the early 1990s:

- *Profits come from taking risks, not avoiding them.*

  A new cadre of employees, skilled in sophisticated trading methods, has emerged that is very willing to take risks. This development has generated, in turn, the need for expensive control systems, for management methods to contain firmwide risk exposures, and for controlling the human-risk element in the business. The techniques of risk control lagged way behind the trading techniques, however, and the enforcement of guidelines varied widely from firm to firm.

- *Rogue traders can be extremely dangerous.*

  Firms committed very large amounts of capital to their various trading activities, and in so doing increased their exposure to large trading losses caused by sudden market movements or human error. Thus the traders had the potential (which their merger and arbitrage colleagues mostly did not) to destroy the whole firm.

- *Firms found themselves increasingly vulnerable to client legal action for various product liability and dramshop claims.*

  This development has two sources, one legal and one financial. Courts became receptive to complaints based on the idea that if there has been a loss, there must have been some misconduct. And the senior management of securities firms may have encouraged excessively aggressive trading and brokerage activities as a means of promoting business.

- *An extreme form of moral hazard developed in firms, with owners and employees having different perceptions and goals.*

  Traders and brokers had very strong incentives to increase the risks borne by their firms, without comparable incentives to protect the firms from harm. Efforts to control high-performance employees were often resisted by threats of resignation, sometimes leading to excessive management forbearance. Compensation programs and performance evaluation became a great deal more complicated.

- *Management's duty to maintain an environment of high professional standards had never been more important in the banking and securities business.*

  The tone of senior management determines whether those in charge look the other way when a profitable but questionable trading opportunity appears, and whether risk managers' views are beaten down or dismissed in favor of an aggressive trader. Management sets the style of the firm, a style that can encourage rogues and imprudent or unsupervised risk taking unless higher standards are known to prevail.

• *Shareholder value in the securities industry is now directly related to the values that management imposes on the firm.*
   During the 1980s and 1990s many firms have suffered serious penalties from employee misconduct, proven as well as alleged. Exhibit 1-1 shows a list of sixteen well-known firms that have been involved in such situations and whose shareholders have paid a price for it. And the price—a combination of damages, fines, loss of shareholder value, and damage to the franchise value of the firm—has been vastly disproportionate to the profits, income, or gains associated with the misconduct.

Has the securities industry really become a sucker's game, one in which the suckers are the owners and shareholders of firms that are operated strictly for the purpose of profiting employees by turning aggressive, risk-oriented brokers and traders loose on the market? Gains, when they are made, are mostly paid out to employees. What's left, after taxes, is paid to shareholders, who supply the capital. If things go wrong, traders may lose their bonuses, but shareholders may lose millions. If traders get their firms into trouble with clients, regulators, or prosecutors, the traders may suffer serious penalties (if caught), but their firms may be ruined. No wonder shareholders are unimpressed with the opportunities to invest in major, highly sophisticated, world-class investment banks, banks with supposedly high franchise values. After all, in the bull market of mid-1996, Morgan Stanley, Merrill Lynch, and Lehman Brothers traded at a puny eight times earnings, and Salomon Brothers at six. Meanwhile, other firms at less risk of self-imposed damage traded at higher relative prices: Charles Schwab at nineteen times earnings; AIG at sixteen; Travelers Group at twelve; and Alliance Capital Management, Citicorp, and J.P. Morgan at eleven. Both groups of firms have similar exposures to changing financial markets, as measured by their "betas" (share price volatility relative to market volatility). But their stock prices are quite different. The stocks of the major investment banks—the most market-dominating of all financial-service firms, where employees are the most talented, sought after, and highly paid—lag well behind the stocks of the other firms.

This observation brings to mind a recent study by Demsetz, Saidenberg, and Strahan in which the franchise value of commercial banks was found to be inversely related to an "all-in" measure of risk based on the banks' stock market returns. Franchise value was found to be a function of efficiency, access to protected markets, and valuable client relationships. The greater the franchise value, the study reported, the lesser the risk the banks exposed themselves to.[16]

Investment banks actually manage their trading-risk exposures well. There are other risks, however, that affect their franchise values. These arise from the firms' reliance on employees who have very strong incentives to produce profits and who operate with large amounts of the firms' capital in a fast-paced, closely regulated business. It is the human risk associated with these employees that is so unpredictable, so hard to manage, and sometimes so devastating.

One might argue, then, that the securities industry's biggest problem has not been handling its market-risk exposures, but lowering its risk of self-destruction. One might also argue that solving the latter problem might make more money for shareholders (by the market's revaluation of the firm's shares) than anything else management might do.

The New Bankers

All in all, people's careers in finance today are a great deal more exciting, well paid, quick developing, and ego enhancing than twenty years ago. But at the same time, these careers have become more uncertain, stressful, accident prone, and short-lived. These changes have taken place not just for traditional traders, brokers, salesmen, and investment bankers, but also for commercial bankers, operations specialists, risk managers, consultants, lawyers, and all of the others, including clients, who have cast their lot with financial-market transactions.

These career conditions may attract too many people with the high-roller mentality of a Donald Trump, rather than with the old-fashioned, Scottish characteristics more appropriate for sober, professional, fiduciary activities involving large sums of other people's money. The most talented individuals in the financial services industry today have perhaps become too concerned with their own welfare to be interested in the welfare of the firm or its clients. If so, more and more revenues, efforts, and skills have to be allocated to management and control systems—"zookeeping," for short—that are designed to prevent fraud and misbehavior by employees, however talented and productive they may be.

The better firms moderate and balance these factors to some degree, trying to find an optimum mix between meeting the most aggressive

Exhibit 1-1 Firms That Have Suffered Serious Damage to Shareholder Value Due to Misconduct, 1986–1996

Firm		Event	Consequence
E.F. Hutton	1986	Check-kiting scandals	Now defunct (sold, 1987)
Kidder Peabody	1986 1993	Insider-trading scandals Falsifying government-bond trades	Now defunct (sold, 1994)
Drexel Burnham Lambert	1987	Insider trading, stock parking	Now defunct
Deutsche Morgan Grenfell	1987	Insider trading, stock manipulation in the "Guinness Affair"	Sold to Deutsche Bank, 1989
	1996	Losses at Morgan Grenfell Asset Management	$930 million in losses and payments for restitution and compensation
NatWest Bank	1987	Stock manipulation in the "Blue Arrow Affair"	Reorganization, major losses at parent; parent management changed; CEO changed
Goldman Sachs	1987	Insider trading (Robert Freeman)	Large legal expenses
	1994	"Maxwell Affair" pension funds	$250 million in fines
BCCI	1991	Various frauds, money laundering	Now defunct (billions lost to investors and depositors)
Salomon Brothers	1991	Treasury-bond auction scandal	$500 million in fines, settlements; $1 billion market cap loss; complete management change; CEO changed

Firm		Event	Consequence
Nomura Securities	1991	Improper payments, market rigging	Large penalties, operating losses; CEO changed
	1997	Improper payments	CEO changed; renewed business and reputation losses
Baring Brothers	1995	Fraudulent trading of Nikkei-index contracts	Now defunct ($1.4 billion loss; sold to ING, 1995)
Prudential Group	1995	Fraud at Prudential Securities	$1.5 billion in fines and settlements
		Fraud at Prisa	$345 million in further settlements
		Fraud at Prudential Insurance	Up to $1 billion left to settle
			CEO changed
Paine Webber	1995	Fraudulent sale of limited partnerships	$300 million in fines and settlements
Bankers Trust	1995	Misrepresentations in derivatives trading	$300 million in customer restitutions; losses; $1 billion market cap loss; CEO changed
Daiwa Bank	1995	Concealed trading losses	Fines of $340 million and loss of US license; CEO changed
Merrill Lynch	1996	Orange County loss of $1.2 billion in leveraged interest-rate products	Pending

demands of the market and maintaining a culture with high standards and based on long-term professional development and retention of valued employees. Addressing this difficult task is a matter of leadership. Not many firms have found this golden balance. It is not easy to strike. And even those that come close are in danger of sudden market shifts or rogue behavior that can cause lasting and perhaps irreparable damage.

Regulation,
Competition, and
Market Conduct

■

Some two hundred years after his death, Adam Smith's ideas dominate the organization of economic activity more strongly than ever. The "invisible hand" guides people, as they seek to improve their own well-being and pursue their own interests, to produce the greatest good for the greatest number and to allocate labor, capital, and intellectual and natural resources in the most efficient way possible.

Adam Smith predicated his analysis on the idea of free markets and perfect competition, in which lots of relatively small players interact, with none sufficiently powerful to affect prices and competition. He was silent as to who would regulate competition, and how, so as to achieve this ideal competitive condition. The interactions of the market would provide for individual success and failure. The winners would indeed win, and the losers lose. However eagerly one wanted to be a winner, fear of being a loser would affect behavior. And those who wanted to be winners at all costs would diminish their probability of succeeding by continually exposing themselves to a high degree of risk. The aim of all of this was to have an economic system with a level playing field that would optimize results for the society, thereby maximizing economic welfare, growth, and opportunity. The system would have its flaws and abusers, of course, but on the whole it would still be preferable to the alternatives.

The world Smith and his disciples such as Walter Bageot, Alfred Marshall, Joseph Schumpeter, Friedrich Hayek, Milton Friedman, and Ayn Rand described has been remarkably robust, repeatedly beating back challenges from alternative visions of society, ranging from the Fabian socialists of the nineteenth century to the Fascists and Marxists of the twentieth century. Even milder forms of government planning and control, such as habitual French intervention in the private sector and the much-touted Swedish welfare state, eventually lost much of their appeal or began to sink under their own weight. Challenger after challenger has risen, only to be discarded into time's trash bin of unworkable ideas.

Maybe there is a lesson here, having to do with human nature. Maybe the free market that Adam Smith described is the one form of economic organization that most closely aligns with what people really do perceive as being in their own interests. Even when an alternative system is imposed for a very long time, as Marxism-Leninism in the Soviet bloc for much of the twentieth century, the invisible hand creeps in again through black markets, minicapitalism, work-minimizing behavior, and a host of other ways. Though they have generated much excitement, the "transition econo-mies" of Eastern Europe and the "emerging markets" of Latin America and Asia involve little more than the invisible hand being allowed more room to apply its touch. Even the most modern writers on business affairs, running the gamut from "new" models of competitive advantage of com-panies and countries and "new" trade theory, to the "new" ideas of core competencies of corporations, usually provide little more than old wine in new bottles—essentially vintage Adam Smith repackaged for a broader market.

If the invisible hand so dominates the landscape of economic ideas, then laissez-faire must certainly be the anchor of national and international policy toward business. People should be left to their own devices, left alone to do what they perceive is best for themselves and to create the kinds of organizations that hold the best promise of moving in that direction. Measures that distort markets should be absent altogether, or at least as nonintrusive as possible. If governments are too intrusive, human ingenuity will find ways around them. Government intervention should be calibrated against its market impact in the cold light of how people are most likely to respond, not according to some social thinker's ideas about how they *ought* to respond. Any such intervention needs to be tested as to whether it makes the market work more efficiently or, if it does not (which is usually the case), whether it works *with* market incentives or *against* them. Do the social gains achieved by the intervention outweigh the loss in market efficiency? Where free markets have been permitted, they have left pow-erful performance benchmarks behind. Recent history suggests that policies that deviate too far from the free market are doomed to failure.

The market itself, in order to thrive, needs a clear and stable set of rules of conduct.[1] When this is absent, as in the "wild west" of yesteryear and in some of the formerly communist countries today, the market is inhibited. When there is a lack of law and order and of personal safety—when there is no sanctity of contracts and private property, no recourse to courts of law, no protection from extortion—the functioning of free and fair markets suffers. These institutions are needed not only to achieve maximum economic performance, but also to create a viable social environment for business. Before the proper balance is struck, however, the process of creation may itself go through phases of vigilantism, self-regulation, and informal market practices.

Some scholars have argued that, fundamentally, what's good for free-market capitalism is good for society—that every other system that has been tried fares less well in creating an anchor for personal liberty as well as for distributive justice and ordinary decency. In the words of one author, Elaine Sternberg:

> Distributive justice requires that organizational rewards reflect contributions made to organizational goals. Inherent in this definition are the concepts of merit and responsibility.
>
> Ordinary decency refers to the honesty, fairness, presumption of legality, and absence of physical coercion essential for the existence of trust and most long-term undertakings.[2]

But does this mean that free markets always produce an economic and social optimum? A look around the world suggests they do not. All free-market countries have chains of social and economic policies that constrain overly aggressive market behavior. In this sense, the *political* process, democratic or otherwise, invariably comes up with ways of guiding the *economic* process in the direction of results that depart (sometimes significantly) from what would happen under free-market conditions. The need for such forms of guidance is to be found in the failure of market mechanisms to produce socially acceptable results. There are several reasons for this failure.

Market Failures

Adam Smith's approach to resource allocation via the free market may well be the most efficient from an economic perspective, but not necessarily from the perspective of politicians who have extensive noneconomic agendas. In a totally free market, some get rich and some get poor. It all depends on your natural endowments, your investment in skills, your saving and spending patterns, your entrepreneurship and ingenuity, your level of effort, and your luck. It's all up to you.

But democratic societies do not see it quite that way. For every perceived success there may be nine failures, and that may be too many in a full-fledged democracy. Myriad public policies try to make sure things turn out differently, principally by diminishing the consequences of being a loser. The poor are lifted up to some sort of tolerable standard of living by means of a social safety net that includes supports such as welfare payments, negative income taxes, food stamps, free medical care, free or subsidized housing, and free or subsidized training and schooling—the basics, and often much more. Few have to live in the streets anymore in any industrial country, at least for any length of time. The unemployed are taken care of for a while, often for quite a long while, and sometimes (especially in Europe) at incomes not too far from what they earned when they were working.

Meanwhile, those who are better off are taxed more aggressively than the rest, usually in ways that likewise promote social concepts of fairness. Progressive income taxes take more from those who are better off than from those less successful—not only in absolute terms as under a flat tax but also *proportionately*—even though many economists see no economic justification for doing so. "People are different," economists say, "and they value extra income differently. So there is absolutely no economic justification for taxing Mr. Smith and Mr. Jones at different marginal rates unless you know much more than tax authorities actually do know. In particular, you need to know how each of these two gentlemen values a dollar of additional income."[3]

In addition to progressive income taxes, there are sales and value-added taxes, real estate taxes, personal property taxes, excise taxes, death taxes, capital gains taxes, "user fees," "sin" taxes on tobacco and alcohol, and more, each reflecting prevailing concepts of "fairness" as much as the need for fiscal revenues. In federal countries like the United States, tax fairness is fine-tuned at the state and local level as well. You are taxed progressively on your income from work at the federal, state, and sometimes even municipal level. You are taxed on your income from interest and dividends (which have already been taxed at the corporate level), assets accumulated from income *already* taxed once. And when those assets appreciate, they are taxed yet *again* as capital gains, even if those gains may be due only to inflation. Then when you die, most of these assets are taxed one last time before they pass on to the kids. All the while, you can deduct donations to charity, mortgage interest, property taxes, and medical bills. You can also claim various other tax breaks that politicians consider to have socially redeeming value.

The result is an involuntary transfer of income and wealth from the richer to the poorer members of society, from "less deserving" to "more deserving," put into effect by the people's representatives, the politicians. This is not all bad, of course, because it can help build up the important middle classes, and the economic safety net that such policies create may shield the economy from extreme unemployment and depressed markets for all kinds of goods and services. It may also address a society's need to treat its citizens humanely and to redress inequalities of opportunity and access to wealth. All well-developed societies have some such system of transfer payments. Many are more extensive than those in the United States. But they come at a price of reducing freedom in the markets and economic efficiency, often resulting in high unemployment and dim prospects for future growth.

In a normal situation, we would expect our politicians to recognize the value of preserving the market system, and not to damage it too much by yielding to the temptations of populism. More-or-less free markets can survive in such climates very well. But what they cannot do is tolerate extreme inefficiencies in resource allocation. When the pendulum swings too far in that direction, the economy sustains critical damage that can take a long time to repair.

Public Goods

The free market is not good at allocating the costs of *public goods*. National defense, parks, and public safety are obvious examples. Others, ranging from public schools and hospitals to airports, highways, and postal services, are often subject to debate. The value of these goods is hard to identify and to allocate among beneficiaries in rough proportion to the benefits received, even as others (as free riders) are able to enjoy them without sharing in their cost. Some of these public goods have been privatized successfully to let market-based actions increase the quality of service and reduce the cost of delivery. Vigorous discussion has developed in many countries about the efficacy of market-based solutions to such problems as environmental pollution, high-quality public education, and maintenance of fisheries. These solutions vest resource users with ownership rights, thus creating an incentive to maintain that resource on a sustainable basis. So even though the market demonstrates some weaknesses when costs and benefits cannot easily be allocated, it can nevertheless be used to provide cost-effective solutions to social problems involving public goods. On the whole, however, government intervention is still needed to allocate the costs and benefits of public goods effectively. But only, of course, to a point beyond which economic efficiency would suffer unacceptably.

External Interference

In a classic paper published almost forty years ago, Nobel prize-winning economist Ronald Coase analyzed a simple situation. Suppose that a candy maker operates noisy equipment next door to a doctor's office. In pursuing his own interests, the candy maker is interfering with the doctor's examination of his patients.[4] Though the candy maker derives benefits from this noise pollution (being able to make candy at a profit), the doctor is injured by it and receives no compensation. Economists call this type of interference a *negative externality*, or a "social cost." The conventional solution to this externality problem is for the candy maker himself to be restrained, maybe even put out of business. Coase pointed out that this completely overlooks the damage such restraint would do to the candy maker, who is making noise only in the pursuit of his own livelihood and with no intent of harming the doctor. There are two possible outcomes: The doctor's business continues to suffer, or the candy maker is forced to shut down. Which causes the greater harm? Coase demonstrated that forcing the candy maker to shut down may be an inferior solution compared to undertaking a freely negotiated arrangement between the two parties whereby the doctor is compensated by the noisy candy maker or the doctor compensates the candy maker to quiet down. The eventual solution depends on the relative size of the gains and losses faced by the two parties. That is, negative externalities can be dealt with most efficiently by means of negotiated arrangements between parties, regardless of how the law would otherwise allocate responsibility and impose liability.

The law should place the burden of avoiding harmful effects on the party that can do so at lowest cost, and leave the rest to private negotiation. This is the famous "Coase theorem." The best legal solutions to social issues and conflicting property rights are those that mimic most closely what people would come up with if they were free to negotiate. This goes for all kinds of rights, ranging from free speech to aircraft overflights, from air pollution to clean streets.[5] Nonetheless, when social costs arise, public policy and institutional arrangements tend to be called into action to deal with them. Their design can lead to more or less inefficient results, however, depending on how closely they align with freely negotiated outcomes.

Negative externalities have played a large part in financial markets from time immemorial, with crises, costly crisis prevention, and questionable practices regularly visiting losses on innocent parties. Finance is and always will be a highly "pollution-intensive" industry, one requiring active and considered public policies to deal with the many forms of interference that affect it.

Contestable Markets and Competition

Adam Smith predicated his description of the operation of free markets on perfect competition (that is, large numbers of small suppliers incapable of affecting prices), perfect information, zero transactions costs, and the like—conditions painfully familiar to any beginning student of economics. In the real world, of course, perfect competition rarely exists for many reasons, including the economies of large-scale production, differentiated products, and "natural" monopolies such as supplying water to homeowners. There is also the fact that producers detest perfect competition and having to sell in "commodity" markets where the sole determinant of success is price. So they busy themselves trying to escape it, sometimes constructively and sometimes not so constructively. In an effort to differentiate themselves from others and command higher compensation, people beaver away in training programs and graduate schools. Sometimes, when they are talented enough, they may even create a unique presence in the marketplace, as Luciano Pavarotti and Michael Jordan have done. In order to command higher prices and larger market shares, companies try to invent better mousetraps and advertise the extraordinary quality of their products. Success stories like Microsoft, Disney, Wal-Mart, and Singapore Airlines abound. All of this is a vital part of the market-driven system of economic organization, especially when economies of scale and economies of scope are important aspects of the production process. Effective competition and the vigorous contesting for market position have to hold out the hope of a pot of gold at the end of the rainbow.

Corporations sometimes try to exploit the market by effectively blocking out rivals in inappropriate ways, shifting economic benefits from others to themselves—what economists call *rent seeking*. Examples include creating monopolies and producer cartels, colluding on prices to drive them far above costs, pleading for protection against imports at the expense of the consumer, and predatory dumping intended to drive weaker players from the market and subsequently permit monopoly pricing. In such cases governments usually step in to regulate prices, to break up the monopolies and collusive practices, or to improve the functioning and contestability of the market. Competition policy itself is almost always imperfect, however. How do we best identify the existence of a monopoly? What is "collusion"? What is a "cartel"? How do we define "predatory"? What happens when the benefits of cooperation among suppliers apparently far exceed the dangers of market exploitation? How do we avoid regulatory interventions aimed at yesterday's failures of competition? What about anticompetitive practices that occur abroad, outside national jurisdiction, yet have a significant impact on the local market? Many of these questions have been answered only imperfectly, although recent advances in the economics of industrial organization have contributed to substantially more efficient regulatory policies.

Information and Transactions Costs

Information is often expensive. It has to be created, absorbed, processed, and acted upon in order to be effectively applied in the market. Sometimes these are not difficult problems. In the foreign exchange market, perhaps the most perfect in the world, dealers can check rates on screens in whichever markets are open on a twenty-four-hour basis virtually year-round. All major players have almost the same information almost all the time, as well as essentially the same costs of doing transactions. Success or failure in this virtually seamless market depends mainly on the dealer's *interpretation* of whatever information is available at the moment. Compare this with the hapless American tourist in France, wandering into a *bureau de change* on a cathedral square forty miles outside Paris, staring blankly at the extortionate posted rates, armed with little or no information and few immediate alternatives.

The fact is that information has value. Those who have it can charge for it through fees, spreads, and other means. Those who don't have it must pay for it, either by incurring the costs of obtaining it for themselves or by meeting the seller's price. A similar analysis applies to transactions costs, including the cost of taking business elsewhere. Doing so may be quite easy and cheap in some cases, but in others may involve establishing entirely new relationships with new suppliers, or what economists call *recontracting costs.*

Information and transaction costs are fairly easy to deal with in interprofessional, or wholesale markets, where solutions can be left to the interplay of competitive forces. Exceptions arise when information is stolen. Proprietary information is imbedded in the value of a firm. When it is misappropriated, there are clear victims, principally the owners of the firm. Stealing information is not a victimless crime. Some people (those who would have bought or sold had they been privy to the same information) are injured in the process. Consequently, coming down hard on people who steal information may well be justified.

Information and transaction costs tend to be far more serious when it comes to doing business with retail customers, who may be poorly informed or find it difficult to shop around, making them ripe for picking by unscrupulous operators. This goes for any market, but it applies especially to financial markets. "Buyer beware" (caveat emptor) is always a good rule, but people who find financial affairs difficult to understand and pretty far removed from their expertise and everyday life tend to be least capable of making complex decisions in their own best interests. For this reason, society protects them—protection that may also serve the public interest. The government requires adequate disclosure in language ordinary people can understand, limits access to certain "toxic" financial products, specifies in detail how certain financial services may be sold, and cracks down on various kinds of financial abuses. These are the purposes of the landmark Securities Acts of 1933–1934, passed after a period of egregious abuses of retail customers in the U.S. financial markets during the 1920s. These acts have been generally regarded as very effective, but of course the regulatory costs they create have to be met by the market.

Finally, while free-market activities may be efficient in the long run, they can cause extreme harshness in the short run for a great many people. Political pressures then develop to interfere in the market—to have government regulation set aside market forces so that a more benign environment may develop in their place.

The main reasons for intervening in markets invariably are the five mentioned here: fairness issues, achieving and paying for the benefits of public goods and services, resolving issues of external interference, the extent to which competition really exists, and the costs and access to information. These things have to be balanced against society's need for an efficient, growing economy, which is best achieved by letting markets work. This is the overarching trade-off of modern economics.

Layers of Social Control

Thinking about all of these things makes clear that unfettered market control of economic outcomes is probably not feasible in any democracy that tries to create the maximum level of welfare for the maximum number of people. Since this is more or less the professed goal of virtually every political system that exists today, constraints on firms, labor unions, individuals, and other economic actors are ever present—and probably always will be.

At the center of these regulatory efforts is the firm itself, whose managers are supposed to be intent on maximizing long-term shareholder wealth, the principal creative force in the free-market system of economic organization. If managers and owners are different, as in a corporation whose shares are publicly traded, the market forces governing corporate control and shareholder value are supposed to make sure this maximization occurs. Waste, inefficiency, and bad management are reflected in share prices. If the stock price drops low enough, it will trigger takeover action by investors or other companies that think they can do better after ousting current management. In short, market-imposed discipline governs the destiny of the firm—its overall performance in the market for goods and services, labor, raw materials, and other resources, as well as for capital and ultimately for corporate control. The firm is the source of economic energy for the system, the goose that lays the golden eggs.

But suppose, for example, that, intent on the pursuit of maximum shareholder wealth, management fails to deal with environmental pollution and so imposes serious costs on others in society. This may create a response among the victims that will ultimately find resonance in the political arena. It could trigger legislation to deal with the problem through taxation, prohibitions, fines, or other enforcement actions. In U.S. environmental policy, for example, the critical point probably came with Earth Day demonstrations in 1970, only a few years after the publication of Rachel Carson's *Silent Spring*. Earth Day was followed in short order by the National Environmental Quality Act and by federal air- and water-quality legislation. A large bureaucracy, the Environmental Protection Agency, was established to ensure enforcement at the national level and to promote consistent enforcement at the state and local levels as well.

Within only a couple of years, the United States had imposed a new layer of social control on corporations, one designed to protect the environment from pollution. Firms had to conform and their costs rose. They had to address efficiency in pollution control as yet another competitive element. Their relative product prices reflected the cost of pollution controls and accordingly influenced consumer behavior. The environment, a public good that previously had been "unpriced," now had to be factored into market decisions and became an important element of U.S. economic life.

Product safety followed a similar path. Firms in pursuit of free-market objectives may well be tempted to cut corners in product design, placing at risk consumers who lack pertinent information when they make their buying decisions. A host of federal legislative initiatives has therefore evolved over the years to protect consumers, including the passage of the Fair Packaging and Labeling Act of 1969 and the creation of the Consumer Product Safety Commission, and at the state and local levels various consumer safety initiatives have been undertaken. The food and pharmaceuticals industries in particular have been affected. With roots in the Pure Food Act of 1906, the Food and Drug Administration was established to ensure that products are safe, if necessary through rigorous testing, in advance of their availability in the market. Again, firms in the affected industries have had to adapt in ways that usually raised costs and prices, influenced product availability and time-to-market, and affected shareholder values. While there is considerable controversy about *how* the regulatory system works or *what* ought to be regulated—such as the FDA's 1996 decision to classify cigarettes as addictive and subject to FDA control while making no similar move on alcoholic beverages—few people today would argue for scrapping the FDA.

Such regulatory or social control initiatives have pertained not only to health and safety, but also to general product quality and sales techniques. Efforts by corporations to skimp on product quality are usually reflected in market forces, with consumers soon defecting to buy from competitors who do better. Even here, however, there have been consumer protection initiatives aplenty, including legislation leading to the creation of the Federal Trade Commission in 1914 and a broad range of state and local measures such as taxi commissions, "lemon laws" for automobiles, and the like. The area of consumer protection has been especially targeted by nongovernmental organizations such as Consumers Union, as well as by consumer activists of virtually every stripe. Producers may not like it, but they have to deal with it.

In matters of labor, the dynamics of corporate relations with their employees gave rise to organized labor in the nineteenth century, with collective bargaining over compensation, job classifications, working conditions, and job rules. Normally, collective bargaining would be left to negotiators, but again government bodies have been created to regulate the process—the National Labor Relations Board in 1935 and much later the Occupational Safety and Health Administration (OSHA).

In various industries, problems at the interface between the market and society have given rise to further constraints on business in the form of very specific control initiatives. In transportation, for example, the Interstate Commerce Commission was established in the 1870s to regulate the railroads, a response to what was considered predatory pricing aimed at farmers who needed the railroads to get commodities to market. This mandate was later extended to other forms of transportation. In air transport the Civil Aeronautics Board (CAB) was originally created to allocate routes, set prices, and define services in what was regarded as a unique industry. Although the CAB was scrapped during the Carter administration, some of its functions were assumed by the Federal Aviation Administration.

Using powers originally granted to Congress under the Constitution and put to use ever since, the federal government regulates virtually all aspects of commerce, industry, and economic life in the United States. State governments have followed the same route. Layers of social control affect all industries. All pay greater or lesser amounts of taxes. All are subject to environmental, labor, consumer health and safety, and antitrust statutes. All are subject to federal and state securities laws. All are exposed to fines and penalties under these laws, and to civil litigation based upon them. The idea is that these various layers of restraint, like the thin threads used by the Lilliputians to hold down the giant Gulliver, will balance out the uneven distribution of power between corporations and their customers, employees, and other constituents in the marketplace. Periodically the balance of power shifts. Too little external restraint permits exploitative behavior on the part of corporations, as was probably the case, for example, at the end of the nineteenth century. Too much restraint, on the other hand, leads to corporate impotence and weak economic performance. Under such circumstances the regulatory burden may be lifted (as began to occur in the United States in the late 1970s) in a gradual process of deregulation. Too much constraint can also, of course, lead to vigorous efforts to avoid the regulatory burden by shifting business activities abroad, or to an increase in black-market or underground economic activities.

Control of Financial Services

Financial services comprise a range of "special" businesses. They are special because they deal mainly with other people's money, and because serious problems that crop up in the industry often have a profound impact on third parties, on people not otherwise involved in the transactions.

Banking

A variety of financial services businesses handle the nation's money and therefore affect interest rates and the availability of credit. Of these, banks are the most important. Because they hold much of the country's savings, the Federal Deposit Insurance Corporation was established in 1933 to guarantee bank deposits. This action was itself part of the Banking Act of 1933, an effort to rebuild the banking system, which had collapsed under the weight of thousands of bank failures and which had been compromised by perceptions of fraud and misbehavior, notably in the securities activities of major banks. The Banking Act also influenced the practices of the Federal Reserve (created in 1913) and provided for the Comptroller of the Currency and state banking regulators as parts of a "dual banking" structure. And it separated, through the Glass-Steagall provisions of the act, commercial and investment banking functions. Because banks were special—they had unique fiduciary responsibilities and also were the corner-stone of the national monetary system—the government insisted that managers of banking institutions be (to use the British phrase) "fit and proper" and that their activities be subject to capital controls, limitations on operations, a variety of other regulations, and frequent inspections to affirm compliance. The system worked well for many years. However, bureaucratic inefficiency, political influence, and fierce market pressures eventually overtook it. Despite the extensive banking regulations and powers of enforcement, the United States experienced in the 1980s its worst financial crisis since the passage of the Banking Act. Hundreds of savings and loan institutions—and many important commercial banks—failed and had to be reorganized, at considerable taxpayer expense, by the government. These failures increased the regulatory pressure felt by all banks, both healthy and unhealthy.

The industry, regulators, and the courts have subsequently invested considerable effort in reforming banking laws to make them more relevant to modern competitive conditions. Though some major breakthroughs have occurred in the de facto repeal of laws restricting interstate banking and of the Glass-Steagall provisions, these efforts have not been rewarded by the enactment of major legislative reform. The old laws and their special regulatory burdens remain in effect. Nationwide banking has been made possible, however, and both the Federal Reserve Bank and the Comptroller of the Currency have asserted their powers boldly by permitting qualified banks to conduct investment-banking operations through a subsidiary. This is possible under a loophole in the 1933 Banking Act (Section 20) that permits banks to engage, to a limited extent, in otherwise nonpermitted activities. Permission must be granted separately by the Federal Reserve for licenses to conduct transactions in corporate debt and equity and municipal revenue bonds. Only a few American banks have sought and received these licenses. And even after the licenses are granted, the Fed retains strict oversight.

Consider an example from the real world of financial markets. In the spring of 1996, the Federal Reserve fined Swiss Bank Corporation $3.5 million for violating conditions of its Section 20 investment banking activities. Like U.S. banks, SBC was permitted through its separately capitalized Section 20 subsidiary to underwrite and trade in corporate securities and municipal revenue bonds up to a limit of 10 percent of the subsidiary's total revenues. Pushing fast into global securities markets, especially after its acquisition of S.G. Warburg of the United Kingdom and its integration into the bank's global wholesale arm, SBC-Warburg, the bank's volume of these activities at one point exceeded the Fed's limit. Whether it was an inadvertent or deliberate violation was irrelevant. The Fed's reaction was swift and sure. For the first time it publicly chastised and fined a major bank in this connection. It was immaterial that the limits had been under attack from many quarters as being obsolete and unjustifiable under current competitive conditions and indeed were later raised substantially. The Fed was determined to step on any violators in order to send a signal to the market. Probably more important than the fine, SBC was now in the Fed's "penalty box" for an indeterminate period, and the bank would be watched even more carefully than usual.[6]

Securities

In recent years the importance of the securities industry has increased considerably. More financial transactions now occur in securities markets than through banks. These transactions and financial flows, including the activities of mutual funds, pension funds, and other institutional investors, now dominate financial behavior. But market developments have overtaken regulatory developments, which have not kept pace with the changed realities of the marketplace.

The differences between banking and securities regulation are important to understand in this context. On balance, banks carry a regulatory burden, in terms of the requirements and costs of compliance, that is vastly greater than that which applies to the securities industry. In part, this results from the different regulatory histories of the two industries. When Congress passed the Securities Act of 1933, it focused on "truth in new issues," requiring prospectuses and creating underwriting liabilities to be shared by companies and their investment bankers. Congress then passed the Securities Act of 1934, which set up the Securities and Exchange Commission (SEC) and focused on the conduct of secondary markets. Later on, in the 1960s, it passed the Securities Investor Protection Act, which provided for a $600 million fund (paid in by the securities industry and supported by a line of credit from the U.S. Treasury) to protect investors who maintain brokerage accounts from losses associated with the failure of the firms involved.

None of these acts, however, provided for the government to guarantee deposits with securities dealers or to guarantee investment results. So there was less need to get "inside" the firms; the taxpayer was not at risk. Though the SEC developed into a regulator willing to use its powers to protect individual investors and ensure the integrity of the markets, most of the discipline to which securities firms have been subject since 1934 has been provided by the market itself. Prices have risen and fallen. Many investors have lost money. Many firms have failed or have been taken over by competitors. Others have entered the industry with a modest capital investment and succeeded. Firms are in fact "regulated" by the requirements of their customers, creditors, and owners—requirements demanding marked-to-market accounting, adequate capitalization, and disclosure of all liabilities, as well as supervisory and legal proceedings. Customers, for example, require good service and honest dealings, or they will change brokers.

These market-driven requirements have proven to be just about as effective regulators as any body established by government.

Insurance and Other Financial Services

In the United States, insurance regulation is undertaken at the state level, conducted by state insurance commissions. Insurance and banking are generally separated; one prominent exception involves insurance holding companies (for example, Prudential, Travelers, and Equitable), which are permitted to own securities firms, provided that such firms are organized as separate subsidiaries. These businesses are set up differently in Europe, where insurance and banking are permitted activities for both sets of providers, with both being regulated at the national level. In a recent departure from these existing regulatory arrangements, however, the European Union (EU) has developed its own insurance-industry directive, which will determine how insurance practices within the EU evolve.

International Regulations of Banking and Securities

As U.S. banking and securities activities have become increasingly integrated with those in foreign and offshore markets, their regulatory regimes have also become more international. New banking regulations were imposed in the 1980s to provide for minimum capital adequacy and for the conduct of banks doing business with the European Union. After the capital adequacy rules were considered by a committee of the Bank for International Settlements, they were adopted by all EU members, Switzerland, the United States, and Japan. The Union's Second Banking Directive permits banks having a license to operate in one Union country to operate in all, subject to home-country regulatory supervision. Banks may participate as they wish in unregulated markets, such as those for foreign exchange and commodities as well as the Eurocurrency and Eurobond markets, but their activities as institutions are still subject to overall control of the home-country banking regulators. The Baring Brothers case provides an example. Although the firm's actions in Singapore and Japan ultimately brought it down, it was the responsibility of the Bank of England, as home-country regulator, to supervise and control the global activities of the firm. The case demonstrated how difficult this is to do. Predictably, it has resulted in closer scrutiny of banks by regulators.

In the securities industry, international regulatory controls are both less extensive and more complex. There is no requirement for home-country regulation of the global activities of U.S. or Japanese nonbank firms. Regulation is thus a matter of compliance with the local regulations in each country where a firm operates. National regulatory requirements are often very different from one another, however. This presents each firm with the massive task of monitoring regulatory compliance in each locale and promotes an inefficient use of regulatory capital. Still, the essence of the regulatory differences between securities firms and banks is that banks are subject to more explicit limitations on their businesses—especially through the requirement to maintain minimum amounts of capital—than are securities firms. The latter, however, have to bear the costs of maintaining expensive local compliance systems. And since securities firms are dependent on banks for much of their funding, they have to meet strict credit standards acceptable to the banks.

Regulatory Dilemmas

As we have seen, financial services have been, and will continue to be, subject to significant governmental regulation and supervision due to the fiduciary nature of the business and the possibility of social costs associated with institutional failure. Indeed, small changes in financial regulation can bring about truly massive changes in financial activity. Such changes can affect the competitive viability and performance of different types of financial institutions spreading their activities across the financial spectrum.

An amazingly difficult set of policy trade-offs invariably confronts those responsible for designing and implementing a properly structured financial system. On the one hand, they must strive to achieve financial efficiency for the financial system itself and to protect the competitive viability of financial institutions that are subject to regulation. On the other hand, they must safeguard the stability of institutions and the financial markets as a whole, often by protecting them from their own mistakes. In addition to encouraging acceptable market conduct—including the politically sensitive, implied social contract between financial institutions and small, unsophisticated customers—regulators must also protect against problems of contagion and systemic risk. The need to maintain an adequate safety net is also beset with difficulties such as moral hazard and adverse selection. These difficulties are especially problematic when financial products and activities shade into one another, when activities both on and off the balance sheet are involved, and when domestic and offshore business are conducted.

Regulators constantly face the possibility that *inadequate* regulation will result in costly failures, as against the possibility that *overregulation* will result in opportunity costs in the form of financial efficiencies not achieved, or in the relocation of firms to other, more friendly regulatory regimes. Since any improvements in financial stability can be measured only in terms of damage that *did not occur* and costs that were successfully *avoided,* however, the argumentation is invariably based on "what if" hypotheticals. There are consequently no definitive answers with respect to optimum financial regulatory structures. There are only "better" and "worse" solutions as perceived by those to whom the regulators are ultimately responsible, in light of their collective risk aversion and reaction to past regulatory failures.

Some of the principal options that regulators have at their disposal include "fitness and properness" criteria, under which a financial institution may be established, continue to operate, or be shut down; line-of-business regulation as to what specific types of activities financial institutions may undertake; and regulations as to liquidity, various types of exposures, capital adequacy, and marking-to-market of assets and liabilities. Regulatory initiatives, however, can have their own distorting impact on financial markets. Regulation becomes especially difficult when financial markets evolve rapidly, with regulators chronically lagging one or two steps behind, and when there is jurisdictional conflict or overlap between different regulators.

The regulatory vehicles that may be used for implementation—the "delivery system"—range from reliance on *self-control* by the boards and senior management of financial firms, to industry *self-regulation,* to *public oversight* by regulators with teeth, including the possibility of criminal prosecution.

There has been lively debate about the effectiveness of *firm* self-control in the financial services industry; firms continue to suffer from incidents of misconduct despite the often devastating impact on their franchises. Control through *industry* self-regulation is likewise subject to substantial controversy, especially in the United Kingdom, which relies heavily on this approach. The self-regulatory body governing pension funds failed to catch the disappearance of the Maxwell pension money. The Personal Investment Authority (PIA) for years failed to act against deceptive insurance-sales practices at the retail level.[7] And there are always political charges of the fox watching the henhouse; the City of London has been much criticized for the very "easygoing ways" that have done so much to contribute to its competitive success in the global marketplace.[8]

Despite its preference for self-regulation and quiet settlement of disputes behind closed doors, there is evidence that the kind of aggressive investor protection that exists in the United States is making inroads. The Investment Management Regulatory Organization (IMRO), which oversees some $2.2 trillion in assets, has been increasingly vigilant in investigating problems, including a 1996 fine of $1.2 million against Jardine Fleming for late booking of trades. This is seen as critical in view of London's role as an international fund management center, and IMRO has interpreted its mandate as including activities of firms doing business anywhere in the world that have ties to firms regulated by the agency. IMRO has taken to issuing press releases on disciplinary actions, maintaining a register of all key individuals such as fund managers and directors, and increasing its training efforts. Instead of politely requesting Morgan Grenfell Asset Management (MGAM) to turn over pertinent files in the scandal discussed in Chapter 1, IMRO investigators raided MGAM offices and hauled files away in a large black garbage bag.[9]

But reliance on *public oversight* for financial regulation has its own problems. Virtually any regulatory initiative is likely to run up against powerful vested interests that would like nothing better than to bend the rules in their favor.[10] Even the *judicial* process that is supposed to arbitrate or adjudicate matters of regulatory policy may not always be entirely free of political influence or popular opinion. Finally, some of the regulatory options, such as capital adequacy rules, are fairly easy to supervise but potentially distorting due to their aggregate, broad-gauge character. Others (for example, fit-and-proper criteria) are possibly very cost effective but devilishly difficult to supervise, in much the same way that some supervisory techniques are far more costly for the industry to comply with than others.

Perhaps the most effective regulatory interventions in the operations of securities firms are those that build upon the dynamic relationship that exists between regulators and the regulated. These interventions often result in healthy and constructive nonlegislative remedies to newly perceived problems. In some cases such interventions are triggered by a perceived failure in the marketplace. In other cases public attention has been drawn to an incident, and a regulatory response is unavoidable. And though some of these interventions result in redundancies or increase costs with little benefit, they nevertheless reflect the reality of the regulatory give-and-take in today's marketplace. Some recent examples are the following:

Problem: Some securities firms were shifting their holdings of individual stocks immediately prior to releasing research reports on the same companies—so-called purposeful trading.

Response: In August 1995 the SEC banned purposeful trading in all securities transactions, a ban that had already been in place on the New York Stock Exchange and been proposed by the National Association of Securities Dealers to cover all other cash and derivatives markets as well. The rule also reinforces the preexisting practice of maintaining "Chinese walls" between research and trading departments.

Problem: Retail investors cannot understand mutual fund prospectuses, which contain long and often incomprehensible assemblages of legal language that befuddles rather than clarifies investment decisions.

Response: SEC Chairman Arthur Levitt prodded several mutual fund companies to issue plain-spoken, "low-fat" prospectuses that would fit on two sides of a letter-sized piece of paper covering eleven points: the fund's goal, its investment strategy, the risks involved, the portfolios for which its investment would be appropriate, fees and expenses, past performance (annual historical returns expressed in a bar chart, and numerical average annual returns), who manages the fund, how to buy shares, how to get money out, how income and capital gains are distributed, and whether other services such as check writing are available. Following successful market tests the format may be made mandatory, although the full prospectus will still be available to interested investors.[11]

Problem: Concerns were raised in the media and in Congress about sales practices for over-the-counter derivatives by unregulated affiliates of SEC-registered broker-dealers and futures-commission merchants registered with the Commodities Futures Trading Commission (CFTC), specifically with respect to the characteristics of the products involved and their suitability for end users.

Response: A Derivatives Policy Group comprising representatives of major firms was formed in March 1995. It presented a "framework for voluntary oversight" covering prudential measures, management controls, enhanced reporting, evaluation of risk in relation to capital, and counterparty relationships (including such issues as transparency in marketing materials and sales practices).[12]

Problem: The rogue trading activity of Nick Leeson at Barings was not detected by British, Singaporean, or Japanese regulators, with special criticism leveled at the United Kingdom authorities, where Barings was based.

Response: The Bank of England (which regulates banks in the United Kingdom) and the Securities and Futures Authority (which regulates securities firms) hastily decided they needed to collaborate in order to prevent any more cases of malfeasance from falling through the cracks. This collaboration was especially urgent because European universal banks have acquired British merchant banks and British clearing banks have invested heavily in their merchant-banking subsidiaries. The two regulators therefore decided to exchange more information and to jointly visit banks engaged in the securities business. According to Richard Farrant, chief executive of the SFA, "If there is integration in the marketplace, then the regulators may have to follow."[13]

Some of the enforcement problems involve plain old criminal activity. For example, the bull market in stocks during 1995 and 1996 was accompanied by vigorous activity in the market for initial public offerings (IPOs) of stock in small companies underwritten by small brokerage firms. Evidence mounted that organized crime had infiltrated the market, involving threats and intimidation, beatings, and gross exploitation of both investors and issuers at some two dozen brokerage firms.[14] As in the legalized gambling business, organized crime goes where the money is and is devilishly hard to dislodge once it gets entrenched. Unlike with casinos, though, the issue here is the integrity of the capital markets and requires aggressive law enforcement initiatives.

The Net Regulatory Burden

It is useful to think of financial regulation and supervision both as imposing "taxes" on and giving "subsidies" to the operations of financial firms. On the one hand, the imposition of reserve requirements, capital adequacy rules, interest/usury ceilings, and certain forms of financial disclosure requirements can be viewed as imposing implicit "taxes" on a financial firm's activities, at least in the sense that these requirements increase costs. On the other hand, regulator-supplied deposit insurance, lender-of-last resort facilities, and institutional bailouts serve to stabilize financial markets and reduce the risk of systemic failure, thereby lowering the costs of financial intermediation. They can therefore be viewed as implicit "subsidies" provided by taxpayers.[15]

The difference between these tax and subsidy elements of regulation can be viewed as the *net regulatory burden* (NRB) faced by financial firms in any given jurisdiction. Financial firms tend to migrate toward those financial environments where NRB is lowest—assuming all other economic factors are the same. NRB differences can induce firms to relocate where transactions are done if the savings realized exceed the transaction, communication, information, and other economic costs of doing so. Since one can argue that, in today's global financial marketplace, transaction and other economic costs of relocating are likely to be small, one can expect financial market participants to be extremely sensitive to changes in current and perceived NRBs among competing regulatory environments. To some extent, the regulators responsible for particular jurisdictions appear to recognize this sensitivity and—in their competition for employment and value-added creation, taxes, and other revenues—have engaged in a form of competition over NRB levels, a kind of "regulatory arbitrage."[16]

Competition will spark a dynamic interplay between demanders and suppliers of financial services, as banks and securities firms seek to reduce their NRB and increase their profitability. If they can do so at low cost, they will actively seek product innovations and new avenues that avoid cumbersome and costly regulations. Doing so may be easier when there are multiple and overlapping domestic regulatory bodies, as well as in the global case of multiple and often competing national regulatory authorities.

A domestic financial system like the United States may have multiple regulatory authorities, too, complemented by a host of other regulators at the state and local levels. For example, financial activities at the federal level could fall into the regulatory domain of the Federal Reserve Board, the Comptroller of the Currency, the SEC, and the Commodity Futures Trading Commission, to name just the major regulatory agencies. Each of the fifty states also has its own regulatory body to deal with banking, securities, and insurance. Every city and municipality has an agency responsible for local income taxes, real estate taxes, transfer taxes, stamp duties, and so on, all of which affect the NRB for financial firms. The situation is complicated still further by ambiguity regarding the definition of a "bank," a "security," an "exchange," and so forth—blurring the lines of demarcation between both products and firms, and raising questions about which regulatory agency holds jurisdiction.[17]

NRB associated with regulations in onshore financial markets creates opportunities to develop parallel offshore markets for the delivery of similar services. Barriers such as political risk, minimum transaction size, firm size, and credit quality help temper the migration of financial activity abroad. Nonetheless, offshore markets can be used to replicate a variety of financial instruments such as forward contracts, short-term commercial paper, long-term bonds, Eurocurrency interest-rate futures, and the like—many of which are exposed to significant NRB by national financial authorities. Offshore markets thus pose a general competitive threat to onshore securities or banking activities. Entry and exit costs, currency conversion costs, and distance-related delivery costs—plus uncertainties surrounding these costs and problems of management control—continue to act, however, as effective barriers to complete NRB equalization across countries.

The rise of regulatory competition and the existence of offshore markets underscore the fact that financial services firms often have opportunities to execute transactions in any of several financial centers. The development of offshore currency and bond markets in the 1960s was a case in which borrowers and lenders alike found they could carry out the requisite market transactions more efficiently and with sufficient safety by operating off-shore, in what amounted to a parallel market. Domestic regulators usually want to have the transactions conducted within their own financial centers. This procedure serves their desire to maintain an adequate level of prudential regulation, to sustain revenues from the taxation of financial services, to support employment and output in the financial services industry and in linked economic activities, and to maximize their regulatory domain. And so the market for financial regulation has become "contestable"; other national regulatory bodies and offshore markets offer rules and opportunities that may be more favorable than those of the domestic regulator.

As any sort of economic activity gains mobility, it becomes increasingly difficult to subject it to regulation. In today's world, because communications costs are low and capital mobility is high, it is becoming less and less feasible for a state or a nation to impose an NRB that stands too far apart from world norms. It is nonetheless likely that a long-run equilibrium can be sustained with a *positive* overall NRB. Financial firms ought to value their being located in an important and orderly market, their access to financing by lenders of last resort, and their being headquartered in a stable and secure political climate. Indeed, markets that are almost totally unregulated, such as the Eurocurrency market (with NRB approaching zero), have not in fact completely dominated financial transactions that are subject to location shifting. Since financial institutions may find it in their interest to pay some regulatory tax, the economic question then centers around the sustainable magnitude of this net regulatory burden.

It seems likely that the progressive convergence in regulation of banks, securities firms, and other types of financial firms will continue. Players based in the more heavily regulated countries will successfully lobby for liberalization, and there will be an emergence among regulators of a broad-gauge consensus on minimum acceptable standards, a consensus that will eventually be accepted by those countries with substandard regulatory regimes. The objective is to optimize the balance between market efficiency and regulatory soundness. Market forces will then be free to determine what transactions are carried out, where, and by whom.

Performance Benchmarks

The conduct of a financial institution, as with all business firms today, is calibrated against two sets of benchmarks: its performance in a highly competitive market, and its performance against the changing standards of social control. Management must work to optimize between both sets of benchmarks. If it strays too far toward meeting the demands of social and regulatory controls, management runs the risk of poor performance in the market, severe punishment by shareholders, and possibly even a takeover. If it strays toward unrestrained market performance, or sails too close to the wind in terms of market conduct, management's behavior may cause disastrous results for the firm and its managers, shareholders, and employees.

These are the rules of the game, and firms have to live with them. But these rules are not immutable. There is constant bickering between firms and regulators about the details of external constraints on corporate conduct. Sometimes firms win battles (and even wars), leading to impressive periods of deregulation. Sometimes it's possible to convince the public that self-regulation is sufficient or that the effects of misconduct on reputation are powerful enough to obviate the need for external control. Sometimes the regulators can be convinced, one way or another, to go easy. Even so, after another major transgression or crisis, the system constricts again, generating a new spurt of regulatory activity. Managers, politicians, the media, activists, investors, lawyers, and accountants all join this battle to define the new rules under which business gets done. Eventually a new equilibrium is established, one that will define the rules until the next crisis or regulatory spurt.

There are also some more fundamental forces at work in society's review and assessment of business conduct. Laws and regulations governing the market conduct of firms are hardly created in a vacuum. They are rooted in social expectations as to what is appropriate and inappropriate, which in turn are driven by values imbedded in society. These values are fairly basic. They deal with lying, cheating, and stealing; with trust and honor; with what is right and what is wrong. These are the *ultimate* benchmarks against which conduct is measured and can be found, for example, in the Ten Commandments imbedded in Judeo-Christian values and in the foundations of other major religions.

But fundamental social or religious values may or may not be reflected in people's *moral expectations* as to how a firm's conduct is assessed. As everyone knows from Hollywood, businesspeople are stereotyped as unattractive—greedy, aggressive, unsympathetic individuals interested only in their own success. Certainly the image of Wall Street professionals in the 1980s, when Ivan Boesky and Michael Milken ruled the headlines, was not favorable. And movies such as *Wall Street* and best-selling books like *Bonfire of the Vanities, Den of Thieves,* and *Barbarians at the Gate* reinforced this image. So there may be a good deal of slippage between fundamental social or religious values and how these are reflected in the public's moral expectations of business conduct. Such expectations, however, are important, and managers ignore at their own peril the buildup of adverse opinion in the mass media, the formation of special-interest lobbies and pressure groups, and the general tide of public opinion that derides one or another aspect of market conduct.

These moral expectations may, indeed, have a profound impact on the formation of public policy. Even while firms conduct their business as usual and without incident, religious organizations, interest groups, and the media generate constant complaints about the inappropriate behavior of a firm or an industry. But then the fateful day comes. Some sort of social tolerance limit is reached. A firm goes too far. An accident occurs. A report is made public. The interests of various groups suddenly converge, and they demand action. The system squeezes, and another set of constraints on business conduct emerges, perhaps complete with implementing legislation, regulation, and bureaucracy. Or maybe the firm is hauled into court to face a massive lawsuit. Or its reputation is seriously compromised and the price of its shares drops sharply.

Further complicating the problems of both guiding and assessing the conduct of firms is the potential variability of fundamental values, of the public's moral expectations, and of the law. Drexel Burnham was crushed, some supporters of the firm say, by a sudden and unexpected reinterpretation of the law. But values and expectations also change, the former much more gradually than the latter. Indeed, fundamental values such as those identified here are probably as close as one comes to "constants" in assessing business conduct. But even in this domain things do change. As society becomes more diverse and mobile, for example, values almost certainly evolve. Values in Victorian England were very different from those a century before or after. They also differ across cultures. And the interpretation of values is often difficult. Is lying wrong? What's the difference between lying and bluffing? Is it only context that determines how behavior is assessed? The same conduct may in fact be interpreted differently under different circumstances, interpretations that may change significantly over time and differ widely across cultures. These uncertainties present difficulties for even the best-run firms.

Management's High-wire Act

As managers of securities firms review the experiences of their competitors, they cannot escape an important message. Most firms can endure the cost of an unsuccessful trade or a broken deal, however large, and still survive. These are business risks that firms have learned to manage by limiting their exposure and by detecting the damage early. Although a few firms in the long history of the securities industry have failed because of disastrous business deals, such cases are rare. Today, the greater danger is in falling afoul of regulators, or in becoming victim to a massive lawsuit for which the penalties may be severe, or in suffering massive damage to the firm's reputation.

Such injuries to firms are often the result of reactions by outsiders that may appear to professionals as unfocused, ambiguous, or even unfair. For example, outsiders may invoke a new reading of the legal rules or a new finding of culpability—requiring something different from what was required before. Though all professionals accept that regulators, litigants, analysts, and journalists have their jobs, too, these outsiders can become especially susceptible to public uproar and political pressure. They may then find it difficult to take the side of an offending securities dealer.

Wall Street has long suffered exposure to public criticism, especially in the early part of this century, after the crash of 1929, during the late 1960s (when many firms could not manage their back offices), and again during the 1980s. Wall Street has never expected to be understood by Main Street, nor much cared whether it was or not. But the difference today is the extensive application of closer surveillance and regulation, aggressive prosecution and plaintiff litigation, unsympathetic media and juries, and stricter guidelines for penalties and sentencing. All of these developments make it easier to get into trouble and harder to avoid serious penalties for mistakes. Global brokerage and trading operations involve hundreds of different, complex, and constantly changing products that are difficult to monitor carefully under the best of circumstances. Doing this in a highly competitive market, in which profit margins are under constant challenge and performance-rewarded employees have a powerful temptation to break the rules, makes the problems far more difficult. Performance-oriented managers, through their compensation and promotion practices, have unwittingly encouraged the unacceptable behavior that has brought many of them down.

The reality is that the value of the firm suffers from these uncertain conditions. Since maintaining (indeed, maximizing) the value of the firm is the ultimate duty of management, it is management's job to learn how to run the firm so that it optimizes the long-term trade-offs between profits and external control. It does not good to plead unfair treatment. The task for management is to learn to live with it, and to make the most of the variables it can control.

If we believe that the present value of any firm is the risk-adjusted discounted cash flow generated by the business franchise well into the future, we are driven to the conclusion that maximizing this value has three fundamental components.

1. *Managing the cash flow itself*—revenues and costs. To maximize cash flow, the firm cannot shy away from tough trading practices or from the need to be aggressive and effective in pursuing opportunities. And the firm must do so at acceptable costs.

2. *Managing the franchise value*—market share, the reputation of the firm, and its ability to obtain mandates, gain access to important clients and customers, and recruit and retain top talent. Obviously, good franchises can withstand a certain amount of scuffing from time to time, but damage greater than that can be extremely costly to the firm's owners.

3. *Managing the risks.* Most firms today can boast of extensive and sometimes impressive risk-management capabilities. But most of

these relate to position risks, settlement risks, default risks, and other customary forms of financial risk that broker-dealers incur. In most firms these risks are managed skillfully. There is growing evidence that institutions with high franchise values pay much greater attention to sound risk management than those with little to lose.[18] But the greatest risks appear now to be the willful or ignorant misconduct of employees and of management itself. Such misconduct can be difficult to detect. It can result directly from deficiencies in employee training, the firm's culture, performance evaluation, and compensation. Perhaps more fundamentally, firms need good leaders at the top, and at the top of the various revenue and cost centers. Leaders are not only people who are respected as top producers. They are also capable of setting high standards, enforcing them diligently, and doing all this in a cost-effective way that increases the firm's fundamental value in the marketplace.

In the end, it is leadership more than anything else that separates winners from losers over the long term. Unfortunately, much of the leadership in the securities industry is selected—perhaps of necessity—because of its highly effective product performance over a relatively short period; those who make money for the firm right now are promoted to become its leaders. This can create a nasty conflict between the firm's short- and long-term goals, usually to the detriment of the long-term interests of its shareholders.

This threat to firms' long-term interests is a matter of concern not just to the leaders and owners of firms in the industry, whose personal wealth may be directly at stake, but also to individuals who wish to have careers at the firm. For such individuals, the long-term value of the business matters greatly. Few truly outstanding employees are attracted to a firm for its immediate, short-term prospects. Most want to become part of a culture that seeks to maximize the value of the franchise. If the firm proves deficient in this respect, the employees with attractive alternatives will leave.

We believe that there is much a firm can do to fortify its franchise value and to modify the risks to which it is exposed. These topics are discussed specifically throughout the succeeding chapters and are brought together in Chapter 11 ("Zookeeping"), which emphasizes management issues. A guiding principle, we believe, is that good professional behavior reinforced by a sense of belonging to a quality franchise is a valuable *competitive advantage* for a firm and will also lower the risks of, and the consequences from, mistakes or misbehavior.

Exhibit 2-1   Basic Rules for Appropriate Conduct in Finance

Basic Responsibilities

Would my actions violate any one of several responsibilities anchored in law, social and ethical norms, professional codes, and company policies?

Infringement of the Rights of Others

Could my actions, or those of my firm, appear to be judged by a well-informed and impartial observer as "unfair"? That is, would they impair the rights of others, rights that have been defined by a consensus of society as a whole and known to everyone?

Franchise Value

Would my actions, or those of my firm, compromise our reputation for fair and honest dealing, even in tough business situations, and thereby cause lasting damage to shareholder value?

Reputation Knowledge

Would I be comfortable seeing a fair report of my own actions, or those of my firm, prominently and widely disseminated in the media?

What If It Were Done to Us?

If this action were undertaken by one of our competitors, would we grudgingly admire their savvy, or would we cry "foul"?

As a starting point we establish intuitive smell tests—rules for personal conduct by employees. The firm has to accept the responsibility for training its employees in laws, expectations, and values and in identifying the many hazards and pitfalls that are characteristic of the securities industry. The firm must also reinforce its goals with management systems and leadership actions that demonstrate leadership's commitment. It must "walk the talk." Employees should know what they need to do when, inevitably, difficult choices or decisions arise. To avoid making serious mistakes, employees must consult first the rules and then, if necessary, their superiors. Exhibit 2-1 is an example of such guideposts.

Sound rules, to be in synch with the environment and the times, cannot be concerned only with the firm's immediate self-interest. They have to establish a balance between the firm's own interests and those of the firm's clients and counterparties. The rules need to reflect the realities of the outside world—what the public's perception would be if the firm's conduct in a particular situation were known. They must fit the times and appear to be responsive to the interests of others. They must be able to survive changing times and markets. And they must, above all, seek to preserve the long-term value of the firm and its franchise, and to set a pattern for employees that will reinforce the congruence of long- and short-term interests.

3

Caveat Emptor
and the
Retail Investor

■

Self-interest and trust. Uneasy bedfellows, at best. But such is the life of a broker: motivated by self-interest to form relations of trust with his clients. Most brokers somehow maintain a balance between the two. Some, though, care too much about trust and too little about self-interest. Some of these don't make enough money to succeed, and often leave the industry. And some brokers care too little about trust and too much about self-interest. They can make plenty of money—until their actions catch up with them. Their clients are the most direct losers. But when this happens, the whole securities industry loses, too. The public comes to distrust brokers, even though most of them do a good, steady job of offering valuable services to clients who appreciate them.

The Client-broker Relationship

The fiduciary duty of care and loyalty that a lawyer or accountant owes a client is defined in terms of standards that have governed and shaped their respective professions over centuries. The professional obligation of a broker is not as well defined. One would like to think that brokers are expected to represent a client's interests, first and foremost, and to act consistently in accordance with the client's needs and wishes. The basic problem is the potentially serious divergence that can develop between the broker's professional obligation to the client and his or her own immediate financial self-interest. This is the classic principal-agent problem encountered in many areas of law, economics, and finance. This problem can generally be avoided in finance if clients take advantage of the open market, which enables them to shop around for investment services, and if brokers remain aware of the value of their own personal business "franchises."

The challenge of providing the best possible advice to clients and carrying out their wishes is complicated by the difficulty of determining what clients actually want (or ought to want). Despite the wealth of information readily available in the public domain, not all clients are well informed about the markets and the alternatives presented to them. Nor, despite their desire to increase the value of their assets, are all clients sophisticated enough to understand the risks they face in investing. Hanging over brokers' heads is another problem, too. No matter how clearly brokers state their advice, clients may see a violation of fiduciary obligation where in fact there is none; for example, when a portfolio performs far worse than expected and the client selectively remembers a truncated version of what the broker advised.

That said, brokers have ample opportunities to exploit clients. Regulators and lawmakers have therefore given primary emphasis to the protection of retail investors rather than sophisticated institutional investors. Caveat emptor—let the buyer beware—may have been good enough for the Romans, but our citizens are aided in their dealings in financial markets by state securities laws, the Securities Acts of 1933 and 1934, the Investment Act of 1940, and rules of the National Association of Securities Dealers and the various stock exchanges. Under current U.S. regulations, brokers are obligated to assess their clients' level of sophistication, history, past exposure to financial investments, financial status, and investment needs. The broker is required to "know the client" and to be sure that any investments offered are suitable and appropriate.

This mighty effort at regulating transactions at the broker-client level is supported by a legitimate national interest in protecting the integrity of the capital markets. Corruption of the functioning of the capital markets—especially at the retail level, which represents the overwhelming source of savings in the financial system—would be disastrous. It would deter the participation of investors, misallocate financial resources, erode liquidity, and impede the operation of critical market mechanisms, with debilitating consequences for economic growth.

Although broker compensation after a year or two of seasoning is usually based entirely on performance, it includes several elements.

Commissions

Salespersons are mainly compensated by commissions or their equivalent. Prior to 1975, commissions on the New York Stock Exchange (and virtually all other stock exchanges in the world) were fixed, that is, subject to minimum levels established by the exchange. On 1 May 1975 ("May Day") the minimums were withdrawn, and all brokerage commissions became negotiable. Large institutions, of course, immediately succeeded in negotiating much lower commissions for their orders. Some modest relief was also passed on to individual customers, depending upon how actively they traded and how large their business was. The smaller customers obtained very little relief. Their accounts were more expensive to maintain, it was argued, so they should pay more. In time, the negotiability of commissions spread. The London Stock Exchange adopted negotiated commissions in 1986, when the reforms known as the "Big Bang" took effect. Commissions are becoming negotiable virtually everywhere today, even in Tokyo.

Securities traded on exchanges involve outright commissions, which are disclosed to customers. For securities not traded on exchanges, such as over-the-counter (OTC) stocks traded on the NASDAQ system and bonds of all types (also mainly traded OTC), commissions are not charged. Firms earn the difference between their quoted buy and sell prices. However, firms include the equivalent of a commission for such trades in calculating salespersons' cumulative compensation.

Firms set the rates of commission for individual customers, and a scheduled percentage of commission dollars (or the equivalent) will be paid out to the brokers. Firms also establish break-points defining the transaction sizes at which commissions decline, and set higher commissions as incentives for the sale of in-house or other profitable products the firms are trying to push. New issues of stock involve much higher sales commissions to assure effective distribution, but these commissions are paid by the issuer, not the investor.

Since the income of brokers is determined by their production of commissions (or the equivalent), they can be expected to work hardest on transactions that will optimize their own bottom line. Salespersons therefore have a built-in temptation to put their own interests ahead of their clients'. Firms try to establish systems and procedures to contain such temptations, although firms' own interests are often complicated by the need to push mutual funds or special investment vehicles that they manage.

The pressure to increase commission income is what creates the motivation and potential for broker misconduct. Commission-based incentives are believed to dominate broker behavior. As the commissions from their trades increase, brokers' incomes increase progressively. According to one account, a broker in 1994 generating $149,000 in commissions at Smith Barney was able to keep just under $50,000 (33 percent), but a broker generating $1 million in commissions was able to keep $425,000 (42.5 percent).[1] Such sliding-scale benefits create a pay structure for brokers that encourages in-and-out trading and similar behavior not consistent with "suitability" criteria associated with clients' best interests.

Sales Contests and Trips

Securities firms have from time to time mounted single-product sales contests in which "winners"—those meeting a certain sales quota for the promoted product—receive trips to Hawaii, Rolex watches, or similar rewards. Such promotions are no different from those used in the automobile and many other industries as a motivational technique. Well-established brokers can fairly easily win several such contests each year. Sometimes the contests are arranged by the firm, sometimes by the management company whose mutual funds are being sold through brokerage firms. The contests certainly help to generate sales. But in the words of one investor, "When a product is part of a contest you run the risk that the broker's interest in, say, a trip to Hawaii, may be placed above your interest in a good investment. The broker goes to Hawaii, and Lord knows where you end up."[2]

Up-Front Payments

In both recruiting and compensation, firms have tended to reward sales skills rather than the quality of financial analysis and advice, and have been known to pay substantial up-front signing bonuses for new hires to attract the best sales talent and to raise internal competition among salespersons. The practice is highly controversial. Critics claim it is predatory; large firms are weakening smaller rivals by attacking their most important asset. The practice pushes up broker compensation for the entire industry and reduces broker tenure (and hence loyalty). The practice also decreases the loyalty of clients to their firms, relationships that have traditionally belonged to the firms rather than to individuals, who may change firms. In defense of the practice, others argue that up-front payments help diminish the potential for conflicts over clients by tiding over new hires until they can develop a viable clientele; new hires are under less pressure to boost commissions through sales to clients of their previous firms.[3] According to one report, a successful branch manager who moved from Smith Barney to Prudential Securities in 1994 lured twenty-five brokers from his former firm with a "70-50-50" plan for the best producers. The plan included a signing bonus of 70 percent of the past year's commission income plus 50 percent of the next fifty months' gross commission earnings.[4]

In May 1994, SEC Chairman Arthur Levitt appointed a committee (chaired by Daniel Tully, then CEO of Merrill Lynch) to make recommendations for changes in compensation practices in the retail brokerage industry that would avoid actual and potential conflicts of interest. The following April the committee issued the "Tully Report," which contained a recommendation "to end up-front bonuses (or pay them over several years)."

Merrill Lynch apparently did not fully subscribe to the Tully Report. In the last quarter of 1994, the firm paid more than $21 million in up-front bonuses (part of which was deferred) to lure successful brokers from other firms. Merrill explained that the payments were partly to compensate these brokers for the loss of commissions on the portion of their book that did not follow them to Merrill. And a year after the Tully Report appeared, Merrill was reported to have lured several brokers from a St. Louis firm, Edward D. Jones. A senior Merrill spokesman noted that the firm pursued all sorts of business opportunities and was in conformance with the letter of the Tully Report because half of the signing bonuses were paid over a ten-year period.[5] Despite its own practices, Merrill has gone to court repeatedly to stop its own brokers from defecting. The clients belong to the firm, not to the broker, Merrill claimed in a recent lawsuit, and for a broker to take them along to another firm would be "nothing short of piracy."

Incongruence of Goals

Life for new brokers tends to be tough, with a bullpen sales environment even among the major firms. Compensation is totally dependent on the sales scoresheet, and underperformance is severely punished. The five-year broker attrition rate among new hires approaches 75 percent at most firms, and even veteran brokers who bring in less than $150,000 in commissions are frequently asked to leave.

The fundamental divergence of interests in the relationship between brokers and clients reflects an incongruence of goals and is a primary cause for broker misconduct. With an eye to the commission scale (including perks) offered by the firm, brokers have strong incentives to make recommendations to clients that increase these payoffs. These recommendations often involve investments that make little sense from the perspective of investor objectives. This relationship between broker and client can be highly asymmetrical. While the client faces unlimited losses, the broker's own risk of loss is negligible, and gains may come at the client's expense.

On the other hand, brokers have their own franchises to worry about, and this concern can offset some of the agency problems the customer faces. Nothing kills a broker's relationship with a client faster than bad investment performance or advice that turns out to be against the client's best interests. The most experienced and successful brokers work as independent business people who, though associated with a firm, see themselves as owning valuable franchises that enable them to sell securities to personal customers over a long period of time.

Peddling questionable products is no better for the long-term value of such businesses than a McDonald's franchisee who lets his restaurant become filthy. Far from pushing any old investment their firm is trying to sell, good brokers sell solutions to their clients' particular financial problems and requirements, provide sound and timely advice, and offer good investment opportunities. Such brokers will refuse to sell unsuitable products to their clients. The long-term interests of these brokers are substantially aligned with those of their clients.

Transparency

Firms are required to disclose all material information regarding any given investment to their retail clients. But many firms do not voluntarily disclose sufficient information to enable investors to determine either the performance of their accounts or the cost of individual trades. Mutual funds may involve front-end loads, discounts charged against the invested principal to compensate the management company for the cost of setting up accounts and investing the money. Customers may also be charged commissions to buy shares in the mutual fund. These commissions are disclosed in the order-confirmation reports sent to customers by the broker. But the "confirms" might not mention certain fees or other expenses charged to investors' accounts. Though brokerage firms disclose aggregate commissions, clients often cannot determine the number or cost of in-and-out trades made. And though no commission is charged for over-the-counter trades in stocks and bonds, the broker has earned the equivalent of a commission by selling the security at the bid side of the market. Neither confirms nor brokerage statements reveal the difference between the cost to the firm of the OTC position sold and the price charged to the customer.

Sometimes investors do not understand the information disclosed, while brokers may feel it is not their duty to explain it. Details may be omitted in order to persuade less sophisticated investors to undertake certain investments. The asymmetry of information regarding investments creates a "power distance" between brokers and clients, and clients may lose control over decisions due to broker omissions (whether intentional or not). If clients do not understand the nature of the brokerage business, the broker's motivation, and the proper interpretation of sales materials, they are potential prey for rogue brokers with the intention to defraud.

Reputation for Honesty

Many people have developed a distrust for the brokerage profession over the years. Even stockbrokers themselves seem to lack high regard for the integrity of their profession. In a survey commissioned by the Securities Industry Association in 1995, only 52 percent of stockbrokers said that "honesty was important" in their jobs. This contrasted with 54 percent for appliance salespersons, 75 percent for real-estate agents, 78 percent for new-car salespersons, 82 percent for used-car salespersons, and 88 percent for insurance agents.[6] The explanation may be that brokers, especially new brokers trying to get started, tend to work the phones calling people they do not know. Many brokers have atrocious manners and may themselves be extremely frustrated by the low success rate of cold calling. And the widely publicized behavior of a few rogue brokers—many of whom hop from firm to firm, seemingly escaping any disciplining at all—has created suspicion and cynicism concerning the brokerage business as a whole. Indeed, the surge of dinner-time telephone calls from neophyte stockbrokers has annoyed so many people that the directors of the New York Stock Exchange voted in May 1996 to limit cold calling (but not too strictly, prohibiting calls only before 8 A.M. and after 9 P.M.). The SEC and NASD have also decided to impose similar restrictions; an industry sweep led by the SEC had found almost half of cold-calling brokers somehow violated existing federal laws.[7] Finally, a study conducted by a private market-research group and published in July 1996 showed that stockbrokers were steering novice investors into high-risk investments, had failed to profile their customers correctly, and routinely failed to explain the long-term nature of the investments and associated risks. The study surveyed the sales practices of twenty-one major firms. Its ratings of the firms for customer service and professional integrity were consistently mediocre, averaging a score of 73.5 of a possible 100. The best-performing firm, Smith Barney, scored only 75.1, a C in any professor's book.[8]

These studies place much of the blame on a small group of rogue brokers, ones who knowingly break the rules. But the public, which constitutes the general market for retail brokerage services, must be in doubt as to the quality of management and control in brokerage firms. How can firms allow these things to happen? Are the rogues so clever? Or is management too often turning a blind eye?

A problem that has plagued the industry for some time is widespread cheating by brokers who pay others to take the basic Series-7 and Series-63 licensing exams that allow them to practice. The NASD response has been to tighten security in the examination process. Among other things, the examination sessions are videotaped, and brokers caught cheating are thrown out of the business. The problem seems to be confined to smaller brokerage firms that provide only minimum training. None of the cheating involved brokers working for major firms.[9]

The integrity of the retail brokerage industry has thus been put at risk. Perhaps partly as a result, the share of commission income attributed to discount brokerages such as Charles Schwab, Fidelity Investments, and Vanguard, as well as to Internet-based trade-execution services, has grown steadily. Discount brokers' share of retail commissions rose to approximately 15 percent in 1995 from less than 2 percent in 1980.

Out of Control at Pru-Bache

Certainly the most dramatic recent case of institutionalized misconduct in the retail investment business involved Prudential-Bache Securities (now called Prudential Securities), whose $1.4 billion legal settlement broke all records. The story has been fully documented in a 1995 book by Kurt Eichenwald, *Serpent on the Rock,* which chronicles what is arguably one of the most sordid chapters in the history of Wall Street. False and misleading information was provided to retail customers of Prudential-Bache Securities—a wholly-owned subsidiary of the Prudential Insurance Group, the self-described financial "Rock of Gibraltar"—about the risks and prospective returns on $8 billion worth of mostly illiquid "limited partnerships," mainly in the real estate and oil and gas sectors.[10]

Limited partnerships are sophisticated investment vehicles that pass through untaxed cash flow and income to investors, who are either general partners (those who manage the investments) or limited partners (those who put up most of the money). Before the 1980s, these partnerships were available only to institutions and wealthy investors. But as the markets pushed up the values of the underlying properties, it was thought that individual retail investors should be offered a piece of the action, too. Pru-Bache's limited partnerships were sold in the 1980s and early 1990s to approximately 340,000, mainly small, often elderly, investors. According to SEC allegations, the sales employed outright lies and deceptions, both in broker tactics and in the promotional material distributed to brokers by the firm itself.

Pru-Bache brokers piggybacked on Prudential's premier name and reputation for honest dealing but behaved like nineteenth-century "snake-oil" salesmen, peddling grossly unsuitable and often fraudulent investments mainly to unsophisticated customers. Clients were given vague information about the investments and promised high returns and low risks. Brokers often implied that the investments were backed by Prudential Insurance's considerable resources. In the words of one broker, the investments were "just like CDs."[11]

At times, entire Pru-Bache branches appear to have participated in various forms of misconduct. Documents were altered to cover up wrongdoing. Trades were undertaken without customer authorization. Customers were not informed of losses, even though brokers were clearly required to do so. Account churning was common. Customers were systematically put into unsuitably risky investments. And employees not licensed to make trades were (improperly) paid commissions.

Perhaps most disturbing was management's failure to supervise employees and its toleration of questionable practices that were occurring on a breathtaking scale. James J. Darr, who was responsible for originating the limited partnership investments, had come under suspicion at his previous firm for being on the take, accepting personal payments from limited-partnership sponsors in exchange for distributing the investments. He allegedly continued this practice of under-the-table payments at Pru-Bache. According to one associate, "The products were dogs, and there was virtually no due diligence to ensure the investment ideas were legitimate. Darr intimidated employees into rubber-stamping harebrained projects." Anyone who questioned the due-diligence process or the performance of the limited partnerships was fired. "It's my way or the highway!"[12]

A number of Pru-Bache employees were indeed fired. Among them were members of a small group of whistleblowers in the limited partnership department who had uncovered Darr's past and raised suspicions about the business and how he ran it. Pru-Bache's CEO, George L. Ball—in the words of an informed observer, "one of the worst chief executives the securities industry has ever seen"[13]—didn't want to know about the allegations. When finally presented with the need to dismiss Darr, Ball took nine months to do so. This delay occurred even though the firm's legal department had already substantiated the charges against him, even as $500 million of new, dubious limited partnerships were being peddled to retail investors.

Many of the brokers knew the products were faulty, but they worked on commission and were subject to the firm's minimum-production rules. The payout for limited partnerships escalated from 37 percent on commissions of $200,000 up to 41 percent on commissions in excess of $450,000. In addition, for selling in-house funds there was a differential of 5 percent over the commissions paid by other investment banks or independent mutual-fund companies.

In the initial settlement with the SEC in October 1993, the firm acknowledged that it had misrepresented investments to clients, that its executives had poorly supervised branches, and that its brokers had abused customers' accounts. It admitted to criminal wrongdoing and was placed on three-years' probation that provided that a criminal indictment would be sought against the firm if it again stepped over the line. Such an indictment would almost certainly lead to the firm's demise. The firm also agreed to appoint an ombudsman to handle future complaints by employees or clients. SEC officials were assigned to be in residence at the firm during the probationary period.

With regard to compensating victims, Prudential agreed to an initial down payment of $330 million on an open-ended federal settlement, and the firm agreed to continue repaying all customer losses caused by fraud, regardless of the total final cost (investors in the Prudential-Bache Energy Income Partnerships alone had lost at least $1 billion). The compensation paid to clients escalated beyond the initial $330 million to $635 million by the summer of 1994 and to $1.4 billion by the end of 1995, the costliest settlement of its type in history.[14] Even the collapse of Drexel Burnham Lambert, which was the largest on record at the time, involved a settlement of less than half that amount.

Victims had several options for recovering their losses. They could submit a claim against the compensation fund Prudential had established for the purpose.[15] They could participate in the $120 million class-action settlement with the firm. Or they could take their cases to arbitration. At this point Prudential decided to play legal hardball to minimize the eventual cost of the settlement.[16] Prudential's lawyers tried to stop victims from opting out of the class-action settlement. According to one securities lawyer, "Despite all their talk about being the 'new' Prudential, they still won't deal honorably with the victims of their admitted fraud."[17] By the end of 1995, Prudential Securities had received over 152,000 claims for compensation, and claims were rolling in at a rate of 3,000 per week in advance of a 10 January 1996 filing deadline. About 56,000 claimants had already received settlements totaling $397 million.[18]

To provide new leadership at the parent company, the Prudential Group hired Arthur F. Ryan, a well-regarded former Chase Manhattan banker, to replace its discredited CEO, on whose watch the malfeasance took place. Hardwick Simmons, who had headed retail sales at Shearson Lehman Brothers, was hired to replace George Ball and began the long, difficult process of rebuilding the firm's reputation. He stopped paying brokers more to sell in-house products over offerings of other companies. He relieved the firm's top legal officer of his duties. He watched as SEC legal actions were taken against individual brokers and branch managers, and he strongly refuted arguments that they were only carrying out management's orders. "That's bull," said Simmons on the firm's squawk box. "I put on notice any manager, any supervisor, any officer of the company who knows such things go on, but one way or another feels unable to execute his personal responsibility because of interference from above." The firm took out full-page advertisements apologizing to the market and announcing the beginning of a new era at the firm. "Limited partnerships were sold by our firm to some clients that lacked adequate information and were not suitable for their investment needs. That was wrong."[19]

What are the lessons to be drawn from the Prudential Securities mess?

- *The broker and branch-manager compensation and incentive structure was clearly at the heart of the problem.* The firm had virtually no restraints in place to hold this structure in balance.

- *Management all the way up the line from first-level supervisor to CEO was inexcusably sloppy in everything from due diligence and marketing to compliance and personnel policy.* As long as revenues from Pru-Bache's only profitable business were rolling in, management didn't want to know of any possible misconduct. Management thereby aided and abetted corporatewide misconduct.

- *Problems with the management at Pru-Bache were compounded by management failures by the Prudential Insurance Company of America.* Prudential had bought a down-market firm it couldn't control in an industry it didn't understand, lending its capital and good name in ways that led to misuse of both, thereby putting its principal asset—its franchise—in serious jeopardy.

- *At almost every turn, especially in selecting and monitoring senior management at Pru-Bache, management at the parent company seemed unaware of what was happening.* Error led to error and compounded the reputational damage. That damage was further worsened when Prudential Insurance had to compensate life-insurance customers to the extent of an additional $1 billion in 1995 (and pay fines of $35 million in 1996) for improper actions of its *insurance* sales force. In July 1996 a year-long investigation into Prudential's sales practices by insurance regulators in thirty states concluded that management knew of the abuses and malpractices and "in many instances failed to adequately investigate and impose discipline" on the insurance sales force.[20]

In the end, no government civil or criminal charges were filed against any of the Prudential executives involved in the scandal after a 1996 federal court ruling in Washington, D.C., set a five-year statute of limitations for offenses covered by the SEC.

Prudential Securities was not the only firm to lose control of limited partnership sales during the boom times of the 1980s. Paine Webber took a pretax charge of $300 million in 1995 to settle claims from some of the purchasers of $2 billion in energy, aircraft leasing, and other limited partnerships it sold between 1980 and 1992.[21] And in a 1996 New York Stock Exchange arbitration, Merrill Lynch was required to pay an airline flight attendant $750,000 (including $500,000 in punitive damages) for misrepresenting limited partnerships sold to her a decade earlier. As serious as these incidents were, the two firms involved discovered them on their own and took corrective action. Prudential failed in both respects, and the firm paid dearly for its neglect.[22]

An Anthology of Broker Misconduct

Society's understanding of the broker's role remains a bit fuzzy, which creates confusion in determining the professional standards to which brokers should be held. These standards range from having an obligation to understand the client to merely executing the investment decisions dictated by an informed, sophisticated customer. To establish broker misconduct, one must also establish an intent to deceive, manipulate, or defraud. In order to decide which professional standards apply in any given case, one must first determine whether the broker was acting as an investment advisor or merely as a salesperson. An investment advisor has a higher degree of fiduciary duty to the client. In showing that a client has been harmed by a broker's actions, a linkage must be established between the broker's conduct and the client's actual loss. The client's level of sophistication is inversely related to the broker's delegated level of control. And the greater the control delegated, the greater the fiduciary duty.

Gouging the Customer

With negotiated commission rates, competition from discount brokers, and the rise of mutual funds, brokers have been able to charge very different prices for their services. This variability is made possible, in part, by the lack of transparency and disclosure, and, in part, by investors' uncertainties about the fees they should reasonably be expected to pay for their broker's advice and service.

A 1996 study of brokerage commissions at different firms revealed startling differences in commissions on a trade of five hundred listed shares at $10 per share for an IRA account. Among the full-service firms, Paine Webber charged $177 while Everen Securities charged $130. Among discount firms, Charles Schwab charged $89 while Pacific Brokerage charged $25. And among deep-discount firms, Marsh Block charged $39 while Wall Street Equities charged $24. The identical trade cost seven times more at the most expensive firm than at the cheapest. (And today E-Trade charges $14.95.) There are similar differences in fees and other charges such as registration-and-delivery fees, inactivity fees, account set-up fees, account-maintenance fees, and a host of specific services. Perhaps not surprisingly, some of the discounters had the highest fees.[23] There are few industries where it is so difficult to comparison shop.

Retail clients seem to get the same second-rate treatment even in markets set up specifically with their interests in mind. The second largest stock market in the world, the National Association of Securities Dealers Automated Quotation System (NASDAQ), was originally set up in 1977 as the electronic market of the future, one that would aid the small investor. Over the years, however, the market has tilted more and more in favor of its five hundred or so broker-dealers. Trades among these firms were done at far better prices than were available to individual investors. For example, investor orders were executed at the current bid or asked prices, with no obligation on the part of market makers to try to get customers a better price. Limit orders—orders to buy or sell at a given price—were hidden by traders from the market and were sometimes not executed at all. Electronic trading systems available to traders to get the best prices were unavailable to small investors. Many of these practices were mentioned in the SEC's sharp rebuke of NASDAQ in August 1996.

A related problem has been "payment for order flow," under which brokerage firms make additional money by routing small orders to specific securities dealers for execution. These dealers then bundle the orders together for execution at better prices. The difference, naturally, is paid by the retail customer. When the market-making unit of Charles Schwab announced it was suspending the practice in 1996, the firm lost so much business that it quickly retracted the move.[24] Nevertheless, the SEC has clearly kept its eye on soft-dollar practices, given the estimate that soft-dollar brokerage business brought to the industry by mutual fund companies is estimated to comprise 40 percent of all stock trading.

The SEC has mounted an ongoing effort to level the playing field. It has repeatedly proposed that all market makers be forced to show the prices they are quoting and to show limit orders when a quote matches or betters the price. The SEC has also proposed that dealers be required to try to get the best price for their clients. Opponents from the brokerage firms have argued that such rules would impede market efficiency, liquidity, and innovation, and work to the detriment of the investment community. Nevertheless, new NASDAQ rules approved by the SEC in August 1996 force dealers to publicly display all investor limit orders of at least 100 shares but not exceeding 10,000 shares, to notify investors of the absolute best prices at which they are willing to buy or sell a stock (previously displayed only in "private" markets), and to expand the size of any offered block of stock to include a customer's limit order at the same price.[25]

This regulatory debate has surfaced time and again. As markets become more efficient, the participants find their profits squeezed. They complain that they have to make a living, too. The regulators back off. But when regulators do make a stand, thinking the changes especially important, the members of the industry must either reengineer their businesses to become more efficient or take more risks in carrying out their work. Either way, the industry changes as competitors adapt to new conditions. After all, most of the benefits of perfect markets go to the market users, not the market's intermediaries.

Churning

Churning occurs when a broker exercises control over the volume and frequency of trading in a customer's account, and abuses this discretion by the disproportionate turnover of investments. The more volume, the more commissions. Such behavior is directly related to the compensation system under which brokers work, including volume-dependent commissions, sales contests, product-of-the-month campaigns, and large up-front bonuses to lure brokers and their client lists from other firms. Churning can be detected by determining the nature of the account activity in view of the customer's stated goals, purposes, and financial resources.

In one 1995 case reported in *Business Week,* an investor entrusted her nest egg of $800,000 to Shearson Lehman for investment in common stock. Her broker made $100,000 of stock purchases against her wishes and undertook large trades on margin in order to generate margin-interest income ($18,124) and commission income ($20,134). The net profit to her was $2,158. The investor then shifted her account to another firm, a discount house. Her broker at that firm also churned her account, this time in OTC stocks. She pulled her account, but the same thing happened at a third and fourth firm. In the end, her stake had shriveled to $370,000. The customer in this case blames herself for her own naiveté. But the question remains: Is there any other industry in which a customer needs to worry about getting taken to the cleaners by four successive vendors?[26]

Jay Goldinger, a self-proclaimed bond-market guru, attracted hundreds of investors to his firm, Capital Insight, with the promise of conservative investment strategies and superior returns. Aided by an uncommon gift of gab and a lavish lifestyle, Goldinger frittered away over $100 million of clients' money in massive derivatives trading based on a horribly wrong bet on the direction of interest rates. Unbeknownst to his clients, Goldinger had been accused of similar unauthorized trading and wrong interest-rate bets more than a decade earlier. Goldinger's 1995 trading in a client's account of $500,000 recorded five thousand trades. In the words of one knowledgeable observer, this level of activity "was per-se churning, . . . blatantly excessive trading."[27] In some months the commissions amounted to 10 percent of the assets under management, which rapidly eroded asset values. The results of the trading were nonetheless misreported to clients as hefty portfolio gains.

Following a joint investigation by the SEC, the Commodities Futures Trading Commission (CFTC), and the FBI, a federal criminal indictment was issued in March 1996 against Refco, one of the country's largest futures brokers, for aiding Goldinger's trading activities. Goldinger had allegedly commingled dozens of customer accounts without their knowledge or consent, allocated trading gains and losses among certain clients, falsified account statements, and failed to disclose the size of trading commissions. Refco's alleged complicity centered on delays between the time trades were made and the time they were posted to customer accounts, delays that gave Goldinger the time he needed to allocate the resulting gains and losses as he wished.[28]

Stuffing

Investor grievances are often linked to their purchases of in-house mutual funds and limited partnerships. These investments may not only entail significantly higher fees, commissions, and expenses, but also turn in substandard records of performance. Three-quarters of the mutual funds sold by Dean Witter, for example, have historically been in-house funds for which its brokers received between 5 and 15 percent higher commissions than for outside funds. Smith Barney has paid brokers a fixed bonus for selling in-house funds, a bonus that is deferred for five years. Branch managers also must meet specified targets for in-house product sales or lose a significant share of their bonuses.

Brokers push these in-house products because they get paid more. But what they push may not be suitable investments for all of their clients. In a 1996 arbitration, for example, Merrill Lynch was ordered to pay two Venezuelan sisters $1 million to settle allegations that a broker had put them into 75 percent margined collateralized mortgage obligations touted as providing 12 percent annual return risk free, a portfolio that lost over 50 percent of its value when rates turned up in 1994. The professional responsibility of a broker is to know the client and make investment recommendations that are consistent with the client's objectives. If a broker's initial recommendations were valid and reasonably formed from a broad base of knowledge, then the broker's professional obligation has been fulfilled. There is no guarantee, however, that the broker's advice will prove correct or that the investor will reap a profit.

Horror stories nonetheless abound. Enzo Lombardi, a Denver railroad mechanic, entrusted $92,000 to Commonwealth Financial Group, which traded him in and out of options and futures contracts despite his total ignorance of the underlying commodities markets or the pricing of the derivatives. Though part of Commonwealth's sales pitch was that Lombardi's losses on options contracts were limited to the premiums paid, his stake shriveled to $6,000, with nearly half of the loss attributable to commissions. Commonwealth argued that customers like Lombardi were gamblers who were fully aware of the risks and complained only when they lost. Lombardi's case was used in a suit by the CFTC against Commonwealth, arguing that the firm deliberately set out to ransack investors. A federal judge initially ruled that the prosecution had failed to show a systematic pattern of fraud. The judge later revised his ruling when presented with evidence that Commonwealth was continuing to use sales practices and to charge fees and commissions that made it impossible for an investor to gain unless he bet heavily, precisely, and correctly on a major price movement. Between October 1992 and August 1994, commissions charged by the firm accounted for 53 percent of customers' losses.[29]

Another good example of investment products that are sold, not bought, is the *retail preferred stock,* a security devised originally for institutional investors but revamped for retail investors when the market appeared to be hot. Retail preferred stock provides no tax benefits to individual investors, no maturity, no call protection after five years, and only a junior position in the capital structure. These features were described by one seasoned investment banker as "stealth junior junk bonds, with no financial covenants or rights in liquidation, which at least the bonds would have had." Yet these instruments were sold to retail investors.

In a sting operation revealed in 1996, the FBI set up a small brokerage firm to catch stock promoters who bribe brokers to buy stock in small companies and charged forty-six people with stock fraud and conspiracy—reportedly the largest single set of securities arrests ever made. Among them were promoters, officers of small companies, and stockbrokers, many of whom had records of previous securities violations and were set to benefit from shares previously issued to insiders at big discounts. Nor did the FBI have to wait very long after it opened the doors of its brokerage for the bribes to come in. "They beat our doors down," according to the head of the agency's New York office.[30] One of those arrested, Joseph V. Pignatiello, had a fifteen-year history of securities charges, dating back to 1982, which included a two-year jail term.[31]

Boiler Rooms and Bucket Shops

Much of the broker abuse of retail clients originates in small, local broker-ages that operate hand-to-mouth, have little reputation to protect, and engage in aggressive cold calling. They can compete in a limited number of ways, none of which serve the best interests of investors.

- Specialize in securities that lie below the big firms' radar screens. Such securities include penny stocks of small, unknown companies subject to inadequate disclosure, which allows selective information to be supplied to clients. Low-priced stocks also have higher-per-centage commissions at most brokerage firms.

- Peddle financial and commodity-linked derivatives such as gold or heating-oil futures and stripped asset-backed securities (often called "toxic waste") that the major firms want to unload. The toxic-waste problem came to a spectacular head in March 1994 with the $700 million collapse of a group of mortgage-backed derivatives funds run by David J. Askin. Investors lost over $400 million. Tape record-ings suggested that some of the major securities firms, including Bear Stearns, Kidder Peabody, and Donaldson Lufkin, had pushed Askin to accept millions of dollars worth of toxic strips, which he then sold to retail clients, who were rarely in a position to under-stand what they were buying.[32]

- Play on the get-rich-quick instincts of exceedingly unsophisticated investors by promising them huge returns and limited risks.

- Take advantage of clients by means of excessive commissions, un-authorized trading, extortionate spreads, churning of accounts, and other illicit practices.

These techniques are not new. In the 1920s, unscrupulous operators rented boiler rooms in office or apartment buildings to launch a blitz of sales calls to unsophisticated local customers. After a few months, the operations often closed down and disappeared with whatever customer funds had been accumulated. By the 1990s, such operations were extremely rare, but activities designed to promote the sale of unknown, highly risky securities to the unsuspecting public continue to be called "boiler rooms" or "bucket shops."

Today such operators, although registered as securities dealers, make their money by charging exceedingly high commissions to customers brought to the firm by brokers who call on some 200 to 450 clients per day. Once hooked, a customer can expect additional abuses before the broker disappears or complaints are filed against the firm, which itself may then collapse.

Many such firms encourage new brokers to build up their client lists by "dialing for dollars." Cold calling from purchased lists or the phone book, using scripted sales pitches, is now the norm. Most of these firms have no meaningful training programs, research support, or compliance infrastructure. And their brokers, though having taken the requisite tests and nominally met professional qualifications, are likely to be permanent occupants of the bottom of the profession. These brokers act as institutionalized predators on naive victims who can be tempted by a cold call or are subject to bait-and-switch tactics. Even somewhat more sophisticated clients can fall victim to the lack of disclosure and unauthorized churning of their accounts. Many clients never notice the deception until, sooner or later, they are rudely awakened by massive losses.

Consider the case of the Denver-based brokerage Chatfield Dean, which in 1991 took over eight offices and two hundred brokers from a liquidating penny-stock brokerage called Stuart James. Important in making its niche strategy work were the firm's sales tactics, which focused on stealing clients from the well-known brokerage houses. For example, brokers at Chatfield Dean used a three-call approach to sell stock (introduction, teaser, and hard-sell), and the firm's employee manual recommended that brokers make two hundred to three hundred calls per day.[33]

Clients often had unwelcome surprises. For example, a college professor bought 1,500 shares of a computer distributor named Random Access. When he called his broker at Chatfield Dean and asked for an account update, he learned he had instead been put into a company called Airship International. Though he had authorized no sales, his shares had already been through various trades before he ended up with that particular investment. In another case, a local couple was taken in by a cold-call promise that they would double their money by investing in Trinity Towne Investments. The couple committed their life savings ($4,700), which disappeared when Trinity Towne filed for Chapter 11 bankruptcy. Chatfield Dean was accused by NASD of using manipulative tactics with the intent to defraud and deceive its clients. Among other things, management admitted to charging more than 2,300 customers excessive markups—as high as 180 percent above the prevailing market price of shares—amounting to $1.3 million in overcharges during 1989–1993. In December 1993 the firm agreed to fines and restitution of almost $3 million.[34] Management admitted that it failed to supervise its brokers and to execute customer orders promptly, delaying trades for up to twenty-four hours. The firm also admitted that its brokers had "exposed customers to an undisclosed market risk" and "breached brokers' implied representation of fair dealing." The SEC levied personal fines on individual employees, including the chief executive, and several were suspended from the industry for various periods of time.

Boiler rooms seem to be going on the airwaves as well. Informed listeners to New York's WOR radio station in late 1994 could scarcely believe their ears as they listened to Irwin "Sonny" Bloch's long-running, nationally syndicated call-in show on financial advice. Bloch was urging viewers to invest in four radio stations and in coins and precious metals through the unknown DeAngelis brothers of Stroudsburg, Pennsylvania. The brothers were subsequently indicted for stealing millions of dollars from investors who fell for the pitch. And it was also discovered that Bloch had a personal stake in the investments. After fifteen years on the air, the program was discontinued. Allegations against Bloch included the fraudulent sale of unregistered securities and participation in a Ponzi scheme (that is, a scheme in which money from some investors is used to pay others). Bloch denied the allegations (including, despite ample evidence to the contrary, that he had any business connection with the DeAngelises). "The allegation is that I was in business with these yo-yos, O.K.? The answer is, I never have been and never will be. . . . The small issue is whether or not I read the ads too well and didn't make it clear enough that these were commercials. The big question is, how much responsibility does an announcer have?"[35] In his case, quite a lot. In October 1996 Sonny Bloch pleaded guilty to lying under oath and evading over $410,000 in federal income taxes, and was sentenced in New York federal court to twenty-one months in prison, three years' probation, and 750 hours of community service. This followed civil tax evasion judgments of $4.5 million, won by the government, and a guilty plea in New Jersey federal court on charges that he defrauded investors, on which he was awaiting sentencing.[36] But regulators remain concerned. Because the Federal Communications Commission is unable to regulate broadcast content (except for obscenity), such "infomer-cials" are increasingly replacing boiler rooms as a means of luring unsophis-ticated investors into various types of scams.

Can't Keep Bad Firms Down?

Like rogue brokers who keep popping up again and again, doing more than their share to damage the reputation of an entire profession, rogue firms have been equally difficult to drum out of the business. For example, in 1996 the SEC pressed its case against A.R. Baron, its chief executive, and head trader for defrauding New York University and other clients. Because the firm had been making unauthorized stock trades and refusing to execute trades, the SEC sought a temporary cease-and-desist order to require a full accounting to the SEC and the appointment of an independent compliance officer. The SEC discovered repeated instances of questionable conduct at the firm. According to an SEC lawyer, "Based on the kind of conduct we have seen at A.R. Baron & Company during our investigation, we're confident that this kind of fraudulent activity will continue and investors may suffer losses they may never recover."[37]

Sometimes different firms that flagrantly violate the rules are set up and run by the same individual. For example, James A. Villa worked for one of the most notorious brokers, First Jersey Securities, and then proceeded to run a firm called Thomas James, a penny-stock operator censured during 1990–93. That firm's successor, H.J. Myers (again run by Villa), had twenty-two of its employees fined or suspended from the business in 1996 (most for a week or less). The firm had sold four initial public offerings with excessive markups, and three of these later proved worthless. The firm admitted no guilt and promised to clean up its act.[38]

Or take the case of Comprehensive Environmental Systems and Alter Sales, two companies dominated by stock promoters who issued millions of shares of stock to bogus foreign companies owned by the group, in exchange for services never provided, and hyped share prices by arranging favorable television coverage of the companies' prospects. The role of the foreign shell companies was to avoid regulatory scrutiny through a loophole whereby unregistered stock issued to foreigners and consultants does not have to be reported. The group then dumped its shares as the price rose, visiting massive losses on hundreds of investors as well as on legitimate entrepreneurs over whose ventures they had gained control. Closely in-volved in the case was a former SEC lawyer who had earlier been assigned to investigate the promoters involved, and who joined forces with them shortly after his suspension for unauthorized disclosure of information.[39]

And then there was Stratton Oakmont of Lake Success, New York. The firm joined NASD in April 1987 and began using boiler-room tactics to peddle penny stock it had underwritten to retail clients throughout the country. Overcharges for the investments vastly exceeded the NASD guideline that anything in excess of a 10 percent markup indicates possible fraud. The chronology is impressive.

- *1990.* Stratton Oakmont was censured for trading more stocks than it was authorized to do. A principal of the firm was fined $2,500. The firm was fined five more times for failure to report its NASDAQ trading volumes, with fines ranging from $250 to $1,500.

- *1992.* In response to SEC allegations, but without admitting wrongdoing, Stratton Oakmont agreed to pay $500,000 in civil penalties and reimburse $2 million to customers for misrepresenting securities it sold in a high-pressure sales operation.

- *1994.* Stratton Oakmont was ordered by the SEC to implement the recommendations of an independent consultant for straightening out its operations. After the firm failed to comply, the SEC took further legal action. The U.S. District Court for the District of Columbia issued a permanent injunction against the firm regarding the practices in question, leading several states to suspend Stratton Oakmont from doing business.

- *1995.* Stratton Oakmont was censured for making customers sign agreements that prevented them from cooperating with investigations into the firm's business practices. The firm was also fined $20,000.

- *1996.* The firm was fined $325,000 to settle a case involving an initial public offering. The CEO was fined $50,000 and suspended from the industry for forty-five days. Both Stratton Oakmont and its CEO denied any wrongdoing.

Over the years, twenty states had banded together to make Stratton Oakmont settle investor complaints, but this collective effort failed. Finally, in 1996 the NASD disciplinary committee voted to eject the firm's president from the securities industry, to suspend the firm's head trader, and to fine both individuals. The committee also fined the firm $500,000, ordered it to return excess profits of $1.88 million to clients, and barred it from selling securities it owned to its customers. Since proprietary sales represent the core of Stratton Oakmont's activities, the NASD action would effectively put the firm out of business. Stratton Oakmont said it would appeal to the NASD national committee, arguing that the firm was now in full compliance with all securities laws and regulations and that the action was a vendetta against the firm. Meanwhile, it continued to do business as usual. But should the NASD effort fail, all fifty state securities regulators would be likely to revoke the firm's license. According to the director of the Alabama Securities Commission, "It appears they view the occasional payment of a fine to some regulatory body or another—even a hefty fine—as simply a cost of doing business. . . . This is their last-ditch effort to straighten out or get out of the business."[40]

Mutual Funds

There were over six thousand mutual funds in the United States at the end of 1996—more funds than there are stocks listed on the New York Stock Exchange. There are money-market funds, tax-free municipal-bond funds, taxable-bond funds, junk-bond funds, balanced funds, global funds, country funds, growth funds, income funds, growth-and-income funds, sector funds, hedge funds, tax-efficient funds, currency funds, and so on. Assets of mutual funds long ago outstripped the total deposits held by banks and thrift institutions. Funds continue to be one of the most dynamic sectors of the financial markets, with average annual growth in excess of 22 percent between 1975 and 1996. The $3.5 trillion of assets under management at the end of 1996 surpassed the total assets of life-insurance companies and approximately equaled those of commercial banks.

Competition for funds under management is among the most intense anywhere, heightened by analytical services such as Lipper and Morningstar, which track performance in terms of risk and return over different holding periods. *Business Week* and *Fortune* periodically publish summaries of the performance of publicly available mutual funds. These mutual fund scorecards are some of the hottest items on the magazine racks.

The bewildering array of products vying for the investor's dollar makes the fund-management business hypercompetitive and the jobs of fund managers among the most challenging in the industry. Despite clear warnings that past performance is no assurance of future results, a rise in the rankings often brings in a flood of new investments, with the manager handsomely compensated and moving on to bigger and better things in the fund-management game. On the other hand, serious performance slippage causes investors to withdraw funds, taking with them the manager's bonus and maybe his job. Still, the fund-management companies do well from their fees, expenses, front-end loads, digressive back-loads, and other charges. Managing funds is one of the most lucrative businesses in the securities industry, despite its highly competitive character.

Performance Pressures and Franchise Value

Fund managers make tough customers for the sales and trading desks of investment banks. For the funds, buying and selling securities is a cat-and-mouse game in which anything less than the best price can, in time, be severely punished in the performance rankings. Sometimes this concern can lead to questionable behavior on the part of fund managers themselves. Consider, for example, the case of Jeffrey Vinik, the former highly regarded manager of Fidelity's flagship Magellan Fund. Over a period of several weeks in 1995, Vinik was actively talking up the value of technology stocks even as he was unloading the fund's own heavy investment in the same stocks.[41] Once Vinik's maneuver became public knowledge, inquiries were made into personal trading by fund managers. It turned out that Vinik and several other Fidelity fund managers traded extensively for their own accounts, sometimes even shorting stocks held in the portfolios managed by the firm. This news followed on the heels of the firing of a star manager at Invesco Funds for violating personal-trading rules.

These embarrassing disclosures, coupled with an SEC investigation, contributed to Vinik's being fired by Fidelity, which also imposed new restrictions on personal trading. Other management companies followed suit, and a blue-ribbon panel was appointed to formulate appropriate restrictions on personal trading by fund managers. SEC Chairman Arthur Levitt, addressing the mutual fund industry at its annual meeting in 1996, raised the issue, too. If he sat on the board of a fund, Levitt said, "I would have reservations about portfolio managers actively trading for their own accounts. . . . With millions of investors migrating from insured bank accounts, this industry cannot afford even the appearance of conflicts of interest."[42] The Vinik affair is a good example of corrective forces emanating from the market itself, obviating the need for regulatory action.

The same thing happened when many money-market mutual funds (MMMFs) "broke the buck" after U.S. interest rates rose in 1994. Large numbers of funds managed by all kinds of firms were jockeying for position in the MMMF boom of 1992 and 1993. Retail clients, miffed by declining interest rates, deserted bank deposits and CDs for higher-yielding assets with equal or greater liquidity and check-writing privileges. Because the funds could invest only in Treasury bills, highly rated commercial paper, and similar short-term money-market instruments, however, MMMF managers found it difficult to produce even the small differences in performance that could lead to dramatic shifts of customers from one fund to another. Managers therefore began using fixed-income derivatives to change their funds' maturity profiles to extend duration and to benefit from declining rates. Since the underlying asset mix remained the same, this change in maturity profiles was perfectly legal and proper.

But rates started to increase in early 1994. This trend continued for the rest of the year, inflicting significant losses on many of the funds. Suddenly, a share bought for a dollar was worth a good deal less than a dollar. Retail clients, having believed that their investments were just as safe as bank deposits, were outraged. Many fund-management firms feared that the investors would sell their MMMFs, go back to bank CDs, and maybe pull out of other funds as well.

The biggest loser was Paine Webber, whose Short-Term Government Bond Fund lost 9.3 percent in a couple of months. Notwithstanding extensive disclosure about the differences between bank deposits and MMMFs (including the absence of deposit insurance), investors applied the old adage "If it looks like a duck, sounds like a duck, and walks like a duck, it's a duck." People thought if a dollar invested in their MMMF looked like a buck, it ought to act like one. They certainly did not expect to see its value fall below a buck. Sensing this discontent, the management of the Paine Webber funds, among others, scrambled to top up their funds with their own money, thereby attempting to prevent wholesale liquidations of MMMFs and to preserve the companies' reputations. Altogether, more than $650 million was put into the funds by management companies to repair the broken bucks, as shown in Exhibit 3-1. Once again the franchise effect was at work. Firms voluntarily incurred significant costs to themselves in order to safeguard their franchises.

Despite the voluntary action by the managers of major funds to protect their customers, the SEC announced in March 1996 that it was changing its rules to improve the stability of money-market funds by prohibiting investments in certain kinds of derivative securities.[43]

Exhibit 3-1   Money Market Mutual-Fund Bailouts by Managers, 1994–1996

Adviser	Reason	Amount ($millions)	Funds
Paine Webber	Purchases of securities to absorb derivatives losses	$268	Short-Term U.S. Government Income; Offshore Short-Term Government Income
Barnett Banks	Purchase of derivatives	$100	Emerald Prime Funds
United Services	Purchase of derivatives	$93	U.S. Government Securities Savings
BankAmerica	Cash infusion to offset derivatives losses	$68	Pacific Horizon Government; Pacific Horizon Prime Money Market
ABN Amro	Purchase of derivatives	$45	Rembrandt Taxable Money Market; Government Money Market
Value Line	Purchase of derivatives	$40	Value Line Cash Fund
Union Bank	Purchase of derivatives	$20	Stepstone Money Market
Piper Jaffray	Invested own assets to provide fund liquidity	$16	Institutional Government Income

Adviser	Reason	Amount ($millions)	Funds
Kidder Peabody	Loss recorded on purchase of $166 million of derivatives	$7	Cash Reserve; Premium Account; Government Money; Liquid Instruments Reserves Money Market; Liquid Instruments Reserves Government Securities
Wilmington Trust	Purchase of derivatives	$5	Emerald Prime Trust Fund
	Cash infusion to offset derivatives losses	$4	Rodney Square U.S. Government; Money Market
Fleet	Cash infusion to offset derivatives losses	$5	Galaxy Money Market; Galaxy Government; Galaxy U.S. Treasury
Wayne Hummer	Purchase of derivatives	$4	Money Fund
Northern Trust	Amount reserved to absorb potential derivatives losses	$4	Benchmark Diversified Assets; Benchmark Government Portfolio; Benchmark Government Select
Zweig	Cash infusion to offset derivatives losses	$0.4	Cash Fund
Retirement Systems Consultants	Purchase of Treasury bill to offset losses from an interest-rate spike	$0.1	Retirement System Fund

Nothing for Something?

The incentives for salespersons in mutual funds are much the same as they are in other types of investments. There are two important differences, however. Because of the various spreads, fees, and commissions, assessing the performance of one's brokerage account is often a complicated task. Assessing performance is much easier with mutual funds. The reason is a higher degree of transparency, especially with eagle-eyed reporters and analysts publicly comparing the performance of mutual funds over various investment periods. The funds' track records are easy to determine, and even small blemishes are clearly identified. The second difference is a consequence of this high degree of transparency. Because fund-management companies (especially the big ones) are extremely sensitive to anything that may damage their reputations, they take fast corrective action when things go wrong.

The mutual-fund business can be treacherous territory for the retail investor. In the first place, how are the uninitiated supposed to pick fund managers? Today, funds are required to disclose who the individual managers are, along with their backgrounds. A fund's track record is easy to check, but on the whole both equity and bond mutual funds underperform the market. Morningstar reported that since 1986 no more than 26 percent of stock mutual funds beat the S&P 500 Index during four different time periods. Performance in other sectors hasn't been much better. Exhibit 3-2 provides a comparison of the performance of different types of funds with their respective indices. Exhibit 3-3 shows the relative performance of publicly available growth-and-value funds (adjusted for management and related fees, but not for sales charges) against the S&P 500 Index and the Vanguard Index 500 portfolio. In all, 233 funds underperformed the indices, but only 53 outperformed them during the eleven-year period covered. Unless the retail investor knows something special about a given fund manager, it seems that a low-fee, passively managed index fund would produce more satisfactory results.

Still, people invest mainly in actively managed funds, despite evidence that these funds offer lower risk-adjusted returns and on average underperform index funds. Why? One possible explanation is the perceived value of professional fund management that is not incorporated into the share price (that is, the net asset value in the case of open-end funds). In a recent study of why people invest in mutual funds, Martin Gruber of New York University examined the performance of 270 open-end equity funds over

Exhibit 3-2   Comparative Mutual-Fund Performance

Stated Fund Objective	Average Five-year Performance Against Relevant Indexes (α)
Maximum Capital-gain Funds	−4.590
Growth Funds	−1.550
Growth and Income Funds	−0.680
Balanced Funds	−1.270
Corporate Bond Funds	−0.033
High-yield Bond Funds	−0.129
Government-backed Mortgage Funds	−0.020
Government Bond Funds	−0.096

Source: Data from Edwin J. Elton, Martin J. Gruber, Sanjiv Das, and Mathew Hlavka, "Efficiency with Costly Information," *Review of Financial Studies* 6, no. 1 (1993) and Christopher R. Blake, Edwin J. Elton, and Martin J. Gruber, "The Performance of Bond Mutual Funds," *Journal of Business* 66, no. 3 (1993).

Note: α is the estimated risk-adjusted return after all transactions costs and expenses, compared to the appropriate indexes using the so-called Wiesenberger-type fund profiles, over various holding periods and adjusting for survivorship bias, 1987–1991 for bond funds and various ten-year holding periods for stock funds.

a ten-year period.[44] He found that past performance is, in fact, related to future performance and that "sophisticated" investors who move into funds that have performed well in the past also do well in the future. Nonetheless, since managed funds do poorly on average, there must be plenty of other investors who do poorly.

So why do people continue to invest in funds that perform poorly? Professor Gruber attributes this phenomenon to "disadvantaged" investors who act on the basis of advertising and broker advice; are too lazy to do their own research or move their money; are restricted by fiduciary obligations from investing in better-performing funds (as with pension

Exhibit 3-3   **Performance of Growth-and-Value Funds versus Standard & Poor's 500 Composite Stock Price Index and the Vanguard Index 500 Portfolio (31 December 1986 to 31 December 1996)**

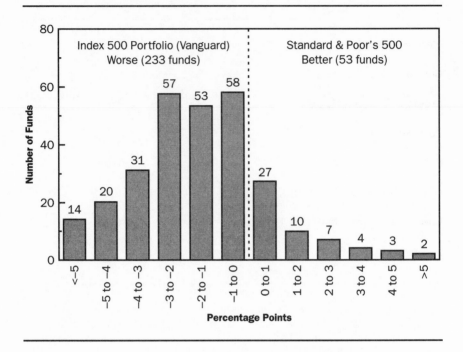

accounts); or are locked into particular investments by a reluctance to realize capital gains. Even sophisticated investors, of course, cannot short the dogs among their fund investments. All they can do is invest their new money elsewhere in order to gradually reduce the weight of the bad performers. By the same token, disadvantaged individual investors tend to rest content with their disproportionate share of underperforming funds. Indeed, Gruber finds that load funds perform just about the same as no-load funds. The disadvantaged investor basically pays the load for nothing, while the sophisticated investor in high-performance funds gets the benefit of professional management for nothing.

Nevertheless, the mutual-fund business is a good example of how regulation and competition can come together to serve the retail investor. Regulations in the United States require strict fit-and-proper criteria for management companies of mutual funds sold to the public, as well as extensive disclosure of pertinent information, such as the identity of fund managers, investment strategies, fees, and expenses. The threat of regulatory action and civil liability lawsuits keeps the pressure on the boards of mutual funds to carry out their obligations to investors and to pursue the funds' objectives in good faith. Some management companies, however, nominate individuals to serve as directors of several, even many, of the companies' funds. One wonders whether such directors can fulfill all of their responsibilities to the funds' investors. If the directors fail to do so, they can expect to be sued by lawyers representing the investors as a class. And since information about board membership is in the public domain, prospective investors can check out such information before they put their own cash on the line. All of these factors, coupled with the transparency of fund performance and the vigorous competition among funds and fund managers, operate together to ensure that investors have a fair and efficient market in which to make their choices. If they fail to choose wisely, it's probably their own fault.

Got a Beef with Your Broker?

As we have seen, the brokerage business is very substantially exposed to conflict with its clients. Few vendors—except perhaps the used-car dealer whose most recent sale disintegrates before it gets halfway down the block—are as exposed to instant client feedback. Assets and portfolios of assets are marked-to-market daily. Losses are immediately apparent, and there is very little that gets people more excited than a financial loss. If something bad happens, the immediate reaction often is to look for someone else to blame and, if possible, to sue. Even when brokers have acted fairly, honestly, and fully in accordance with their fiduciary responsibilities, conflicts arise. Clients sometimes simply don't want to hear what their broker has to tell them, or don't want to remember it. Mix in horror stories of high-pressure sales tactics, inappropriate investments, commission-based compensation, sales contests, and all the crooks and rogues that are attracted by the investment business, and the resulting brew has a distinctive character all its own.

Mandatory Arbitration

When people open brokerage accounts (or take jobs as brokers), they sign waivers of the right to sue. Instead, disputes are adjudicated under a mandatory arbitration process run by NASD. This arrangement is designed to avoid lengthy and expensive dispute resolution proceedings in the courts, where the issues would be decided by lay jurors unfamiliar with the many complexities of the securities markets. According to a 1987 Supreme Court ruling allowing arbitration in place of civil lawsuits in the brokerage industry, complaints filed against an individual broker or a firm are subsequently heard according to NASD rules by a panel of individuals selected by NASD, at least one of whom must be from the brokerage industry itself. In practice, the findings of these arbitration panels are rarely explained, and successful appeals are infrequent. Investors pay their own legal fees, and complaints are routinely dismissed if they are not filed within a time limit that is far shorter than for civil lawsuits.

Many people think the deck is stacked against the small investor.[45] Of course, the industry does not see it that way. The industry had argued before the Supreme Court that the NASD arbitration process is both more efficient and faster than civil suits, and precludes excessive damage awards. Of special concern to the industry is that it not be held responsible for market losses incurred by its customers, even when they have acted on advice from their broker. No market can succeed if all the gains go to the customer and all the losses are absorbed by the broker. The industry wants the public to believe that the securities markets are fair and safe and that misconduct will be addressed appropriately. The industry fears, however, that if it is seen as too generous to unhappy customers, the frequency and cost of settlements will increase dramatically.

Both the industry and its clients tend to agree that arbitration panels are often poorly constituted and include people who are incompetent, out of touch, biased, overextended, or ignorant of the law. These problems cast a bad light on the whole process. A few years ago, for example, a nineteen-year-old San Diego Marine Corps sergeant, Rodney Cook, whose wife had died in a car accident, invested the $85,000 insurance proceeds with Dean Witter. Later he found that most of this nest egg for his child's education had evaporated after more than one hundred trades in options and other complex investments by a rookie broker. Mr. Cook duly filed a complaint alleging excessive trading and other malpractice, which was heard in a Beverly Hills hotel room by an NASD panel. The chair was a seventy-two-year-old former broker who repeatedly referred to him as "Rodney King" (Mr. Cook is black). Dean Witter argued that Mr. Cook, a high school graduate, was a "sophisticated" investor and knew exactly what he was doing. After two days of hearings, he received nothing. Another panel member later said, "People go into brokerage firms to make a quick buck mostly, and it doesn't always work out."[46]

In another case a seventy-one-year-old Florida retiree, Gordon Newell, got himself into a Catch-22 situation in a 1992 complaint against Merrill Lynch. Newell alleged that broker misconduct had cost him the bulk of his retirement assets through limited-partnership losses. The mandatory NASD arbitration agreement he had signed when opening his brokerage account made a lawsuit impossible. Because prearbitration discovery took a year, Merrill's lawyers persuaded a New Jersey judge to throw out key aspects of the complaint on the grounds that they were no longer timely. Newell appealed, but at that point he was left with no recourse either to arbitration (which he had, in effect, already lost) or to the courts (a forum precluded by his initial waiver upon opening his account). Ironically, Merrill had itself resorted to the courts in its successful effort to avoid arbitration. Mr. Newell ultimately took a philosophical view of his experience with Merrill: "I look at the actuarial tables, and I realize they're just waiting for me to die."[47]

Overall, according to a report in the *Wall Street Journal,* about six thousand arbitration cases were heard in 1995, 85 percent of them with NASD (the rest with the New York and American Stock Exchanges). Most were settled. Of the cases that were decided by arbitration, 53 percent of the investors were awarded compensation. The average award, 60 percent of the compensation claimed, was substantially lower, however, than compensation awards in comparable civil suits. Punitive damages against brokers or firms occurred in less than 2 percent of successful arbitration cases, and these damages were generally less than $100,000 (a Supreme Court decision in 1996 upheld the authority of arbitrators to award punitive damages, rejecting a brokerage-industry argument to the contrary). The threat of stiff penalties for nonpayment has been sufficient to ensure the enforcement of damage awards imposed by arbitration panels. Enforcement of settlements has been problematic, however, with many clients not receiving the promised compensation. As a consequence, NASD has cracked down on firms that fail to honor settlement agreements. NASD threatens these firms with suspension or cancellation of association membership and withdrawal of brokerage registration. But there is yet another complication here. Some settlements provide for several payments over a period of time if clients agree to drop their complaints. With the complaint withdrawn and NASD jurisdiction over the dispute thereby eliminated, some firms have failed to make the additional payments. The apparent lesson in dealing with brokers: Don't drop the complaint until the last check has cleared.[48]

There has been widespread criticism of the SEC for its failure to oversee the NASD arbitration process. Critics argue that the Supreme Court expected such oversight when it approved mandatory arbitration in 1987, but that the SEC has neglected to intervene because it has been excessively influenced by the securities industry.[49]

A NASD task force on arbitration policy (the so-called Ruder Commission, headed by a former SEC chairman) issued a confidential draft report in early 1996. The report supported the brokerage industry's long-standing desire to cap punitive damage awards by limiting them to twice compensatory damages or $750,000, whichever is less, and to have this rule enforced in New York State, which has disallowed punitive-damage awards against brokers. The task force recommended barring brokers from going to court prior to arbitration, a tactic that imposes long delays and heavy expenses on clients.[50] It also recommended that brokerage firms and investors be given the right to veto the appointment of specific individuals to arbitration panels, that arbitrators be better trained and compensated, and that timely disclosure of relevant documents in arbitration proceedings be assured.[51] It failed to recommend, however, that arbitration decisions be made in writing or that they be explained. The commission believed that these changes would compromise the finality of arbitration decisions and encourage appeals to the courts. In the words of one commission member, "We're interested in increasing the chance of a quality process. If you're going to require investors to arbitrate and you don't have a quality process, you're going to shoot yourself in the foot."[52]

How to Check Up on Brokers

NASD has for some time run an investor hotline to tap into the Central Registration Depository (CRD) and obtain information on disciplinary actions against individual brokers, their firms, and fines levied in excess of $5,000. Pending actions, which have not been accessible through the CRD, must be obtained from individual state securities regulators. In June 1995 NASD announced a $25 million investment to facilitate tracing the disciplinary history of brokers. With the CRD data available electronically by the end of 1996, investors can easily check the records of prospective firms and brokers. Major parts of the plan, however, were opposed by the

Securities Industry Association, which favored a system that would make only adjudicated complaints available to the public, while complaints still pending would be available only to regulators. The industry argued that excessive data containing unsubstantiated allegations would be misleading and that information on individual brokers should be expunged after a reasonable period of time.[53] The 1996 report of the Ruder Commission argued that the time limit within which complaints have to be filed should be increased in order to encourage brokerage firms to settle with clients.[54] In 1996 NASD adopted limits on the size of punitive damage claims against brokers to twice actual damages up to a maximum of $750,000 and at the same time lifted the six-year eligibility limit covering what the industry called "stale claims." It also allowed claimants to choose three from among fifteen arbitration panelists and raised the size of the claim that can be heard by just one arbitrator to $25,000.

Class Actions and Safe Harbors

Balancing the rights of shareholders against those of a corporation is often difficult. It is especially difficult in so-called strike suits, legal actions of dubious merit that professional litigants or lawyers themselves instigate to obtain either rich out-of-court settlements or massive judgments by juries impressed by courthouse theatrics. Because of the arbitration requirement, most brokerage complaints are not addressed by litigation. In cases involving alleged violations of the Securities Acts of 1933 and 1934 and related statutes, however, litigation may be permissible. In such cases it is common for lawsuits to be bundled together so as to avoid rehearing the same case hundreds of times. As a consequence, when a possible violation is identified, lawyers usually try to assemble a class of plaintiffs; for example, all of the investors in the shares of a company between certain dates. Lawyers then invite those eligible to join the suits, which in the United States are typically brought on a contingent-fee basis. After the lawyers obtain settlements or damage awards, which the class needs to approve, they get their fees.

Many have argued that the litigation process, initially set up in the 1930s, is tilted too far in the direction of plaintiffs; the process has had significant adverse effects on economic efficiency and growth, while redistributing income and wealth from consumers and shareholders to those who distort the system to their own advantage.[55] In 1995 Congress put forward bipartisan legislation to redress this imbalance, legislation that was initially supported by the Clinton administration. The president unexpectedly vetoed the legislation, however, in response to pressure from the plaintiffs' bar and from some academic advisers, who argued that the bill contained harmful ambiguities.[56]

Congress overrode the Clinton veto in December 1995. The main provisions of the new law include:

- A safe harbor protecting companies from suit in the case of performance predictions that turn out to be wrong. This provision especially benefits high-tech companies and those introducing new products by constraining investors who say they were defrauded by misleading forecasts.

- Reducing access to deep-pocket securities underwriters and accounting firms by raising the threshold for successful conviction of such firms.

- Requiring judges to determine whether a suit is frivolous or abusive, in which case the plaintiff would be liable for the other side's costs. This provision protects companies from investors and lawyers on fishing expeditions but does not threaten legitimate suits by investors.

- Imposing a three-year statute of limitations after the violation (and one year after its discovery), despite an SEC request to extend it to five years.

- Allowing judges to select as lead plaintiff the one with the greatest financial stake in the outcome, thereby rejecting the "race to the courthouse" engaged in by members of the plaintiffs' bar and a small group of professional plaintiffs who hope to hit the jackpot.

Efforts to limit the authority of state securities regulators, especially over mutual funds, were defeated in this bill, but a House subcommittee voted 25–0 the following year to introduce another bill that would achieve most of the same objectives.

Regulating Brokers

Given the damage that misconduct in retail transactions can have on the securities industry and on the operation of the financial markets in general, what can be done about it? There are three paths to reform that can be and are used simultaneously: self-control, industry control, and regulatory control.

Self-control

We have already noted that major brokerage houses have much to lose from broker misconduct, not only in terms of their current earnings but also by damaging their reputations. Nothing leads to client defections faster than a major scandal that seems to be systemic; that is, which can be traced to management failures, as opposed to a single individual who was able to avoid or evade an otherwise appropriate control process. Since the cost of shifting a brokerage account is very low, informed customers find it easy to head for the exits.

The big firms are especially aware of this exit phenomenon. For example, Merrill Lynch continues to have the world's largest securities sales force, numbering some thirteen thousand brokers in 1996. These salespersons increasingly act as new-age financial gurus, as "soft-sell adviser[s] to restructure your portfolio, plan your estate, and whip up minor miracles like an interest-only mortgage for your new ski chalet."[57] They are compensated by a flat percentage of assets under management. They are the shock troops in achieving Merrill's target of $1 trillion in total assets under management by the year 2000, up from $703 billion in 1996. Borrowing a leaf from the airlines' book, Merrill Lynch in 1996 announced its Financial Advantage client-reward program with its bronze, silver, gold, and platinum tiers—depending on assets maintained with Merrill—under which clients benefit from commission-free stock and bond trades and various other services in return for a relatively modest annual fee, depending on the level of assets under management. The intent is to hold existing clients and draw business from independent financial advisers, discount brokers, banks, mutual fund companies, and pricier "wrap" accounts of competitor brokerage firms.[58]

The retail distribution business provides the firm not only with a 20 percent return on equity, but also with far more earnings stability than rival investment banks. The firm has unbeatable placing power for securities targeted to the general public (as well as institutional investors). It has ranked as the world's top underwriter for several years running. The last thing Merrill needs is significant broker misconduct and client defections.

Merrill invests heavily in training, research, generation and dissemination of product information, and accounting and back-office systems. The firm continually rethinks broker compensation. Indeed, its salespersons (called "financial consultants," not "stockbrokers") are required to sign a Draconian agreement that forbids them from contacting clients for one year after leaving the firm. Its 60 percent retention rate for accounts of departed brokers is far in excess of the industry average.[59] This policy not only benefits the firm's market share, but also helps cement the clients to the firm and gives new brokers a hand in developing their client bases.

A number of firms have introduced statements that make available rate-of-return information to investors, and most have done away with single-product sales contests. Nonetheless, large firms may have a limited capacity to police what goes on in far-flung branch offices. Smaller firms may be unwilling to implement reforms in a highly competitive sales culture. And firms of any size can always dress up sales contests as educational trips to the Galapagos Islands or as seminars in Tahiti.

Even in the face of market pressures to the contrary, some of the big firms have shifted the basis of broker compensation. Dean Witter was the last of the major firms to pay its brokers a differential for hawking in-house mutual funds. The firm discontinued this practice in 1995, following similar moves by Merrill Lynch, Smith Barney, Paine Webber, and Prudential Securities.[60] As with Merrill Lynch, various securities firms have introduced broker compensation based on fees and assets under management rather than commissions. Firms have also toned down sales contests and stopped favoring in-house products. Indeed, in late 1995 Merrill announced that it was considering whether to compensate newly recruited brokers by salary rather than commissions.[61]

Firms are beginning to crack down on individual brokers who step over the line. Houses like Merrill Lynch and Smith Barney have fired million-dollar brokers following allegations of wrongdoing. In 1996 Paine Webber fired one of the members of its exclusive Chairman's Club, a response to allegations that, in trading for his wife's account, he had exceeded trading limits in a small company's stock. Going after top producers, who would normally be coddled by the big firms, is an obvious attempt to signal that a firm's reputation has to be protected even at a very substantial cost in lost production.[62]

Still, a year or so after stating that it would cease paying its brokers extra compensation to push in-house mutual funds, Dean Witter continued to have its branch managers' compensation linked to new investments in the company's funds and to subject them to sales quotas for in-house funds. Failure to sell 75 percent in-house funds would mean loss of compensation and attendance at "training sessions" to improve performance. The apparent result of this practice and of applying higher overhead charges to investments in nonproprietary funds: not much change.[63]

Industry Control

Whenever an industry subject to allegations of misconduct says, "Leave it to us," public skepticism about the fox guarding the henhouse quickly follows. Even so, the securities industry has every incentive to clean up its act and keep it that way. The industry has taken several approaches.

One has been to work closely with the SEC to improve standards for broker education and qualification. There are also plans to develop "super brokers," a new generation of salespersons trained and compensated to put themselves in the shoes of their clients and to think beyond the next trade.

In 1995 NASD proposed rules to limit cash payments and noncash compensation to brokers for selling mutual funds or variable-rate annuities (although trips to Hawaii would still be winnable for selling all of the products that a firm offers).[64] Further, NASD has substantially reorganized itself to address criticisms that it was too lax in policing brokers in its dual role of regulator and operator of the NASDAQ trading system. Mary Schapiro, head of the newly formed NASD regulation unit, reportedly favors small-investor protections that would be quite unpopular with the industry, including "airing a bigger chunk of brokers' dirty linen on the Internet" and imposing more severe penalties on supervisors who fail to control brokers with bad disciplinary histories.[65]

Still, there seems to be plenty of room for slippage. Magically, the crackdown on broker sales contests gave way to contests for fee-based "independent" advisers held by mutual-fund companies for steering investments in their direction. The signs at posh resorts in Cancun or Palm Springs that read "Welcome Brokers" rapidly changed to "Welcome Advisers," and invitations that used to say "Vacation of a Lifetime" now enticed winners to a "Due Diligence Conference." Needless to say, Buffalo and Cleveland were not among the most frequent venues.[66]

Regulatory Control

Striking a proper balance between protecting retail investors from abuse and straightjacketing a fast-moving industry is very difficult. Too much control hampers the efficiency and dynamism of financial markets, with negative implications both for optimum investor portfolios and the cost of finance for those who tap the markets. Too little control risks financial disaster for individual investors and encourages the flight of investors to more level playing fields. Too little control may also contaminate and undermine the financial system itself.

Recent initiatives by SEC Chairman Levitt, a former broker and chief executive of the brokerage firm of Hayden Stone, have included customer education initiatives and the streamlining of regulatory burdens. He has also supported the use of criminal sanctions. In 1995 the Justice Department, operating in cooperation with the SEC, indicted eleven stockbrokers for defrauding retail investors in ten states of amounts ranging from $10,000 to $1.2 million. At no other time in memory had the government used criminal charges against brokers on such a large scale. The charges included siphoning money from client accounts, selling nonexistent securities, forging checks, and issuing fictitious account statements. In one case a broker stole $114,000 over a four-year period from the accounts of two clients, one of whom was confined to a nursing home. The Justice Department-SEC action was intended to send a message that rogue brokers would no longer be tolerated. "People who do this are the same as people who go into a store with a handgun," said Levitt. "The penalty for swindling American investors is severe. Those who do so will not just be barred as brokers; they will be prosecuted as criminals."[67]

The action followed a report by the General Accounting Office suggesting that rogue brokers who were disciplined in one situation soon popped up again somewhere else doing the same thing. The indicted brokers, all of whom were dismissed, worked not just for small firms, but also for the largest houses, including Merrill Lynch, Paine Webber, Prudential Securities, and MetLife Securities. In almost all cases the misconduct was reported to NASD and the regulators by the firms themselves, who subsequently reimbursed the defrauded clients. About half of those charged soon pleaded guilty.

Another SEC initiative involved the creation of the blue-ribbon committee on compensation, headed by former Merrill Lynch chairman Tully.[68] The committee's report (discussed earlier in this chapter) noted that incentive-based broker compensation works well on the whole but generates a conflict of interest that may seriously damage individual investors. The report advocated a set of "best practices," including compensation formulas that align (over the long term) the interests of the client with those of the broker and the securities firm; that require the broker to understand clients' objectives and to educate clients about markets and risks; and that improve training, education, and supervision of brokers. Through its examples of best practices, the committee in effect rejected broker compensation based on salaries. This position was a response to industry objections that the resulting fixed costs would drive many firms out of business in down markets. Instead, the committee favored compensation based on the performance of client portfolios, and the elimination of the most questionable incentives (some of which have been discussed earlier). The committee also suggested deferring part of broker compensation and making payment contingent on a clean compliance record, compensating via stock options to tie brokers better to their firms, beefing up compliance departments (including checks on the alignment of investor objectives and actual transactions), and informing investors of their rights in ways they can understand.

Levitt has directed some of his more important efforts toward mutual funds. He has been especially concerned that the offering material of such funds be comprehensible to unsophisticated investors. In an October 1994 address to the National Press Club in Washington, he illustrated the problem by reading a representative excerpt from a mutual fund prospectus.[69]

Maturity and duration management decisions are made in the context of an intermediate maturity orientation. The maturity structure of the portfolio is adjusted in anticipation of cyclical interest rate changes. Such adjustments are not made in an effort to capture short-term day-to-day movements in the market, but rather are implemented in anticipation of longer term, secular shifts in the levels of interest rates (i.e., shifts transcending and/or not inherent in the business cycle).

He asked the audience whether they understood what this meant to a retail investor making decisions about where to place his or her money. Faced with confused silence, he then read a translation of the excerpt, one that he had asked Warren Buffett to prepare.

We will try to profit by correctly predicting future interest rates. When we have no strong opinion, we will generally hold intermediate-term bonds. But when we expect a major and sustained increase in rates, we will concentrate on short-term issues. And if we expect a major shift to lower rates, we will buy long-term bonds. We will focus on the big picture, and won't make moves based on short-term considerations.

Which will Aunt Millie understand? Will she read the prospectus in the first place before she sends money? Does it matter if she doesn't read anything anyway?

At Levitt's initiative, the SEC put out for comment in March 1996 a sweeping set of proposals to overhaul how mutual funds may be sold to the public. These proposals included:

- A brief (two-page) profile prospectus in plain English that cuts through the legal gibberish and makes it easier for investors to understand what they are buying (but not precluding the availability of the full prospectus)

- Raising the percentage of fund assets that must be invested in asset classes implied by the fund's name from 65 percent to 80 percent

- Disclosure of a measure of fund risk, such as the standard deviation of annual returns in the prospectus

- For bond funds, disclosure of duration to reflect the interest sensitivity of fund assets

- A requirement that fund performance be compared with an appropriate benchmark, such as the S&P 500 Index, in the prospectus

- Discussion in simple language of the principal risks the investor faces, rather than a legal muddle of every conceivable risk that might be encountered

The mutual-fund industry was broadly supportive of the SEC initiative but opposed disclosure of both performance against benchmarks and disclosure of risk measures. Notwithstanding firms' frequent use of both statistics (when favorable) in promoting their mutual funds, the industry argued that such statistics were misleading.

Few industry sectors are as complex as the retail distribution of securities. Many people are involved, and they are spread all over the country. Effective sales performance requires strong production incentives and tough managers. The business attracts those who respond to financial incentives and want to be rich. Most are honest and professional. Some are not. Short-term performance tends to dominate longer-term matters. "Long term," said one senior investment banker in the 1980s, "is what we do after lunch." This short-term focus makes it hard to balance reputational effects and today's trades.

Still, the industry strives to provide a level playing field and fair markets that investors can trust. This financial environment is maintained in no small measure because of the many effective federal and state securities laws, strong regulators, active legal remedies, and other similar equalizers that aid unsophisticated investors. The financial markets are probably better in the United States than any other country, but abuses still happen. Some, as in the case of the multiple problems at the Prudential, can be devastating or even fatal to firms. Especially dangerous, too, are those situations in which rogue brokers are tolerated, even promoted, by their supervising managers. Rogue, timid, corrupt, or ill-chosen managers are the underlying problem, one that boards of directors often fail to identify until it is too late.

4

Playing with the Big Boys— Wholesale Transactions

■

In the old days, if you worked for an investment bank, your clients respected your judgment and expertise. They accepted what you said. The deal was closed and the clients were happy. But things are different now. Deregulation and competition have made it possible for clients to get into the markets on a moment's notice, virtually to issue securities on the phone whenever a deal seems especially attractive. Anybody can call and offer whatever he or she wants. So the clients shop around now. They ask for your best rate and time stamp it. To get the business, you have to call all over the world to find the cheapest source of funds. You may still lose the deal because some other firm, somewhere else in the world, may offer a price that is better than yours by only the smallest of fractions. Or you may win it, but at a price that the market won't buy so you lose money on the deal. Often it seems irrelevant that your firm has been the client's primary investment bank for a quarter of a century, irrelevant that you personally have been dealing with the client for years. Yes, you still have to have a relationship to get to them to listen to you, but lots of firms have that much of a relationship. Occasionally a really good idea, something proprietary, will win out, but most decisions get made on the basis of price. Just price.

Today bankers know the wholesale business is tough. Every trade is like wrestling with a 600 pound gorilla. Win or lose, you always get the breath squeezed out of you. It sure is a different business from the way it was.

The Way It Was

Until about 1980, corporate and government clients worked with bankers in much the same way that they worked with other professionals, such as lawyers and accountants. They had relationships with a particular firm—or maybe two or three firms—many of which were inherited by one management group from its predecessor. Morgan Stanley had the most illustrious list of clients, many going back to old J.P. Morgan himself. Goldman Sachs had the largest list of clients, most of which had been added since the mid-1960s, when the firm began an aggressive effort to market itself to corporations. Commercial banks offering wholesale banking services like loan syndications—for instance, Morgan Guaranty, Chemical, Citibank, Chase Manhattan, and Manufacturers Hanover—tended to have institutional relationships, too, with top executives often serving on each others' boards. Most large companies, however, used several banks, so that the companies' prospective financing needs could be covered by the aggregate of the banks' maximum legal lending limits.

Goldman Sachs stirred things up by calling on their competitors' clients, which other investment banks then began doing in self-defense. By the end of the 1970s, considerable competition for "relationships" had developed. Companies also became more approachable, as CEOs and CFOs, moving around within their industries, built finance "teams" of their own—including fresh investment-banking relationships. Some relationships between clients and banks were altered by mergers or new board appointments. Most were affected by the growing sophistication of companies' finance departments, which wanted to use the best firm for each purpose—commercial paper, equity issues, mergers, and so on.

But nothing changed the relationship between bankers and their clients as much as the Eurobond market, which emerged suddenly in the early 1980s as a powerful alternative to domestic financing for U.S. corporations. The Eurobond market had existed as a market of convenience for U.S. firms during the 1960s and early 1970s, when domestic capital controls required that foreign investments be financed abroad. The first Eurobonds were denominated in U.S. dollars and purchased mainly by non-American holders of Eurodollar deposits, such as Swiss banks (usually on behalf of their overseas private banking clients), quasigovernmental investment bodies, and pension funds. (Eurodollars are deposits or other accounts maintained outside the United States that are denominated in dollars.) After the 1971 collapse of the Bretton Woods system of fixed exchange rates (with the dollar tied to gold and other currencies to the dollar) and, in 1973, of its somewhat more flexible successor, the Smithsonian Agreement, the dollar began to float freely against major currencies. Thereafter, capital controls on U.S. companies were no longer necessary and were progressively removed. With U.S. companies relying more on the domestic capital markets, the slack in the Eurobond market was taken up by European and Japanese issuers, who wished to avoid the costs and inconveniences of registering securities in the United States.

All other things being equal, investors ought to require a premium rate of return to purchase securities denominated in a currency other than their own; these securities typically provide limited secondary-market liquidity, skimpy disclosure of investment information, and questionable home-country legal recourse in the event of a dispute. U.S. investors did, indeed, receive such a premium. But for companies located in countries with poorly developed or overregulated capital markets, the rates offered in the Eurobond market were better than those available at home. So the market continued to operate in the 1970s for such issuers, despite that period's exceptionally high interest rates and the weakness of the dollar.

The situation changed dramatically under President Ronald Reagan. First, tight money and reduced inflation began to lower nominal interest rates. New legislation then reduced taxes by 25 percent over three years, considerably enhancing market liquidity and sharply accelerating economic growth. A bull market in both stocks and bonds suddenly emerged. Bolstered by low inflation, high real interest rates, and Reagan's confident, get-tough policy toward the Soviet Union, the dollar began a four-year climb (pushing the yen, for example, from 202 to the dollar in 1980 to 260 in 1985). American investors were making money, but foreign investors in dollar securities were making more—appreciation not only in the value of securities, but also in the dollar. The Swiss and Japanese could not get enough dollar investments, preferably Eurobonds. The Swiss obtained high-grade U.S. corporate paper (which they preferred over French or Italian issues) in confidential bearer form and free of U.S. withholding taxes. The Japanese bought either prime U.S. corporate names or the Eurobonds of familiar Japanese companies whose issues were not available in Tokyo. The American companies, just entering the "debt decade" of the 1980s, were more than happy to oblige by issuing more paper. They were also attracted by the aggressive rates and by the absence of a waiting period before entering the market.

The Securities Act of 1933 requires that companies issuing bonds to the public in the United States register them with the Securities and Exchange Commission. In accordance with the rules in force at the beginning of the 1980s, the SEC's staff would then review the registration statement before clearing it to become effective, at which time the offering could commence.

The waiting period from filing until effective date was about thirty days. To minimize underwriting risks, the issuers and underwriters negotiated the issue's price on the night before the effective date. But in the Eurobond market there was no SEC, nor did the SEC apply its rules to U.S. companies operating in that market. A company seeking funds could therefore do the deal as quickly as its banker was willing to proceed with an issue.

Prior to the 1980s, bankers in the Eurobond market insisted on having a week or two to market an issue before setting the price. This practice, which followed that of the U.S. domestic market, generated sales interest in the issue. In the 1980s, however, bankers became more aggressive. Crédit Suisse-First Boston was the first bank to offer a bought deal, one in which the bank waived the normal marketing period and priced the deal as part of the solicitation of the client. The first issuer under this arrangement, a governmental entity from Canada, jumped at the opportunity to lock in what was a very attractive rate. The issue was not especially successful; the market had never seen a prepriced deal before, but one assumes Crédit Suisse's numerous portfolio managers in Zurich got a good look at the deal. Once the bought deal was done, it became the standard, much to the regret of other underwriting firms, especially those with no "captive" placing power of their own.

The genie was now out of the bottle. Big corporate and governmental issuers insisted on similar treatment. And aggressive European banks such as CSFB (which was on its way to becoming the Eurobond market leader) began calling on U.S. companies to offer them deals at rates they couldn't refuse. Smaller firms suffered because they could not compete with the rates offered by larger, better capitalized ones. Clients' longstanding loyalties to their bankers suddenly gave way to a new era of fierce competition on the basis of price. U.S. investment banks, which at first believed themselves insulated from what they saw as an exclusively European phenomenon, found that they were not. In Europe, U.S. companies could avoid registration, eliminate waiting periods, obtain financing wherever their operations took them, and get much better rates as well. AT&T, for example, shunned the U.S. market and opted for the Eurobond market instead, where its bonds were issued at a rate significantly *below* that of U.S. Treasury Bonds, the most secure and lowest-priced issue on the domestic market. Even at this rate, the company's bonds were, to the Swiss, an exceedingly attractive alternative to Treasury Bonds, which were subject to U.S. withholding taxes and had to be registered in their clients' names.

In 1982, the first year of these new banking practices, U.S. companies that were rated single-A or better issued more bonds in Europe than domestically.

Many investment bankers active at that time believed that the SEC enacted Rule 415 in 1982—the rule that allows shelf-registrations—specifically to combat the appeal of the Eurobond market and to bring business back to the United States. With a shelf-registration, a company can eliminate the waiting period, go directly into the market, and do bought deals. Instead of making clients go to Europe to catch the new wave, relationships be damned, the SEC lets them do the same thing at home. This transformation took only about a year, and the U.S. bond market and its underwriting spreads have never been the same since.

Nor have the relationships between investment banks and their clients. There are no more exclusive banking relationships. With the exception of deals involving proprietary elements (which are uncommon), everything gets put out for competitive bidding. Even middling companies now work with several bankers, and increasingly pick the cheapest one. Bankers used to have a different idea of the value they created for their clients. They offered a lot of attention, service, information, and expertise. In return, the clients accepted what the bankers told them and didn't fuss too much about rates. Bankers could price deals with a built-in cushion against risk. But not any more. Today, many companies no longer value bankers' advice and counsel. Companies have their own experts and don't need bankers to tell them what the markets are doing. They have the same screens as the bankers, and they know how to use them.

Corporate Gorillas

The wholesale market for finance poses a host of new competitive (and standards-of-conduct) problems for banks and securities firms. Because their clients value relationships less and keen pricing more, firms find it increasingly difficult to compete along old-style service lines. As their products—particularly capital-market products—become commodities, the relationship between client and supplier changes drastically. The banker becomes a mere counterparty to a trade, rather than a trusted adviser who has arranged the transaction. As a trading counterparty, one becomes concerned about risk, spreads, and potential profit. This creates a conflict. The best interests of the firm, rather than the best interests of the client, become paramount in the transaction—and the client knows it.

The client no longer expects the firm to provide its total, undiluted effort on its behalf. As a consequence, the client no longer trusts the firm in the same way, holding the firm at arm's length, instead. Indeed, the client eagerly cultivates relationships with competing firms to avoid becoming dependent on just one or two. One result of this trend in the United States is the virtual disappearance of investment bankers from the boards of directors of major public corporations. A few bankers remain members of boards they have served on for years, but very, very few are newly invited to join boards of well-established companies. Another result is that the loyalty between clients and firms has substantially declined.

Firms make less money from underwriting than they once did, and each deal involves much more risk. Investment banks have to think of their corporate-finance clients as opportunities, not as annuities. Relationships with clients nonetheless remain very important. Each client has a stable of four or five investment banks it first turns to for quotes and ideas, and being among those four or five—being "inner-circled"—is a matter of relationship. Modern relationships with clients also provide bankers with information they can use to generate useful ideas that may ultimately lead to future deals. But the relationship has to be managed on the basis of mutual respect *and* convenience. Clients have to expect even their most enthusiastic bankers to decline bidding for some deals. An angry response to insufficient loyalty has no proper role here.

Most securities firms today have reorganized their corporate-finance delivery capability around capital-market desks, where a group of intense professionals contact issuers of debt or equity to present useful ideas and the firm's best rates. Their corporate-relations generalist counterparts are supposed to find out when a client is likely to be interested in doing something. After being notified of this potential interest, the capital-market desk will regularly contact the client's finance department or treasury in an effort to snatch a deal away from other firms. All eyes tend to be attracted to the big deals that might be coming down. One already visible effect of this change in the system is larger firms' perceptible neglect of smaller companies and of those that finance infrequently.

Other consequences of today's corporate-finance world range from over-promising and misleading of clients (in the case of nonbought deals), to badmouthing of competitors, and occasionally to offering inappropriate side payments to get assignments. It has now become fairly common for banks to exaggerate the price at which a deal can be done in the future and to inflate the level of downstream services—such as coverage by one of the firm's research analysts and market making in the security to be sold—they will provide.

Investment banks have also become more comfortable in criticizing their competitors and putting them in a bad light—even when such communications are not completely truthful. The firm's marketing representatives and salespersons are, after all, encouraged to do whatever it takes to land a substantial deal. Though inappropriate payments in this increasingly rough-and-tumble world occur infrequently, they do occur, especially when government officials or public employees are involved. As discussed in Chapter 8, political contributions by investment bankers soliciting municipal-bond business in the United States ("pay to play") have been highly embarrassing (and expensive) to such firms as Merrill Lynch and Lazard Frères. And many large privatization deals around the world have led to charges of improper payments and official corruption.

Though sometimes effective, such tactical ploys and maneuvers are often discovered, resulting in a loss of professional reputation and good will. If the profit on deals is high enough, some people—perhaps those at Drexel Burnham Lambert in the 1980s—do not care very much about the loss of respect. But if firms want to be seen as professionally sound, reliable, and respectable, then they must act accordingly. They must learn to manage the conflicts that increasingly exist between their interests and those of their clients. Such conflicts are almost impossible to handle without some negative repercussions, but they must nonetheless be addressed.

Institutional Gorillas

Block trading of equity securities with institutional investors began in the 1960s. On May 1, 1975 ("May Day"), the New York Stock Exchange abolished minimum commission rates, leading to an immediate drop of about 40 percent in brokerage commissions paid by institutions. This was only the beginning. Over the next few years commissions continued to decline to their present level, which are only 10 or 15 percent of their pre–May Day levels. The erosion of commissions contributed to a vast increase in trading volume in stocks, a trend already underway as pension funds built up their holdings following the 1974 enactment of the Employees Retirement Income and Security Act (ERISA). Average daily stock turnover on the New York Stock Exchange increased from 11.6 million shares in 1970 to 44.9 million in 1980, reaching 346.1 million shares in 1995. This increased volume meant that institutions were coming to dominate the secondary equity markets. The percentage of total trades done in units of ten thousand shares or more—the NYSE definition of a block trade—increased from 15.4 percent in 1970 to 29.2 percent in 1980, reaching 57.0 percent in 1995.

Trading in fixed-income securities (bonds) also grew rapidly during this period. Although reliable trade-volume data are not available, the combined value of the world's bond markets currently exceeds the combined value of the world's stock markets: approximately $20 trillion outstanding for bonds versus $16 trillion for stocks. Moreover, large parts of the global bond markets have become seamless, with foreign exchange transactions and swaps cross-linking various national and offshore markets. Anomalies are quickly arbitraged away. Only the best-informed, most opportunistic, and highly capitalized firms have the information and other resources needed to produce a sustained profit in this most globalized of financial markets.

In the United States today, institutions hold 52 percent of all stocks (in dollar terms) and a much larger share of bonds. Of the various types of institutional investors, pension funds (private and public) are by far the largest, representing 25.9 percent of all institutional stock-market holdings. Mutual funds hold 12.2 percent, and foreign investors as a group, 5.6 percent. Insurance companies and banks are also players. There is a great deal of competition among institutions for assets to manage. This competition is based mainly on the performance of assets managed against benchmarks (such as the S&P 500 stock index or the Salomon Brothers U.S. bond index) commonly called "bogeys." It is also based on the different types of investment possibilities offered, such as passive (indexed) investments, international and emerging-markets investments, and various other specialized types of securities. These specialized investments include funds concentrating in various types of fixed-income securities and derivatives.

The compensation of institutions is usually based on the performance of assets under their management. Portfolio managers, therefore, are typically sophisticated, aggressive, and demanding. They know the markets well and demand that their brokers and advisors go all out for them. They insist on the best research ideas, the best trading execution, and the best follow-up service. They expect to utilize the firm's capital in facilitating trades and require their brokers to trade large blocks of securities at the most competitive prices.

To capture this business, most of the large broker-dealers have developed very modern departments that include intense sales coverage of the big institutions, research support, and aggressive market making in listed, unlisted, and, increasingly, international securities. They have also been willing to bid for whole portfolios of securities, often without knowing much about what securities the portfolios contain. In such cases, the successful bidder has to perform a masterful job of quickly selling, swapping, and hedging the component parts in order to make money.

Institutional investors believe that unless they play brokers off against each other, they will not get the best rates or execution. They do, however, want to retain the attention of some of the smaller research-oriented houses with good investment ideas. Because these small firms may not have the appetite or the muscle to participate in large-scale block trading, they have to be rewarded in "soft dollars," that is, through directed brokerage business in return for good research service.

This pattern of institutional activity has now been largely established in London as well, following the deregulation of brokerage commissions and stock-exchange rules there in October 1986 (the "Big Bang"). As in the United States ten years earlier, trading volume increased sharply in London, and in the new Stock Exchange Automated Quotation (SEAQ) trading system the London Stock Exchange attained a strong international capability; SEAQ became the principal market maker in Europe for many large European corporate securities. The Big Bang has since induced competitive responses from exchanges throughout Europe, mirroring what has happened in New York and London. Tokyo lags behind these changes, but Japanese financial institutions (including foreign broker-dealers) are nevertheless becoming more competitive. The fact is that countries that don't develop highly competitive markets for stocks and bonds will lose business to those that do.

Who Is a Wholesaler?

A wholesaler is a middleman—a direct buyer from manufacturers or bulk suppliers who distributes to retailers. Banks and investment banks have been wholesalers from the beginning; they provide large-scale loans or financings in the securities market to major users of credit. Banks refinance these transactions with bank deposits or sales to buyers of securities, the end-suppliers of credit in financial systems. The users of credit in wholesale markets are rarely everyday users, however. Because they come to the market only occasionally (perhaps once a year or so), they do not know the market well and rely on the middleman. The suppliers of credit often lack expert knowledge. Even some large institutions are not fully informed about all the lending or investing possibilities available to them. Only the middlemen know all the rates and adjust them every day.

Middlemen live on their market contacts, the flow of orders or inquiries that comprise their unique pool of market information. This valuable information enables the middlemen to function as market makers. Every market maker quotes a price at which he is willing to buy a commodity and another at which he is willing to sell it. The difference is the dealer's spread. This spread is the difference between what the market maker thinks a prospective seller will accept for the commodity (the bid price) and what he thinks a prospective buyer will pay (the offer price). The less sophisticated he believes a potential seller to be, the lower the market maker's price. The reverse is true on the offer side. Spreads therefore depend heavily not just on immediate market supply and demand, but also on who the trading counterparties are. Trading in tiny lots with retail customers facilitates wide spreads. Block trading with other banks or securities firms—so-called interdealer trading—and with large institutional investors who are sensitive to even the smallest price penalty that will influence the performance of funds under management involves hair-thin spreads. Market makers also need to take large positions on the firm's books in order to provide liquidity for the customer. No wholesale price or no commitment, no deal.

Bid-offer wholesale spreads exist in all kinds of interdealer markets. In the foreign exchange market, the interdealer spreads quoted in the *Wall Street Journal* or the *Financial Times* often differ dramatically from the exchange rates quoted to tourists at airports. Similarly, in the London market for Eurodollar deposits, the rates at which major banks offer to take deposits from other major banks (the London Interbank Bid Rate, or LIBID) and to place deposits with other major banks (the London Interbank Offered Rate, or LIBOR) differ significantly from those for a medium-sized company to borrow Eurodollars (most likely at a hefty margin over LIBOR) and from the interest rate available to a medium-sized depositor. These examples reflect the difference between wholesale and retail spreads.

In securities underwriting, the price at which an underwriting group deals with an issuer is the wholesale price. The price at which the underwriters resell to clients (individual or institutional) is the retail price. This retail price, by custom and agreement in the United States, is a fixed price. Until recently it was not fixed when dealing in Eurobonds. Once an underwriter had bought bonds from the issuer, the firm was free to sell to its clients at whatever price it could get. The underwriting spread tended to be larger in the Eurobond market than in the United States. Because of the price flexibility in the Eurobond market, institutional accounts in particular began to shop around among syndicate members to find an underwriter willing to sell at a price only slightly above what he had paid. This price was much lower than that at which the underwriter hoped to sell the bonds to retail customers. The larger institutional buyers were quickly able to force themselves into the interprofessional market as well. Similarly, once European opportunities became clear alternatives to domestic finance, corporations and institutions began benchmarking against the best alternative rates available to them. For example, borrowers from banks began to look at opportunities in the U.S. commercial paper market, which usually offered lower-cost money than either LIBOR or prime-rate-based borrowings. In time, the other markets would have to find a way to offer equivalent rates through discounts, or risk losing business. The lowest rate for all large clients and dealers soon became the wholesale market price. Retail investors and smaller corporations and institutions, lacking both access and economic power, still had to pay the higher rates.

Today we define the wholesale market for financial services as comprising those borrowers and issuers who have easy, independent access to capital markets and therefore can obtain the best rates available. Individuals and companies that are too small, unsophisticated, poorly rated, or poorly understood by investors are required to obtain their funds at posted, retail rates. Wholesale borrowers are well informed, know their options, and accordingly can be discriminating and tough. They rely on the market mainly for execution and price. When and if they want advice and loyalty, however, they may find themselves transacting at the retail rates of old.

Unlike those on the wholesale side, retail investors expect to pay the full rate, especially when they want advice, explanations, and time-consuming services or when they trade in small lots. In recent years, even the retail investor market has been stratified into those who want execution only and those who want different types of services and attention. For example, your bank transaction now costs more if you talk to a teller than if you execute it mechanically via ATM or a PC-linkup. Brokerage commissions are much lower if you use a discount broker that offers execution but few other services, and lower still if you use an electronic broker via the Internet.

In almost all cases, we can assume that the wholesale market consists of well-informed, qualified players and that the retail market does not. Competition for wholesale services, coupled with the limited need for hand holding and other attentions, have brought the rates way down. Well-informed, qualified buyers should be able to look out for themselves, much as the players in any interprofessional market are expected to do. Fiduciary duties to fellow professionals are simple: "We will trade at the price we agreed, and we will conform to the laws for disclosure and accepted market practice regarding payment and delivery unless we agree otherwise. If tomorrow you don't like what you bought today because interest rates went up, or the company went bankrupt, or something else, it's too bad! If you think you have a beef, then we'll listen to the tapes. And if we still can't agree, then you can sue me and we'll see how the courts or the arbitrators look at it."

For the most part, regulators have accepted that self-regulation works well for wholesale players who operate in many countries and markets simultaneously. Over the past decade, the worldwide regulatory direction in most financial services has therefore been to back away from the wholesale market and to focus instead on ensuring that retail markets work fairly and efficiently. Modern society does not offer much sympathy to victims who should be able to take care of themselves but do not. Public attention and sympathy is saved for the innocents of the retail sector and for those supposed innocents (for example, Gibson Greetings or Procter & Gamble) who act as wholesalers but are not.

Market Sanctions

Disputes occasionally arise over what was said when a trade was agreed. People may remember things differently, especially when there is considerable money at stake or no love lost between the trading parties. In the early 1980s, as the volume of securities trades shot up rapidly, most firms installed telephone recording devices in their trading rooms. When a trade dispute arose, the principals and their superiors would sit down together, listen to the taped conversation, and decide—usually on the spot—what to do. Rarely did such matters go to litigation.

It is often claimed that the wholesale market needs little regulation or, indeed, that regulation is harmful to market efficiency. Neither the foreign exchange market, the world's largest wholesale market, nor the Eurocurrency market has significant regulation. It is argued that the market itself is capable of imposing severe sanctions. If shunned because of unacceptable behavior, you could be cut off from trading, underwriting, and credit facilities. You could possibly be driven out of the business altogether.

Fearing such sanctions, wholesale market players conform to the rules of the market.

Or so the argument goes. But does the market control behavior in the way the argument requires? The answer is both no and yes. Few firms have ever been explicitly shunned by other market participants. Ivan Boesky traded until the very end. Bob Freeman had Goldman Sachs' unequivocal support until he admitted to a criminal offense. Drexel Burnham wasn't widely shunned by clients or by competitors after apparently misbehaving. Nor was E.F. Hutton after its check-kiting episode that resulted in criminal charges for mail fraud, or Salomon after its problems concerning Treasury-bond auctions. Many professionals involved in controversial areas of activity simply move from one prominent firm to another. Witness Howie Rubin, once a reckless Merrill Lynch trader of mortgage-backed securities. Though he evaded risk management controls and cost the firm hundreds of millions in 1989, he is now productively employed at Bear Stearns. Many of the takeover and leveraged buyout figures of the 1980s are still in business (or have retired, rich). In sum, there is very little evidence of sanctions by market cohorts.

Nonetheless, the market has done its job when sanctions are required. There are big losers in such situations: the owners (stockholders) of the firms themselves. E.F. Hutton, Drexel Burnham, BCCI, and Kidder Peabody are all out of business. Morgan Grenfell (Guiness scandal in the United Kingdom, 1986), County NatWest (Blue Arrow scandal in the United Kingdom, 1987), and Baring Brothers have ceased to be independent firms. In the 1990s, major losses of shareholder value befell Salomon Brothers, General Electric (in Kidder Peabody), Bankers Trust, and Daiwa Bank, among others. The market values of these companies (or their parents) have in all cases dropped far more than the aggregate value of the direct losses and expenses related to the scandal provoking the change. The market, in effect, revalued the prospects of all of these firms based on a lower assumed future value of the corporate franchise.[1]

The Bankers Trust case (discussed in Chapter 1) is an instructive example. In the wake of the derivatives scandals, the firm experienced damage to its reputation and prospects, and the erosion of customer confidence in one of its core businesses. The impact on shareholder value was substantial. One way of measuring the damage is to compare the returns on Bankers Trust stock to the Standard & Poor Money Center Bank Index and to the returns on J.P. Morgan stock, its most comparable rival, both before and after the scandals broke (around February 1995). Prior to the scandals, the price of Bankers Trust stock tracked the index very closely and actually outperformed Morgan's stock. After the scandals, Bankers Trust stock traded at a substantial discount from both the index and Morgan's stock. At the end of August 1996, the return on Bankers Trust stock purchased in early 1995 lagged the index by 46 percent and the J.P. Morgan return by 25 percent.

Even in the absence of obvious and specific misconduct, traders know that they may suffer severe consequences if they take advantage of a client's inexperience or ignorance. (It doesn't matter whether the client is retail or wholesale, as in the case of Gibson Greetings or the State of West Virginia's Consolidated Investment Fund.) When a client complains loudly and publicly about substantial losses resulting from an undisclosed risk, a firm may agree to an out-of-court settlement (which may run into the millions of dollars) rather than continuing to litigate and facing an uncertain outcome in court. In either case, the publicity associated with such a complaint may wreak havoc on a firm's reputation, on the valuation of its future prospects, and on its franchise value.

Most people in the securities industry now understand that clients can be dangerous. You need to know your wholesale clients just as well as you know your retail clients, maybe better. If clients do not know what they are doing but persist in trading anyway, then you had better stop dealing with them. If you do not, you may end up guaranteeing their losses. In this context, only one mistake with one client is enough to devastate a firm.

Succeeding with Wholesalers

Operating a successful business in the wholesale sector of any market—the interprofessional sector—depends on being able to create *value added* for the clients. This may be the most difficult thing there is to deliver, but it is also the most important.

- *Being good.* Creating value means being substantively and demonstrably good at what you do. Those firms with good research, good ideas, and good execution stand out. Such firms can charge full rates for their services because they have something to talk about with their clients when making sales calls. By contrast, businesses that depend more on personal relationships, the exchange of favors, inside information, or other such nonsubstantive features have a hard time keeping up and are not likely to last. Owners and top managers must find a way to deliver *substance*. The wholesale market being served is very much aware of it, and the long-run relationship between the firm and clients depends on it.

- *Being first.* Part of being good is being first: first with a new idea, first to call the client. In an industry in which information is so valuable—and so quickly worthless—communicating quickly and accurately is essential. But being first can also create conflicts. How many companies can be the first to know that a client company is for sale? Which of several possible buyers does the firm choose to represent when a merger transaction involving an attractive target comes along? How many can be shown a new, proprietary financing idea? How many can get a call during times of market turmoil asking if there is anything they would like to sell? Developing the capacity to resolve such conflicts quickly and in the best interests of the client (and hence of the firm's own long-term franchise) is another significant management challenge.

  A further aspect of being first involves putting the client's interests ahead of the firm's own interests. Whenever the firm acts on behalf of a client, that client must be allowed to trade first, ahead of the firm itself and ahead of other clients who subsequently engaged the firm to act for them. The firm cannot set aside the first client's interests simply because other clients have deeper pockets.

- *Being consistent.* The Michelin Red Guide to restaurants in France points out that there are many wonderful chefs to choose from, many wonderful meals to try. But only a very few receive Michelin's coveted three-star rating. These, says the Guide, are very special because they can deliver the same wonderful meal day after day after day. Their consistency, not just their potential for a flash of genius, is what gets them this coveted rating. Financial service companies should read the Michelin Guide carefully to learn more about this unique quality and how it is maintained. The answer, of course, is through good management and good training, coupled with uncommon talent and creativity.

- *Being loyal.* The nature of the relationship between banker and client is special. It is vested in the banker, who receives a great deal of private information from the client about its business. Such information usually covers descriptions of future plans, sometimes including information shared on a confidential basis. Companies discuss their funding plans, acquisition goals, and difficulties with rating agencies or with investors. Investor clients, for their part, discuss their portfolio holdings, research ideas, and preferred areas for investment. Both sets of clients, in this sense, expect bankers to help them achieve their goals, to protect the confidentiality of the information provided, and to support them generally. Nothing seems to infuriate a bank's longstanding client more than to discover that the bank is financing another company's effort to take it over. Accordingly, some banks—especially Goldman Sachs—kept their distance from hostile takeovers and emphasized the defense of target companies. This strategy, deemed wasteful by many bankers, has helped Goldman Sachs convince its clients that they could rely on the firm's loyalty. It remains today the firm with the largest number of corporate investment-banking clients.

- *Being willing.* Loyalty also shows up when investor clients want a market maker during difficult market conditions. Often large block-trading firms take losses as part of an effort to provide the necessary liquidity to clients, and these losses are often not repaid by a disproportionate flow of business after the markets have improved. Firms that do this (and not all do) believe that their reputation for being a loyal counterparty for trades is important and will be reflected in future business.

- *Being trustworthy.* Unless they have no choice or, not valuing the virtue, are untrustworthy themselves, clients don't do business with people they don't trust. Dealing with untrustworthy clients involves its own set of risks. Recognizing the value of mutual trust reminds us that we do not want clients to cheat us any more than clients want us to cheat them. This trust extends to not misleading each other and to not making unreasonable demands that would comprise either of our interests. In soliciting business, a firm's representatives may promise substantially more than should be promised, only to confront the disappointed client after the fact with the news that "the market has changed." A client's effort to ensure that research reports about his company are favorable can create much stress. Expectations of side deals or co-investment opportunities can be major impositions. Any such behavior can seriously compromise mutual trust.

In 1995, the Federal Reserve Bank of New York, in conjunction with securities-market regulators, published a committee report on Principles and Practices for Wholesale Market Transactions. In the report are twenty-seven conclusions and recommendations for administrative practices and control procedures to be adopted by wholesale market banks, brokers, and dealers. These conclusions and recommendations incorporate the lessons learned from recent cases such as Kidder Peabody, Barings, and Bankers Trust. Although initiated by U.S. regulators, it was hoped that the principles—all voluntary so far—would eventually be adopted throughout the global securities marketplace to cover many different types of transactions. Most dealers accepted the proposed principles as useful, but not binding, in their own relations with clients. "The way we treat our clients," one London dealer said, "will be dictated first and foremost by their individual needs." Others reacted to the new principles with greater skepticism. A representative of a large U.S. pension fund, claiming to be an end-user of derivative instruments, asked, "Whose interests are being served? . . . We agree that self-regulation is preferable to government regulation, but let's not confuse self-regulation with dealer regulation."[2]

Creating added value—and getting business as a result—is only half the job. Working with wholesalers also involves risks; some effort has to be spent on enlightened defense.

- *Being alert.* Most mistakes and accidents occur because someone who might have prevented them was not alert enough to do so. The best firms have managers at all levels who are alert to everything that goes on in their arenas. They pick up on irregular cash flows, erratic client or employee behavior, and the like—all tips that something is amiss. As Ace Greenberg, former chairman of Bear Stearns has said, "All of our officers and employees are just as honest as any on Wall Street—but they're more honest because they know we're watching them all the time."[3]

- *Being "prudential."* The word "prudential" is not often used in U.S. financial markets, but it is in Britain, where it has become key to self-regulation in the financial services industry. A prudent person managing a firm will be careful, cautious, and honest, acting as if his or her own money is involved. In the United States it is part of one's fiduciary duty to be prudent when acting in any capacity with other people's money. (And it may be up to you to prove that you were in fact prudent if it comes to litigation.) Prudential conduct can be expected only if it is extensive and very visible at the top of the organization. Sometimes, of course, it is not.

- *Being diligent.* All financial people know the term "due diligence." Not all know that it relates to a legal term that defines a possible defense in cases involving securities-related civil liability. If one is obligated to be informed about a matter and has made an effort to do so, what determines whether the effort is sufficient to pass muster? The effort is sufficient, under the law, only when it has been duly diligent—that is, when the effort has been as serious, unflagging, and completely thorough as the circumstances require. Most people who attempt to mislead are clever enough to avoid detection under half-hearted efforts to undertake due diligence. Many banking and investment-banking professionals are sufficiently independent and difficult to manage that only the most vigorously applied efforts to implement due diligence policies or enforce tough standards will succeed.

- *Being tough.* Being tough means being insistent when your subordinates and associates resist doing something they should. Examples are turning down a lucrative piece of business because of a possible conflict rather than trying to fudge it, disciplining top producers when they misbehave rather than looking the other way, turning down easy money from a client that is ignorant or devious rather than rationalizing the transaction. Many such cases occur regularly in the business. The toughest calls involve turning down clients and deals and making your most productive employees toe the line. But if you can't be tough, you can't be good.

These points focus on protecting value, rather than creating it. None are easy to implement or enforce, despite their importance to a firm's long-term future. Successful firms are those that can handle these management challenges and that can formulate an overall business strategy in terms of the firm's fundamental client relationships. What kind of clients do we want? What kind of relationship do we want them to have with us? What minimums do we expect from the client in order to continue doing our best? What price are we prepared to pay in order to maintain these relationships? What price are we *not* prepared to pay?

Such matters are never precise. But frameworks can be constructed and senior employees can be educated to manage their associates and the clients—even difficult ones—within these frameworks. However spectacular a single deal or series of transactions may be at the time, and however mesmerizing the profit opportunities, their long-term value to the firm may be trivial if they fall outside these carefully established frameworks.

These issues are further complicated when a firm decides to act as an investor in a transaction that may put it at odds with its wholesale clients. As investment banks have increased their portfolios of merchant-banking investments—investments in minority positions of usually illiquid assets—

these conflicts have become more common. When large firms invest as principals, they will displease other players, including sometime clients of the firm, whose positions are in opposition to the firms'.

Goldman Sachs faced two such situations in 1995, both involving invest-ment activity by the firm's limited-partnership affiliate, Whitehall Street Real Estate. One case was about the restructuring of the failed Canadian real estate company, Cadillac Fairview. Whitehall bought some of Cadillac's debt securities and maneuvered in the complex bankruptcy proceedings to increase the value of the assets it had bought. Investors in Cadillac's junior debt securities were unhappy. Some of these large institutional investors subsequently announced that they were reducing their brokerage business with Goldman. If offending a past or future client of the firm was a bar to its acting as a principal investor, then Goldman could never participate in merchant-banking investments. Some years ago the firm may have felt this way, but it no longer does.

The realities of the market have changed. As wholesale market players deal with one another increasingly at arm's length, the more likely it is that they will, from time to time, get in each other's way as investors. That does not mean, of course, that in doing so they would be willing to violate conflict-of-interest rules (and therefore to ignore their duties to clients). The reality, however, is that wholesale players will unavoidably find them-selves opposing each other in their efforts to maximize investment returns.

5

Market Rigging

■

Almost always, it seems, the first thing that happens after a new financial market is formed is that someone tries to manipulate it. It happened in the United States and in markets in Europe and in Japan, and is now fairly common in countries with emerging financial markets. When markets are sloppy, volatile, poorly regulated, guided by corruptible people, and not very transparent, then anything can happen. Indeed, it may be that if market rigging *can* occur, it will. The economic incentives to rig markets are plentiful, especially if the manipulation is not easily detected. It can be checked only by a strong counterforce by those who run the market. They must be vigilant and willing to bring offenders to trial. Regulations must be well conceived and strictly enforced through appropriate sanctions. Even the Amsterdam Stock Exchange, formed in 1645 as the world's first, needed to impose a rule prohibiting market manipulation. The exchange was able to enforce this rule effectively because the trading community recognized that an offense against the market was an offense against them all, individually and collectively.

Market manipulation has many forms. Misuse of information is a common one, as are trading on inside information, fabricating stories about companies, cornering markets, concealing trades, and watering stock. Early American financial history is rich in examples, beginning perhaps with insider trading in about-to-be-redeemed Continental Bonds just after the Revolutionary War and continuing into the nineteenth century, when financial markets developed rapidly and created ample opportunities for some to swindle others.

Jacob Little was perhaps our first financial rogue to be recognized as such. He pioneered the large-scale manipulation of stocks by cornering the market for shares in the Norwich & Worcester Railroad in 1835. He had joined a group of Boston railroad investors and promised them to do everything in his power to raise the price of the stock and not to sell his

121

own shares below $90. He secured the promise with a $25,000 bond. Later on, Little began to worry about a possible market decline and devised a way to sell his shares secretly to his own associates, who had to buy them to maintain the price. When the market subsequently crashed, Little simply sent them the amount of his bond—a pittance compared to his gains from dumping the stock early and at a much higher price. Little's coinvestors were furious and threatened to relieve him of certain body parts if he ever set foot in Boston again.

Jacob Little had his ups and downs in the market, rationalizing that if he failed to lead the lambs to slaughter by artful manipulation, others would do it instead.[1] By the time he finished, this forerunner of such famous speculators as Daniel Drew, Commodore Vanderbilt, and Jay Gould had succeeded in creating the stereotype of stockbrokers as shrewd businessmen who put their own interests ahead of those of their clients.

It was not until late in the nineteenth century that rogues began ripping off the unsuspecting public by forcing stock prices up (or down) by concerted market action. The typical strategy was to start the price moving upward with some modest but concentrated buying, coupled with the aggressive circulation of false stories that would justify the price movement and suggest that even greater price increases were imminent. The public would then rush in, pushing the stock price to frantically inflated levels. By that time the manipulators would secretly be selling. Soon afterward the bubble would burst and the stock would plummet.

Such manipulation remained common into the 1920s. An article in the *New York American* noted that "by artful management, assiduous plugging, manifest predictions, and supplies of stock skillfully curtailed as the demand increases . . . stocks may be blown up to an absurd rate and offered, as a favor, to the public."[2] One consequence of the manipulated and overheated financial markets of the 1920s was the great crash of October 1929. The crash was so severe (some blamed it for the Great Depression of the 1930s) that it came under congressional investigation. A host of serious market abuses was discovered, and the Securities Acts of 1933 and 1934 were passed as a result. American markets have since benefited from these constraints on the likes of Jacob Little and the many swindlers who followed the same path. The regulatory cycle was complete. Abuses begin, are initially tolerated, then become serious. After major losses occur, the public reacts and adopts new rules and regulations. The market enters a new phase of regulatory equilibrium.

But the system is not airtight. In any nearly perfect market, ferreting out the tiniest pockets of inefficiency is the crux of profitable trading. Each time a trader succeeds in making a gain, though, he helps to destroy that inefficiency. In this hypercompetitive setting, it is obviously tempting to stack the deck in one's own favor by bending the rules (written or unwritten) and manipulating the market. Ironically, the more efficient the markets become, the greater the temptation to cheat and to create profitable trading opportunities by manipulating the market.

A Squeeze by Salomon

By 1991 Salomon Brothers had become the most powerful bond house in the world. Its dominant share of the global market in new issues and secondary-market trading assured the firm of access to governments, corporations, and large institutional investors everywhere.

The heart of Salomon's power lay in the U.S. government securities market, where the firm had specialized since its beginnings as a partnership in 1910. By 1990 the firm controlled more assets than all but a few of the largest American banks. Well capitalized and profitable, "Solly" was especially known for its highly competent pool of talent and its fiercely competitive willingness to take risks and to back innovative and high-tech approaches to market making and proprietary trading. It was also characterized by a loose, spontaneous management style that cut through organizational formalities to identify and reward top performers. The firm was the world's most formidable and intimidating trading machine at a time when trading had become the principal source of profits on Wall Street.

Salomon's tough-talking chairman John Gutfreund was at the peak of his thirty-eight-year career, one which had already generated many laurels. He had been declared the "King of Wall Street" by *Business Week* in 1985. On the strength of billionaire Warren Buffett's confidence in Gutfreund, Buffett's Berkshire Hathaway invested $700 million in Salomon. But Buffett's confidence in the firm may have been disturbed if he had read Michael Lewis's best-selling *Liar's Poker*, which described in rude and ugly detail the culture and environment of Salomon Brothers in the 1980s. By the time the book came out in 1989, however, the firm was already very different. Many of the more colorful characters had left. Gutfreund had also committed himself to better management and control procedures, and had put the firm through a major strategic review in 1987. Nonetheless, by the end of 1991 the firm was left in shambles, with its survival in doubt.

Salomon had pushed its trading revenues to more than 80 percent of the firmwide total in 1991 (versus 57 percent in 1987). Its nontrading results were quite acceptable, too, ranking fourth in U.S. underwriting and third in mergers and acquisitions that year. But trading was driving the firm more than ever, and driving its "trading engine" was its government-securities department. This group personified Salomon at its best and at its worst. Its brilliant, aggressive, workaholic young professionals were devoted to preserving Salomon's leading position and powerful market reputation. They were also arrogant, ruthless, and so obsessively focused on beating the competition and making money that they lost sight of everything else. As Floyd Norris of the *New York Times* put it, "At Salomon Brothers, trading has always been a form of war in which the opponent is entitled to no pity and rules are viewed as impediments to be side-stepped, if possible."[3]

Before any U.S. government bond auction, participating securities firms' traders attempt to estimate what the winning price will be and how much of the paper can be sold at that price (that is, the rate of interest). Traders build a book of orders from customers and then make their bid. Only firms designated by the Federal Reserve as *primary dealers* can submit bids for new issues. In 1991 there were about forty such firms, which had the benefit of prebidding discussions with the Treasury to exchange views about market demand and factors affecting it. These dealers would aggregate their own bids for bonds with those of large institutional customers that had authorized them to bid on their behalf, which enabled dealers to present the largest possible block of orders to the Treasury. To minimize their position risks, dealers would sell (short) the as-yet-unissued bonds to customers at a price judged to be a good bet. Dealers would then have to count on being allocated bonds in the Treasury auction to supply their customers with the securities that they had already pre-sold to them. Any shortfall would have to be covered later by purchasing bonds in the open market.

Aggressive traders often bid for more bonds in Treasury auctions than they have orders for, and at a higher price. The more orders traders have at higher prices, the more bonds they are allocated. The more they are allocated, the more of the market for the issue they control. According to one former Salomon trader, "If you build a book of $3 billion, $5 billion, $8 billion, then you really control the situation. Then you use your muscle, your big war chest of dollars, to force the thing with a drop-dead bid."[4] The idea is to control the market and to force other dealers and those covering short positions to buy from the dominant player at whatever price that firm sets.

Cornering the market in Treasury securities is prohibited, although technically it was allowed until July 1990, when the Treasury imposed a limit of 35 percent on how much any firm or consortium of firms could bid for in a single issue. Prior to that time, no single firm, or so it was thought, had enough resources to purchase a market-cornering position in Treasuries. But in view of the increasing dominance of a few large firms, the limit was imposed to maintain maximum competition among primary dealers and to achieve the highest possible price and lowest possible funding cost to the government over the long run. Those opposing the 35 percent limit nonetheless felt that the government could be preventing itself from receiving the lowest-cost bids.

Paul Mozer, a fast-rising trader at Salomon with an MBA from the Kellogg School at Northwestern University, was one of those who opposed the 35 percent limit. After his first assignment working in Salomon's Chicago office, Mozer had been transferred to New York in 1983, where he worked at the bond-arbitrage desk under John Meriwether, the firm's trading boss. (Meriwether is the now-legendary figure who, according to author Michael Lewis in *Liar's Poker,* countered John Gutfreund's 1986 challenge to a hand of poker—"one hand, one million dollars, no tears"— with an offer to play for "real money instead, ten million, no tears." Gutfreund refused, and his confrontation with Meriwether was taken to demonstrate that even powerful, high-placed executives lack the right stuff, the capacity to stand up to the Cool Hand Lukes of the trading room.) When Meriwether was made Salomon's vice chairman and head of bond trading in 1988, he appointed the thirty-three-year-old Mozer head of government securities, one of the most important and visible trading positions at the firm and, indeed, on Wall Street.

Highly self-confident, aggressive, and impatient with bureaucracy, Mozer soon found himself in sharp conflict with Treasury officials and their rules, including the 35 percent limit on any individual issue of securities to be auctioned. Mozer became obsessed with outsmarting or otherwise getting around the new regulations, which themselves were in good part enacted in response to his own aggressive bidding. If he could somehow win all, or almost all, of an issue, other dealers would have to come to him to obtain the bonds they needed to fill customer orders. Mozer could then sell the bonds to them at higher prices. In order to achieve this goal, Mozer misidentified bids in excess of 35 percent as orders coming from bona fide Salomon customers, when in fact they did not. These false bids totaled over $15 billion from 1989 to 1991.[5]

A probe by the Treasury Department in April 1991 alarmed Mozer, and he reported one of his violations of the rules to John Meriwether, who informed John Gutfreund, Tom Strauss (Salomon's president), and Donald Feuerstein (the firm's general counsel). Mozer admitted to falsifying a customer order that Salomon had presented at a February auction. This order, plus other phantom orders, pushed Salomon over the Treasury's limit. Gutfreund and the others chastised Mozer but did not alter his position or investigate his activities. Gutfreund said he would report the matter to the Treasury, but neither he nor anyone else did so. Things cooled down.

Within a month of this meeting, Mozer violated the rule again. At the 22 May auction of two-year Treasury notes, "Salomon and its customers collectively purchased approximately $10.6 billion out of $11.3 billion in notes that were to be available for purchase by competitive bidders."[6] Salomon thus controlled 94 percent of the notes. In the process, the firm bid $2 billion for at least one customer and simultaneously repurchased $500 million from that same customer at the auction price, while "inadvertently" failing to disclose its own position. Dealers charged that Salomon then forced up prices of the notes, putting the squeeze on competitors who had sold notes to customers in the when-issued market with the intention of covering their positions in the auction. Because no notes were available, competitors had no choice but to go to Salomon and pay a much higher price. The squeeze was no secret. Many dealers were complaining openly, and the Treasury's price data showed abnormal price patterns, provoking yet another inquiry. In June, the SEC and the Justice Department requested information from Salomon and certain of its clients about the bids. One Treasury official, noting Salomon's arrogant disregard of the bidding rules, said that it was shocking that Salomon "could do it at the February auction, learn about it in April, not tell us, and do it again in May."[7]

The Treasury and the Federal Reserve were outraged and suspended Salomon from submitting customer bids in further government auctions. Salomon's board asked for the resignations of Gutfreund, Strauss, Meriwether, Mozer, and some lesser figures on 16 August 1991.

Accused of truly scandalous conduct, Salomon was threatened with a criminal indictment for bid rigging and for misreporting required information to government authorities. A criminal conviction or plea bargain would almost certainly have put the firm out of business because of the customer defections and civil lawsuits that would have resulted. Neither Drexel Burnham nor E.F. Hutton had survived criminal charges in the 1980s.

In late August of 1991, Salomon admitted publicly that its trading activities had become too aggressive and that it had indeed made several illegal bids (noting, however, that the firm had made less than $20 million in profits from all of these activities). Salomon's board of directors, consisting of seven outside directors and six from within the firm, held an urgent meeting; the outsiders, led by Warren Buffett and his long-term colleague at Berkshire Hathaway, Charlie Munger, took control. Berkshire, the firm's largest share-holder with a 16 percent stake, did the necessary firing and also elected Buffett himself as chairman. Buffett skillfully avoided the criminal indict-ment of the firm by localizing the blame on Mozer and his superiors, by unequivocally accepting responsibility for Salomon's actions, and by prom-ising internal reforms and future good behavior.

Buffett resolutely began the process of putting the firm back together. To help him do so, he selected forty-three-year-old Deryck C. Maughan as chief operating officer in charge of day-to-day activities. Maughan, who until a month earlier had been head of the firm's highly successful Tokyo operations, was not a trader, nor even an American. Indeed, he was an Englishman who, though he had been an official in the British Treasury for ten years, had had nothing to do with government securities at Salomon. Maughan was seen as a good choice to look at matters objectively. Buffett told Salomon employees that the firm would be taking fewer risks in the future and that it would not be operating as close to the edge as it had in the past. Compliance was to be emphasized. He would be ruthless in protecting the firm's reputation. Buffett and Maughan pledged to improve the firm's internal controls, to renew its commitment to integrity and high standards, and to reform its excessive, somewhat haphazard compensation system, which some felt was at the root of the firm's problems. The two new leaders were able to convince the Treasury and the Fed to allow Salomon to participate once again in auctions—for its own account but not, until later, for the accounts of customers.

As 1991 drew to a close, the scandal abated. But Salomon's actions had set off an avalanche of protests and complaints about the low level of ethical and professional standards on Wall Street. The media, politicians, and competitors all jumped onto the bandwagon. Buffett was required to appear before Congress, where the scandal was investigated by various committees. The financial community appeared shocked by the revelation that the world's leading trading firm, feared and respected in all major markets, was guilty of flagrant illegal behavior and that its top managers had been aware of it and done nothing. Adding insult to injury, Salomon was itself a respected member of the Treasury's debt-finance advisory committee.

A settlement was soon reached with the SEC in which Salomon paid $290 million in fines. The firm also had to compensate investors who had suffered losses because of its actions. In addition to its two-month suspension from acting as a primary dealer by the Federal Reserve, Salomon was blacklisted for a time by several important underwriting and investing clients. The firm announced a charge against earnings to establish a reserve against civil liabilities that could have reached $400 million (more than forty suits had already been filed).

Mozer, the young superstar just entering the high-performance years of what could have been a long, remunerative, and distinguished career, pleaded guilty to two counts of lying to the Federal Reserve Bank of New York. He was fined $30,000 and sent to prison for four months. U.S. District Court judge Pierre Laval noted that "in the world of financial crimes, deterrence of others is an extremely important aspect of sentencing."[8] Mozer has since returned to Wall Street, where he was last seen trying to raise money for a hedge fund that he would manage.

A tough guy to the end, John Gutfreund reportedly told his top executives at a closed-door meeting: "I'm not apologizing to anybody for anything. Apologies don't mean shit. What happened, happened."[9] Gutfreund was fined $100,000 and barred for life from heading a brokerage or investment firm. In addition, he ultimately lost an effort to secure $14 million of accrued compensation from Salomon and faced a variety of civil lawsuits brought by disgruntled investors. Strauss and Meriwether were fined lesser amounts and suspended from the securities industry for six and three months, respectively. Strauss has not resurfaced since, but Meriwether is now head of a successful fixed-income hedge fund.

Hostage to the Dealers?

What factors had a role in the Salomon scandal? Central to any explanation is the explosive growth in the auction system for Treasury securities, whose new-issue volume grew from $59 billion in 1980 to $1.5 trillion by 1990. Likewise, refundings of outstanding Treasury securities grew from $62 billion to $2.2 trillion over the same period (from 33 to 64 percent of American GDP). The main conduits for this massive task are the forty primary market dealers licensed by the Federal Reserve Board to purchase Treasury securities at auction. American public-debt financing has taken on a life of its own, virtually dominating the capital markets and the financing options of private and municipal borrowers. It influences worldwide interest rates and exerts a powerful impact on government policy decisions. Every hiccup in the market, from shifts in the Japanese appetite for dollar securities to events in Eastern Europe, sends policymakers into frenzied meetings on its implications for the next Treasury refunding.

Getting to the right price for a new securities issue is no simple task. Reliable information regarding investor demand—with thousands of potential investors worldwide, each having a variety of investment choices—has to somehow coalesce every few weeks. And the Treasury needs to be able to use this information effectively to obtain the highest prices (or the lowest interest rates), thereby minimizing its funding costs for each issue of debt.

Different countries use different methods for achieving this objective, but the primary-dealer approach is generally regarded as both efficient and fair. The notion of having a limited number of such dealers bidding for their own accounts and for those of customers reduces the number of buyers with whom the Treasury has to deal; the primary dealers make up an easily manageable group of well-informed players. Rules such as the 35 percent limit are designed to ensure that no one bidder gains sufficient control to depress prices and thereby raise the Treasury's funding costs. In order to enhance the information flow needed for the Treasury to get to the best price, and as long as there is no collusion, premarket exchanges of information are permitted, both between dealers and between them and the Treasury. Mozer and Salomon may have considered the Treasury incapable of punishing the firm's infractions because of the firm's importance to the market as the largest of the primary dealers. It may also be that the legal powers of the Treasury to mete out punishment were not sufficiently well defined to create a credible deterrent.

Bidding for new Treasury issues is a tough business and requires tough people. The more efficient the auction market, the less likely it is that the primary dealers as a group will make much money. All of the major players have essentially the same market information, although they may not all interpret it the same way. Misinterpretation of that information and unexpected changes in market conditions can lead to large losses. For a firm like Salomon to achieve extraordinary profits from this business, it had to take large position risks, develop new techniques for trading or hedging its positions, or react faster than everyone else to changes in market information. Although firms try all of these alternatives, none is easy in an environment of cutthroat competition. Most dealers are content to accept these difficulties and to conduct their business honorably within the rules. Salomon and perhaps some others disguised improper activities and tried to exploit regulatory loopholes to squeeze their competitors and clients, and to gain an illegitimate edge on the market.

With razor-thin risk-adjusted profits, many dealers have activated firmwide efforts to cut costs. Some firms cut back on the capacity of independent internal auditors to ensure compliance with laws, regulations, and rules. Until the Salomon revelations, however, abuses had not often been detected, and penalties for self-reported rule violations were few and usually fairly modest.

In accordance with rules long in effect, the Treasury itself, not the SEC, has jurisdiction over all auction-related activities. It is the Treasury's sole venture into securities regulation. In a loose partnership with the Federal Reserve Bank of New York, it monitors and regulates the activities of primary dealers. The rules for auctions and other activities are both numerous and complex; they can easily be violated inadvertently. The Treasury requires self-reporting of any such violations. Firms are always embarrassed to report a serious misstep, even if accidental. For its part, the Treasury has a very limited capacity to detect violations or enforce its own rules. This limitation is one justification for the system of primary market dealers; only the most qualified dealers of good reputation are permitted into the club. It is a sensible rule, one that is practiced in most other developed countries.

In the Salomon case, the Treasury did match up customer bids and detected an anomaly that subsequently led Paul Mozer to confess what he had done. Later, after the May 1991 auction in which Mozer exceeded the 35 percent limit again, both the Treasury and the Fed detected evidence of a squeeze. They turned the investigation over to the SEC, which had already requested information from Salomon after the first announcement of a violation. One could complain about the speed of the process, but in fact the wrongdoer was caught and punished by the regulators.

Salomon itself also paid a heavy price. In addition to the regulatory penalties, its stock price dropped by one-third, or $1.5 billion in terms of the firm's market capitalization. To avert a possible financing crisis of its own, the firm liquidated almost a third of its asset portfolio. It dropped from fifth to tenth in stock underwriting. Its credit standing as a trading counterparty took a major hit. Big customers, including the World Bank and the State of California, suspended trading with the firm. It settled a variety of contested legal actions at significant cost. It lost key employees and had to pay well above the market to retain others.[10] In effect, what punishment was not meted out by the government was left to the market, and Salomon shareholders paid dearly. Still, the firm survived and remained a primary dealer and was permitted to resume bidding at Treasury auctions on behalf of customers after 1 August 1992. But the firm still faced a battery of civil lawsuits in connection with the scandal.

Having guided Salomon through the crisis, Buffett returned to Omaha, leaving Maughan in charge as CEO of Salomon Brothers. And as business returned to normal, Wall Street asked itself how the scandal could have occurred. Salomon was warlike, domineering, and arrogant, but few thought the firm was actually venal or dishonest or stupid (which is what you'd have to be to think you could get away with the illegal manipulation of Treasury auctions).

The extent to which Salomon and other firms failed to police themselves created the potential for problems. The control function within the firms (the ticket processors, record keepers, and compliance officials) must be totally independent of the traders. Mozer and his chief clerk, however, were able to get around the firm's control procedures, which were weak, chaotic, and outdated. In addition, the people enforcing them had insufficient power and influence to stand up to Mozer, and neither Meriwether nor anyone senior to Mozer seemed to know or care what he was doing. All they wanted to know was that the firm was making money. After all, the Street glorifies its successful traders, not its compliance departments. Good compliance and surveillance are expensive, and not always thought to be worth the money. But as the Mozer episode demonstrates, a strong, independent compliance group empowered with the highest authority by the firm may be one of a trading firm's best assets.

In time, Salomon recovered, but it was never quite the same. The firm reported record profits in 1993, but 1994, a difficult year for all of the industry's trading firms, was a different story. Salomon lost nearly $1 billion before taxes, more than any other firm, at a time when it was also undertaking major reforms in its internal organization, management controls, and compensation system. The poor performance and ongoing reforms caused serious turmoil and a considerable defection of talent. At the annual meeting in May 1995, one unhappy shareholder announced that the firm had been a bit rough edged before and may have stepped on the rules too often, but at least it made money. Would the firm that Buffett and Maughan were trying to build from the ashes of the old Salomon be too nice and law abiding to compete effectively?

The Economics and Law of Speculation

Efficient markets allocate returns in proportion to the amount of risk borne by a market participant. Any excess return other than an amount commensurate with risk is known as an *anomaly* if it occurs on a consistent basis. When investors speculate in an efficient market, they make undiversified, unhedged bets on assets, such as stocks or positions in derivatives, in order to maximize expected gains (from intuition or results of trading models) regarding future market movements. The idea of an efficient market, by definition, rules out the possibility of making sustained excess returns; investors will immediately take advantage of any costless and riskless possibilities for gain by taking simultaneous long or short positions in an asset.

Investors have been reassured over the years by pragmatic regulations designed to protect the honesty and integrity of the market. Regulations that have displaced a pure laissez-faire philosophy in financial markets were motivated more by the objective of improving investor confidence than by the intent per se of imposing restrictions on financial activities. Among other things, regulations attempt to ensure that participants have equal access to information. "Innovators and speculators have found each other in securities markets and nurtured the enterprises that have made great breakthroughs."[11]

The central role of speculators in financial markets is to assume the risk of price fluctuations. Market manipulation represents an attempt to eliminate that risk by controlling prices through deception. Before the 1930s, manipulation was virtually undetected and also heavily institutionalized in the United States. Because it did not violate any specific legal statutes, it was accepted as a risk of participating in financial markets. Indeed, manipulation was regarded as a bold and admirable skill, and successful manipulators boasted of their enterprise and daring foresight. As opposed to watching the swinging pendulum—a metaphor for prices—manipulators themselves attempted to influence the pendulum's end position. A market rigger who successfully manipulated this pendulum reaped all the gains from bets placed on the direction of its movement. This type of manipulation has occurred in and between all markets where securities, assets, or other sophisticated products or commodities are for sale.

Speculation increases turnover in capital markets. It can therefore be viewed as a lubrication factor that ultimately increases the efficiency and liquidity of the market. It raises trading volumes, smooths price fluctuations, encourages more active market participation, and increases the potential for optimum capital allocation. Primary issuers or corporations seeking to raise capital are, for their part, indifferent as to whether the stock is initially purchased by an investor seeking to hold long term or by a speculator seeking to sell immediately. As potential purchasers, investors know that shares will have an active market because of speculative activity. Investors can therefore convert their shares to cash and buy new issues more easily. As manipulation-linked losses undercut investors' confidence in the marketplace, however, the long-term effect will be a loss of market liquidity and efficiency.

The role of technology in integrating and linking markets in real time should make market manipulation increasingly difficult; the relationships between asset prices, exchange rates, interest rates, macroeconomic conditions, and economic policies will play a more immediate role in setting prices. Arbitrage possibilities across international stock markets also tend to reduce the effect of any domestic manipulative activity. Still, even broad and deep financial markets are subject to potential manipulation.

Spread Skimming at NASDAQ

In August 1996 the National Association of Securities Dealers entered into a settlement with the SEC (without admitting to wrongdoing) to resolve charges of price fixing and collusion among market makers. This settlement followed earlier settlements between the Department of Justice and two dozen major NASDAQ dealers of alleged antitrust violations associated with their "pricing convention." Repeated complaints had also been made that NASDAQ dealers regularly backed away from the firm quotes they were required to make for customers. Some companies were reportedly defecting from NASDAQ to the New York Stock Exchange because they were fed up with NASD's inability or unwillingness to discipline its members. Civil suits alleging collusion were filed against thirty-three major NASDAQ dealers accused of running the market more for their own benefit than for the benefit of investors.

The SEC settlement required NASD to spend some $100 million on improved policing of NASDAQ, the second-largest stock market in the world (after the New York Stock Exchange). In addition to the improved policing of member firms, NASD filled 50 percent of its governing board with independent, nonindustry representatives. It appointed a professional hearing officer to preside over disciplinary proceedings and established an independent auditing staff to review all aspects of NASD operations. NASD also prohibited the coordination of quotes by members, regulated trade reporting by and among NASDAQ market makers, and prevented NASDAQ dealers from refusing to honor quoted prices by backing away.[12] The SEC settlement was accompanied by a stinging rebuke from SEC chairman Arthur Levitt.

The investigations of NASDAQ were triggered by a 1994 study by professors William Christie and Paul Schultz, which suggested that NASDAQ dealers were enriching themselves by quoting unnecessarily wide spreads between buy and sell orders.[13] The wider the spreads, of course, the greater the dealers' profits. But for wide spreads to persist in a competitive marketplace in which many dealers quote prices for the same stock, some sort of at least tacit collusion, they argued, would have had to exist.

NASD initially ridiculed these findings and commissioned studies to refute the research of Christie and Schultz. These new studies were unable do so, however. A number of prominent Wall Streeters nonetheless charged that the two professors and subsequent investigations by the SEC were biased against NASDAQ and the dealer market that it offers (versus the NYSE's auction market). Further investigations followed, which produced evidence of tape recordings of dealers manipulating customers into buying at artificially high, and selling at artificially low, prices. Dealers who rejected this practice (that is, who quoted better, more competitive prices) were harassed and threatened with sanctions by their competitors and by NASD.[14] As one observer noted, "A trader who offered too good a deal to customers was deemed to have violated the ethical and professional standards of the NASDAQ market. Such a trader would be subject to a variety of sanctions. Others would try to nail him in trading, or would refuse to trade with him if at all possible."[15] This kind of behavior was evidently known to senior NASD officials, who either did nothing, took part in the questionable activities themselves, or helped in arranging coverups. At best, officials pleaded with dealers to stop the harassment, usually to no avail. In response to the need to quote more competitive prices, one dealer reportedly said in a taped conversation, "Why should I do that? You know, we might as well milk it for as long as we can."[16]

As the investigations were progressing, NASD convened a governance committee to recommend actions to improve the system. Chaired by former Senator Warren Rudman, the committee recommended splitting NASD's functions into two independent units, one the NASDAQ market operations themselves and the other a regulatory arm to supervise and control that market. The governors of NASD then appointed Mary Schapiro, who had a strong track record on enforcement as director of the Commodities Futures Trading Commission, as the new head of NASD's enforcement arm.

None of these measures was sufficient, however, to ward off harsh SEC censure of earlier misdeeds. In the words of the SEC enforcement chief William McLucas, "No one examining the record will be able to stand up and say, 'This is a product of Commission bias.' The only thing the Commission has in mind is investor protection and fair markets."[17] There were dire predictions of layoffs and profit erosion in the NASDAQ departments of major securities firms; it would be nearly impossible, some claimed, to make decent profits in the more competitive markets to come. Time will tell, of course, whether this is so. But perhaps most disturbing about the NASDAQ affair is that its prevailing standards of professional conduct tolerated the rigging of markets in ways that damaged clients, undermining the credibility of the whole market, one of the most innovative and successful in the world.

Ramping, Cornering, and Other Popular Manipulations

Webster defines manipulation as "controlling or playing upon by artful, unfair or insidious means, especially to one's own advantage."[18] In financial markets, manipulation involves fooling others into paying a higher price (or receiving a lower price) than they would if the manipulation had not taken place. Because the manipulators are positioned on the other side of the transaction, they pocket the gains. Here are two examples:

1. A fund manager gets the word out that he is bullish on a particular stock. Investors buy shares on the strength of his views and the price rises, even as the fund manager himself quietly begins to dump the shares in the market. He wins, they lose. This example is a classic illustration of *ramping,* or *frontrunning.*

2. An investor group quietly buys up a large proportion of the shares of a company and then puts out the word that the company is likely to fail, inducing some investors to sell shares at prices below the real worth of the company. Some investors will be induced to sell shares short, or to sell futures that eventually have to be covered by delivering the underlying stock. The manipulators buy the stock being sold on the market and obtain control of most of the outstanding shares. Manipulators can now charge the unsuspecting

short sellers a stiff premium to buy shares from them to avoid de-
faulting on their positions. This example is a classic illustration of
cornering a market.

In both cases, there is premeditation. That is, the manipulator has a plan
to make windfall profits by either driving prices up and forcing others
obligated to deliver securities or commodities to pay exorbitant prices, or
by squeezing prices down when the manipulators themselves have obligations to sell at a later date. Both of these strategies are illegal in the United
States and in most other countries with well-developed financial markets.

The *manipulator* is the initiator of the scheme, whose success depends
on how much of the underlying asset is under his or her control. But the
attempt to manipulate a market is not without risk. For example, failed
attempts to corner can leave manipulators with large blocks of the underlying asset, which may then have to be sold under adverse market conditions. The famous case of the Hunt Brothers' efforts to corner the silver
market in the 1970s is an example.

The *manipulatee* is the victim of the scheme. It is a role shared by the
investor, first and foremost, as well as by the issuer of the securities, by the
marketplace, and by the economy as a whole. Even though the company
may not be issuing shares in the primary market, the loss of confidence as
a result of the secondary-market manipulation of its securities will affect
the share value and hence the value of the firm as a whole and its cost of
capital. While the manipulated investor loses in the short term, the cost
and ability of the issuer to raise funds in the marketplace may be impaired
in the long term. More generally, manipulated markets suffer investor
defections, illiquidity, and an eroded ability to allocate capital, with potentially serious consequences for national economic performance. Manipulation also drives transactions abroad, into markets deemed less susceptible
to manipulation, with potential long-term damage to the competitiveness
of the domestic securities market.

Ramping at Sterling Foster

During the 1996 bull market in stocks, the NASD brought the largest
disciplinary case in its history against Sterling Foster and several of its
brokers in connection with massive stock manipulation in an IPO for
Advanced Voice Technologies, a small company developing a voice-mail
system to help teachers and school officials communicate with parents and

students. Insiders controlled the bulk of the shares and allegedly bilked hundreds of small investors out of some $51 million through misrepresentation, unauthorized trading, and ramping the shares. NASD's new "Radar" trade-detection system and improved linkages to trade-processing firms allowed the NASD to identify victimized investors and put together a case against the firm, located on Long Island in a nondescript building next to a vegetable stand, with a parking lot full of BMWs and Mercedes-Benz convertibles.[19]

Frontrunning at Magellan

On several occasions in 1995 Jeffrey Vinik, the highly reputed manager of the Fidelity Magellan Fund (which had been heavily invested in technology stocks and was being carefully watched for any sign that it was souring on the sector), talked up technology stocks while at the same time unloading these stocks in the market. In the ensuing months, the SEC investigated Vinik's actions, especially in the case of Micron Technology and Goodyear Tire & Rubber, both of which he had talked up even as he was selling Magellan's holdings of the two stocks. But according to one observer, market manipulation is much more complex. "There is a big hole in any notion of market manipulation here [in the Vinik case]. How would it work? He couldn't have known when, or what, or even if anything was going to be printed [about what he said or did]. So how could he have counted on a market impact that would enable him to do something wrong?"[20] In any case, Fidelity's management quickly muzzled Vinik and other fund managers, and placed their trading activity under more intense supervision. This intervention was obviously intended to prevent further damage to the firm's reputation. Vinik later resigned under pressure to start his own fund-management business. The episode is a good example of corrective forces emanating from the market itself, obviating the need for regulatory action.

Sumitomo's Metal

Not long after this, Sumitomo Corporation lost roughly $1.8 billion because a senior copper trader, Yasuo Hamanaka, speculated on the London Metal Exchange for a decade or more. The exchange had long been known as a gentlemen's club of opaque rules and lax enforcement far removed from the rough-and-tumble of the usual commodities trading pit. Lack of transparency in Hamanaka's trades on the exchange and in the over-the-counter market allowed him to mask the trades, the size of his holdings, and the market equilibrium in copper. In the end, Hamanaka's efforts to keep the price of copper up and squeeze his competitors collapsed in the face of withering attacks from other speculators and short sellers, ultimately driving prices from $1.40 a pound in mid-1995 to $.80 a year later. It may seem reassuring that even massive efforts to rig markets ultimately fall victim to the forces of supply and demand, but Hamanaka's positions were financed by huge, highly structured bank credits (which, along with suspicions of systematic market rigging, led the U.S. Federal Reserve and Commodities Futures Trading Commission to become involved). In the words of one observer, "One of the beauties of this market is that it has limited regulation, which allows it to function fluidly. And one of the bad things is that it has limited regulation, which allows people, if they're big enough and rich enough, to abuse it. Somewhere there has to be at least a narrow path between those two extremes."[21]

Rigging Chase Medical

On 25 January 1989 the Securities and Exchange Commission filed charges in U.S. District Court alleging that two New York salesmen, Vincent Militano and Milton Sonneberg, had cornered the market for and manipulated the price of Chase Medical Group, a holding company operating a network of family-practice medical centers. Both defendants worked for Moore & Schley, Cameron & Co., a brokerage firm. The two brokers were accused of manipulating the stock, defrauding customers, and failing to disclose share purchases in excess of 5 percent of Chase Medical's outstanding shares.[22]

The Chase Medical stock price was artificially inflated through a classic short squeeze designed to defraud investors. The stock, which was trading around $4 per share in August of 1988, suddenly jumped from $8¼ on 28 November to $13⅝ on 23 December, despite the absence of any positive news about the company during the period. Indeed, on 16 November the company announced a loss of twenty-five cents per share for the quarter that ended 30 September. The price surge was therefore unexpected and certainly unjustified by any information that became available to the market.[23]

Militano and Sonneberg had accumulated 1.4 million out of a total of 2.6 million shares outstanding. It was estimated that customers of Moore & Schley controlled more than the total number of shares actually outstanding; because some 340,843 shares had been sold short, the stock controlled by Moore & Schley amounted to 108 percent of publicly available shares on 13 January 1989, when the American Stock Exchange suspended trading. The intent was to force those with short positions to buy stock at the price set by those who had cornered the market.

Neither Militano or Sonneberg held any of the shares in his own account. Instead, they placed shares in customers' accounts without their authorization. In order to maintain their corner on the market, they also refused to sell the stock when ordered to do so by their customers. And because many clients were unaware of the situation and how their accounts were being used, they failed to make margin payments in the face of rising prices. The damages to victims totaled $10 million.[24] The SEC sought a preliminary injunction to freeze the assets of the defendants,[25] as well as a permanent injunction and disgorgement of all commissions and profits derived from the transactions. In addition, a number of clients filed civil suits.[26]

Trading did not resume after it was suspended because there was concern that Chase Medical stock was no longer sufficiently widely held to support a viable market.[27] Most of the Chase shares were eventually sold for $1 apiece. Moore & Schley did not survive the episode and was subsequently acquired by J.T. Moran Financial Corporation.[28]

Militano and Sonneberg colluded to move the market by mimicking the role of investors, using their positions as brokers as a cover for executing unauthorized transactions. Regulators did not become aware of the scheme until the two brokers controlled more than the amount of shares outstanding through client accounts or through short positions.

Rigging via the Internet

Not very long after the Internet became a popular means of communication its potential for ferreting out suckers became clear to people with market rigging on their minds. In 1996 the SEC launched its first lawsuit involving this medium. SGA Goldstar, an electronic newsletter distributed via the Internet, touted the stock of a company called Systems of Excellence (ticker symbol SEXI), evidently in exchange for illegal allocations of shares in the company to the publisher of the newsletter. Insiders (including the company's chairman, members of his family, stock promoters, and the newsletter's publisher) then dumped the shares once the price had risen from a mere 25 cents at the beginning of 1996 to $4.75 in mid-June. The SEC cited the electronic newsletter as "highly promotional, strongly urging investor accumulation of the stock, discouraging sales and even discouraging investors from independently verifying SGA's information."[29] Stung investors later groused on the Internet bulletin board about the mess, although some of the complaints sounded decidedly sheepish.

Market Manipulation Abroad

Since the passage of the Securities Acts in the 1930s, the United States has operated a legal and regulatory environment that has progressively clamped down on market rigging and other offenses in financial markets. The markets, as a whole, have benefited as a result. American markets are the world's most active, not least because participants have confidence that the markets are honest and fair. But in most other countries, the requisite legal and regulatory environment has not existed until quite recently. Financial markets involving the retail public were not well developed or widely utilized abroad, or the incentive to cast away self-regulatory notions in favor of more rigorous, adversarial forms of regulation was low. And in some countries such as Japan, where the retail markets are in fact highly developed, the regulatory inertia has been so durable and strong that not even the financial scandals in the so-called bubble economy of the 1980s could induce lawmakers to effect significant reforms against the entrenched opposition of the bureaucrats and market manipulators.

The growing connections between the world's markets and the shared need to participate in globalized transactions have brought about a significant amount of regulatory convergence. There is still a large variation, however, in the quality of financial regulation in marketplaces around the world. Major manipulations continue to occur, as is evident from the following examples from Britain, Japan, and China. Nonetheless, to the degree that such countries then take steps to remedy the conditions that allowed the manipulations to occur, the process of regulatory convergence continues.

Stock Parking and the Blue Arrow Affair

Blue Arrow was an aggressive employment agency that was a valued client of County NatWest, formerly the securities affiliate of Britain's National Westminster Bank. In early 1987, Blue Arrow decided to make a $1.3 billion hostile raid on an American competitor, MAI, a company much larger than itself. The raid was successful because Blue Arrow offered a very high price in cash, which was to come from a $1.4 billion stock issue to be placed by County NatWest. The issue was the largest stock offering of its type ever done, and it reflected an extraordinarily high ratio of new money to preoffering market capitalization. The issue, amazingly, appeared to go well and seemed to be a coup for County NatWest, a second-rate investment bank trying hard to make itself first-rate.

Unfortunately for the parties involved, the market was not as dumb as it seemed. Only about 50 percent of the stock offering was purchased by investors, with the underwriters taking up the slack. To support the issue, County NatWest itself bought the stock, in the end owning 9.5 percent of Blue Arrow. Contrary to law, the bank did not report its stock ownership to regulators. The Blue Arrow stock price, already sagging as a result of the unsold shares, was then flattened in the market crash of October 1987. By the end of the year, County NatWest had to report a loss of $80 million on its Blue Arrow position and another $150 million of other losses, mostly in trading and attributable to the crash. NatWest, the parent bank, had to report in turn, that its profits were off by 30 percent for the year, due to these losses and additions to loan-loss reserves.[30]

This stock-parking debacle led to an investigation, during which it was discovered that County NatWest's parent was itself involved in the financing and finagling of the Blue Arrow shares, as were Blue Arrow's broker (Phillips & Drew) and its parent (Union Bank of Switzerland). County NatWest's chairman and its chief executive both left the bank early in 1988, but their departures did not end the scandal. Various resignations and criminal indictments followed. The cases came to trial late in 1991; the defendants were found guilty and given suspended sentences in February 1992. The trial had also raised additional questions about the performance of NatWest's personable chief executive, Tom Frost, who resigned in March 1992.

Flying Stock in Tokyo

Probably no major financial market has suffered more from rigging and manipulation than Japan's. This market became a true powerhouse during the 1970s and 1980s on the back of Japan's superlative performance of manufacturing efficiency, international competitiveness, and economic growth. The Nikkei-225 index, which tracks the so-called First-Section Companies listed on the Tokyo Stock Exchange, rose to dizzying heights. Companies came to be valued at many times what similar U.S. or European companies were trading at, and urban real-estate prices reached truly astronomical levels. Bank credit was plentiful, and the market couldn't get enough of Japanese equity issues or corporate debt linked to equity warrants. It was a go-go era in which those who warned that trees don't grow to the sky were ridiculed and shouted down. But more than this, it was an era during which it was easy to mask all kinds of shenanigans, ones that the market regulator—the all-powerful, inbred, and exceedingly arrogant Ministry of Finance (MOF)—was unlikely to detect and that it would otherwise simply ignore. Then came the 1990s. The game was up.

In the summer of 1990, a Tokyo newspaper published an account of payments being made by the Big Four securities firms—Nomura, Daiwa, Nikko, and Yamaichi—to reimburse some of their major clients for losses incurred during the market drop of 1990, the beginning of a market decline that eventually took almost half the combined value of all Japanese stocks.[31] Several important institutional clients were unhappy because they had lost so much money. Nomura and the other brokers felt they had to make good on at least some of these losses to retain their clients' loyalty. After all, they reasoned, "We put them into these stocks in the first place—soliciting their business pretty aggressively—and if our competitors offer to reimburse them, and we don't, we'll be dead meat with important customers when the market recovers."

These compensation payments were not against the law. Indeed, there were very few laws regulating the securities markets in Japan. Regulations were imposed as needed by the MOF through its informal practice of "administrative guidance." The ministry tended to permit or prohibit activities as it saw fit. Apparently it knew of these payments and did nothing to stop them. The Big Four made the payments by creating mispriced trades that guaranteed profits for their select customers, a practice considered outright market rigging and prohibited by law in other countries. There were also reports that the Big Four had rigged additional trades in listed stocks and other securities, including U.S. Treasury issues, to make money for favored clients.

Disclosure of the compensation payments and other suspicious transactions created a stir. Interest was especially intense because most of the brokers' clients—their enormous number of retail customers, who ironically were the Big Four's largest source of profits—had received nothing for their losses. The firms initially denied the charges but then admitted that a small amount of compensation had in fact been paid. The media's chase after the "real story" was soon on.

By midsummer 1990 the scandal was Tokyo's hottest item. Reporters were covering it from all angles and digging up new disclosures at a furious pace. Reluctantly, the Big Four admitted that the compensation payments were greater than originally indicated. Indeed, they totaled nearly $1.5 billion and were paid to some two hundred large clients of the firms, including company investment funds, institutions, and a few influential individuals. The scale of the compensation and market-rigging operation was staggering, even to U.S. observers who, in the wake of the savings-and-loan crisis and insider-trading revelations at home, had grown accustomed to sizable scams. It was equally shocking that the MOF, guardian of financial markets in Japan, had turned a blind eye to the Big Four's problematic conduct.

The press was soon onto other suspected market manipulations as well. For example, in September 1991 Meiji Milk Products announced it had discovered a drug that was 100 percent effective in curing AIDS. Although the drug was untested and, even if shown effective, would not be available for years, the company's stock price shot up from ¥777 to ¥1,200 per share. The press subsequently determined that a large number of Meiji Milk Products stock-purchase warrants had been about to expire, worthless because their exercise price was ¥790. Instead, the warrants were exercised during the artificial spike in the stock's price (which later collapsed). The company saved about $50 million that it would have had to pay to retire the bonds tied to the warrants.[32]

In another case, Nomura and Nikko had each paid $120 million to Susumu Ishii, the boss of a major *yakuza* (organized-crime syndicate) before his death in September 1991. Ishii had apparently sold worthless golf-club memberships to the two securities firms and used the proceeds to buy shares in Tokyu Corporation, a railway and construction company that Nomura Securities subsequently promoted aggressively. Ishii acquired about 30 million shares, the stock went up, and he sold out a good part of his position for a large, riskless profit.[33]

The story set the media aflame and led to several hearings before an outraged Diet. A number of Nomura's top executives resigned, including the firm's chairman, Setsuya Tabuchi, and its chief executive, Yoshihisa Tabuchi (no relation). The latter took a parting shot at finance minister Ryutaro Hashimoto, who he claimed knew about the compensation payments all along. Nikko's president, Takuya Iwasaki, likewise resigned when his firm's continuing involvement with the gangster became known. Minister Hashimoto, trying to calm the situation, admitted that his ministry could have done better and cut his own salary by 10 percent. But by November he, too, was gone. Hashimoto later reappeared, however, becoming prime minister in late 1995.

Setsuya Tabuchi explained that the resignations represented an effort to take responsibility for the scandals, adding cryptically that the actions were the result of "innumerable discussions about Japan's position in the world and the drastically changing role of our nation's stock market." He went on, however, to suggest that "The bubble economy hasn't only been a problem for Japan's securities companies. The difficulty is that there is a mismatch between the rules in Japan and the rules in the rest of the world."[34] The two Tabuchis were later reinstated by Nomura.

About the same time that the Tabuchis were in the spotlight and the MOF was promising tighter regulation, another now-famous scandal was taking place. Daiwa Securities, Japan's second-largest brokerage firm, had a number of clients that accumulated large stock losses following the market collapse. A reporting date was approaching, and the clients did not want to book the losses. So Daiwa offered to "park" their stock with other clients by arranging a sale of the shares at a greatly inflated price, about equal to the original owners' initial cost, together with guaranteed repurchase agreements at a somewhat higher price to compensate the obliging parkees. Such schemes are called *tobashi,* or "flying around" to avoid being caught by accountants. The practice was well known in Tokyo, and it was understood to be widely used by favored customers. Stock parking is illegal in the United States.[35]

One of the *tobashi* trades that Daiwa arranged was with Tokyu Department Stores, a large retailing company controlled by the Tokyu Corporation. Tokyu Department Stores bought a portfolio worth about $225 million through Daiwa for roughly $675 million, disguising $450 million of losses for its owner, a Daiwa client. Daiwa agreed to repurchase the portfolio from Tokyu at a profit. But the market declined further, and the portfolio's original owner was financially unable to repurchase the portfolio from Daiwa. The firm then told Tokyu that it had a problem and couldn't pay the full price. A very un-Japanese dispute ensued. Both desperate and angry, Tokyu took Daiwa to court, a hitherto unthinkable course of action in a country where everything tends to be settled behind closed doors. Daiwa admitted the offense and several others like it. In the end, a typically Japanese solution was achieved. The two parties worked out a settlement, and at a news conference broadcast on live television, Masahiro Dozen, Daiwa's president, resigned to take responsibility for the event.[36]

Although many Japanese may have otherwise shrugged them off, these market-manipulation scandals needed to be publicly redressed once they were widely publicized. Those involved had to be punished despite the fact that, except for the unproven market-rigging charges, no laws had been violated. Indeed, there *were* no relevant laws and no prescribed penalties for such abuses. Penalties were assessed on the basis of what would satisfy the press, which had disclosed the scandals in the first place.

After some desultory efforts to impose lesser penalties, the MOF finally required Nomura to close 87 of its 153 branch offices for a period of one month, to shut down its research department, and to discontinue trading for its own account. The penalties were deemed appropriate (in a Japanese context) and were uncontested, although the punishment was neither required nor necessarily even legally authorized. "This kind of behavior is indicative of the lack of rule of law in brokering," according to an American lawyer in Tokyo. "The system as it currently operates is very obviously beneficial to the privileged players and is difficult, if not impossible, for the less privileged or foreign players."[37] Incredibly, in 1997 Nomura was again involved in payoffs to organized crime and client defections. Evidently, memories are short.

Sisco's Fiasco

By 1995, Shanghai International Securities (Sisco) and its principal competitor, Shen Yin Securities, controlled over 22 percent of all stock trading on the Shanghai Stock Exchange and underwrote the vast bulk of China's initial public offerings. Sisco had over two hundred shareholders spread throughout the privileged few in Chinese industry, government, and military circles, and a close alliance with Hong Kong billionaire Li Ka-shing. Shen Yin was controlled by the state-owned Industrial and Commercial Bank of China and the City of Shanghai's treasury department. Sisco had grown in six years from one small room, ten employees, one telephone, and a bicycle into China's most dynamic securities firm, with nationwide representation even before the Shanghai exchange officially opened in late 1990. Together, Sisco and Shen Yin effectively controlled access of foreign firms to the Chinese securities underwriting and trading business (and split commissions with them). Merrill Lynch and Bear Stearns were said to be allied with Sisco, while Daiwa Securities and Goldman Sachs were allied with Shen Yin.[38]

At the end of 1994, the Shanghai market was experiencing a severe letdown. Market prices had sagged, and the numerous new issues of Chinese shares, launched in Shanghai, Hong Kong, and even New York, were performing poorly. To replace the lost volume in share trading, the dealer community and the government cooperated to bring forth a new financial product, government-bond futures. These contracts became one of the few bright spots in the otherwise lackluster Shanghai market. Average daily trading volume in futures increased from $1 billion in 1994 to $6 billion in early 1995.[39] Interest rates on an increasing supply of government bonds (the government deficit was 24 percent of GDP in 1994) included an inflation-adjustment premium in order to make them attractive to investors. Bets on the futures market were, in effect, bets on China's inflation rate.

In mid-February 1995 daily futures volume skyrocketed to $102 billion, over four times the previous high, in response to a newspaper report that accelerating inflation would trigger a higher premium. Sisco then took an enormous short position on bond-futures contracts in the expectation that rates would continue to rise and prices decline. When, instead, prices rose dramatically, the firm was forced to cover its short position in a sharply rising market. The firm, with a registered capital of only $120 million, faced a loss of between $80 million and $150 million.

Staring financial ruin in the face, Sisco and another securities firm in similar straits tried desperately to orchestrate massive sell orders ten minutes before the Shanghai Stock Exchange closed on 23 February 1995. Prices dropped like a rock.

On the following morning, the authorities responded by suspending all trading in bond futures and by unilaterally canceling the final eight minutes of the previous day's trades, worth about $37 *billion*. Those with remaining futures contracts to settle were required to settle them privately or be stuck with the losses, effectively shifting the remaining burden of the market manipulation to Sisco's trading counterparties. For its part, Sisco (with its close ties to the Shanghai municipal government) accused the China Economic Trust and Investment Development Corporation (with close ties to the Ministry of Finance in Beijing) of having inside information on the inflation statistics. This accusation was hotly denied by others, however, who pointed out that every securities firm in China was controlled by one government entity or another.

After two months of uncertainty, Guan Jinshen, Sisco's founder and chief executive, resigned from the firm. So did the chairman, Xu Qingxiong, ostensibly because of old age. Both resignations were part of a government-orchestrated package to save Sisco, which pleaded guilty to a minor infraction of the rules and was briefly suspended from trading bond futures, and to rebuild the market's badly tarnished reputation.[40] Not long thereafter Wei Wenyuen, head of the Shanghai Securities Exchange, was likewise replaced. In July 1995 Guan Jinshen was arrested and charged with embezzling public funds. "The Government has punished violators in order to preserve the normal development of the securities markets. It was a necessary step."[41] In mid-February 1996 Sisco was forcibly merged into Shen Yin, making that firm China's dominant securities company. Unable to operate independently because of its heavy debt and damaged reputation, Sisco became another name on the lengthening list of Chinese companies to fail in the wake of misconduct.[42] Guan Jen was found guilty of misappropriating public funds and bribery in February 1977 and was sentenced to seventeen years in prison. Wei Wenyuan was rehabilitated and appointed adviser to the newly formed Shanghai Securities Association.

The Sisco scandal evidenced both weak market supervision and the failure to enforce trading limits even when they were subject to flagrant violations. There was also a reluctance to let the chips fall where they may when corrective action was required. The scandal was thus symptomatic of a recurrent cycle in China: creation of a new capital-raising vehicle, regulatory indifference, active trading, speculative frenzy, collapse, market meltdown, and, finally, political crackdown. According to one observer, "The central Government is afraid of crisis. They'd rather see a far smaller trading volume than a crisis. We think stricter management is needed, but we're concerned that the government may be overreacting."[43] It did. Previously ranging from 1 to 2.5 percent, margin requirements increased to 10 percent, driving away many of the 250 institutions and several thousand individuals formerly engaged in trading bond futures. Another observer noted, "Like the rest of the economy, the stock system is laced with corruption that alienates many ordinary citizens. Most of the trading is speculative froth that bears little relationship to fundamentals, and some of the excitement seems to be flavor-of-the-month variety. . . . Many Chinese buy stocks with the giddy excitement they might show entering a casino. . . . The losers keep quiet."[44]

Caveat Investor

These examples of manipulation in domestic and foreign markets are only a few of many. Scandals accompanied the 1994–95 market meltdown in

Mexico, and investors have been hammered by market rigging and corruption in all possible forms in Russia and some other Eastern European markets. Even seemingly sophisticated and safe environments, like the international oil and copper markets, have been manipulated, the former by a German commodities company, Metallgesellschaft, and the latter by Sumitomo Corporation. In both of these cases, as in the others discussed, the perpetrators were severely punished by market and regulatory forces. Such responses to misconduct have improved the quality of the global marketplace, in which all major players now operate.

The international dimensions of market rigging were also apparent in May of 1995, when Edzard Reuter, the CEO of Daimler-Benz, and Manfred Gentz, its CFO, announced that the company would show a profit for the year and was expecting to pay a dividend, as usual. Gentz later acknowledged that he already knew the company would soon announce a record loss and omit the dividend. This behavior may have been acceptable under the German standards. But since Daimler-Benz was listed on the New York Stock Exchange, it was subject to stringent U.S. disclosure rules. Article 10b-5 of the 1934 Securities Act makes it unlawful to issue any untrue statement to investors. This incident triggered investigations by both German and U.S. authorities under antifraud statutes, and shareholders filed civil suits for damages. An NYSE delisting is unlikely, however.[45]

Two conclusions may be drawn from this exploration of the international dimensions of market manipulation. First, the regulatory environment of the future will be more like that of the United States than it is now. Traders and firms taking advantage of its frailties need to wise up. International markets need the kind of monitoring, control, audit, and internal investigative procedures that are already established in the United States. The market exposures are considerable, and the legal and regulatory hazards are growing. Second, it is nonetheless foreseeable that many overseas markets will continue to be subject to periodic manipulation by indigenous participants and others who wish to bet on being able to operate undetected unpunished. People who wish to invest or trade in such markets without engaging in shady and manipulative activities need to bear this possibility in mind. Many markets today, especially those that are just emerging, are neither honest nor fair. Anyone who enters them must bear the risk.

Trading on
the Inside

■

Ever since the insider-trading scandals of the 1980s, securities firms have come under increased scrutiny by the SEC. The slightest irregularity in trading can trigger an investigation. Files are subpoenaed. Employees are interviewed. The firm's lawyers are galvanized to focus on the urgent task of protecting the firm against a potential legal onslaught. Quite often, the investigators find nothing and, after the temporary disruption, the firm returns to normal. But if investigators decide to file charges, the disruption is far more serious and long term. The firm is suddenly in the news. All hell breaks loose. There is no telling how many clients will defect, and whether they may ultimately return. There is no telling how much money the firm will lose to lost business or legal damages. And even if the charges are dropped or the firm is vindicated in court, the firm's integrity may have been seriously questioned and its reputation tarnished. The task of recovery from such an event is slow and painful.

Before the Law

Before 1934, insider trading was not a crime in the United States. Indeed, it was a common practice among the market operators in the early part of the century. Many people believed that investing in common stock was too risky for ordinary people without privileged access to price-sensitive information. Bernard Baruch, a famous speculator in the 1920s, actually bragged in his 1957 autobiography that he traded on inside tips. So did Joseph Kennedy, the first SEC chairman (and father of JFK). Prior to the 1930s, the market depended on laissez faire to guide its invisible hand, especially during the swashbuckling years of the late 1920s.

Although the Securities Acts of 1933 and 1934 enacted under the

Roosevelt administration were responses to the rampant and severe abuses of the previous decade, the acts are now generally considered to be sensible, restrained, and constructive. The new regulations did not interfere with the market's ability to set prices. In fact, they improved transparency and price discovery by requiring material information to be disclosed in a timely manner for the market's benefit. The 1934 Act, which authorized the establishment of the SEC and defined corporate insiders as "officers, directors or holders of 10% of more of a company's shares," discouraged profit taking by insiders on securities held for less than six months.

At first, enforcement of the insider-trading rules was, at best, lax. The markets were still sunk in the mire of depression. Much of the financial community had sullenly opposed the new laws and was not especially cooperative. In any event, radical changes could not be made quickly. It was not until 1942 that the staff of the SEC developed its Rule 10(b)5, a very general provision that prohibited fraud in securities transactions. The SEC has subsequently used this provision as the basis for its enforcement actions against trading on undisclosed information, although it is hard to see just from reading it how the SEC and the courts could have squeezed so much from this one source.[1]

The SEC established the basic elements of a 10(b)5 insider-trading violation in a landmark case, *Cady Roberts,* in 1961. First, there had to be a relationship that afforded access to nonpublic information relating to an important corporate development. And second, an insider could not fairly (and legally) trade on that information without first having disclosed it to the investing community at large. The presumption was that this ruling would apply to stockbrokers and bankers who came into possession of inside information in the course of their duties, as well as to corporate officers and directors. Here things remained until Wall Street was rocked by the *Texas Gulf Sulfur* case in 1968.

That case was one of the first to demonstrate that when the SEC pounces, it often does so without warning and as a reaction to a newly uncovered, seemingly scandalous incident. The SEC is, after all, a political institution with a mission to protect ordinary investors against the abuses of the powerful and well-connected. When it strikes, it acts in the full glare of the public eye and is seen as defending the interests of the many against those of the few. Under such circumstances, many would expect the SEC to be a vengeful, possibly dangerous institution that may act too quickly and without due consideration and legal standing. The SEC has generally not done so, however, although some observers believe it has occasionally been excessively harsh.

Texas Gulf Discovers Insider Trading

Texas Gulf Sulfur was a U.S. mining company that discovered in November 1963 a potentially major copper, zinc, and silver deposit in Timmins, Ontario, a remote area 350 miles north of Toronto. Almost immediately after the initial discovery, the extent of which was still quite uncertain, several employees of the company purchased shares. The exploratory pit was then closed for the winter. After reopening the mine the following April, the company confirmed the discovery of a major deposit and quickly organized a press conference. Another group of employees purchased shares in Texas Gulf Sulfur at this point, just before the press conference announcing the discovery. In addition, two directors of the company bought shares just after the press conference. One of them, Francis Coates, bought shares for family trusts right after the announcement. The other, Thomas S. Lamont (a former vice chairman of the Morgan Guaranty Trust Company and son of a famous J.P. Morgan partner), advised the bank's trust department to buy. He then bought some of the stock in the company himself an hour or so after the press conference.

All three sets of investors were charged in 1966 with insider trading. All were clearly insiders, and they had traded on the basis of price-sensitive information. The first group (those who had bought before April 1964) were exonerated by the trial judge, Dudley J. Bonsal. Up until that point the extent of the discovery was unknown, and the employees had based their actions on educated guesses. Bonsal also exonerated the third group, the two directors who traded after the press conference, because the duration of an appropriate waiting period after an announcement was not clearly defined. Only the two individuals who bought just before the press conference were convicted.

In reviewing the lower court's decision, the U.S. Court of Appeals reversed Judge Bonsal in the cases of the first two "winter" investors and of director Coates (Lamont died before the government's appeal). Coates's mistake was in trading before the market had fully digested the news of the discovery. In other words, he had not waited long enough before calling his broker. (In those days, it took much longer for the news to get out to market participants than it does today.)

The Court of Appeals took a much tougher line than Judge Bonsal on whether a material discovery was known before April, and on the fairness of the brief waiting period employed by Francis Coates. The effect of these rulings was to convict *all* of those accused by the SEC (except for Lamont, who would undoubtedly have been convicted had he lived), thus establishing that the courts were seriously concerned about insider trading. The Court of Appeals reversal also helped define inside information and appropriate behavior on the part of those in possession of such information. The conviction of Coates demonstrated that no one, however high in the corporate firmament, would be exempt from prosecution.[2]

More Efficient or Less?

Over the next decade *Texas Gulf Sulfur* generated considerable debate in academic, legal, and financial circles about whether insider trading was actually harmful to anyone and, if not, whether it should be illegal. Studies were produced to demonstrate that insider-trading laws made markets less efficient by slowing the speed at which the market assimilated important information. It was also argued that the gains from having markets that quickly reflect true values would likely outweigh any costs, or opportunity losses, borne by investors who were not in the know. Many of the investors losing such opportunities, these arguments continued, were only short-term speculators, anyway. Society owed them nothing. Besides, those benefiting were entitled to entrepreneurial rewards, and the more these rewards were made available, the more entrepreneurial the American economy would be.[3] Critics of insider-trading limitations also voiced concern that market surveillance and litigation were too expensive and could lead to police-state tactics. No other market anywhere in the world, they continued, imposed similar legal sanctions for trading on inside information—not the securities markets in London, the foreign exchange market, or the commodities market. So why us?

If one accepts these arguments, the decision in *Texas Gulf Sulfur* may be the first time that economic efficiency was overridden by considerations of general fairness for market users. The harm done by insider trading was to deprive unknowing sellers of gains that they would have received had they not sold. To permit such harm would violate the basic spirit of the Securities Acts of 1933 and 1934: if individual investors who are not plugged in to the gossipy circles of the financially savvy were to be included in the country's financial market, then standards fair to all would have to apply regardless of their impact on short-term economic efficiency. What good, the acts seem to inquire, is a capitalist economic system when the vast majority of those on whom it depends for political legitimacy end up on the short end of the stick? This argument went on to note that government has a duty to provide a financial marketplace of high quality and high integrity, which would, in turn, generate greater participation by the investing masses and produce more liquid and efficient markets. John Shad, a former head of E.F. Hutton and the SEC chairman in the late 1980s, thought insider trading was a true market killer. "If people get the impression they are playing against a stacked deck," he said, "they're simply not going to be willing to invest."[4] Accordingly, Shad beefed up the enforcement arm of the SEC. From 1982 through 1985, an average of twenty cases of insider trading were brought annually, including the sensational case of Paul Thayer, a former deputy secretary of defense in the Reagan administration, who was charged with leaking to eight people, including his mistress, inside information he had obtained as a director of two major corporations.

It Oughta Be a Crime

The legal issues involved in defining and prosecuting insider-trading cases are complex, not quite as simple as the moral issues appear to be. Because criminal charges are involved, there has to be credible evidence that a crime has been committed before a prosecution can be initiated and an indictment handed down. Wrong-footing the market had never been a crime before, nor had it been common to prosecute people for not telling everything they knew about a commercial matter to their counterparts. Common law tends to rely on the breaching of a basic duty—a fiduciary duty in financial cases—in defining criminal wrongdoing. Thus, it may be unethical, despicable, and unfair for someone to attempt to deceive and mislead others in financial transactions, but it is not criminal unless it involves the breach of a fiduciary duty.[5]

The Supreme Court had a chance to analyze insider-trading issues in 1980, before the great burst of related cases that arose during the merger boom later in that decade. *Chiarella v. United States* was a landmark case that involved an employee of a company that printed confidential tender-offer announcements. Prior to publication the employee had been openly trading on the information contained in the documents. The SEC tracked him down, brought him to trial, and secured a conviction. Chiarella was identified as a "tippee," or one who (though not an insider himself) obtains or "inherits" inside information from someone who is. On appeal the Supreme Court overturned the trial court's decision. The Court agreed that a fiduciary duty had to be present in order to anchor insider-trading offenses to the common law, and that Chiarella would have had to engage in "manipulative or deceptive" practices in order for such a duty to be breached. The Court also found, however, that Chiarella had no fiduciary duty to the companies being taken over or to their shareholders. The decision rejected the doctrine of "parity of information," which maintained that all insider information, as well as the burdens associated with it, was the same regardless of who held it. The Court reasoned that this doctrine defined the scope of fiduciary duties too broadly. These duties depend on specific, not general, relationships.[6]

Chief Justice Warren Burger dissented. He argued that information obtained through independent research and effort was valuable personal property that could be misappropriated illegally by others. He believed that Chiarella had misappropriated property (information) belonging to his employer's client, and that he should have been convicted under 10(b)5.

Using the Chiarella ruling as a guide, the SEC in 1980 promulgated its Rule 14(e)-3a, which states that in the case of tender offers, "it would be manipulative and deceptive" for a person to trade while in possession of nonpublic information acquired directly or indirectly from a party to the tender offer or anyone acting on that party's behalf.

The Supreme Court soon confronted the problem of tippees again in the 1983 case *Dirks v. SEC*. Ten years earlier Raymond Dirks, a financial analyst covering the insurance industry, ran across information from a former executive of Equity Funding Corporation of America, a company he had covered closely and had recommended to clients. The information Dirks uncovered suggested that Equity Funding had been committing extensive fraud and misreporting its financial results for years. Dirks investigated the matter for several months and persuaded many of his clients to sell their shares. He did not own any shares himself. He also attempted without success to interest a reporter from the *Wall Street Journal* in the story. The journalist did tip off the SEC, however, which began to investigate Dirks. When the fraud was made public, Equity Funding stock plummeted. The New York Stock Exchange filed charges against Dirks for spreading rumors and trading on inside information. The SEC also charged Dirks and his clients with insider trading, noting that "when tippees come into possession of material information that they know is confidential, and know *or should know* it came from a corporate insider, they must either publicly disclose that information or refrain from trading." The SEC secured a conviction, and it was upheld by the U.S. Court of Appeals. But in 1983, ten years after the date of the alleged offense, the Supreme Court (by a vote of six to three) overturned the conviction.

The Supreme Court held that Dirks was not an insider himself but a typical tippee. He did not have a fiduciary duty of his own to the corporation but inherited one from his source, who, as a recent employee of the corporation, did have such a duty. If Dirks had simply obtained his information from the market through his own analytical work, he would not have had a fiduciary duty. The Court went on to say, however, that the tippee assumes the fiduciary duty of an insider *only* when the insider has breached his or her own duties (that is, behaved in a deceptive or manipulative way) and the tippee knows or should have known that there has been such a breach. Whether the insider, or tipper, has committed a breach depends, in turn, on how much of a "direct or indirect personal benefit," or "secret profits," he or she received as a result of the disclosure of sensitive information. In this case, because the tipper had not benefited personally, Dirks was not guilty.[7]

Still another landmark insider-trading case, *U.S. v. Carpenter,* was brought by the SEC in 1987 against a *Wall Street Journal* columnist, R. Foster Winans, who was then writing the popular "Heard on the Street" column, which reports on current stock-market trends.[8] Winans and several associates were convicted of misappropriating information from his forthcoming columns in order to trade on their content. The trial court held (based on Chief Justice Burger's dissent in *Chiarella*) that although Winans owed no fiduciary duty to the companies involved, he did owe an obligation to his employer, Dow Jones, not to steal material nonpublic information (namely, Winans's own unpublished columns) from it and use that information to purchase securities. The appeals court upheld the conviction, which the Supreme Court chose not to review.

Nearly a decade later *Business Week* was involved in a similar incident. In early 1996 it appeared that someone was gaining access to forthcoming articles in the magazine's "Inside Wall Street" column. *Business Week* goes to press on Wednesday evenings and is not available to the public before 5:15 P.M. on Thursdays, after the markets close. Nonetheless, a suspicious Thursday trading pattern developed, with unexplained increases in volume that reflected the nonpublic information contained in the article. The magazine notified the American Stock Exchange, NASDAQ, and the SEC.

Whether or not insider trading was actually going on in this case, *Business Week's* internal monitoring was the product of an earlier, 1988 trading scandal traced to its printing plants in Connecticut and California and to a graphic-arts contractor in New Jersey. As part of that scandal, S.G. Ruderman, the magazine's radio correspondent, was convicted of insider trading and went to jail. According to its publishers, "Our readers have a right to know. And we are determined to protect the integrity of the magazine."[9]

However, in September 1996, the SEC's confidence in the application of the misappropriation theory from the U.S. versus Carpenter case was dealt a serious blow when a three-judge panel of the Eighth Circuit of the U.S. Court of Appeals overturned a conviction of a lawyer who, while acting for Grand Metropolitan P.L.C. in its acquisition of Pillsbury Company in 1988, made $4.3 million from trading in Pillsbury shares and options. The judges opined that the misappropriation of information by the lawyer did not violate any actual law, only so-called judge-made law related to misappropriation. The Fourth Circuit had earlier in the year overturned a similar misappropriation case, but in a less sweeping manner. The Eighth Circuit judges requested a review by the full circuit court to affirm their position. Depending on how this case evolves, the Supreme Court may be asked to hear the case, at which time another important decision likely to affect the course of insider trading can be expected. However, not everyone expects a Supreme Court ruling to be helpful: James Cox, a law professor at Duke University, claimed that the Supreme Court, which has stunned experts in securities law before, "just makes things worse, in terms of certainty and clarity."[10]

The Scandalous 1980s

The procession through the courts of insider-trading cases in the 1980s was interrupted by a chain of events that stunned financial centers all over the world and no doubt changed them forever. This was the incredible sequence of confessions and convictions involving insider trading, stock parking, and other offenses such as mail fraud that was begun after the apprehension in May 1986 of Dennis B. Levine, a thirty-three-year-old managing director of Drexel Burnham Lambert who was earning over $1 million a year in mergers and acquisitions. His was the biggest, most flagrant case of insider trading uncovered by the SEC up to that point. The offenses had extended over a period of six years and involved known profits of $12.6 million. Levine had initially opened bank accounts in the Bahamas with a

Swiss bank, Bank Leu, and secretly traded in the stocks of companies involved in deals his own firm was handling. He subsequently formed a ring, the so-called Yuppie Five, of bright and promising young lawyers and bankers from other firms who passed on merger information to Levine for his insider-trading activities. He managed to trade undetected via Bank Leu in Nassau because, in part, he stuck to buying or selling small amounts of shares and generally spread the business around. In addition, the NYSE's StockWatch surveillance system had not been set up yet, and the SEC's own computerized market-surveillance activities were not yet fully up to speed.

Levine's system collapsed in May 1985, when an anonymous letter received in the New York offices of Merrill Lynch suggested that two employees in Merrill's Caracas, Venezuela, office had been trading on inside information. The firm investigated and found that the individuals named in the letter were copying trades that another broker there was making on behalf of a legitimate customer, Bank Leu. Merrill smelled insider trading and notified the SEC. Almost a year later Bank Leu, after a futile effort to hide behind Swiss banking laws protecting customer secrecy, was required to divulge the names of the people involved. The SEC had Levine red-handed. He was not-so-gently asked if he would like to cooperate with the SEC in order to reduce a likely jail sentence and fine, and he agreed.

However well paid and active, Levine was an unknown, minor figure on Wall Street—an overeager, undertalented M&A gofer who promoted himself as having a good nose for business and being able to get close to deals being done by other firms. Drexel had been his third firm. He had previously worked for Smith Barney and then Lehman Brothers as an M&A scout. In cooperating with the SEC, it was no surprise that he was able to point the finger at the Yuppie Five. But it was a surprise that he also pointed at Ivan Boesky, New York's most flamboyant risk arbitrageur, to whom he had been secretly passing inside tips. (Risk arbitrage is an activity that financial firms, typically limited partnerships or departments of investment banks, engage in to profit from the difference between the current market price of a target company's stock and the final deal price in announced merger-and-acquisitions transactions.) Boesky was extremely well known and extremely wealthy from the profits of the risk-arbitrage partnerships he had managed for years. He was a shameless self-promoter who gloried in attention and is generally thought to be the first Wall Streeter to publicize risk arbitrage widely to attract money that he would manage for his clients. Risk arbitrage, he said in his 1985 book *Merger Mania,* was an art form, not a regular business. Only special people could succeed in it, he added, omitting that in his case "special" meant "crooked." Perhaps it was difficult for him to meet the investment expectations of all the new money pouring into his funds. Perhaps he felt he needed an edge.

When confronted by the SEC, Boesky immediately confessed and of-fered to cooperate. He agreed to disgorge profits, pay a fine of $100 million, and spend time in jail. Just how long would depend on how helpful he was in turning over others. Ultimately, Boesky gave the SEC both Martin Siegel, head of M&A at Kidder Peabody, and Michael Milken, Wall Street's junk-bond king, then operating out of a personal office complex in Beverly Hills.

Siegel, a 1971 graduate of the Harvard Business School and Kidder's thirty-eight-year-old investment-banking superstar, confessed to passing information to Boesky about Getty Oil's acquisition by Texaco and about various other deals in exchange for briefcases stuffed with cash. Siegel immediately agreed to disgorge $4.25 million, surrender his interests in Drexel and various Drexel partnerships, and cooperate with the govern-ment in an effort to reduce his jail sentence. He told the SEC of extensive inside trading at Kidder and of a conspiracy to exchange deal information with Robert Freeman, a partner and head of risk arbitrage at Goldman Sachs.[11]

All this success led U.S. Attorney Rudolph Giuliani to become over-confident. He ordered Freeman and Siegel's assistant at Kidder Peabody, Richard Wigton, arrested in their offices during the workday, in plain sight of all the other employees. Wigton resisted and was hauled off in handcuffs. Another Siegel associate, Timothy Tabor, a Rhodes Scholar with a brilliant career ahead of him, was also arrested and kept overnight in jail. Rather than simply caving in, all three denied the charges and fought back as best they could. Giuliani's office found that it did not have enough evidence to proceed to trial, and asked for the indictments to be lifted without prejudice (meaning that the charges could be reinstated later if the government came up with what it needed to go forward).

The investigations of Wigton and Tabor were eventually dropped, but only after bringing them many more months of financial hardship and personal discredit. Freeman did not fare as well. Maintaining his innocence, he fought strenuously against the charges and was supported by his partners at Goldman Sachs throughout the battle. After two-and-a-half years, he finally confessed to one count of mail fraud, for which he was sentenced to $1 million in fines and four months in jail.

With Boesky, Levine, and Siegel all cooperating with the government, prosecutors closed in on Milken and Drexel Burnham. When confronted with the charges against them, both Milken and Drexel Burnham denied everything and put up a fierce legal battle. The firm, confronted with compelling evidence against it and also threatened with charges under the Racketeering Influenced and Corrupt Organizations Act, finally conceded and paid fines of $630 million. It subsequently went bankrupt following the collapse of the junk-bond market, which without Milken's services the firm was unable to sustain. Milken, a man richer than the firm that employed him, was totally uncooperative and continued to fight all ninety-eight counts of market manipulation, stock parking, fraud, and insider trading with which he had been charged. In the end he also conceded, ostensibly to protect his brother and his family. Milken pleaded guilty to six felony counts (none involving insider trading), was fined $600 million (later increased by civil damages and expenses to about $1 billion), and was sentenced to ten years in jail. He subsequently did cooperate to some degree and was paroled after less than three years in jail. Despite the fines and damages he had paid, Milken remained a very wealthy man.

The story of these dozen or so famous but corrupt Wall Streeters, graphically and controversially told by former *Wall Street Journal* writer James Stewart in *Den of Thieves,* was both shocking and disgusting to the American public. The amounts of money and the numbers of people involved in the scandals were stunning. The unrestrained greed and im-morality was alarming, as was the corruption of so many of the country's best and brightest young people in finance. The public was outraged. There were recurrent calls for reform, and the misdeeds on Wall Street were used by the Bush and Clinton administrations to help justify politically the 1990 and 1993 tax hikes, which especially affected those who had done well financially in the dynamic 1980s, no matter how far removed from the sleaze of Wall Street. The prosecutors became heros, avenging angels of the democratic system. Giuliani was elected mayor of New York City.

Despite all the legal activity, the prosecution of the Wall Street invest-ment bankers and arbitrageurs broke no new legal ground. The scandals involved insider-trading violations, to be sure. The offenders admitted acting on information that was price-sensitive, that emanated from inside sources, and that had been obtained either through breach of a fiduciary duty or by misappropriation. And all of them had profited substantially from their violation of the law. The offenders' plea bargains obviated the need for trials, however. There were consequently no appeals, no new case law.

Though the prosecutions set no new legal precedents, there were many questions raised afterwards about the prosecutions themselves. Central among these was whether the prosecutors had acted too ruthlessly in pursuing their quarry. By invoking RICO, Giuliani had made the suspects in an insider-trading investigation feel like Mafioso Dons accused of drug trafficking. Many observers, including a goodly number of people hardly sympathetic to Michael Milken, believed that the federal prosecutors, motivated by the desire to feed both public opinion and their own political ambition, had embarked on a vendetta at the expense of the civil rights of the defendants. Such bullying practices, these observers note, continue to this day. Others argue that the public hardly wants its prosecutors to be wimps, and that a market-based system with aggressively enforced rules is likely to be better and more efficient than a system in which enforcement is lax. In 1994 and 1995, the SEC brought 45 cases against alleged insider traders, a number that exceeds the previous peak of 43 during the take-over-boom year of 1989. In 1995 NASD referred 113 cases to the SEC for possible insider-trading scrutiny, which was 24 percent higher than the previous year.[12]

The SEC, in November 1996, also sanctioned broker-dealer Fox-Pitt, Kelton for failing to have established and implemented anti-insider trading compliance policies, which presumably permitted some illegal trading to take place. The broker-dealer must demonstrate through its actions, the SEC said, that the firm is committed to preventing misuse of any material nonpublic information.

Legacies

Over a decade later, the legacy of the Den of Thieves era is apparent in five distinct trends in the financial marketplace.

1. Securities firms are spending much time and money on compliance and detection systems.

   Firms are much more careful and thorough in preventing and de-tecting insider-trading violations. Most firms involved in M&A activities today severely restrict the amount of risk arbitrage that they undertake, and have firmwide restricted-trading lists that prohibit transactions by employees in stocks of certain companies, usually those in which the firm has an advisory assignment pending or which are subject to takeover rumors.

2. The SEC and the NYSE have substantially increased their capacity to detect irregular trading patterns in stocks subject to takeovers.

Computers scan all stocks listed on exchanges or on the NASDAQ, and report abnormal patterns of trading activity that precede a takeover announcement. Once the computers have spotted something, the SEC works backwards to locate the offender. It looks for connections between people involved in the transaction and those who traded in the stock. When connections are found, a broadside of subpoenas is issued. These are sent to everyone even remotely involved with the deal and to those connected to them. "If we are told the information was disseminated at a dinner party, we get the guest list," said an assistant director for enforcement at the SEC's New York office. "Then we turn the suspects upside down and really shake them."[13] Through investigation of this sort, the SEC has been able to bring dozens of successful cases against employees of firms and their family members or friends who have traded on information available only to insiders.

3. The SEC has found ways to curtail insider trading through foreign banks that were previously protected by secrecy laws and blocking statutes.

   During the 1980s, the SEC and other arms of the U.S. government arranged treaties with Switzerland and other countries to waive bank-secrecy laws and blocking statutes if evidence of specified crimes committed in the United States (for example, insider trading) could reasonably be presented in accordance with local due process. As a result, said one SEC official in November 1995, "The Swiss [banks] can only delay us from finding out the identity of [their customers] for about a year. We almost always find out who they are. It just takes a long time."[14] In the meantime, the SEC tries to freeze the suspect's accounts. In some cases, the SEC even blocks multiple bank accounts and files charges against "certain [unknown] purchasers" of the securities in the expectation that some will come forward to explain themselves—or perhaps to plea-bargain—in order to unblock the accounts.

4. Detection by the SEC is further facilitated when it apprehends an individual suspected of insider trading because the individual is so likely to give up and implicate others in order to save his or her own skin.

   The 1980s cases are thick with friends squealing on each other to reduce their own difficulties. Since it is virtually impossible to commit insider trading all by oneself and without anyone else knowing or suspecting it, the probability of getting caught rises simply because there are other parties involved who, if questioned, are typically unwilling to protect co-conspirators.

5. Coupled with the increased likelihood of detection, the penalties for insider trading have become so substantial that no reasonable person should knowingly trade on inside information.

Before the 1980s no one had ever been sent to jail for insider trading. The fines and related penalties were modest in comparison to what they later became. If caught today, one can expect to be required to disgorge all profits, pay fines, and sometimes be subject to civil suits by shareholders or others who lost money because of the actions in question. The legal costs are horrendous as well, especially if the SEC drags things out or if it charges an individual with RICO violations. Rarely will one find a firm willing to pay the defense costs of an employee charged with insider trading. More likely, the employee is fired and left to get by on his or her own resources, which may be difficult. Also, under the revised federal sentencing guidelines, jail time is not unusual for insider trading. These penalties can be so severe, some observers of the scene say, that they force innocent people to agree to offenses they did not commit in order to end the nightmare once and for all. If so, then surely the expectation of penalties should serve as a deterrent to future cases of insider trading. No doubt it has, but there are always a few people out there who never seem to get the word or who think they are too smart to be caught.

The SEC Turns Nasty and Plays Rough

An SEC investigation can be tough. Once underway, the SEC will seemingly talk to everyone you know, trying to figure out exactly who received what information from whom. Many in the industry think that the investigations can be unfair or even arbitrary and tyrannical, especially in cases involving tender offers. One example involves the 1990 tender offer for Motel 6 by a French group, Accor. For months, rumors had circulated about a possible takeover; the word got out to some people who talked to their friends, and the friends talked, too. They were caught up in the SEC's investigation of connections, and a year or so later they began to bargain for a settlement. Then the SEC said that the individuals can be liable to return not only what they made themselves (plus penalties), *but also what everyone they might have told about the tip had made.* Persons being investigated often find themselves in a Catch-22 situation. They can settle the case and get on with their lives, or they can destroy a few years of their lives fighting the case, spending hundreds of thousands of dollars in legal fees in the process. Not much of a choice.

The legal uncertainties concerning insider-trading make it all the more difficult for the target of an investigation to decide whether to fight, or to concede and settle. The case of Robert Chestman is emblematic of the uncertainties. Chestman was a stockbroker with a client who was married to a daughter of a sister of Ira Waldbaum, the controlling shareholder of the Waldbaum supermarket chain in New York. In 1986 Waldbaum decided to sell the company to A&P and told his sister, who told her daughter, who told her husband. The husband, in turn, called Chestman and asked for advice on whether to buy Waldbaum shares. Chestman said he could not give advice under the circumstances but then bought some Waldbaum stock for himself. The SEC ultimately caught up with him and prosecuted him under Rule 14e-3(a). He was convicted in the U.S. district court, but the appellate court threw out the conviction. Because of a legal technicality, however, the case was reheard by the Second Circuit Court of Appeals, with all of its twelve judges present. The result was a mishmash. Five judges voted to reinstate Chestman's conviction under 14e-3(a) but to throw out any fraud conviction under Rule 10-b(5). Five judges voted to convict on all counts, including the 10-b(5) counts. One judge voted to affirm the reversal of all the counts. The result was a conviction under 14e-3(a) but not 10-b(5).

The Supreme Court has yet to rule on the extension of Rule 14e-3(a) to cases such as Chestman's. In the meantime, however, anyone who trades on information relating to a tender offer may potentially be held liable under the rule if that person knew or *should have known* that the information was from an inside source.[15] This rule creates a vast and as yet indeterminate scope for prosecutorial discretion in initiating investigations. Individuals and firms need to keep a safe distance. Playing things close to the edge invites disaster.[16]

The World Watches

While the SEC was prosecuting its insider-trading cases, the rest of the world looked on in wonder. It must be some sort of special American mania, Europeans thought, to prosecute important people in society just for doing what important people have always done, that is, to take advantage of their privileged positions. In most other countries there was no special opprobrium associated with insider trading. One perk of membership on the board of directors of a large corporation or bank was the exceptional access it provided to price-sensitive information on which a board member could trade. For years, the compensation levels of such directors were low, certainly by U.S. standards, because it was assumed that they would compensate themselves in this and other ways. Employees of financial institutions were not viewed much differently.

Attitudes abroad began to change with developments in the United States. If nothing else, as financial markets became more global, transactions would increasingly shift to the more transparent and honest markets. Who, indeed, wants to play against a stacked deck when there are honest games in town? The U.S. fetish for a level playing field therefore gave the country a competitive advantage in the global "market for markets." In 1967 France became the first European country to outlaw insider trading, followed by the United Kingdom in 1980, albeit without the same prosecutorial zeal as the United States. But as the insider-trading scandals unfolded in the United States during the 1980s, European countries began to reexamine their own regulatory structures, which remained antiquated and lacked effective enforcement powers. Even the London Stock Exchange openly admitted that, before the Financial Services Act was passed in 1986, it could not act against organized rings of insider traders using offshore accounts even when the Exchange knew who they were.

The Financial Services Act was passed in anticipation of the general market reform in Britain that has been called the "Big Bang." New market rules, which triggered much greater competition and resulted in dramatically increased trading activity, took effect in October 1986. Detection of insider trading remained a problem, however. One of the first developments after the Big Bang was the arrest and conviction for insider trading of Geoffrey Collier, head of equity trading at the British merchant bank Morgan Grenfell. Collier had not been caught by market surveillance authorities. Rather, suspicious dealers made calls that ultimately trapped him, after which he openly confessed to his superiors. Soon afterward, a major scandal in the United Kingdom was uncovered by an SEC investigation in the United States. Ivan Boesky had admitted to the SEC that he, together with several Morgan Grenfell associates, had helped Guinness PLC, the brewery company, manipulate stock prices during its 1986 bid for Distillers PLC. The SEC then furnished this information to the British authorities, who otherwise would have been oblivious to the manipulation.

The news rocked London and resulted in several prosecutions and convictions. Ernest Saunders, chairman of Guinness, was sentenced to five years in prison, and Boesky's friend and investor client, Gerald Ronson, was sentenced to serve a year.[17] The Morgan Grenfell man, Roger Seelig, got off on a fluke.[18] But he and his chairman lost their jobs in a dramatic downfall and reorganization of the firm, which led to its acquisition by Deutsche Bank a few years later.

The Big Bang, although it directly affected only the U.K. markets, triggered major reforms in virtually all European financial markets, which for all intents and purposes were considered safe only for professional investors who could expect to be in the know. The reforms made the U.K. markets much more efficient, and growing volumes of institutional securities business from France, Germany, Italy, and other countries came to be done in London on the international sector of the new NASDAQ-like market system called Stock Exchange Automated Quotations (SEAQ). Most of the major continental European countries introduced Big Bang-like reforms in their own markets during the second half of the 1980s, in an effort to recapture the local business being attracted to London and to provide a better market for the large privatization issues that were beginning to be launched. As the quality of the continental markets improved, increased investment by Anglo-American institutions developed, and before long the issues of minority rights, legal recourse, and prevention of market abuses came to be openly discussed in places where such matters had never been raised before. And with better markets and greater pressure for improved economic performance, European mergers and acquisitions mushroomed. In 1985, $20 billion of intra-European and European cross-border mergers and acquisitions were completed. In 1995 the total was more than $150 billion. More mergers, of course, meant more opportunities for insider dealing.

In 1989 the European Union's Council of Ministers approved a directive that all of the member countries harmonize their regulations on insider trading by 1992 along the lines already agreed to by Britain and France. All but Britain and Germany complied by the deadline. Britain was able to do so with the passage of the Criminal Justice Act in 1993. German securities laws were adjusted in August 1994.

The early 1990s were big years for insider-trading scandals and prosecutions in Europe. During 1995, for example, about one thousand investigations into possible insider trading occurred in Britain, with forty-five being forwarded to other agencies for further investigation. Many involved detection of abnormal trading patterns after the London Stock Exchange's IMAS (Integrated Monitoring and Surveillance) system went live in July

1993. The system was improved in 1996 by the addition of artificial intelligence for sensing unusual trading patterns, especially by city brokers and lawyers.[19]

In France, about one hundred investigations and twenty-five referrals to the enforcement agencies occurred in 1993, but the most sensational stories did not appear until the 1994 publication of the best-seller *Mitterrand and the Forty Thieves* by Jean Montaldo. This book capped a period of extensive press reporting in France of corruption among government officeholders, mayors, other officials, and senior corporate executives. Companies such as Saint-Gobain, Alcatel-Alsthom, Schneider, and Lyonnaise des Eaux were implicated in various allegations of corruption and insider trading. The chairman of the Schneider Group was held for twelve days in a Brussels jail for fraud, and the chairman of Yves St. Laurent, a close friend of the late President Mitterrand, was convicted of insider trading and fined three million francs, although the fine was later reduced on appeal.[20]

In Germany the markets were shocked in 1985 when the chairman of the supervisory board of electrical-equipment giant AEG was found by the Frankfurt Stock Exchange to have engaged in insider trading during a takeover bid for AEG by Daimler-Benz. Subsequently, Deutsche Bank made insider trading a violation of official policy and discharged a number of executives thought to have participated in such activity. In 1993, before the final insider-trading law was cleared in Germany, Daimler-Benz announced that one of its supervisory board members, Franz Steinkühler, head of the giant IG Metall trade union, had engaged in insider trading and was forced to resign. Perhaps more than any other case, the Steinkühler affair helped accelerate Germany's war on insider trading.

In other parts of Europe some, if slower, progress was signaled by the conviction in March 1994 of the first insider-trading case in Italy. In Ireland, a case of suspected insider trading was forwarded to the public prosecutor, and in Spain and Switzerland investigations of trading abuses connected to merger transactions were launched. Throughout Europe, an increasing number of cross-border investigations were begun and concluded as a result of cooperative efforts between enforcement officials of different countries.

In Japan there has been considerably less progress in dealing with insider-trading issues. The country's need to address these issues may, in fact, be less urgent because there are only a few mergers or acquisitions of publicly traded companies. Nonetheless, Japan has virtually no systematic method for monitoring suspicious trading and lags well behind the United States and Europe in both the scope and the efficiency of securities-market regulation. Most financial-market regulation is performed directly by the Ministry of Finance, not through the legal system as in the United States and the United Kingdom. The Securities and Exchange Law of 1948 is the governing statute for financial regulation in Japan. This law was amended in 1988 to prohibit insider trading but, according to one Western authority, "The enforcement of insider trading in Japan has proven unsatisfactory and the system for exposing insider trading is poor."[21] Recently, efforts have been made to improve the situation. Japan's first insider-trading case was brought in November 1994 against a fifty-six-year old doctor who sold stock in a pharmaceutical company after learning of the deaths of patients using an anti-shingles drug developed by the company. A second case was brought by the Securities and Exchange Surveillance Commission in February 1995 against a regional bank and a large trading firm involved in the sale of shares of a construction company about to go into bankruptcy.

What It All Means Today

Insider trading is serious business. Generally, of course, these offenses reflect the actions of individuals, not firms; for example, rogue employees who are seeking to make secret profits from information obtained either from a tipper or through misappropriation. But even when the firms are not accused of wrongdoing, the cost to them of employing such rogues can be extraordinary. There are substantial legal and administrative costs, the substantial reputation effect of being publicly associated with the accused, and the fear that a new interpretation of the law might hold the firm to be responsible for all or some of the damages. In any case, the firm can expect to be penalized publicly for failing to supervise its employees and perhaps for tolerating sloppy standards. Indeed, the 1980s demonstrated the importance of effective management on the part of firms of their M&A, arbitrage, and trading activities. Such management would include these efforts.

- *Demonstrate convincingly from the top that the firm has no wish to earn profits from insider trading* and will neither reward those who do nor continue to employ them.

- *Eliminate conflicts and exposures to insider trading.* Undoubtedly this begins with a good understanding of the changing legal and regulatory landscape by everyone in the firm exposed to such activities. But the process doesn't end there. It has to be reviewed and renewed continuously. The firm must remove inappropriate practices and abstain from business where the chance of an insider-trading violation is significant.

- *Maintain and continually update a restricted trading list.* Such a list would prohibit trading, by either the firm or its employees, of the stock of any companies involved in takeovers or about which there have been takeover rumors. (Many firms now enforce their trading restrictions electronically by stopping any trades in securities appearing on the restricted trading list. Those wishing to avoid these restrictions must do so by trading in an account outside the firm. However, such accounts for employees and members of their households are prohibited except when written approval of the firm is obtained). Compliance failures of this sort led to the 1997 resignation of Louis de Bièvre, head of ABN-AMRO's investment banking activities. Insider trading activities by his wife came to light some four years after the fact, ending a distinguished thirty-five year career with the bank.

- *Invest in compliance systems.* Today's compliance systems are much more sophisticated than those of a decade ago. But to be effective, they have to be installed, however expensively. Compliance systems need plenty of people trained in the law and regulatory practice of insider trading. These people set the standards for the firm, and the standards have to be high to be effective.

- *Train new people and reacquaint older ones with changing developments.* The firm does not want to get involved with accidental insider trading, in which the full wrath of Rule 14e-3(a) is brought to bear. The legal standard for determining the firm's obligations is evolving toward responsibility for ensuring that employees do not act inappropriately regarding matters about which the firm knew *or should have known.*

- *Encourage whistleblowing.* Anyone suspecting misbehavior on the part of a fellow employee should be encouraged to report it. Whistleblowers should also be protected against reprisals.

Because of the uncertainties of the law and the vagaries of SEC enforcement, even the most diligent firm cannot insulate itself fully from an SEC investigation of insider trading. Nor can any firm totally eliminate the chance that one or more of its employees may use inside information for their own selfish advantage. Nonetheless, firms can and must take aggressive steps to protect inside information and to minimize the likelihood of employee misconduct.

7

Conflicts of Interest

■

Conflicts of interest are a fact of life. And they have become increasingly common in the securities industry as financial transactions become more complicated and as individual clients work with a wider range of firms—one for a stock offering, another for a merger, yet another for helping the firm develop a strategy for surviving a financial crisis. Firms manage interest conflicts in various ways and with varying degrees of success. What is clear, however, is that a mismanaged or unidentified conflict of interest can be as damaging to a firm as overt and knowing misconduct.

Managing a conflict of interest is, in a way, an unnatural act. Firms are in the business of making money. What do fiduciary duties and clients' interests—the building blocks of conflict—have to do with that? Not much, perhaps, at first glance. But as we shall see, it is just these duties and interests that a securities firm must understand if it is to avoid conflicts of interest or emerge unscathed when they arise.

Fiduciary Roles

Clients have interests—as corporations, governments, or individuals. As clients of a bank or securities firm, they are entitled to hold certain expectations, namely, that the contracted services will be performed according to the agreed terms and that the firm will be bound by fiduciary duties during the contract period. These duties essentially involve care and loyalty. The client has the right to expect that the firm will act with the same care and thoroughness that prudent persons would in conducting their own affairs as a matter of self-interest. The client may also expect that the firm will put the client's financial interests ahead of its own, should the two conflict, and that the client's privacy will be respected and defended if necessary. If a firm offers a service to a client for a fee or a commission—that is, if it is acting as an *agent* for the client—the firm knows that it is expected to perform accordingly. These expectations have their origins in the earliest days of English common law.

By way of contrast, if a firm is acting as a counterparty in a trade with another entity—that is, as a *principal* in a transaction—the obligations to meet all of these expectations do not necessarily apply. If a pension fund buys a block of shares from another pension fund in the market, for example, it has no obligation to consider the other pension fund's interests as if they were its own. It has not been paid to do so. Instead, the fund is responsible for looking after its own interests first. On the other hand, if one pension fund deals with another by buying a block of shares from a dealer who just bought it from the other fund, the dealer inherits some, if not all, of the fiduciary obligations that it would have had if it had been acting as a broker. The pension fund relies on the dealer to quote rates fairly and accurately, and to adhere to customary market practices.

In the financial business there are many ambiguities as to whether and to what extent one is acting in a fiduciary capacity. A deep-discount stock-broker that offers no services other than the execution of buy or sell orders may have very limited fiduciary obligations to its customers. A bank, on the other hand, making a loan to a client (as principal) may be doing so in the context of providing a variety of services bundled together, such as advising the client on recapitalizing or on M&A transactions.

For example, Den Danske Bank, Denmark's premier bank, in July 1992 had a significant credit exposure to the Hafnia Insurance Group, which was quickly deteriorating financially. According to a newspaper report (based on documents leaked by a former employee), the bank underwrote a 1.9 billion Dkr equity issue for Hafnia, with much of the proceeds being used to reduce Den Danske's lending exposure. This transaction took place only one month before Hafnia went into receivership. The stock was sold widely to individuals and institutional investors, who subsequently lost their shirts. The bank lost very little. In the United States such an event would have been a regulatory violation and have led to a class-action suit against the bank, with severe reputation losses.[1] Under such circumstances, fiduciary obligations are stretched to include activities and roles that might not otherwise be covered by them. Among the ambiguities: How broadly do the fiduciary obligations extend? How long do they last? And, one of the toughest questions, who decides these things?

Establishing Interest

None of these questions can be answered without analyzing what clients' interests are. The reason for this connection is simple. It is precisely these interests that a firm is obligated to protect in its fiduciary role. So what are they? Though many and varied, the interests of clients center on economic consequences and the protection of confidential information. The economic issues are usually straightforward. They mainly concern the assessment of strategic opportunities, the effects of specific actions on profits, and the potential exposure to risk. The confidentiality issues are straightforward, too; namely, protecting company secrets that could be of benefit to competitors. Agents acting as advisers or intermediaries (and in some cases, even other principals) must treat their own interests as secondary and give priority to clients' economic interests and to their interests in protecting confidential information. As British soldiers serving in India during the nineteenth century used to say, "You take the King's shilling, You do the King's willing." The primacy of the client's interests thus precludes conflict with the self-interest of the financial-service provider. But as straightforward as these obligations to clients may seem, ambiguities can easily complicate a situation. Reasonable people can differ over these ambiguities, and aggressive reasonable individuals acting under intense competitive pressure can differ even more. Indeed, because clients' interests have a way of expanding in their own eyes and of shrinking in the eyes of service providers, conflicts arise almost continuously.

Agency Conflicts

When a firm is acting as an agent for another party, it has fiduciary duties. How extensive these fiduciary duties are depends on the particular circumstances. Most of these "agency conflicts" seem to revolve around employees, executives, or directors of firms who put their own interests ahead of those of their clients, customers, or shareholders. The opportunity to do so is created by the agency relationship itself. Clients trust their agents to look after their interests with care, and because of the natural and considerable information asymmetries between agents and their clients, agents typically have both the knowledge and the power to use what they know to their own advantage. Such behavior can be extremely abusive to clients. And when it is, it can expose firms and individuals to charges of violating securities laws and related lawsuits.

Commission Conflicts

Almost all financial businesses reward those who produce revenues with commissions, bonuses, and profit-sharing, based mainly on the volume of transactions generated or processed. The industry regards production—doing deals and making trades—as paramount. This is true no matter how production is measured: commissions, fees, assets under management, or some combination of these.

Employees handling investment products have access to information not generally possessed by customers. As a result, all financial activities carried out with customers contain a built-in bias toward the potential misuse of information and the abuse of trusting clients. This bias encourages aggressive sales efforts. It also results in thousands of customer complaints every year and in a continuous flow of damage payments back to customers through arbitration rulings, civil suits, out-of-court settlements, and monetary settlements involving charges brought by the SEC against individuals and firms.[2] The issue involves "moral hazard": an employee benefits from aggressive activity (as does the employer), but the risks of fines and penalties are borne disproportionately by the employer and shareholder. This moral hazard not only takes away from the basic returns of the business every year but does so in particular during periods of intense competition, tighter spreads, higher costs, and adverse market conditions—when the firm can least afford it.

Consider the case of Xylan Corporation and its investment bankers, Robertson Stephens & Company. The stresses of rapid growth and internal disputes led this computer company's CFO to resign. The information was shared with the investment bank but not announced to the investing public until the following day. However, certain Robertson Stephens stockbrokers—having somehow obtained this sensitive information—began calling major clients, who proceeded to sell Xylan stock. The price dropped nearly 12 percent that day. Xylan's management was furious at this exploitation of the inherent conflict of interest between corporate finance and sales, a breach of the most basic of Chinese walls within an investment bank. According to a Xylan spokesman, "We had several discussions with them. ... We would like to make it very clear that we are unhappy with Robertson Stephens."[3]

It is vital for those in the securities business to recognize that the incentive to produce maximum revenues (even at the customer's expense), coupled with the moral hazard that makes the firm's owners and shareholders financially responsible for employee misbehavior, makes for an explosive mixture.

Owner-Manager Conflicts

Conflicts between owners of corporations and their managers occupy a central part of the literature on corporate governance, going all the way back to the famous Berle-Means work in the 1930s.[4] If an individual who owns a business also runs it, such problems do not exist. Likewise, conflicts are rare when a single individual owns a business and hires another individual to run it. If the results are not what the owner wants, the manager either straightens out or is replaced. There are few policy issues to divide owner and manager for long. The owner decides the policies, and the manager carries them out. But if the owner is absent or incapacitated, or is replaced by a group of individuals as shareholders, the manager's authority to set and implement policy is considerably extended.

When a company goes public and appoints a board of directors to represent ownership interests, the power of the manager becomes even greater. The manager, nowadays typically called the chief executive officer, is charged with acting on behalf of the company's owners, its shareholders. But what this delegation of authority entails is often left unclear. In time, the manager sets the corporate goals and strategic plans, suggests new board members to replace those who are leaving, and controls the flow of information about the company's activities and performance. Most American companies impose standards of corporate governance in order to protect shareholders from managers who might abuse their position or otherwise pursue activities inconsistent with shareholder interests.

Managers, however, encounter frequent conflicts of interest with shareholders. A company with an accumulation of cash greater than current needs might best serve its shareholders by paying the cash back to them as dividends or share repurchases. Instead, the company could make a value-enhancing acquisition or invest in R&D or some other project for the future. If an acquisition is ill chosen, however, the company's fortunes may sag, its stock price will tend to decline, and shareholders will be annoyed with management. If such a situation persists, some shareholders may urge replacement of management, or another company may step into the breach with a takeover bid. So proceeds a common economic progression in which the well-intended but unsuccessful performance of management leads to a conflict of interest between shareholders and managers. The takeover boom of 1984–1989 is often used as an example of what happens when shareholder value is undermined by ineffective management. There are forced mergers and reorganizations, as well as voluntary efforts to restructure companies to improve their performance.

A more recent example involves the Chase Manhattan shareholder Michael Price (chairman of the Mutual Series Fund), who wanted what he regarded as an undervalued and poorly managed bank to "be broken up or sold." In the spring of 1995 he became very vocal in his views about the bank and encouraged hedge funds and opportunistic institutional investors to buy into Chase as well. By July of that year these investors—acting independently and not as a group—had accumulated nearly 30 percent of Chase's stock. When these stock purchases became public knowledge, most observers believed that Chase had very little choice but to restructure or be sold. Its merger with (or more realistically, its takeover by) Chemical Bank was announced the following month.

The conflicts of interest in this case involved no violation of fiduciary duties. But consider the contrasting case of a company weakened by actions of management through which management itself directly benefited. The situation is very different; a violation of fudiciary duties may well have occurred. Examples of such problems include overcompensation, excessive management perquisites, and transactions in which management develops personal interests and agendas that may well conflict with the interests of shareholders.

It is only the board of directors that has the authority to contain excessive management spending on expenses and perks, golden parachutes, and lavish stock options and pension arrangements. When boards fail to exercise this authority effectively, they become the focus of shareholder discontent.

In 1995 the boards of W.R. Grace and Morrison Knudsen were said to have been especially lax in resisting management demands for perks and conveniences that couldn't have been in anyone's interest but their own. After much unwelcome press attention and subsequent shareholder pressure, both boards sacked their managers and reformed themselves. Many managers and boards of directors believe that boards need to maintain high standards of independence and shareholder representation. Others seem to believe that if other companies act a bit excessively, why shouldn't they?

During the second half of the 1980s, the extensive takeover activity resulted in an array of owner-manager cases being brought before the Delaware Court of Chancery (Delaware being the state of incorporation for many major U.S. corporations). The chancery court (and then the Delaware Supreme Court) ruled on many cases concerning the adequacy with which directors have represented the interests of their shareholders. A road map of acceptable corporate-governance procedures has emerged through these cases, which paid great attention to the fiduciary duties of directors to exercise care and loyalty. The court prohibited deals if they resulted from directors' neglect of these duties. Directors were also made well aware of their associated personal liabilities. These Delaware cases helped to raise the standards for judging directors' performance.

Duties of Directors

Three rulings stand out as examples of this shift toward the greater accountability of directors. In *Smith v. Van Gorkom* (1985), the directors of Trans Union Corporation decided on short notice, without the benefit of advice from an investment banker or any other outside expert, to accept a takeover offer from the Marmon Group. The directors believed that they were free to accept a higher bid if one was made, and that if none was forthcoming, a market test would have shown the price to be fair. The court did not agree. It held the directors personally responsible for violating their duties of care to the corporation and its shareholders. This ruling was controversial, but in subsequent cases the court never reversed it or shied away from it. The director's duty could *not* be taken lightly. From then on, all deals had plenty of outside advice about valuations, and very few deals were pushed ahead without full board deliberation.

In *Revlon v. Mac Andrews & Forbes* (1985) the Delaware Chancery Court ruled that, of two deals offered to the board of directors of Revlon, the board was not free to accept the one it liked best (largely because of better arrangements for management) unless that deal also carried the higher price, which in this case it did not. The court went on to add that when a company puts up a "for sale" sign, the board's duty of loyalty to its shareholders compels it to shop for the highest offer. Period! From that point on, if the board of a U.S. company wanted to accept any offer, it had to determine that the offer produced the highest value for its shareholders.

A third major case involved the attempted takeover of publishing giant Macmillan in 1988 both by leveraged-buyout experts Kohlberg, Kravis &

Roberts (KKR) and by Robert Maxwell, the flamboyant British media operator later unmasked as a fraud. The Delaware Supreme Court overturned a ruling by the Court of Chancery that would have narrowed, but still permitted, the deal with KKR that was preferred by Macmillan's management. The supreme court believed Macmillan's conduct to be "neither evenhanded nor neutral," noting that "there must be the most scrupulous adherence to ordinary principles of *fairness* in the conduct of an auction." Without such fairness, the board cannot know it is obtaining the highest possible offer. Its duty of loyalty requires that it not place any other interests ahead of this objective.

Going Private

In cases in which a buyout of a public company is under consideration, and the CEO of this target company is slated to become part of the LBO's management team, a clear conflict of interest exists. The CEO, as a director and key employee of the public company, has a duty to do everything possible to maximize shareholder value. As a member of an LBO's team, on the other hand, the CEO has a strong incentive to undervalue the company in order to buy it at a good price. And because of the CEO's influence over the rest of the target company's management team, he or she could very well sway them to accept the deal. Under such circumstances, the only legitimate option available to the CEO would be to abstain from voting on the sale of the company and to refrain from exerting any influence one way or the other.

Such discretion was not apparent in the RJR-Nabisco LBO, the most famous deal of the 1980s. This deal was distinguished not only by its $24.7 billion price tag and by its complexity, but also by the conflict of interest in which the company's CEO, Ross Johnson, was mired. This conflict of interest was exacerbated by a rival bid for the company from KKR. The most responsible thing that Johnson could have done, once he decided to join one of the bidding groups for the company, was to resign from the board. Johnson did not resign, however. How could he have done so without neglecting important duties to his new LBO associates? They needed his advice on what price to bid for the company and on how to squeeze additional cash flow out of it after the LBO. He also had to negotiate his own employment contract with the investors, especially the incentive bonuses he and a small team of key managers would receive.

Johnson not only failed to resign from the board but continued to report to work every day and to use the company's facilities and its internal information for his own purposes. He also continued to recruit key RJR-Nabisco executives for the buyout's management team. He appeared to believe that the interests of the shareholders would be adequately protected by the company's outside directors. It was they who would decide on the bids offered and on the tactics involved in the deal. In any case, he may have reasoned, the board was well advised by lawyers and investment bankers working exclusively on its behalf.

The press portrayed the LBOs of the 1980s and their sponsors as enmeshed in conflicts of interest, ones that were ignored because of the parties' boundless greed. Ross Johnson, already notorious for his free-spending, extravagant lifestyle, was pilloried in the media. He was depicted on the cover of *Time* for the magazine's lead story about greed in America. The deal he had made with his LBO sponsors and with the investment bankers, Shearson Lehman Hutton (as the firm was then called) and Salomon Brothers, was portrayed as the theft of shareholders' wealth. Johnson and six associates had arranged to receive up to 8.5 percent of the new company, with the possibility of receiving much more if certain performance measures were met.

The press had one thing wrong. The shareholders of RJR-Nabisco were going to be bought out at a price that had been reached through competitive bids. Whatever Johnson received would have come out of the pockets of Shearson and Salomon, and no one thought these two firms were unable to look after their own interests. As things turned out, however, KKR won the deal and the Johnson group did not, so none of this ever came to pass. But everyone is now more aware, at least, of the difficulties involved in having a CEO and other key executives who are part of a group seeking to take the company private.

Excessive Payments to Management

Another chord was struck in the RJR-Nabisco case with the extensive publicity given to Ross Johnson's lavish ways—his compensation, fleet of airplanes, runaway expenses, and habit of surrounding himself with celebrities on retainer to the company. All of these expenses were charged to the shareholders of RJR-Nabisco. Because the board itself was lavishly taken care of, it had no incentive to complain.[5] After all, board members might have said, the stock was trading at $50 when the first LBO deal was announced, and the final offer was valued at $108. Since the shareholders did quite well, what reason could they have to complain?

But maybe they would have done better, or perhaps not needed to sell the company at all to capture its intrinsic value, if Johnson and the others had run the company more honestly and professionally. Certainly the investors in the Prudential Securities energy and real-estate limited partnerships (discussed in Chapter 3) would have been better off had the managers of these funds not charged them for millions of dollars in excess commissions, marketing expenses, and sales junkets.[6]

The trend toward highly excessive compensation of U.S. executives began in the early 1990s, when CEOs of poorly performing firms were often reported to be receiving tens of millions of dollars in compensation, mostly from stock options and deferred compensation. The options frequently had lives of ten years and could be exercised at the market price of the stock at the time of issue. Such options had values (according to modern option-valuation models) of between 15 and 30 percent of the stock's price at issuance, but under then-standard accounting practices, their values were not disclosed to shareholders or even recorded on the company books.

Many boards of directors that approved the issuance of such options had no idea of their real value. In some cases, more stock was awarded when the options were exercised than was ever intended. In other cases, boards of directors would cancel a manager's options when the stock price fell well below the exercise price, and reissue them for the lower price. Perhaps the boards felt that the managers were underincentivized with their original options. In any event, the boards created a de facto floor for the value of the options. Though not intended in the original grants, this floor greatly increased the options' value to the recipients.

Executive-compensation programs and awards are decided by the board of directors of U.S. corporations based on the recommendations of management and occasionally of outside compensation consultants.[7] Many boards have resisted the idea of attempting to fix a market value on the options they grant. They have also objected to reporting such values as a cost to be deducted from annual operating profits in determining a firm's net income, as proposed in an exposure draft circulated by the U.S. Financial Accounting Standards Board (FASB). In December 1994, after a year and a half of fierce corporate resistance to the proposed reporting requirement, the FASB withdrew its recommendation and substituted disclosure in the form of a footnote instead.[8]

Executive compensation has not been the only area in which management has pursued its objectives in apparent defiance of shareholders' interests. In September 1995, after the controversy over excessive executive compensation had abated, Time Warner announced its controversial plan to merge with Turner Broadcasting System (TBS) in a stock deal worth $7.4 billion. Time Warner shareholders might have wondered about the supposed synergies to be captured through the merger, and how a volatile Ted Turner—sometimes called "Captain Outrageous" in the media—would fit in with Time Warner's long-range plans. They might also have wondered why their company had to offer last-minute sweetheart deals worth an additional $1 billion to the Captain and to John Malone (head of Tele-Communications, Inc. (TCI), which owned 21 percent of TBS) to obtain their consent to the merger.

The deals negotiated as part of this merger were excessive by any standard. Time Warner was to purchase a TCI distribution company (reportedly worth about $130 million) for $360 million and offer TCI a special twenty-year programming-services deal worth $500 to $700 million. In addition, Time Warner granted Ted Turner a five-year compensation package worth $100 million (while offering no contracts to *any* of Turner's top associates). The final insult was Time Warner's promise to pay $40 million to one-time junk-bond king (and now ex-con) Michael Milken, who claimed to have spent six days offering Turner strategic advice on the deal. Milken was at the time enjoined by the SEC from offering financial services. Some of these arrangements were later modified in favor of the shareholders in order for the deal to close, but perhaps it was because of such outrages that the Time Warner stock price declined by almost 15 percent during the two months following the first rumors of the TBS deal. By the end of that same period, the proposed merger had generated fourteen shareholder lawsuits.[9]

Loyalty Conflicts

Relations between firms and their clients can have their disappointing moments. Clients and firms are not constrained only by a rigid and legalistic conception of the duty of loyalty. Indeed, conceptions of loyalty are somewhat in flux today, and the duties of clients and firms to each other are what they choose to make them. For example, a once-steady client of an investment bank will occasionally decide to do a deal with another firm. Few client relationships are now exclusive, and shopping around among a group of banks is normal client behavior. Despite this common practice, however, clients sometimes feel deserted by their banks, especially when they then turn up representing companies trying to take them over.

For example, in 1988, the Swiss pharmaceuticals giant Hoffmann La Roche put in a bid for the Sterling Drug Company. J.P. Morgan was named as Roche's adviser for the transaction. Sterling Drug was shocked; it had used Morgan Guaranty Trust Company as one of its banks for years (though there was no ongoing advisory relationship at the time). Sterling manage-ment complained and raised a major fuss by publishing a letter from its chairman to Morgan's chairman. In an attempt to embarrass the bank with its longstanding, conservative, blue-chip clients, the letter charged Morgan with disloyalty and misuse of privileged information. Morgan argued in response that it had not acted improperly. Although Sterling insisted that Morgan had outrageously violated its duty of loyalty, this charge seemed unfounded. Hoffmann La Roche was also Morgan's client—and a very loyal client willing to use Morgan's investment-banking arm for merger advice at a time when Morgan was trying hard to develop its position in the M&A market.

Morgan had a choice of working with one or neither of its clients. It had a conflict of loyalty but resolved it in favor of Roche. This decision offended the other client and perhaps some others who read the newspapers. Sterling hoped that its public blasting of Morgan would cause the bank to back down as Roche's adviser, but Morgan stuck with Roche. It is reasonable to infer that Morgan felt greater loyalty to Roche, the client that had hired it for the assignment. In the end, another Morgan banking client, Eastman Kodak (represented by someone else), entered the bidding and won the deal as a "white knight."

Although Morgan may have wondered whether the public relations damage was worth the potential gain, the bank had to free itself from obligations of loyalty that were no longer fully applicable in the wake of the ongoing changes in the industry. Most investment banks have adopted the same approach to the takeover business. Certain types of conflicts may require that a firm not act in a particular deal, but there is no *general* conflict that precludes the representation of one client that wants to make a hostile bid for another client. Target companies have not always appre-ciated this rather transactional and opportunistic approach, but they seem to accept it as a feature of the times. A bidder one day and a defender the next, a company has to select the best *available* adviser for each transaction that arises.

An investment-banking firm with a somewhat distinctive approach is

Goldman Sachs, which prefers to avoid representing clients that want to launch hostile takeover bids for other companies. For years, this policy was explicit. The firm did not assist in the raiding of its present or potential corporate clients. Since the firm had more corporate clients (and therefore more takeover targets) than any other investment bank, this policy served the practical business objective of maintaining client loyalty.

The Goldman Sachs anti-raid policy nevertheless had its sticky aspects. In 1987 the British tobacco conglomerate BAT Industries told Goldman Sachs that it wanted to acquire the Farmers Group, a U.S. insurance business. BAT was one of the largest companies in Europe and one of Goldman Sachs's most important international clients. Farmers was also a Goldman Sachs client. The firm sensed a familiar problem: BAT wanted to take advantage of Goldman's close relationship with Farmers and use the firm's contacts to gain a friendly deal with the company. BAT indicated that it very much wanted a friendly deal. If Farmers said it preferred independence (which was not unlikely), BAT might then want to "go hostile," however, and expect its banker to advise it on how to proceed. Because such a transaction was expected to be valued at $5 billion, the fee to Goldman would be very substantial.

Goldman Sachs advised BAT against an unfriendly approach, but the firm was willing to approach Farmers in an attempt to arrange a friendly deal. If Farmers resisted, Goldman recommended that BAT look for another U.S. insurance company to buy. BAT hired Goldman Sachs on that basis. Goldman then approached Farmers, which firmly denied any interest in being acquired. Afterward, BAT decided it wanted to go forward with an unsolicited tender offer for Farmers. Goldman advised BAT to find another investment bank to make the tender offer. Although Goldman was acting precisely as it had agreed, BAT was irritated. The firm felt that it was entitled to Goldman Sachs's full loyalty and, in any case, wanted Goldman to continue its work on the transaction. Goldman then agreed to share the assignment with another bank, which would handle the hostile tender offer. In the end, the Farmers Group decided that BAT's offering price was high enough to turn the deal back into a friendly transaction, and everyone was happy. But Goldman Sachs ended up as a co-adviser with a split fee.

Information Conflicts

Information can create serious conflicts of interest. In order to trigger such conflicts, however, information has to be inside information, which if known to the market could affect the price of a company's securities. Obviously, if an investment bank accepts a package of confidential company documents, forecasts, or other data, it has an obligation to retain the confidentiality of the information. Banks usually sign agreements to protect clients' confidential information and not to use that information for any purpose contrary to the company's own interests. When the transaction is completed, the bank usually returns confidential documents to the client, although the bank's obligation to protect confidentiality continues.

This simple obligation has at least two major ramifications. First, the firm cannot use the confidential information for its own purposes or, without the consent of the client, represent any other client for whom the information would be useful. For example, suppose that Bullseye Corporation gave confidential documents containing forecasts of sales and earnings to its investment bank to get advice on avoiding bankruptcy. Then, not knowing this, Bidcorp asks the same investment bank to represent it in a friendly takeover of Bullseye. However much it might want to do so, and even if the information is properly protected, the investment bank is unable to "forget" the important price-sensitive information it has received from Bullseye. The bank must therefore decline Bidcorp's invitation.

Banks rarely request permission to act on both sides of a transaction at once. Even if the parties' interests coincide at the time that permission is sought, they may not in the future as negotiations proceed. Perhaps a so-called Chinese wall between two different parts of the firm would enable the firm to justify a decision to represent Bidcorp in the above example. But Chinese walls are not completely reliable, and the burden of proof that there was in fact no leak would fall on the firm itself.

The second major ramification is that information, once received, must be protected for as long as it is relevant. What if Bidcorp did not succeed in its offer and Bullseye continued in business independently? Three years later another company, Countercorp, approaches the bank about Bullseye. If the information originally delivered by Bullseye contained financial forecasts of three or more years, then that information may still be current, even if returned or set behind a wall. Again, the burden would fall on the investment bank to demonstrate that the information was not used in a manner contrary to Bullseye's interests.

The Many Roles of Research

Problems concerning the use and misuse of information can be especially complex in the context of a firm's ongoing research, which plays a critical role in determining the competitive performance of individual securities firms. Unlike what happens in other information-intensive industries, however, research within the financial services sector plays a dual role. The research is simultaneously used by the firm itself and disseminated to its clients. This duality sets up the potential for conflicts of interest.

Suppose that a firm's economists think interest rates are about to rise. If the firm decides to act on this information, it will shorten the maturity profile of its assets (to take advantage of rising rates and protect itself from a drop in securities values) and lengthen the maturity profile of its liabilities (to lock in today's low cost of funding). If the firm passes the same information on to its clients, they will do exactly the same thing. But their assets may well be the firm's liabilities, and the firm's liabilities their assets. And if the clients can position themselves faster and more effectively than the firm itself, the firm will end up with precisely the reverse of the asset-and-liability profile it wants. If the firm therefore decides to delay sending its research findings to its clients, or misleads them in any way, the clients may start shopping for a new firm.

Such potential conflicts of interest exist whenever research (whether involving macroeconomic developments, fixed-income instruments, or equities) serves both the firm and its clients. The importance of these conflicts has risen with the changing nature of competition in financial markets. As in any type of financial intermediation, competitive performance depends on three things.

1. *Information asymmetries.* Suppose one party to a transaction has much less information than the other. Since information has value, market participants with more information can profit from dealing with those who have less. Unfortunately for intermediaries, information has become far more easily accessible in financial markets as a result of technology and competition among firms in the information-infrastructure industry, like Reuters and Bloomberg.

2. *Transaction costs.* A firm may be able to undertake a financial-intermediation transaction more cheaply than another either because it pays less for the resources it employs or because it operates more efficiently. These lower costs can be an important source of competitive advantage, especially in financial services that are commodities, in which competition is essentially price-driven. Process and applications technology sold by everyone from IBM to Andersen Consulting has helped make financial intermediaries' cost structures more and more similar.

3. *Interpretation advantages.* Even if someone has the same information and can execute a deal at pretty much the same cost, it is still
possible to make money as a financial intermediary if a firm can interpret information more accurately than is possible for a client or
trading counterparty to do. Interpretation is largely dependent
upon the quality of the people the firm employs, which explains
the increasingly intense competition between firms to secure the
best talent.

The growing focus on the last of these competitive elements has elevated
the role of research in financial services firms, particularly in the securities
industry, where the half-life of information tends to be very short. And the
greater the fault lines across markets and market participants (that is, the
less integrated the markets), the greater the advantage gained through the
superior interpretation contained in research, and the more likely it is that
conflicts will arise among the various users of that research.

The area of stock-market research provides a good example of this
dynamic. Equity researchers in securities firms have at least four different
roles. In the case of new stock issues, the researcher is supposed to help
in the solicitation of underwriting mandates from corporate clients, assist
in the due-diligence process, support the sales effort in placing new issues,
and provide unbiased information and interpretation to investor clients.
The conflicts of interest imbedded in these roles can be troublesome.
Which investors get the first call? What happens if the research information
is unfavorable regarding an important client?

Though troublesome, the potential conflicts do not have to be unman-
ageable. But for them to be well managed, the analysts must be truly
independent of the investment bankers and aligned with the investors. This
independence may occur naturally to the extent that the analysts involved
are influenced by forces emanating from their own marketplace.

- *Bad advice.* Recommendations that turn out not to be in the interest of investors will sour the relationship with the analyst and the
firm, and will cause investors to deal with competitors.

- *Analyst ratings.* Competitive ratings of researchers by institutional
investors, including elaborate star systems based on accuracy of
earnings forecasts and stock-picking ability, make analysts especially
sensitive to investor reactions to their recommendations.

- *Market for analyst talent.* The hunt for talented analysts is so intense that the best of them have, in effect, their own independent

franchises based on giving outstanding advice to investors. Providing anything but the best possible advice would so devalue an analyst's reputation that he or she is likely to resolve conflicts in favor of unbiased recommendations.

- *Journalistic commentary.* Journalists are constantly on the lookout for corruption in financial markets, which makes front-line actors like analysts shy away from even the appearance of impropriety.

- *Chinese walls.* Firms work hard to prevent research recommendations from being contaminated by other business interests, as in the 1994 Merrill-Conseco case. Merrill Lynch had been retained by Conseco to do an $800 million debt underwriting in connection with that firm's effort to take over the Kemper fund-management group. A Merrill researcher coincidentally downgraded Conseco's stock, potentially making the acquisition more difficult, whereupon Merrill was fired as lead underwriter for the bond issue. Merrill's comment: "There may be times when a research opinion conflicts with a business transaction, but our practice is that our research department remains independent."[10]

On the other hand, several forces increase the likelihood that conflicts of interest will be resolved in the firm's favor.

- *Compensation and budget structure.* The research budget of the typical securities firm is carried by a number of business units, including corporate finance. When an individual researcher or a research department is characterized as unhelpful, the implications should be clear. It may also be a matter of firm policy for analysts to "behave." For example, a 1992 Morgan Stanley internal memorandum noted, "Our objective . . . is to adopt a policy, fully understood by the entire firm, including the Research Department, that we do not make negative or controversial comments about our clients as a matter of sound business practice."[11]

- *"Booster shots" for new issues.* Analysts are sometimes pressured to help sell a stock being underwritten by their firms, usually by releasing a favorable research report soon after the offering.

- *Threats of punishment.* In the mid-1990s Donald Trump threatened a major lawsuit against a Philadelphia brokerage firm, Janney Montgomery Scott, unless an analyst who had predicted tough times for one of his casinos was fired. He was, but was later awarded $750,000 from the firm in arbitration.[12] More common is "penalty box" treatment for an analyst who falls into disfavor at a company he or she covers, stops being invited to briefings, and is prevented from having regular access to the firm.

Evidence suggests that analysts working for underwriting firms tend to do what they are told. In a 1996 study of initial public offerings of stock in 1990–1991, stocks with "buy" recommendations from underwriting firms underperformed those with "buy" recommendations from nonunderwriters by 4.9 percent after one month and by 17.7 percent after a year.[13] This does not mean that researchers in the underwriting firms were being ordered by their seniors to put out puffy reports, but it does suggest that built-in conflicts and temptations can influence analysts, and their seniors constantly must be aware of this.

Making Choices

Information often determines what actions an investment bank can take in accepting a new client. Before a firm can sign on to represent a client in a specific deal, it must first clear the deal for conflicts with other clients. A typical case is one in which a group of bankers is working to develop a new piece of business, say, a merger assignment representing a potential buyer. After putting in much effort the team is awarded the assignment, but before it can accept, it must check with the firm's "conflict book." Frequently, despite the commendable efforts of the team, the assignment has to be declined. Why? Because another company spoke earlier with the firm about the specific target company and disclosed its interest in making an offer. It may have also indicated its price thinking and shared pro forma financial information with the investment bank. There actually have been times when prospective clients have come to visit a bank in order to give it information that would disable the firm's ability to act for others. The wise banker today will not advance a solicitation very far or accept any information from a client without first clearing for conflicts within his or her firm.

Conflicts as Principal

When a firm acts as an investor, not as a service provider, it is acting as principal. In such cases the firm is entitled to give first priority to the interests of its own shareholders and investing partners. It is expected to negotiate for the best price and other terms in deals, and it is generally free of fiduciary obligations to clients.

Conflicts arise, however, when a firm's actions as principal interfere with its actions as service provider, or agent. It is difficult to operate a financial services business of any size without experiencing frequent examples of this kind. Conflicts can also appear when firms find themselves in situations where the interests of one group with which the firm is associated as principal clash with the interests of another such group.

Account Stuffing

A simple example of conflict between the roles of principal and agent is that of a bank taking in funds to be managed on behalf of clients and investing these funds in a manner that is beneficial to the bank itself. Swiss banks manage a large portion of the world's liquid private wealth, much of it at their discretion. The banks have every intention to manage the money safely and in accordance with the instructions received from clients, as fiduciary obligations require. Having control of these vast funds, however, is the source of a potential conflict of interest, especially in relation to these banks' considerable placing power in the international securities market. Seeking to take advantage of this placing power, a Swiss bank may embark on an effort to become a market leader in international bond and stock deals. It may offer to acquire bond and share issues at very competitive rates. When it is successful, it is able to earn substantial fees for itself, but its clients may not fare as well.

Until recently, most Eurobond issues bore underwriting commissions of two to three times the comparable commissions in the United States. In competing for business, coupon rates would be lowered so that (after discounting for the larger, Eurobond underwriting commission) the net cost to the issuer of the securities would be fully competitive with the cost of funds available in the United States or in other markets. Many underwriters would sell such bonds to their institutional customers at rates that reflected a substantial rebate of the large underwriting spread. Swiss banks, however, normally did not rebate the spread to their customers (or to anyone else). They retained it all, and the customers received lower returns on their bonds than they might have in other markets. There were other factors involved, of course, such as administrative and service costs, financial secrecy, and tax avoidance. In the end, however, Swiss banks were able to use their customers' funds to place aggressive bids and thereby generate fee business. Although the banks bundle their customers' money, which works to their advantage, these customers might still do better by investing in a mutual fund with a manager that has no aspirations also to act as underwriter.

In recent years, many U.S. investment banks have entered the invest-ment-management business, and foreign banks have acquired big U.S. fund managers as well. This business is very extensively regulated and transpar-ent in the United States. Some firms manage mutual funds, some maintain in-house funds for clients to invest in, and some manage client money on an individual basis. In addition, more substantial clients might be invited to participate in one or more limited partnerships, investing alongside the firm itself. Under these circumstances, conflicts of interest can easily arise.

Serving the Client by Acting as Principal

Firms often assist their clients by acting as principal while simultaneously performing services for them. Underwriters act as principal. So do banks when they make loans. And so do commercial-paper "dealers." Block trades of stocks and bonds with clients are also done by the firm as principal. In these situations, the period of time in which the firm is functioning as principal is relatively brief, although a firm will be doing so with many different clients every day. In such situations, the opportunity for conflicts of interest to develop is fairly limited.

Conflicts of interest do occur when the time and risk exposure is much greater. In the later stages of the 1980s' takeover boom, many investment banks organized bridge loans for clients in the midst of doing LBOs. In such transactions, the acquiring company (the LBO operator) would often make a tender offer for a controlling interest in the target company. Then, after control was assured, the acquiring company would arrange a second-stage, or back-end, merger; shareholders would vote to merge the target into a shell company established by the LBO operator in order to finance the deal. Once merged (but not before), the considerable financing and other costs of the deal could be charged against the pre-tax income of the target company. Several months were usually required to complete the second step of the merger, and during this period the LBO operator needed to finance the front-end cash tender offer. Commercial banks were willing to make such bridge loans, but the more aggressive investment banks also saw bridge loans as a way of increasing their incomes. They arranged the LBO in the first place and tied themselves in to the process of funding the bridge loans with long-term financing (usually through issuing junk bonds once the second-step merger was completed).

When the junk-bond market collapsed in 1990, it became virtually impossible to refinance the bridge loans. Needless to say, this problem generated bitter conflicts between the bankers and their clients. The bridge loans ultimately had to be sharply discounted on the books of the investment banks providing them, causing large losses to be recorded. Many of the acquiring companies fell apart, leaving the banks with paper that was next to worthless. Several investment banking firms, including four major ones (First Boston, Kidder Peabody, Shearson Lehman, and Prudential Securities), had to be rescued from financial failure by their corporate parents.

Many observers believe that when securities firms begin to act as investors—instead of service providers—they invariably come into direct or indirect conflict with clients who are seeking the same investments. Firms do not want to compete with their own bankers for the best opportunities. And the more principal-investment situations that exist, the more likely it is that such conflicts will require banks to exclude themselves from otherwise desirable and lucrative client-service transactions. In moderation, or when confined to privately owned companies, well-managed principal investing can be a profitable adjunct to an investment-banking business. Beyond that, however, principal investing may be a serious inconvenience to a firm whose primary objective is to maximize its opportunities in the financial-services business.

Acting as Predator

In 1986 principal investing in LBOs captured the interest of many Wall Street firms. Merrill Lynch was especially active, acquiring Jack Eckerd Corporation for $1.5 billion and (together with management) Fruehauf Corporation for $1.1 billion. The following year Merrill Lynch bought Borg Warner Corporation for $4.7 billion and Supermarkets General for $2 billion. Morgan Stanley led groups that purchased Container Corporation of America for $1.2 billion, Burlington Industries for $2.6 billion, and several other smaller companies. Many such investment banks had sold their clients limited-partnership funds for investing in such LBOs. These firms were perhaps envious of KKR; unencumbered by having to run a financial-services business, KKR had invested more than any other firm in leveraged takeovers. The investing principles first laid down by Jerry

Kohlberg at KKR's inception—no hostile deals, the importance of management cooperation, and no investment in highly cyclical businesses—began to be ignored after Kohlberg left the firm. If you couldn't get what you wanted on a friendly basis, then most investment bankers knew how to turn up the pressure. And when they did, they were not only competing with their clients but starting to intimidate them.

In 1986, Shearson Lehman teamed up with a British client, Beazer PLC, to attempt a $1.6 billion hostile takeover of the Koppers Corporation. Koppers resisted fiercely, going to such lengths as to publicize that Shearson was then owned by American Express, whose millions of credit-card and other customers no doubt included many who disapproved of aggressive takeovers. Through advertisements, meetings with public officials, and a continuous onslaught of media events, Koppers did everything it could to exert pressure on American Express, which finally backed down and called Shearson off. The investment bank's predatory attack on a respectable American company was severely censured in corporate circles; such behavior by Shearson could hardly be consistent with the bank's efforts to attract these companies to become clients. Companies do not do business with firms that they don't trust or that they find reprehensible. Even a company that did not mind the tactics might nevertheless wonder whether it should enter or maintain a banking relationship that was potentially so unpredictable. For Shearson, conflicts arose not out of fiduciary duties and obligations, but out of a nonlegal conflict concerning long-term strategic goals.

In 1990 Goldman Sachs started the $780 million Water Street Corporation Recovery Fund for institutional clients to earn high returns from investing in securities (mainly junk bonds) of distressed companies. The fund did well, but it soon became obvious that such "vulture investing" required aggressive tactics to position one's securities favorably (relative to other holders of securities) in working out the reorganization of a company. The size of the Water Street fund—and its willingness to concentrate its investments to achieve maximum power in reorganizations—meant that the fund had enormous clout and could often block reorganizations of companies that were not to its liking. Clashes arose with other investors, banks, finance companies, and some other institutions.

The Water Street fund also invested in securities issued by some of Goldman Sachs's own corporate clients, which occasionally put the firm in conflict with its own clients during a reorganization. The firm therefore found itself trying to charm a client one day and bashing it the next in negotiating a reorganization. Goldman believed, however, that it could maintain two separate identities in the marketplace and that, in view of the small size of the Water Street fund relative to the rest of its activities, it could smooth over the occasional conflicts with clients. It was mistaken. Many clients complained, and the press picked up the conflict between the firm's own interests and those of its clients. After a year of operation, Goldman decided to eliminate the conflict, whether real or perceived, by liquidating the Water Street fund.

Determining whether a conflict exists is sometimes difficult, however, and the press often perceives a conflict when in fact there is none. In 1994 Goldman Sachs had assisted Rockefeller Center Properties (RCP) in staving off bankruptcy, and the firm's Whitehall Street Fund, a real-estate investment fund, had invested $225 million in RCP. As part of that deal, Goldman Sachs itself had also received purchase warrants for 19.9 percent of RCP stock. The following year, the firm organized a group to bid for the outstanding shares of RCP and to oppose another bid, which RCP had already accepted, submitted by real-estate developer Sam Zell and two major Rockefeller Center tenants, GE Capital Services (on behalf of NBC, a wholly owned General Electric subsidiary) and Walt Disney, which leased Radio City Music Hall. Zell and his two partners had themselves been occasional clients of Goldman Sachs. In view of these relationships and the firm's ongoing connections with RCP, many members of the press recalled the conflicts associated with the Water Street fund and accused Goldman Sachs of another such conflict of interest.

The press's understanding of this situation was relatively simplistic, however. Zell and his group had not been involved in the 1994 reorganization of RCP and had not dealt with Goldman Sachs in that context, and there was no confusion whatsoever about Goldman's ongoing role and interests. The firm was now acting as principal investor in RCP and was looking out for its own interests, which were aligned with those of the rest of RCP shareholders. Moreover, although Goldman Sachs had had a representative on the board of RCP, this representative resigned when the firm decided to make a bid on behalf of the Whitehall Street Fund. Having resigned from the board and not serving as a financial adviser to RCP, Goldman no longer had fiduciary duties to RCP. But it did have continued fiduciary duties to Whitehall and its investors. The Zell group surely could not have expected Goldman Sachs to abandon those obligations simply because Zell,

Disney, and GE appeared on the scene to make a bid that Goldman Sachs thought was too low. Goldman, joined by David Rockefeller, ultimately outbid the Zell group.

Undermining Your Partner

Partnerships and joint ventures are hard to hold together in periods of great change, shifting fortunes, and unequal opportunities and talents. Conflicts can occur between partners sharing the same interests, especially when one partner acts in such a way as to put his own interests ahead of the others; for example, by acting on information for one's own account before conveying that information to the partnership. Even when these conflicts develop inadvertently, they can create big problems between partners. For example, in 1970, a group of six large international banks—Chase Manhattan Bank, Royal Bank of Canada, National Westminster Bank, Mitsubishi Bank, and two other banks—formed Orion Bank, a "consortium bank" to operate in international financial markets on behalf of its parents. Orion, one of many consortium banks formed at the time, was very active in Eurocurrency and Eurobond markets. But later in the 1970s Orion's parent banks all began to develop their own independent international strategies. Few among them were then willing to contribute their best people, largest clients, or last dollar to a joint venture in which they had only one-sixth of the profits. Before long, Orion Bank was competing with its own parents and losing money, despite arguably much better knowledge of international markets. Finally, Orion was bought out by one of its parents (Royal Bank of Canada) in 1981 and subsequently liquidated. All of the other consortium banks of the time were liquidated, too, and the consortium experiment was judged a dismal failure.

A similar problem in accommodating partnership and individual interests occurred with a series of complex transactions involving Crédit Suisse, First Boston, and the New York investment bank White Weld. In 1978, after White Weld failed, its 30 percent interest in a joint-venture international investment bank, Crédit Suisse-White Weld, was sold to First Boston and the joint venture was renamed Crédit Suisse-First Boston. First Boston, which was in financial straits at the time, paid for its stake by transferring a 30 percent interest in itself to Crédit Suisse-First Boston. Over the next few years, First Boston became increasingly dissatisfied with the resulting lopsided arrangements for distributing both business opportunities and profits in what was nominally a cooperative venture. The firm also found itself competing with its own affiliate, Crédit Suisse-First Boston. After a decade of conflict, First Boston and Crédit Suisse-First Boston merged into a new Crédit Suisse holding company in 1988. Some conflicts remained, however, and there was yet another reorganization in 1996.

Managing Conflicts

Most duties, interests, and conflicts are obvious to financial professionals. Some are not, however, either because the issues are subtle and complex, requiring consultation with the most sage members of the firm, or because the individuals involved do not have all the facts. The latter are much more common. Ironically, they sometimes occur just because firms have been successful in protecting the confidential information of clients. One part of the firm may not realize that its activities are creating interests adverse to what the firm is doing elsewhere with the same or other clients.

From the earliest moments of a firm's history in the securities business, it must have a system for deciding conflicts of interest. Senior representatives of the firm's corporate finance, mergers, research, and trading should be involved. All transactions in process and those involving prior assignments must be carefully tracked. A clearly defined process for handling new business enquiries must be established and adherence to this process strictly enforced. The process has to start with gathering information that is relevant to the case, including legal input where necessary. Decisions to accept new business should not be made until authorized persons have cleared the transaction for conflicts. All sorts of other potential conflicts, such as those related to brokerage account management, expense allocation, and related matters, should be subject to internal auditing efforts and be part of the scope of the firm's outside auditors' report to management.

But the most important thing is that the top people in the firm put their backs into the program and support it, even when it means they have to turn important business down. If they don't, nobody else will. If they're not tough, then nobody else is going to try to be tougher. And nothing makes a bigger difference to the firm's long-term value than avoiding conflicts and temptations to put its interests ahead of other people's. The only decision a firm's employees should be able to count on in a conflict-resolution case is one that is best for the firm over the long term.

8

Kickbacks,
Payoffs,
and Bribes

■

In the early 1990s emerging markets were the rage. Securities firms and banks from the United States, Europe, and Japan became heavily involved in privatizations and secondary-market transactions in shares of companies in Latin America, Eastern Europe, and various parts of Asia. Special interest was drawn to Mexico, Brazil, Argentina, China, and India. The firms were looking for solid research capability and the opportunity to secure mandates from governments for underwriting the shares of companies about to be privatized. Many of the countries involved, however, were rather opaque environments. Much of the important information needed to pursue such transactions was not publicly available, and the decision-making processes were usually cliquish and hardly transparent. To know what was going on, and to have any kind of chance to succeed, firms had to be plugged-in. They had to know the right people, and the right people had to tell them what was going on. Firms were especially disadvantaged if they lacked such critical access and the information it provided, and their competitors—of which there were many, from all over the world—did not.

Some investment banks set up branches in the countries involved. Others formed joint ventures with local securities firms or banks. These corporate outposts would be staffed and also often run by local nationals whom the firms had hired and trained. In China, for example, one major U.S. firm formed a joint venture with a government bank. Another hired a well-connected former Red Guard officer (from the days of the Cultural Revolution) to head its office in Beijing. Another used a Chinese-American lawyer to travel in and out of China from a base in Hong Kong. All of the firms had senior investment-banking and research personnel traveling into the various Asian and Latin American countries on a regular basis, but most of these people were responsible for activities in several countries and expert in the affairs of none.

The enthusiasm for emerging-market investments was not destroyed by the market crash after the Mexican peso devaluation in early 1995. Joint ventures continued to be considered, even in countries as difficult to work in as India and the successful states of the former Soviet Union. But these ventures—and indeed all business activities in these countries—presented some special problems not usually confronted by major securities firms. Many of the countries with the best investment opportunities had business environments that were among the world's most corrupt. Firms choosing to enter these markets would have to confront issues of payoffs, kickbacks, and bribes.

What makes these issues especially difficult to address is the difference in cultures between industrialized nations and many emerging-market countries. What we may see as corruption abroad is often, from a local perspective, no more than well-entrenched custom. We may want to do things differently, but that just isn't how things are done there. We don't understand why they can't change, and they don't understand why they need to. How does one solve this conundrum? Or are we just mistaken in thinking that everyone should do things our way?

Questionable Payments

In late 1994 the *Financial Times* carried an exposé of what it called "a year of corruption," cataloguing events that had come to light during that year. The list is impressive but hardly unique. Indeed, it is fairly representative of what surfaces in just about every year. The locations, the people, and the character of the events change, but not the role of "questionable payments" (QPs). In its editorial, the paper noted:

> For anyone who still believed that corruption was primarily a problem of the developing world, and not the developed, the exposés . . . should have provided a belated awakening. Scandals ranging from petty 'sleaze' to substantial bribery have broken out across the globe, from Japan in the east, through Britain, France, Italy and the former communist countries, to the U.S., Brazil and Mexico in the west. It is clear that bribery and corruption know no frontiers.[1]

In the words of World Bank President James Wolfensohn, commenting on the role of corruption in his organization's financing programs, "When voters think their money is going into a few people's pockets and Swiss bank accounts, that erodes the whole quality of the overseas assistance package. . . . Countries that are fundamentally corrupt should be told that unless they can deal with it they are not getting any more money. That is part of governmental reform."[2] But when Peter Eigen, a World Bank director in Kenya with experience in various Latin American countries, suggested drafting an anticorruption code of conduct as a cooperative effort between the World Bank, national governments, and international companies, he was stopped dead in his tracks by his superiors. Evidently the World Bank bureaucracy was not ready to walk the talk. So Eigen took early retirement and founded Transparency International, based in Berlin, which collects information on bribery and corruption, and publishes the "Corruption Index."[3]

The World Bank's *World Development Report* for 1996, which focused almost exclusively on the transition economies of Eastern Europe and Asia, reported that corruption was rampant.

> In many transition economies the public's perception of widespread corruption—including the misappropriation of public property—is undermining government reform efforts. . . . Bribes may help business avoid burdensome regulations, but they also create incentives to make regulations even more complex and costly. Officials may block further reforms to entrench their power and maintain their illicit income. State managers may realize that they can purchase or divert enterprise assets more cheaply if they delay privatization and make their companies underperform. Corruption can divert resources away from vital areas such as education, where the potential for bribes is smaller. It also undercuts governments' ability to enforce legitimate regulations and collect revenues as activities shift into the shadow economy in order to avoid the government altogether.[4]

In 1996 Transparency International's Corruption Index identified Nigeria as the world's most corrupt business environment, followed by Pakistan, Kenya, Bangladesh, China, Cameroon, Venezuela, Russia, India, and Indonesia. New Zealand, Denmark, Sweden, Finland, Canada, Norway, Singapore, Switzerland, The Netherlands, and Australia were identified as least corrupt. The United States ranked fifteenth among the least corrupt, slightly behind Israel.[5]

Corruption is the bane of economic development, associated as it is with massive misallocation of resources. Contracts are systematically awarded to those with higher prices and lower quality or performance. Licenses are given to firms that make payoffs instead of to those most qualified. Protection rackets flourish, and the cost is passed on to consumers. Subsidies or protection against imports is provided for decrepit firms or industries that maintain their positions through payoffs and whose continued survival is a blemish on the economic landscape. Legislation and its enforcement is suborned, with sometimes horrific consequences for construction projects, health, and safety. Government officials are included as silent partners on all kinds of business ventures, bringing to the table nothing but their connections and ability to twist public policy. The examples are legion. Corruption is a cancer on the global economy, one that affects the poorest nations the most.

With progressive globalization of the securities industry, financial firms operate in many countries, including emerging-market countries. Many of these activities are joint ventures or involve strategic partners. Others involve subsidiaries and key employees operating abroad. It is rare for a firm today not to encounter problems related to questionable payments in getting new clients, trading opportunities, or necessary licenses and permits.

What Payments Are Questionable?

For U.S. companies there have been no more painful and explosive episodes involving questionable payments than the revelations of numerous payoffs and bribes by major corporations in the late 1970s. Under an SEC voluntary-disclosure program, over four hundred companies admitted making more than $700 million in payoffs to foreign heads of state, cabinet ministers, legislators, judges, mayors, generals, and such lesser functionaries as tax assessors, immigration officials, and appointment secretaries. The disclosures, in turn, triggered large-scale investigations in Canada, Venezuela, Spain, Germany, and dozens of other countries. The investigations led to the arrest and conviction of Japan's former prime minister Kakuei Tanaka, to the disgrace of Prince Bernhard in The Netherlands, to the overthrow of the chief of state in Honduras, and to the forced resignations or demotions of senior executives in firms ranging from Gulf Oil, Lockheed, and Conoco to Japan's Marubeni Trading Company. The revelations caused damage to companies and diplomatic relations, dismissals of numerous foreign defense ministers, cancellations of contracts, expropriations of foreign-owned property, and changes in the military procurement decisions of allies. Not least important, they severely eroded public confidence in the conduct and responsibility of business management, and led to the passage of the U.S. Foreign Corrupt Practices Act (FCPA), a statute that has influenced the conduct of global business for some two decades.

Questionable payments have been variously described as those that might be "corrupt," "illegal," "improper," "irregular," or "unusual." QPs come in all shapes and sizes—in cash and in kind, direct and indirect, legal and illegal, voluntary and extorted, large and small, on and off the corporate books, lump sum and installment, prepaid and *post facto,* inside and outside the country, fictitiously and factually entered into corporate records.[6] The variety boggles the mind. The best we can do is profile four basic kinds of QPs, recognizing nonetheless that there is no clear line dividing one type from another.

Grease

Pot de vin in France. *Mordida* in Mexico. *Dash* in West Africa. *Baksheesh* in the Middle East. *Bustarella* in Italy. *Cumshaw* in much of Asia. Everywhere there are palms to be greased. These lubricating payments, usually small bribes, are given to low-level government officials to induce them to perform such normal duties as issuing work permits and driver's licenses, expediting tax returns, accelerating building permits, obtaining customs clearances, and authorizing financial transactions efficiently and expeditiously. Grease surely accounts for the vast majority of questionable payments made worldwide.

Bribery, Kickbacks, and Extortion

Outright bribes most often involve the payment of relatively large sums to senior public officials. Companies have used bribes to procure or maintain contracts or concessions, reduce tax assessments, settle tax liabilities, and obtain product approvals or price increases. The classic case was that of former Japanese prime minister Tanaka's receipt of $1.6 million from Lockheed to encourage the purchase of L-1011 TriStar transports by All Nippon Airways. In 1994, Prime Minister Morihiro Hosokawa likewise resigned after allegations that he had accepted bribes from Nippon Telephone and Telegraph as well as from a trucking company. Such large-scale bribery has captured the lion's share of media attention. Some recent cases include the following:

- The Justice Department initiated an investigation of Boeing on allegations that a former Canadian subsidiary paid $1.14 million in bribes and fees to senior government ministers in order to sell five De Havilland Dash 8 turboprop aircraft to BahamasAir in 1990. The scheme included the hiring of a consultant (a politically influential businessman who had no aircraft experience) for the sole purpose of passing along the bribes to Bahamian officials in return for a $90,000 kickback.[7]

- In 1995 the Manhattan District Attorney's office and the Federal Reserve launched an investigation of kickbacks in the trading of third-world loans. The traders cheated their own banks by selling loans in the secondary market at discounts from arm's length prices in return for kickbacks from the purchasers, who retained a share of the illicit profits. Under specific investigation were sales by First Chicago of loans to Argentina, Mexico, and Brazil during 1988–1990—a time when the secondary-loan market was pretty murky and regulators showed virtually no interest in its operation. In 1996 a trader formerly at Manufacturers Hanover Trust pleaded guilty in connection with the loan sales.[8]

- In a 1995 investigation into bribery at Adam Opel AG, General Motors' German subsidiary, 65 employees were suspected of taking bribes from suppliers.[9] Similar revelations at other firms involved bidding cartels, payoffs, private services billed to supplier firms, and similar questionable practices. These discoveries suggested that corruption in the private sector was widespread in Germany, a country with strong free-market traditions but with some of the most lenient anticorruption laws in the world. Corruption in industry has been a misdemeanor, not a crime, there is a three-year statute of limitations, and bribes have been tax-deductible under German fiscal rules. Prosecution must be triggered by a complaint from the affected firm, and unlike Opel, most refrain from coming forward. By August 1995, 244 people at forty other companies in Germany had been implicated in schemes such as the one at Opel. In the German state of Hesse, an anticorruption squad estimated that cash bribes doled out to clinch deals add 3 to 5 percent to the cost of every building contract, and that kickbacks cost German taxpayers billions of dollars annually. Evidently the German public has become fed up with reports of the corporate elite lining their pockets, ultimately at their expense. There have been increasingly strident calls for reforms.[10]

A 1996 Commerce Department study documented almost one hundred cases between April 1994 and May 1995 in which U.S. firms lost an estimated total of $45 billion in contracts to foreign rivals that paid bribes illegal under the U.S. Foreign Corrupt Practices Act.[11] A 1996 study released by the National Bureau of Economic Research estimated that reduced U.S. business activity in countries where government officials routinely receive bribes—where U.S. firms are prohibited from bribing under the FCPA but their competitors are not—causes the equivalent of a 30 percent drop in those countries' GDP. In the aircraft industry alone, the study found that U.S. exports dropped by 21.2 percent in corruption-prone countries after the FCPA was enacted, versus 6.4 percent in other countries.[12] American efforts to raise bribery for discussion in the World Trade Organization were strongly opposed, however, by a number of Asian countries as "ordering rivers to reverse course."[13]

The kissing cousin of bribery is extortion, where the improper influence originates at the other end. For instance, Ashland Oil paid $190,000 to two high government officials in Gabon after being informed that "certain outstanding obligations" of very dubious validity had to be satisfied. And Translinear, a Dallas real-estate development company, was told that things would become "unhealthy" if it chose not to meet demands for $250,000 by Haitian officials in connection with the development of a port facility. It refused, and was duly forced to terminate the project.

Agents' Fees

Another important kind of payoff is exorbitant fees or commissions paid to sales agents, consultants, lawyers, and marketers abroad. In the early 1970s the Northrop Corporation paid out more than $30 million in agents' fees and commissions. A private report written by the public accounting firm of Ernst & Young disclosed that during this period the big aircraft manufacturer had employed between four hundred and five hundred consultants and agents, many of whom were either members of royal families or closely associated with the military. Northrop's president, Thomas V. Jones, described the typical agent as "the stethoscope on the workings of government."[14]

What makes such payments "questionable" is that the amounts far exceed the value of the services performed. Some portion of the fees may also be used for bribery (with or without the principals' knowledge) or rebated to executives for use as slush funds off the companies' books. So the trick is to determine what fees are appropriate for the services agents provide.

Political Contributions

Lastly, there are contributions to politicians and political parties. In many countries it is legal for corporations to make such contributions. As always, there is the quid pro quo. Contributions help make new friends and retain old ones, and they may even soften up old enemies. Even if legal, however, such payments may still be questionable if they aren't acknowledged or disclosed. There is always a thin line between contributions that represent a legitimate interest in the political process and those patently aimed at improperly influencing government actions.

The experience of Exxon in Italy has become a classic. Exxon's Italian affiliate, Esso Italiana, funneled a total of $46 million to Italian political parties from 1963 to 1972. Contributions authorized by the parent firm averaged about $3 million a year, for a total of $27 million—big money in those days. The rest was siphoned out of the company without authorization by the managing director of the Italian subsidiary, ostensibly for political purposes. Some of these payments coincided with the oil industry's receiving specific legislative benefits, such as subsidies to offset the higher transportation costs caused by the closing of the Suez Canal during the 1967 Arab-Israeli War, the reduction of the manufacturing tax on petroleum products, and the delay of the government-owned electric utility's conversion to nuclear power. These political contributions were made, as was the custom, without disclosing the recipients, and most were camouflaged as payments to newspapers, publicity agencies, and similar fronts.[15]

In the United States, of course, political contributions are *de rigueur* and highly resistant to reform by politicians who have grown to depend on them to defray escalating campaign costs. For example, virtually all congressional leaders responsible for overhauling federal securities law and regulation have been heavy recipients of legal gifts from the affected brokerage firms, banks, and insurance companies. In 1995 over $5.5 million in contributions were made to the six senior congressmen on key financial oversight committees. According to one consumer advocate, "This congress has put the legislative process up for sale to the highest bidder. . . . The debate over policy is shoved to the side and you get to a debate on who has more influence."[16] The degree of influence (measured largely by the amount of political contributions) is especially important because complex tradeoffs are involved; for example, support for limitations on clients' ability to sue broker-dealers (favorable to the securities industry) versus repeal of barriers to entry by commercial banks (unfavorable to the securities industry).

In its assessment of trends in questionable payments, the *Financial Times* noted that "the common cause behind many of the recent cases has been the need for ever-increasing campaign funds for political parties, rather than individual venality. The soaring costs of campaigning for political office in a televised democracy have put ever greater financial pressure on the participants. In the U.S., as in Japan, the purchase of political favors with campaign contributions has long been almost an accepted part of the system."[17]

Domestic Questionable Payments

The need for political contributions has long been a troubling issue in the $1.5 trillion U.S. municipal-bond business. Thousands of state and local officials have to be reelected periodically, and many of them have very limited access to campaign funds. They do, however, sit on boards or head other bodies that dispense mandates for underwriting the bonds issued by their municipalities and that contract with investment bankers for various services. It is not difficult to imagine situations in which campaign contributions are requested from, or offered by, investment bankers.

By statute, municipal securities in the United States are exempt from registration with the SEC. And though most municipalities agree to a minimal level of disclosure about their affairs and finances, these disclosures do not include discussion of political contributions or other payments made or received. Also, price information in the muni market usually involves calling a broker for a quote; only a handful of the most actively traded munis are listed in the newspaper. The price of any particular bond can vary widely among dealers. The systematic lack of disclosure provides ample scope for questionable dealing, so brokers can overcharge investors as a means of paying for their own political contributions.[18]

As a result, the municipal bond area has become an unusually opaque corner of the normally transparent U.S. financial system, in which a host of unseemly practices has developed. Government officials press investment bankers for campaign contributions in return for appointments as underwriters; investment bankers who have secret back-scratching or fee-sharing arrangements with other underwriters are hired to be objective "advisors" to municipalities; and investment bankers sell overpriced investment services such as mispriced interest-rate swaps to unsophisticated municipal treasurers.[19]

Pay-to-Play

The practice of major securities firms to pay off state and local officials arguably has precluded smaller firms from obtaining mandates that they might have won through a fair competitive-bidding process. Smaller firms can't compete effectively against larger underwriters with established connections and war chests for political payoffs. The politicians on the receiving end gain both personal and political benefits. What results, however, is a distorted and biased election process that clearly works against the interests of the general public. In 1994, for example, the husband of Kentucky governor Martha Collins demanded that Wall Street firms pay him if they wanted to do municipal-bond business in the state. He received $35,000 from Donaldson, Lufkin & Jenrette, which he used to buy a grand piano for the governor. Another widely reported case involved Mary Landrieu, then the Democratic gubernatorial candidate and ex-Treasurer of Louisiana, reputedly a major player in her state's pay-to-play game. In mid-1990, First Boston hired a "consultant" who in reality served as a political lobbyist for Landrieu. Later that year, First Boston won the mandate as lead underwriter on a $78 million bond issue. In May 1991 Smith Barney won a $125 million deal, soon after which the firm contributed $5,000 to Landrieu's reelection campaign. In spite of these and other documented "coincidences," Mary Landrieu won the governorship in 1995 on a platform of being against "fiscal irresponsibility, corruption, and cronyism."[20]

It is only a small step from political contributions to kickbacks. In February 1995 an ex-aide to former New Jersey Governor Jim Florio pleaded guilty to a single count for having shared in more than $200,000 in payments from firms doing bond business in the state. It appears that Camden County retained a firm called Consolidated Financial Management as its adviser for "a buck a bond" (.1 percent) to help find funds for it in the muni market. That fee was later reduced and replaced by payments from underwriters, part of which were passed on to the governor's aide in order to influence underwriter selection.[21]

The arrangements for a kickback are sometimes complex and indirect. In a routine 1993 deal in which the state of Louisiana sold $604 million in general obligation munis to investors, the underwriting was co-managed by Lazard Frères and First Boston. In the underwriting agreement, however, there was a side deal that required the two banks to send $115,000 (half their fees) to First Commonwealth Securities, a New Orleans minority-owned firm. Why? Lazard and First Boston said they were told by state officials that they had to give First Commonwealth 50 percent of their fees to win the job, ostensibly to allow the state to fulfill affirmative action goals.[22]

In 1993 the industry's self-regulatory group, the Municipal Securities Rulemaking Board (MSRB) adopted Rule G-37, which stopped municipal-bond firms and their employees from contributing more than $250 to any politician in a district where the firm does underwriting business. This rule complemented an earlier agreement by the major securities firms to stop contributing to state and local political candidates.[23] Firms that violate Rule G-37 are barred from underwriting deals for two years—although there is a loophole whereby "consultants" are not banned from contributing to politicians. But state and local officials are still reported to be aggressively soliciting Wall Street firms for pet projects, for "soft-money" accounts set up to defray certain political costs, and for other solicitations, none of which make reference to the bond business.[24] Since the MSRB is prohibited from regulating the state and local issuers themselves, politicians are able to continue extracting campaign contributions and side payments, the "mother's milk of state, county, and city politics."

It would be wrong to infer that Rule G-37 is unenforceable. In 1996 Merrill Lynch was barred for two years from the negotiated underwriting of debt issued by the state of Indiana and its agencies; an executive in its private-clients group made a $1,000 campaign contribution (later returned) to the lieutenant governor, who sat on a number of state authorities that issued municipal bonds (and was also running for governor). Merrill, which could have applied for a waiver of the ban and continued to be eligible to bid for auctioned issues, stated that the executive had violated the firm's policy and that "Merrill Lynch does not intend to do further negotiated public finance issues with the state of Indiana without the appropriate regulatory approval."[25]

Bent Advisers

Even though it had been ranked tenth in municipal-bond underwriting in 1992, Lazard Frères shut down its municipal-bond business in 1995 after paying $12 million to settle charges brought by the SEC in a case involving fee splitting with Merrill Lynch. Mark Ferber, a Lazard Frères partner, had been retained to advise the State of Massachusetts on muni bonds, but steered deals to Merrill without disclosing the fact that his firm was receiving a kickback. Merrill paid a similar fine, making the settlement the largest in municipal-bond history. Ferber was indicted on sixty-three counts and faced a jail term of up to three hundred years.[26] In August 1996 he was convicted on criminal charges of defrauding his clients by failing to disclose the kickbacks to Merrill Lynch.

Ferber was sentenced to a thirty-three-month prison term and fined $1 million in December 1996 by U.S. District Court Judge William G. Young. "You are a man without honor," the judge said, "You have lied through your teeth to save your skin. It is not a pretty picture. This is not aberrant behavior. Look at how long it went on. You were lining your own pockets. Greed was the motivator. The money was just flowing in." Nor did the two firms come off very well. "Once Merrill found that Mr. Ferber was ethically defective," the judge continued, "they played him for a sucker. They played him like a patsy. When faced with criminal behavior, they were his co-conspirators. . . . [Yet] I am struck by the disparity in the sanctions on Merrill. They bought their way out for $12 million and none of them are going to jail. A $12 million civil settlement doesn't cause them much pause on the way to the tennis courts or the yacht club." Ferber's sentence was slightly reduced because of the judge's view of the disparity in treatment. As for Lazard Frères, Judge Young concluded that the firm was "totally bereft of internal quality controls. . . . At least Lazard had the decency to get out of the municipal bond business." And he characterized the two firms' municipal bond lawyers as "the most sorrowful, evasive excuse for legal advisers." In response, Lazard issued a statement noting its regret and the heavy price the firm had paid for its involvement, while Merrill responded, "We strongly disagree with the judge's characterizations, which are unfortunate and unfair."[27]

The Ferber conviction represented a key victory in the SEC's effort to reduce corruption and cronyism in the $1.5 trillion muni market. It represented the highest-profile government victory since the insider-trading convictions of Ivan Boesky and Michael Milken in the 1980s. The SEC has nonetheless been heavily criticized by major securities firms and by state- and local-government officials for its aggressive moves to try to clean up the market. In the Ferber case, according to one of the prosecutors, "The jury has said that people who hold positions of trust will not leverage them for private gain. This case has caused significant reform in the way that municipalities borrow."[28] Since none of the muni clients actually lost money, the government had to build its case that fraud occurred by depriving clients of "the right of honest services." The head of the Public Securities Association, the industry's trade group, commented, "It's like a hanging in a public place. Nobody likes it, but it certainly brings home what the penalties are."[29] And the executive director of the Municipal Securities Rulemaking Board commented, "The end of the Ferber case brings a huge sigh of relief to the industry. It has been one of those clouds hanging over this industry. This is not normal behavior. And the industry felt it was being tarred with the same brush. If anyone ever felt there was some wiggle room on conflict-of-interest issues, this is a signal that there isn't." A Lazard Frères statement noted that there was no evidence that any other partners had known or approved of Ferber's actions, but acknowledged that "it is nonetheless a sad day when any former partner of the firm is convicted of a crime."[30] One commentator noted that "other than this area, they [Lazard Frères] were very scrupulous. This is a major exception . . . like if you heard a bishop was going out with a prostitute."[31]

Merrill suffered further adverse consequences from its involvement in the Ferber affair. New York City put the firm in the "penalty box" for several months, barring it from any role in underwriting the city's bonds during that period.

Mispricing

Like a butcher putting his thumb on the scale, a practice known as "yield burning" has also been used by investment banks to pad the bill for Treasury securities they buy on behalf of municipal clients. When interest rates drop, municipalities often refinance their debt by issuing new bonds at the lower rate and investing the proceeds in Treasury securities. The securities are held in escrow to redeem the old bonds when they become callable. The municipalities are therefore able to make a nice profit by raising municipal money, say, at 5 percent and investing it in 6 percent Treasuries. Knowing this, the underwriters sometimes mark up the price of the Treasuries beyond the arms-length market price. Municipalities are nonetheless eager to take the resulting profit and overlook the overcharge, which the taxpayer pays anyway. According to one investment banker, "Yield burning? That's been going on for years."[32]

The IRS and the SEC have recently begun scrutinizing municipal-bond deals and are offering potential solutions to prevent taxpayers from being stung. In order to minimize yield burning, all escrow payments are now required to be made in state securities and in U.S. government bonds with yields designed to meet those of the maturing bonds. There is also an ongoing effort to recoup an estimated $2 billion in unpaid taxes from muni-bond issuers; the government argues that Wall Street firms and their municipal customers rigged prices of securities during refunding operations to avoid federal taxes. Under the program, municipalities are encouraged to pay the amounts owed to the IRS and then to sue the Wall Street firms in order to recover the funds attributable to yield burning.[33] There are signs that the crackdown is having some impact on the muni market, including problems trading and pricing some bonds, due to uncertainty about who will have to come up with the additional taxes related to the bond refinancings of the past.[34]

Though obviously well intended, these efforts by the SEC and IRS have been controversial. The ambivalence of treasury secretary Robert Rubin, former co-chairman of Goldman Sachs, was apparent in his statement to the National League of Cities that he would try to "work with all of the parties" affected by the IRS ruling, including the municipal-bond dealers.[35] After being widely criticized for this position, he recused himself from further involvement in the program to recoup lost tax revenues.

Muni-watchers noted with some amusement as the National League of Cities complained to the SEC that its zeal to clean up the municipal-bond business was excessive and too costly, particularly with regard to enforcement of disclosure requirements against "smaller cities with inadequate resources to defend themselves." The National League of Cities took this position after the SEC initiated its first enforcement action against a local government, Orange County, California. The SEC had charged that the county's board of supervisors failed to disclose material facts in muni issues that were used in part to finance speculation in the derivatives markets. The SEC responded with little sympathy. According to Enforcement Director William McLucas, "You can't lie and you can't disregard facts you know to be true. . . . You can't just say: 'I hired a lawyer and an investment banker.'"[36]

Corrupt Payments as Market Failures

Why do questionable payments occur? Economists find a ready answer: market failure. In a completely free market for goods and services questionable payments *cannot* occur. Why? Because in such markets decisions are made between buyers and sellers in the presence of full information, low transactions costs, complete understanding of price and quality, and other competing buyers and sellers. Transactions proposed at off-market prices or quality are immediately apparent for all to see and will be avoided. How much bribery is there, for example, in the interprofessional foreign-exchange market? Virtually none, because the economist's free-market assumptions basically hold true. Violate them—as when central banks impose draconian exchange controls—and watch how quickly questionable payments thrive. This economic perspective suggests that we ought to look for imperfect markets as a root cause of questionable payments around the world. What are some of these imperfections?

Opaque or Ambiguous Rules

In developed and developing countries alike, an important stimulus for QPs is ambiguity in legal and regulatory systems. Virtually all nations have laws against corruption, bribery, and extortion. But in dozens of countries these laws are obscure, untested, or unenforced.

In his famous book *The Italians,* Luigi Barzini describes his country's regulatory structure as a "tropical tangle of statutes, rules, norms, regulations, customs." Barzini quotes a local economist as calculating that "if every tax on the statute books was fully collected, the state would absorb 110 percent of the national income." *Bustarella* is often the only way for a business to cope with this statutory and bureaucratic nightmare. U.S. companies filing tax returns in Italy have a choice: the American way or the Italian way. The Italian way seems easy and inexpensive, but look what happened to hundreds of Italian businessmen in 1994–1995, when political authorities decided to crack down on tax evasion and payoffs. Many people, including some of Italy's most prominent businesspersons, were arrested and charged with corruption. Any manager of an American company following similar practices would, if caught in the net, have hell-to-pay when the news got back to the head office and the SEC.

Statist Regimes

Prospects for making payoffs appear to be brightest in political regimes that concentrate economic, political, and social controls in the hands of the state, whether tribal, militaristic, totalitarian, autocratic, or oligarchic. In statist regimes, after all, those in the seat of power see themselves as dispensers of privileges and exceptions, and civil servants are vested with discretionary authority to grant or withhold permits for almost every kind of commercial activity. In short, the ordinary workings of consensual political processes or free markets cannot be relied upon to safeguard legitimate business interests. Firms need to dispense goodwill or yield to extortion to protect themselves. Research sponsored by the SEC supports this view. In the 1970s an estimated 90 percent of the QPs occurred in nations *not* included in the list of the twenty-three nations, both developed and developing, ranked most free in political rights by the influential Freedom House Comparative Survey.

Cultural Complexity

In some cultures interpersonal behavior is covert; in others it is quite open. In *Beyond Culture,* anthropologist Edward T. Hall finds that in Asia, around the Mediterranean, and in the Middle East, much information is implicitly, rather than explicitly, conveyed. Personal bonds are strong. Great distinctions are made between insiders and outsiders. Ingrained cultural patterns are slow to change.[37] For the American or European business executive psychologically attuned to his or her home environment, these barriers to understanding and communication are formidable. One way to get around the problem is to use "cultural bridges," such as friendly local agents, consultants, or governmental officials who can make things happen.

Of course, not all the services of these cultural bridges involve bribes or influence peddling. Local agents and consultants understand the social, economic, political, and psychological patterns of their countries and regions, and the need for businesspersons to understand these patterns in places like the Middle East is compelling. While the remuneration involved may appear questionable to American observers, it is at least in part a legitimate payment for legitimate services.

Payoff-prone Industries

Some industries, such as those requiring extensive government approvals in order to do business, appear to be more prone to questionable payments than others. The President's Council on Economic Priorities found large-scale bribery to be particularly common among the pharmaceuticals, health care, oil and gas, aerospace, chemicals, rubber, and food industries. Other surveys have added construction, mining, communications, and shipping to the list.

The market structure within which firms operate seems to be central in explaining large-scale QPs. Both the aerospace and petroleum industries are ones in which a relatively small number of firms compete tooth and nail for market share. Because such circumstances may lead to collusion, companies have occasionally coordinated their QP behavior. For instance, the five of the storied "seven sisters" of the oil industry that operate in Italy—British Petroleum, Exxon, Gulf, Mobil, and Shell—appear to have acted in concert, via their trade association, in making contributions to local political parties over the years. In Jamaica, the aluminum producers Alcoa, Reynolds, and Kaiser apparently made coordinated contributions to political groups. And in Mexico, six tire companies made a $420,000 joint payoff to get a price increase approved. The payment was arranged by the Rubber Industry Chamber, a trade association, and was apportioned among the companies according to market share.[38]

Payoff-prone Firms

Independent of the industry in which a firm is involved, the nature of each firm has considerable impact on whether it engages in QPs. Roderick Hills, a former chairman of the SEC, pointed out that "we find in every industry where bribes have been revealed that companies of equal size are proclaiming that they see no need to engage in such practices."[39] Why are some firms clearly more resistant to QPs than others, even within the same industry? One obvious consideration is that international firms, as compared with mainly local firms, seem more susceptible to QPs. International firms tend to be bigger, to have more at stake, and to be subject to more regulation. Individual bribes are usually negligible in value in relation to the firm's overall revenues, costs, and financial resources. By the same token, these firms may be viewed as having a greater ability to pay than purely local firms. International firms may also have unusual opportunities to engage in off-the-books and slush-fund financing.

Competitive Strength

Eric Hoffer, the late homespun philosopher, once said that "power corrupts the few, while weakness corrupts the many." And so it is with QPs. Companies having clearly advanced technology, powerful market positions, and particularly strong product superiority usually find it less necessary to engage in QP behavior than their less fortunate competitors. For example, IBM for many years had the luxury of being able to say "no" to extortionate demands of government officials. Other companies in the same sector appear not to have been nearly so fortunate, at least according to revelations made in the SEC's QP disclosures.

Size of Transactions

For companies that depend heavily on one-shot, big-ticket deals, the pressure for payoffs can be intense. For some companies, satisfactory annual revenues depend on the procurement of just a few big contracts, which are therefore make-or-break transactions. When individual deals are this huge, payoffs represent only a tiny fraction of the overall price and can easily be incorporated into it. And if the company is on the rocks financially and one large contract can spell the difference between survival and disaster, management may be driven to take desperate measures. The pressure gets even stronger during recessions. When business is bad and there is excess production capacity, firms will scramble frantically for sales to maintain output levels.

Inadequate Internal Control

Another critical factor explaining the tendency for firms to engage in QPs is the degree of control exercised by corporate headquarters; tight managerial control and oversight is easiest when affiliates abroad are wholly owned subsidiaries. When affiliates comprise a potpourri of distributors, dealers, suppliers, subcontractors, licensees, agents, consultants, and joint ventures, however, control becomes difficult or impossible. Paul Orrefice, former president of Dow Chemical's U.S. operations, insisted that he was "one-hundred-percent sure no one in Dow has made one payment. . . . I would fire anyone who did,"[40] only to reveal a few months later that the company had made QPs totaling more than $3 million over a six-year period. Why the embarrassing contradiction? Dow's control seems to have been a bit flabby. Whereas total QPs made by the parent itself and its wholly owned subsidiaries amounted to barely $200,000, the remaining $2.9 million in payments were made by partially owned foreign affiliates. QP problems may be less serious with wholly owned subsidiaries whose senior managers are generally citizens of the firm's home country. Even in such situations, however, the subsidiaries often come under heavy political and cost pressures to increase the proportion of local ownership via joint ventures and to use host-country nationals for top management jobs.

Management Indifference

Views on questionable payments among top management differ widely. Some managers consistently refuse to engage in any sort of payoffs what-soever. They have sometimes paid a heavy price, but they seem to consider the cost worthwhile. Others have apparently focused almost exclusively on the bottom line, without worrying very much about how results are achieved.

Senior management's attitude toward QPs evidently determines the over-all climate within an organization. After examining Senate testimony re-garding Lockheed's payoffs in Japan, author Anthony Sampson concluded that, to most of the firm's executives, "Lockheed was [former chairman Daniel J.] Haughton. It was Haughton who inspired Lockheed men to go abroad to sell their planes with single-minded determination. And it was his drive and impatience that pressed them to use whatever hard-selling methods they could employ, including bribery."[41] Such attitudes may be reinforced, in turn, by outside directors on corporate boards who may not care, who allow themselves to be hoodwinked by management, or who adopt a "hear no evil, see no evil" attitude.

Tackling Questionable Payments

What can be done about questionable payments? And by whom? The zero-base option is to do nothing. The logic here is that QPs are such an entrenched part of global business that it is naïve to expect any real improvement. We might also argue that the storm of publicity and com-motion, coupled with increased legal scrutiny, has already helped curb some of the most blatant cases.

The largest constituency for doing nothing (besides the lucky QP-recipi-ents) seems to be the stockholding public itself. An SEC-sponsored statis-tical study of trading in the common shares of seventy-five companies, conducted right after the QP disclosures of the 1970s, detected only faint signs of market reaction. Most shareholders seem bored by the whole thing, having overwhelmingly rejected proposals, placed on proxy ballots in one company after another, to guide management in this area.[42]

Further, there are some powerful arguments for at least tolerating, if not necessarily condoning, QPs. For one thing, as many businesspersons are quick to point out, operating globally requires at least some exercise of the old maxim "When in Rome, do as the Romans do." Another rationale heard frequently from business and labor leaders is that QPs by U.S. firms that win orders away from foreign firms undoubtedly pay at least short-term dividends in income and jobs. Probably the most sophisticated defense for QPs is that, in societies with severe structural barriers to free markets, QPs may actually improve the functioning of the system. That is, in countries where social systems are systemically chaotic, such as in Russia today, a certain amount of corruption may be the one thing that makes the system work tolerably well. And in a very poor developing country, grease payments may arguably produce a more equitable distribution of income. So QPs can be socially useful insofar as they help to remove obstacles that themselves distort efficiency.

But too often those who defend QPs underrate their enormous costs and destructive consequences. QPs raise the cost and lower the quality of goods and services. They help to preserve existing class and other discriminatory relationships, to the detriment of society at large. Perhaps most seriously, tolerance of corruption at high levels inevitably fosters broader lawlessness and can undermine the moral fabric of a society. In concluding his book *Asian Drama,* the late Swedish economist and Nobel laureate Gunnar Myrdal observed that in developing nations, corruption paves the way for authoritarian regimes, military takeovers, and totalitarianism. "The extent of corruption has a direct bearing on the stability of governments."[43]

The effects of QPs on firms themselves are equally far-reaching. No doubt executives believe they are advancing corporate interests by spurring sales or protecting assets. Yet payoffs require enormous time and effort invested in what ought to be routine transactions, and thereby consume prodigious amounts of the firm's scarcest single resource—managerial effort. Payoffs also drive up operating costs and, if everybody bribes, often fail to provide the hoped-for advantages. And once a firm reveals a willingness to comply with demands for QPs, it risks being considered an easy mark susceptible to pressure for still more and larger payoffs. Public exposure in a *host* country where the firm operates can cause retaliatory pressure on the company. Public exposure in the firm's *home* country can induce stockholder suits, legal action by regulatory agencies, and outright dismissal both of those directly involved and their bosses. In the minds of many people, these pernicious effects of QPs seem to far outweigh their claimed necessity.

Unilateral National Reform

In the early 1970s SEC investigations, originally directed at corporate nondisclosure of funds used for illegal political campaign contributions in the United States, revealed that over three hundred American companies had made questionable payments to foreigners. The SEC found that U.S. corporations had altered financial records to disguise the use of corporate funds for illegal purposes both domestically and abroad. In failing to record improper payments to foreign officials or in failing to reveal their underlying purpose, companies violated the nation's securities laws. It is against this background that Congress came to view such payments, or bribes, as causing potentially major problems for the United States. In particular, the payments could create embarrassing foreign-policy situations with friendly nations or aggravate the suspicions of nations whose relations with the United States were already strained.

Prior to 1977 the United States had no explicit statutory authority to prosecute corporations and their officers for bribing foreign officials. With the enactment of the Foreign Corrupt Practices Act in that year, however, the United States took a leadership role in the battle against questionable foreign payments. Reflecting the findings of SEC investigations earlier in the decade, the act's provisions focused not just on foreign payments themselves, but also on corporate accounting and record-keeping procedures.

The bribery provisions prohibit corporations from transferring or promising to transfer money or gifts to a government official, a politician, or agent of another country to promote the corporation's own business dealings or to influence that country's laws. Minor "grease" payments are still permitted; payments to policemen and customs officers, for example, are excluded from the act because their duties, unlike those of more senior government officials, are "merely ministerial or clerical." The FCPA's requirement of "corrupt" motives or intent has created some uncertainty concerning what acts come under the law and constitute bribery, but it is nonetheless clear that whether or not a given transaction takes place is less important than the corporation's intent to influence foreign officials through it.

The accounting and record-keeping provisions of the FCPA were drafted as amendments to the Securities and Exchange Act of 1934. The wording requires only that the company keep books and records in "reasonable detail" and that the books "accurately and fairly" reflect the company's transactions. By increasing the accuracy and credibility of corporate records, Congress hoped to renew confidence in public corporations.

The FCPA creates both criminal and civil liability. The Department of Justice is authorized to conduct both criminal and civil investigations, though most of its investigations have been directed at alleged civil violations of the act. In addition, the SEC is authorized to bring actions against companies for civil violations such as the failure to maintain adequate internal accounting. The designated penalties for violating the FCPA include both fines and imprisonment (a maximum of five years).

The fines can be substantial. As part of a guilty plea for making a $1.5 million payment to an Egyptian official to facilitate the sale of three C-130H aircraft, Lockheed paid $24 million—roughly three times its profit on the sale. Goodyear Tire & Rubber was fined $250,000 after pleading guilty to offering bribes in the guise of advertising expenses to an Iraqi trading company. Vitusa was fined $100,000 for paying $50,000 to a government official in the Dominican Republic to obtain the remainder of the $3 million owed to the company under a contract for powdered milk.[44]

Given the FCPA restrictions on business conduct abroad, U.S. companies have had to use their ingenuity to compete effectively against foreign companies not subject to similar restrictions, especially in markets where the rules of competition are unclear or still evolving. For example, in order to help in its effort to gain access to the Chinese insurance market, Chubb set up a $1 million program to teach insurance at Shanghai University. Boeing undertook a $100 million program to train Chinese aircraft-maintenance workers in the company's technology. IBM donated $25 million in computer equipment and software to Chinese universities. Other companies have used training visits to the United States. Visits to Disney World and Niagara Falls are highly prized, and per diem reimbursements for expenses can, for frugal trainees, add up to a large bonus by home-country standards. Some companies have also used local agents abroad, though this course of action may generate its own risks under the FCPA: "One U.S. consumer products company discovered that its Chinese partner paid kickbacks to government officials when the Americans left the room. If the U.S.

company legitimately didn't know, it would not be liable [under the FCPA] as long as it fired the agent when it found out."[45]

In the area of securities law enforcement, in 1996 the SEC opened a case against Montedison, one of the big Italian firms caught up in the corruption scandals, alleging that the firm had filed false financial statements between 1988 and 1993 fraudulently misstating its financial condition by concealing over $400 million in bribes.[46] The argument was that if a firm had its shares traded in the U.S. public markets (in this case, in the form of American Depository Receipts, or ADRs), then it has to be held to the same disclosure standards as domestic firms and therefore come under SEC jurisdiction.

Elsewhere in the world, the U.S. approach to QPs, especially its provisions for criminal prosecutions, has won few friends. Many have argued that this approach, aside from involving a dubious extension of American law to sovereign foreign countries, may present extraordinarily difficult enforcement problems and make it harder for U.S. firms to compete effectively with less scrupulous foreign firms—especially since no other nation except Canada has followed the American lead. Charles Bowen, former chairman of Booz Allen and Hamilton (a management-consulting firm) reportedly characterized proponents of the criminalization approach as "a bunch of pipsqueak moralists running around trying to apply U.S. puritanical standards to other countries."[47] Even if so, QPs are objectionable to most Americans and generally considered to be an inappropriate use of corporate assets.

A few other countries besides Canada have also begun to take aggressive action. For example, Japan undertook a number of anticorruption measures in the mid-1990s. A meeting of vice-ministers in 1995 decreed that civil servants could no longer invest in companies that come under their supervision. The decree was a direct reaction to the revelation that a senior Finance Ministry official had helped a health-foods company obtain an import license for a Chinese herbal tonic. But the vice-ministers' action also complemented earlier measures taken by the Fair Trade Commission in order to prevent bid rigging on public contracts. In this context, their decree was part of a more fundamental effort to deal with the highly publicized spate of bribery, bid-rigging, and other scandals involving public officials in Japan. As part of this same effort, Japanese officials involved in public procurement were required to undergo training on how to avoid corruption, and each ministry was required to submit a list of sensitive positions in which bureaucrats might be tempted by bribes.[48]

Korea has also taken aggressive action in response to pervasive corruption. A recent investigation there revealed that thirty-five business groups, including Samsung and Daewoo, gave some $369 million in bribes to former President Roh Tae Woo to obtain specific government contracts. The chairmen of seven major corporations were indicted in December 1995 in President Kim Young Sam's unprecedented frontal assault on corruption. If successful, this effort could help Korea post better growth performance in the years ahead.[49]

Comprehensive International Reform

Many lawyers and business executives have issued a call for comprehensive international reform: the creation and enforcement of stringent laws or agreements that would govern commercial and political corruption in all countries. This approach would avoid the adverse competitive consequences of unilateral action by home countries whose firms encounter pressures to make questionable payments abroad. But there is a potentially fatal flaw in this approach. There is precious little inclination for countries to enact the requisite laws, enter into effective agreements, or even to enforce bribery laws that are already on the books.

The World Trade Organization has made an effort to have stricter anticorruption rules adopted in order to promote greater competition and transparency in government procurement, which accounts for around 10 percent of global output. As the *Financial Times* noted in an editorial, however, such initiatives are helpful but incomplete. The WTO's anticorruption rules now cover only about twenty countries, most of which are already industrialized and are therefore less likely to have significant problems with QPs. Others countries seem reluctant to sign on. "As long as there are willing takers of bribes, there will be enthusiastic givers. Curing the cancer of corporate corruption depends heavily on reform within countries. Increasing privatization should help that process. Removing companies from government control, and requiring them to respond to commercial imperatives, greatly reduces the scope for illicit inducements."[50]

Despite the obvious obstacles to achieving comprehensive reform, former U.S. Trade Representative Mickey Kantor argued that bribery and related practices undermine the integrity of the international trading system and need to be fought in every way possible.[51] The following proposals have received the most attention:

- *Home-country sunshine.* Perhaps no other approach has won more support from government officials than full disclosure. In their speeches on QPs, SEC officials have often quoted the famous maxim of Supreme Court Justice Louis D. Brandeis that "publicity is justly commendable as a remedy for social and industrial disease. Sunlight is said to be the best disinfectant." The SEC has been sold on the prophylactic effects of disclosure. In the SEC's view, business does not welcome payoffs and would be happy to have a defense against the arm twisters of the world. Management should be systematically forced to expose QPs and then to face whatever stockholder suits, public embarrassment, and governmental penalties might follow. Present laws, in fact, require such disclosure.

- *Home-country oversight.* Some have proposed that the QP problem could be adequately managed if corporate boards of directors, auditors, and lawyers took a more activist approach to enforcement. At one point Stanley Sporkin, then chief of the SEC's enforcement division, declared that corporations should have autonomous "business practices officers" charged with blowing the whistle. He also called for an expanded role of auditors in detecting illegal and questionable acts on the part of their clients.[52] Certainly, vigilant boards and truly independent auditors can ease the QP problem, especially in conjunction with more vigorous regulatory enforcement. But there are still more important questions. Costs could be astronomical if, for example, auditors were forced to explore every nook and cranny of their clients' businesses to try to catch all forms of management misconduct.

- *Multilateral regulation.* The limitations inherent in unilateral approaches have prompted calls for international cooperation in dealing with corrupt practices. Almost everyone in the United States likes the international approach. Yet the American effort to export the campaign against bribery isn't finding many buyers abroad. The *Wall Street Journal* has reported that "some foreigners view it as a mixture of woolly minded idealism and hard-headed Yankee guile," and that "there are signs that the search for ways to eliminate payoff competition could become as frustrating as the search for new international rules to govern the use of the seas, which has produced many conferences but few agreements."[53] Besides being unenforceable, any code negotiated, say, under U.N. auspices would be so watered down to gain general acceptance that it would be ineffective. The problem of QPs is a political bombshell everywhere, and most nations seem disposed to let the United States run with this particular hot potato by itself.

• *Collective self-regulation.* To combat corrupt practices, the International Chamber of Commerce (ICC) prepared an international code of conduct more stringent than the laws of most countries. Skeptics see such business codes as "prescriptions for doing nothing," and many believe that QPs will remain a fact of life no matter what such codes say. Others put little stock in codes other than the ones companies are able to formulate for themselves.

• *Corporate self-regulation.* Various techniques are available for internal cleansing—self-regulation by corporate management. Some corporations have established new codes of conduct or reaffirmed old ones that prohibit the use of company funds for political or illegal purposes. Others have improved internal reporting systems and controls by establishing special audit committees composed of outside directors and by adopting stringent policies governing the solicitation, use, and payment of international agents and consultants. Still others have reorganized to gain control of their foreign operations, and asked executives to sign annual pledges that they and, to their knowledge all employees reporting to them, have complied with their firm's policies on questionable payments.

There are signs that international initiatives are picking up steam. The World Bank has implemented procurement rules allowing it to investigate allegations of corruption and to blacklist firms found to be making payoffs in connection with some of its $19 billion in annual financial disbursements—overcoming its traditional position that this would constitute interference in the internal affairs of member countries. According to President James Wolfensohn, people increasingly "know that corruption diverts resources from the poor to the rich, increases the cost of running businesses, distorts public expenditures and deters foreign investors."[54] Meanwhile, the International Monetary Fund has made investigating corruption one of its priorities as well, presumably taking the view that corruption adversely affects economic policies and the reflow of IMF resources into offshore bank accounts. The Organization for Economic Cooperation and Development has been working on an anticorruption proposal that would end tax deductibility of bribes and make bribery a criminal offense, and the Organization of American States has come up with a convention outlawing cross-border bribery and "illicit enrichment" of public officials, complete with investigative protocols and extradition provisions.

Questionable Payments in Banking and Finance

Because banks and securities firms are really no different from other firms doing business domestically and internationally, they tend to be subject to the same kinds of pressures to make QPs. Because firms providing financial services are highly regulated in most national environments, local markets are often imperfect and leave ample room for questionable payments. Problems are most likely to arise in the following areas:

- Procuring operating licenses

- Establishing joint ventures (especially with the government as partner)

- Setting up additional banking or brokerage outlets, ATMs, and other distribution vehicles

- Securing regulatory and supervisory forbearance to avoid crackdowns in problem situations and in the application of safety and soundness policies

- Securing foreign-exchange allocations in cases where exchange controls are applied

- Avoiding certification requirements (for example, as being "fit and proper"), thus enabling firms or bankers to operate in markets from which they would otherwise be excluded

In addition to the above examples, which are similar to those that may arise for any corporation doing business abroad, some special problems arise in the financial-services sector:

- Using financial firms as conduits for questionable payments

- Using QPs to suborn regulatory standards that are needed to prevent the financial system from being contaminated by unscrupulous operators

- Using QPs for kickbacks to relevant government or corporate authorities in an effort to secure financing assignments

Because government agencies both at home and abroad have often turned a blind eye to QPs, financial institutions have grown accustomed to making them with very little difficulty. For instance, the U.S. Export-Import Bank once made more than $50 million in guaranteed loans for a Hughes Aircraft project in Indonesia despite the bank's knowledge of alleged payoffs.[55] And there has occasionally been a distinct coziness between the big accounting firms and the companies they audit, with auditors failing to report unusual items and sometimes even transmitting QPs on behalf of clients. Much more troubling, however, are the financial institutions that serve as vendors of secrecy, as havens for slush funds and money laundering, and as repositories used by the recipients of QPs. It is only because financial institutions are willing to take on these roles that most forms of QPs are able to continue. Since QPs are typically either illegal or otherwise unacceptable, few would withstand public disclosure and the scrutiny such disclosure would entail.

Is There a Solution?

Our discussion of the dimensions of international corporate payoffs—in terms of the home and host countries, industries, and firms involved—leads us back again to the root of QPs: the inability of markets to work well. Efficient markets need a large number of buyers and sellers competing with each other. They also need low transactions costs, good information, freedom from artificial impediments, and products that are easily identified and priced so that people know what they are buying and selling and can tell when they are getting value for money. We have concluded that QPs are invariably the product of things that *prevent* markets from working efficiently. Sometimes there are only a few sellers trying frantically to peddle their wares. Sometimes there are only a few buyers in a given market, or only a single one, as in government procurement. Many regulatory mechanisms also interfere with free markets; for example, tariffs, taxes, foreign-exchange and price controls, and labor restrictions. Sometimes language or sociocultural barriers make it difficult or even impossible to do business. All of these factors give rise to the incentive structures that underlie QPs.

What this analysis suggests is that the various proposals for dealing with QPs are no better than second-best solutions to the problem. The proposals do no more than raise obstacles to QPs—plug holes in the dike—without attacking the heart of the problem: improving the ability of markets to do their job. To be sure, some obstacles to market efficiency (like language or cultural differences) can never be eliminated; to the extent that such obstacles remain, middlemen will continue to have opportunities to exploit monopoly positions. And some obstacles, like restrictions on controlled substances, may be viewed as socially and economically necessary; QPs that undermine these restrictions should rightly be attacked head-on. But aside from such cases, we are convinced that the real solution to the payoff problem fundamentally hinges on removing barriers to market efficiency.

The need to prohibit QPs has to be balanced against the need to promote and maintain legitimate, socially useful business practices, especially in countries with emerging financial markets. In formulating policies on QPs, the unique circumstances of each country or market must be taken into account in the short term, keeping in view the longer-term goals of eliminating QPs altogether and of increasing economic efficiency. Such policies should also be realistic. Since penny-ante grease is probably ineradicable, attention should focus instead on curbing the most egregious kinds of QPs, such as major bribery and extortion. And since unenforced or unenforceable laws create little more than contempt, we ought to accept that nations and corporations alike are limited in the degree to which they can control what people do.

Nothing about QPs is simple or straightforward—neither the problem itself nor its potential solution. This hardly means that patent remedies like criminalization cannot be effective to some degree. But such remedies by themselves offer only partial solutions that may backfire or create a false sense of security. Real progress is likely to come only through a complex and gradual process that attacks both the symptoms and the root causes of the disease. Unfortunately, a war fought on many fronts appeals to nobody, least of all to politicians. Firms and their managers and employees are therefore likely to run into QPs well into the foreseeable future.

Financial Secrecy
and Money
Laundering

■

Private banking has developed into an important segment of global finance—a very special, very discreet, very lucrative niche. The clients are typically wealthy members of their countries' economic or, in some cases, political elites, and they usually want their money—often tens or hundreds of millions of dollars—to remain safe and out of sight. For a private banker, the prestige and financial rewards are substantial, but so is the potential risk, some of which concerns clients. Private clients are looking for someone they can really trust with their money, someone in whom they can confide important and confidential financial and personal information, and someone who can manage the money for them conservatively and well. Their real interest is in protecting wealth, rather than aggressively increasing it, and that includes keeping it from unduly coming to the attention of tax authorities.

There are many wealthy but corrupt and crooked people out there—some of them very elegant. Private bankers have to steer clear of the worst without asking too many questions of the best. Most good private clients would pull their money out in a flash if they thought their bank was willing to take in other people's dirty money. They certainly don't want the firm to be subject to an investigation that might reveal their own account relationships or threaten the stability of the firm itself. But it's often hard to know for sure where money came from.

Financial Secrecy

Financial secrecy—the nondisclosure of financial information concerning individuals, firms, financial institutions, and governments—represents an integral part of the market for all banking and financial services, fiduciary relationships, and regulatory structures. It also constitutes a product that has intrinsic value and that can be bought and sold separately or in conjunction with other financial services.[1]

The Demand for Financial Secrecy

A variety of services, both legal and illegal, is available to people willing to pay for the assured nondisclosure of financial information:

- *Personal financial secrecy* usually remains in substantial compliance with applicable laws and regulations. Many countries have long-standing traditions of banking confidentiality. Indeed, it is often regarded as a cornerstone of individual liberty.

- *Business financial secrecy* involves withholding financial information from competitors, suppliers, employees, creditors, and customers. Release of such information is undertaken only in a tightly controlled manner and, where possible, in a way that benefits the enterprise. Financial information is proprietary and capitalized in the value of a business to its shareholders.

- *Tax evasion* is a classic source of demand for financial secrecy. Some people are exposed to high levels of income taxation. Others are hit by confiscatory wealth taxes or death taxes. Still others feel forced by high indirect taxes or by quasi-taxes like price controls to escape into the underground economy. And some people believe that the only fair tax is none at all.[2] Tax evasion requires varying degrees of financial secrecy in order to work.

- *Capital flight* refers to an unfavorable change in the risk/return profile associated with assets held in a particular country sufficient to warrant active redeployment of assets in another jurisdiction with a more favorable profile. It usually involves significant conflict between the objectives of asset holders and their governments. It may or may not violate the law. It is always considered by the authorities to be undesirable.[3]

- *Proceeds from bribery and corruption,* discussed in the last chapter, need to be kept secret as they are received, and kept that way until the heat is off. Corrupt former public officials from many developing countries use the proceeds from secret assets to live out their retirements in luxury in places like Cap d'Antibes or Monaco. If the cover of secrecy is blown and a successor government gets its hands on such officials, very bad things can happen to them.

- *Criminals,* such as drug traffickers, not only accumulate large amounts of cash but regularly deal in a variety of financial instruments and foreign currencies. So do gun runners and terrorists. And there is organized and unorganized crime—robbery, burglary, theft, illegal gambling, prostitution, loan sharking, protection, extortion, and other forms of racketeering.[4] All of these activities require ways to launder funds and eliminate paper trails that might be taken as evidence of criminal activity. Money needs to disappear and stay that way.

No matter what the motivation of the people involved, the value of secrecy depends on the probability of disclosure and on what may happen if the secrecy cover is blown, or what economists call the *damage function.* Damage can range from execution, prison, exile, and political ostracism to confiscation of assets, fines, incremental taxes, social opprobrium, and familial tension. Avoidance of damage is the secrecy seeker's goal. Since damage resulting from exposure usually is a matter of probabilities, the attitude toward the risk of exposure is a critical factor in how this benefit is valued by an individual.

Most people agree that personal and business demands for financial secrecy are fully legitimate and that capital flight is mainly the symptom of misguided macroeconomic policies that encourage people to safeguard their hard-earned assets abroad. Most people also agree that the demand for hard-core criminal secrecy, whether to launder drug money or to hide the proceeds of organized crime or the stash of corrupt public officials, is illegitimate. In between are a couple of debatable motivations for the demand for financial secrecy, notably tax evasion and political corruption.

Tax Havens. A dramatic example of the sensitivity of the tax issue involved the estimated $10.7 billion flow of German investment funds into the Luxembourg bond market following announcement that a 10 percent withholding tax would be imposed beginning in January 1989. Luxembourg levies no withholding tax on interest and maintains strict banking secrecy. As German investors sought to escape the new withholding tax, the price of Euro-DM issues sold in Luxembourg skyrocketed. In early 1989 it was actually cheaper for PepsiCo than it was for the German government to borrow in deutsche Marks. The government ultimately decided to allow "coupon washing," which enabled investors to escape the new tax by selling bonds prior to the interest-payment date and by buying them back immediately afterwards.[5]

In the early 1990s Germany, hard pressed by the cost of reunification, again went after interest income with a 30 percent withholding tax at source, triggering an estimated $215 billion capital outflow, again mostly to Luxembourg. Helping their clients to flee the tax became, once again, good business for the German banks' Luxembourg affiliates. This time, however, the German tax authorities reacted much more aggressively, investigating a number of banks for aiding and abetting tax evasion. There was a nationally televised raid on the Dresdner Bank branches in Dortmund and Frankfurt. Hypo-Bank in Munich was charged with helping customers avoid taxes. Even Merrill Lynch's Frankfurt operation came under investigation.

The first conviction in the investigation of eight thousand Dresdner Bank clients came in February 1996: a German dealer in sausage casings was fined DM 1.3 million and sentenced to almost four years in jail for evading DM 6.3 million in taxes. Using an account with the Luxembourg branch of the Dresdner Bank and following the bank's advice, he had submitted false invoices in the name of a nonexistent company registered in Panama.[6] In addition, the father and the tax adviser of tennis star Steffi Graf were jailed after having posted $14.4 million in back taxes allegedly owed on Steffi's income of some $177 million since 1983, on which only $7.2 million in taxes had been paid. Her colleague Boris Becker was smarter, having long ago moved to Monaco to escape Germany's punishingly high taxation.

The most entertaining investigation involved Commerzbank, which was blackmailed in 1995 by a disgruntled computer consultant in possession of a stolen list of 1,500 clients with Luxembourg accounts. He demanded DM 5 million to keep the list under wraps. With good cooperation between the bank and the police, the blackmailer was duly tracked down and arrested, and the list was recovered. Picking up where the blackmailer left off, prosecutors then turned the list over to German fiscal authorities for investigation of tax evasion, causing consternation among all, confessions among the meek,[7] a search for higher-quality secrecy among the bold, and renewed calls by German authorities for intra-EU tax harmonization in order to eliminate Luxembourg's role as a tax haven. Former EU President Jacques Delors responded ominously, "We will deal with Luxembourg when the time comes."

The effectiveness of the aggressive German probes of tax evasion remained in question. Some investors turned themselves in, hoping for leniency, and indeed the banks' Luxembourg business appeared to have fallen off a bit. Prosecutors, meantime, say that building cases takes time and effort, in the Commerzbank case involving over 40,000 customers and bank employees.[8]

The Swiss are special. Where's an honest tax evader to run? The Swiss banks stand ready to be of service; in a 1993 plebiscite the Swiss rejected participation in a European economic area affiliated with the EU. Secrecy still protects the accounts of nonresidents evading foreign taxes. The Swiss franc has looked rather strong against the deutsche Mark, which has come under pressure because of the uncertainty regarding the future of European monetary union and the value of the prospective EU currency that is slated to replace the DM—with Swiss long-term interest rates in mid-1996 some 2 percent below equivalent German interest rates. Perhaps coincidentally, German banks have targeted private banking in Switzerland as an area for rapid expansion.[9]

The future may not be so rosy, however. The Swiss federal prosecutor, Carla del Ponte, has called for an end to banking secrecy in the case of suspected evasion of other countries' taxes. "If we do not make tax evasion illegal, we cannot distinguish between tax evasion money and money that is being laundered," said the controversial prosecutor. "That set off alarm bells at many private banks, because a large part of their clientele is believed to be high-earning professionals who avoid high tax rates in their home countries by directing a portion of their income to a Swiss bank."[10] In del Ponte's view, however, the biggest problem is not with the banks but with nonbank secrecy vendors like finance companies, trustees, fund managers, and even gas stations that offer foreign-exchange services as a sideline. "Some banks have set up finance companies to handle deposits they can no longer accept."[11] Indeed, it is estimated that Swiss accounts still hold some $400 billion in drug money, and virtually all known cases of U.S. insider trading have involved Swiss financial institutions of some kind.[12]

The battle between Swiss authorities and the financial community is ongoing. An amendment proposed in 1994 would have obligated Swiss banks to report suspicious clients to the authorities. But the Swiss Bankers Association successfully opposed the amendment, arguing that it duplicated banking rules that already existed and would lead to needless bureaucracy, higher compliance costs, and greater laxity. The association also noted that in the year since Swiss banks obtained the right (but not the obligation) to report suspicious clients to the authorities, twenty-six such reports had been filed in the canton of Zurich alone, which led to nine criminal prosecutions.[13] But Swiss authorities have persisted. In an attempt to strengthen and broaden a 1994 law that enabled, but did not require, banks to report suspicious transactions, the Swiss cabinet passed in 1996 a draft law expanding the existing one in three ways. First, the coverage of the draft law was expanded to include not only banks, but any institutions or individuals responsible for managing funds. Second, rather than simply being permitted to report suspicious transactions, institutions and individuals covered by the draft law would be legally obligated to report such transactions. Third, in addition to the reporting requirement, these institutions and individuals would be required to maintain proper records and to freeze suspect accounts.[14] Whatever the outcome of this skirmish, the battle will certainly continue.

Swiss banks also had a role in the dealings of Imelda Marcos, the favorite example of those citing questionable political activity as a source of demand for financial secrecy. U.S. juries and courts awarded ten thousand Philippine plaintiffs (many of whom signed on with no evidence of any claim) about $1.9 billion—the largest personal injury award in history—against Ferdinand Marcos, to be collected from assets the late president had presumably secreted away in Switzerland. Unable to make a criminal case that would lead to Swiss disclosure, a U.S. appellate court judge decided to go after the U.S. assets of Crédit Suisse and Swiss Bank Corporation to satisfy some $475 million in Marcos assets covered by the award. This move spontaneously extended the court's jurisdiction from Los Angeles and Honolulu, where the case was heard, to Manila and Switzerland and finally back to the United States. The case was contested by the Philippine government, representing sixty-five million citizens, all of whom had presumably been damaged by the Marcos regime. Imelda Marcos, appealing a twenty-four-year prison sentence for graft, offered to return some of the money voluntarily to obtain immunity from prosecution. Caught in the middle were the Swiss banks. A Zurich court ruled that the two banks place the funds in escrow in Manila pending a final ruling by a Philippine court as to ownership, a ruling that was appealed by both banks. Swiss officials were quoted as saying, "Any effort by United States courts to enforce the order through imposition of sanctions against the banks would conflict with Swiss sovereignty, international law and Swiss criminal law."[15]

The Supply of Financial Secrecy

As with the demand for secrecy, the supply of secrecy-oriented financial services encompasses a complex patchwork of intermediaries, conduits, and assets that provide varying degrees of safety from unwanted disclosure.[16] According to a Citibank estimate, the world's private wealth amounts to $15.45 trillion, about half of which is in the United States, $3.1 trillion in Europe, and $3.4 trillion in Japan, with smaller but rapidly growing pools of wealth in emerging-market countries.[17] Somewhat less than half this amount is in liquid form. Private wealth can be classified into onshore financial assets, offshore financial assets, and physical assets held either onshore or offshore.

Onshore assets. Bank deposits and certificates, cashier's checks, securities of public or private issuers, and interests in privately held or family enterprises are standard forms of onshore assets. All normally yield market rates of return yet provide the asset holder with some degree of protection from unwanted disclosure. Traditional banking practice in most countries provides confidentiality with respect to unauthorized inquiries, which gives adequate protection from disclosure for "personal" and "business" needs. But once the law gets involved—whether in civil, tax, or criminal matters—much of this protection is lost.

Using existing legal procedures, the state can force disclosure not only in criminal prosecutions, but also in civil cases concerning divorce, creditors, inheritance, and taxes. Although a certain amount of added protection against discovery can be obtained through cash or through bearer certificates of various types, there is the added risk of theft, loss, and accidental destruction. Onshore beneficial ownership—placing financial assets in the names of friends, associates, or family members—can also provide greater protection against discovery, assuming the third parties can be trusted and will not themselves face legal or other costs as a result. Shell companies and even legitimate businesses can also be used to hide assets.

Offshore assets. Offshore assets may offer a good deal more secrecy because national sovereignty halts at the border. Extraterritorial investigation requires the satisfaction of specific conditions that have been negotiated between governments. As with onshore assets, offshore assets can take various forms, each of which has its own benefits and risks. Bank deposits may be made abroad, preferably in jurisdictions that will serve as tax havens. Foreign equities and debt instruments may provide similar security but may also be subject to host-country withholding taxes. Disclosure of ownership may be possible, too, at the request of the home country. Bearer certificates, beneficial ownership, and foreign shell companies provide added protection and increase the complexity of any future paper chase. In all cases, the attributes of the host country—judged by its history, traditions, and proneness to corruption—are of critical importance in determining whether secrecy is apt to be maintained.[18]

An alternative to the financial secrecy sought in the domestic environments of other countries is provided by offshore assets. These assets may be held in the form of bank deposits in Euro-banking centers such as New York, London, Singapore, Panama, the Cayman Islands, and Luxembourg.[19] All provide substantial exemption from taxation for nonresidents as well. If deposits are made in the offshore branches of domestic banks or in foreign banks that do business domestically, however, the secrecy of the assets may be compromised; authorities may be able to force disclosure through the domestic entity. Deposits in offshore branches of foreign banks that do *not* do business domestically may avoid this problem, but such institutions could prove more risky. Another form of offshore assets is provided by Eurobonds, available in bearer form, which can be purchased by individuals at retail. Offshore shell companies and beneficial-ownership structures can be used to draw the veil further over offshore assets.

All sellers of financial secrecy, whether individuals or financial institutions, have an important stake in limiting disclosure as far as possible to avoid damaging, perhaps irreparably, the value of what they have to sell. Similarly, governments use strict secrecy laws and blocking statutes to support their banks in generating real economic gains from private banking activities in the form of employment, income, and taxes.

Physical assets. Standard forms of physical assets include collectibles, precious metals and stones, other forms of tangible property, and banknotes (domestic or foreign) secreted away in walls, mattresses, safe-deposit boxes, and holes in the ground. Physical assets may also be held offshore, consigned to an individual or an institution. All such assets provide effective secrecy as long as they remain undiscovered, but they are at risk of theft, fraud, extortion, and physical damage.

Market Distortions and Financial Secrecy

Taxes, exchange controls, interest-rate controls, price controls, and trade barriers all give rise to economic incentives for the formation of parallel markets intended to avoid or evade them. Although these markets are often very narrow and inefficient, they are sometimes highly profitable.[20] Public procurement without an open and competitive bidding process; the awarding of permits to do business; and the markets for police protection, other public services, and, of course, for controlled substances such as alcoholic beverages and drugs share similar ills. The symptoms are familiar enough— smuggling, the emergence of domestic and cross-border black markets, tax evasion, bribery, and the corruption of public officials. The best way of profiting from such market inefficiencies is to find the most heavily distorted national economies and then ferret out viable ways to do business in them. The obvious choices are countries bent on pursuing misguided macroeconomic policies using direct controls, often with heavily overvalued currencies, where many public and private transactions are undertaken far removed from transparent markets. Bribery and corruption have always thrived in such environments because market inefficiencies and prohibitions generate more than enough profits to support even extortionate payoffs.

Secrecy-seeker's Surplus

While secret domestic and physical financial assets are generally available to anyone, many types of offshore assets that may be less susceptible to disclosure may be less accessible to some people. Lack of information and financial sophistication, exchange controls, inertia, fear of getting caught, and the size of the required transactions are some factors that inhibit access to some of the best secrecy alternatives available around the world. These factors lead to considerable market segmentation, which in turn gives rise to both constraints and profit opportunities in the international secrecy business.

"List prices" such as bank interest rates, bond yields, and equity returns are established by broad market forces that extend well beyond seekers of secrecy. The returns and costs involved in making such investments secretly may well incur an opportunity cost on the secrecy seeker. The net returns may nonetheless be higher than what individuals would have been willing to sacrifice in order to achieve the degree of financial secrecy actually obtained. They thus enjoy an unearned benefit, which economists call *secrecy seeker's surplus* (SSS).

Financial products specifically tailored to the secrecy market involve substantially higher opportunity costs and hence smaller SSS than other investments. Anonymous bank accounts abroad, for example, may involve high fees and low interest rates, and otherwise have high opportunity costs. Yet even these are in large part "list priced" so that, despite the expense, much of the SSS may remain intact. Not so, however, in the case of custom-tailored secrecy services whose prices are set largely through bargaining. Secrecy vendors try to ascertain how much their products are worth in view of the apparent motivations of the individual secrecy seeker. Vendors adjust their asking price accordingly, after which there may be some negotiation before a final agreement is reached. Vendors will never, of course, threaten to breach the confidential relationship, since any such threat would seriously and perhaps fatally impair the value of their products. In the final negotiated price, much of the SSS may evaporate, drawn off by the vendor.

There are widely divergent secrecy products and vendors, many of whom compete with one another. Because a few vendors have products with no good substitutes, however, demand for such products may well be inelastic. Some traditional secrecy products (gold, dummy companies, holes in the ground) are easily available in some places but less so elsewhere. Others have been built up over the generations as secure repositories and can therefore command high premiums. But high premiums also attract competitors, whose entry may alter the structure of the market. It is probably safe to conclude that higher levels of secrecy involve successively greater degrees of monopoly power in the organization and competitive structure of the market for financial secrecy. Needless to say, many sellers of secrecy make out very well indeed.

Buyers, Sellers, Market Equilibrium

Like any other financial service, secrecy is bought and sold in an active market defined by supply and demand characteristics not dissimilar from those of other financial markets. Holders of financial assets, broadly defined, are generally thought to be driven by considerations related primarily to the size of risks and returns. The behavioral characteristics of asset holders are thoroughly addressed in modern portfolio theory. Beyond this, investor behavior may also be influenced by a concern for confidentiality regarding the nature, location, and composition of financial or other assets that comprise a portfolio.

If confidentiality is not a free good, it must be "purchased" by putting together a portfolio of assets (or a single asset) that yields the desired level of nondisclosure. So one cost of confidentiality to asset holders requiring secrecy is the difference between the expected yields on their confidential portfolios and the yields on the benchmark portfolios these same individuals would assemble if confidentiality were not a consideration.

Besides the cost of confidentiality that may be imbedded in the differential expected real returns on assets, there is also the matter of differential risk. It is likely that portfolios of assets with greater degrees of financial confidentiality may also be more risky. For example, assets may have to be held directly or indirectly in certain countries, resulting in increased foreign-exchange or country risk. Or the portfolio may be forced into a configuration that is susceptible to increased market risk. Various ways of hedging risk, including the ability to diversify or shift risk by means of futures and options markets, may not be available to portfolios subject to a high degree of confidentiality. One could argue that the degree of risk, driven by the correlations of expected future returns on the assets contained in the portfolio, will tend to increase with the degree of confidentiality imbedded in that portfolio.

Conventional views on the creation of efficient portfolios in modern portfolio concepts can easily be adapted to take confidentiality into account. An efficient portfolio is one that maximizes investor returns relative to a risk constraint or that minimizes risk relative to a particular return target. The basic elements in the design of efficient portfolios are the individual's attitude toward risk and the risks and returns available in various asset markets. What happens when one incorporates a concern for confidentiality? Asset holders should be willing to accept a reduced rate of return or be willing to accept a higher level of risk. From a risk/return perspective they will be worse off. But the welfare gains from the enhanced degree of confidentiality may well outweigh the welfare losses incurred in the risk/return dimension. An optimum combination can be defined once the individual's preferences in each of the three dimensions, as well as the availability and cost of alternatives in the market, are known.

Beyond portfolio effects, charges levied by suppliers of secrecy can add to the cost of secrecy. Banking fees may be raised for asset holders known to be driven by the secrecy motive. Transactions may have to be routed in clandestine ways, through narrow markets with wide spreads, or through inefficient conduits, any of which will increase transaction costs. Foreign-exchange transactions, perhaps repeated several times or involving black markets, may add further costs. People may have to be bribed. Third parties, beneficial owners, and shell companies may have to be used to enhance secrecy, all of which produce additional costs. Since many of the counterparties in such transactions know the game very well, they may not be shy about pricing their services. Such charges must be taken into account in determining the cost of secrecy.

Secret Agents in Pinstripes

Agency costs create an additional dilemma for the secrecy-seeking asset holder. An agency relationship exists whenever an investor delegates decision-making authority to the manager of a discretionary account. If such a relationship exists, there will be monitoring and bonding costs such as finding the right person to run secret money and then watching from a safe distance to determine how he or she performs. These costs tend to be financial, although there may also be a divergence between the agent's decisions and ones that would maximize the principal's welfare. Usually, however, contracts between principals and agents provide appropriate incentives for the agent to make decisions that will maximize the principal's welfare, given existing market uncertainties.

In standard agency relationships, agents have to interpret investors' wishes and carry them out as best they can. But interpretation of these wishes is not always easy, which may lead to serious disputes later. In addition, the investor's objectives may change, either explicitly or implicitly, with the agent being uninformed or poorly advised. Or the investor may psychologically reposition his or her objectives after the fact. If the value of the assets has underperformed an alternative portfolio, for example, the principal may unjustifiably blame the agent. Or the agent may abuse the client's mandate by churning the portfolio or stuffing it with substandard securities the agent no longer wants. Or the agent may simply not be very competent.

The role of agent becomes even more complex when principals demand secrecy. Agents must do all in their power to safeguard secrecy, whether within or, depending upon the character of the services being provided, outside the limits of the law. Any failure to maintain secrecy would, at least in the eyes of the principal, be perceived as a breach of the agent's fiduciary obligations, triggering potentially serious disputes between the two parties and threatening to erode the ongoing value of the agent's confidential financial services.

However, agents also have some leverage against their principals. Ordinarily, agency disputes are settled through arbitration or civil suits. But how can the secrecy seeker take the agent to court? Not only is a foreign country usually involved, but the jurisdiction of its courts may not be well defined. Any attempt to invoke legal process would, moreover, compromise the very secrecy the client is seeking to protect. Agents therefore acquire a certain immunity from the sort of redress usually available to asset holders confronted by agent misconduct. Although agents might therefore be tempted to abuse the agency relationship and to enrich themselves at the expense of their clients, such abuse could also expose agents to other types of sanctions such as physical punishment—or worse.

An interesting example in 1996 involved a Swedish foreign exchange scam that victimized large numbers of ethnic Chinese. Fairbank, an investment firm not authorized to undertake foreign exchange trading but affiliated with Pagoda, a British company that was (at the time Pagoda was under investigation by the U.K. Serious Fraud Office), placed ads in Chinese-language newspapers for entry-level currency traders. Almost all applicants were accepted, and two weeks into the training program were told to place Skr 50,000 with the firm in order to gain experience by trading for their own account—money often borrowed from friends and relatives—with the inevitable losses made up by commissions from pulling in other investors. After the scam was revealed, surprisingly few of the investors came forward. Investigators suspected that most of the money they lost was undeclared income, enabling Fairbank and Pagoda to exploit their clients and employees.[21]

The central question is whether the quasi-immunity attributable to secrecy influences the behavior of the agent. To be sure, this quasi-immunity provides a strong incentive for agents to maximize their own welfare. But clients who demand highly confidential services are, in general, fully prepared to pay any normal agency costs that come with secrecy, as long as there are no large unaccountable losses. And the competition that secrecy vendors face from other vendors, coupled with their traditions of prudence and competence, tends to impose constraints on abusive behavior. Still, this problem puts a real premium on selecting an agent. Careful selection can minimize but not eliminate the possibility that a "secret agent" will take undue advantage of his quasi-immunity from legal sanctions.

Roberto Polo

Roberto C. Polo was a founder and head of a New York money-management firm, Private Asset Management Group (PAM), which handled funds primarily for Europeans and Latin Americans seeking nontaxable investments. He was sued in 1987 by his clients for misappropriating some $130 million. It was alleged that the high-living and prominent figure in New York and European social and art-collecting circles had diverted the funds to his own accounts in order to support his extravagant lifestyle. The majority of the assets came from personal holding companies based in the Cayman Islands for investment by PAM in time deposits at banks.[22]

As early as May 1984 Polo's former office manager, Ramona Colón, suspected that all was not as it should be. Apparently at around the same time that Polo bought an impressive town house in New York City, he had transferred from his clients' deposits a sum roughly equivalent to the purchase price. The funds went to an account named ITKA at Crédit Suisse in the Bahamas, which Colón believed was Polo's own personal account. She began to fear that the financial statements being sent to clients were fraudulent, and that their deposits no longer existed. Her fears increased when her boss began a major cleanup of client files, taking them home in shopping bags and demanding the erasure of all related computer records. When Colón challenged Polo, her duties were curtailed. In May 1986 the firm's operations were transferred to Geneva. By the fall of 1987, even PAM's clients were becoming nervous, wondering how Polo could possibly afford his way of living. After clients' requests to withdraw their funds went unanswered, they sued.

By that time Polo himself was thought to be in France; he had been spotted at a Parisian auction house. Lawyers sought legal help in Geneva to track him down (he was believed to hold Swiss citizenship). Although the legal proceedings in New York were civil, not criminal, Swiss authorities issued an arrest warrant for financial fraud. French police attempted to serve the warrant, but Polo escaped and has not been found. In the meantime his Paris apartment was seized, and a New York state court granted a temporary restraining order barring him from disposing of any assets.[23] Polo's clients had learned a valuable if painful lesson about secretive relationships with agents.

Antonio Gebauer

Antonio Gebauer was a senior New York banker who suddenly resigned in May 1986 from his position with Drexel Burnham Lambert, the now-defunct New York investment bank. He had left Morgan Guaranty Trust Company the previous August in order to help Drexel develop a secondary market for Third World bank loans.[24] At the time, he was under investigation for the unauthorized diversion for his own use of over $4.3 million from six private accounts he was managing at Morgan.

A native of Venezuela, Gebauer had played a significant role in the 1970s in building up Morgan's business in South America, especially Brazil, which was then considered perhaps the most profitable market for commercial lending in the world. Gebauer's own estimates suggested that the bank's outstanding loans to Brazil increased from just $50 million in 1964 to approximately $2 billion in 1984.

In 1981 Gebauer was appointed senior vice president in charge of Morgan's South American business. A year later, he was chosen to act as co-chairman of the advisory committee that U.S. commercial banks set up in an attempt to restructure Brazil's $83 billion foreign debt.[25] His contacts in South America, and especially in Brazil, were at the highest level. His first wife, Fernanda de Souza Querioz, was the stepdaughter of a leading businessman. Her family connections provided the base of a social network that included some of the wealthiest and most powerful people in Latin America. These contacts were useful not only in arranging deals, but also in advising on their quality. Gebauer used this latter asset to the fullest and, judging from the bank's superior loan-loss record in Brazil, was justified in doing so. A key member of the Brazilian-American Chamber of Commerce, of which he was president for a year, he was also named an honorary citizen of Brazil. It is understandable, given this background, that Gebauer should have been a natural choice as private banker to a number of his Brazilian friends and contacts. Unfortunately, he was not as reliable as they might have hoped. Over a period of seven years, he systematically siphoned funds from six accounts under his care.

Central to understanding how Gebauer was able to misappropriate millions of dollars is the nature of the accounts in question and the consequences for the manner in which they were managed. All six accounts involved flight capital (except in certain circumstances, it was illegal for Brazilians to hold accounts abroad).[26] None had been declared to the Brazilian authorities, and all were set up in Panama with a hold-mail arrangement. In such situations, secrecy becomes vitally important, with the result that the client, who must keep a low profile, tends both to grant discretion to the banker to facilitate asset management and to forgo receipt of the usual information, such as bank statements. It thus becomes easy for the banker to move funds and difficult for the client to monitor them. Gebauer appears to have exploited these factors to the full, facilitated by the high degree of trust Morgan placed in its bankers.

Gebauer arranged for other employees to issue unauthorized treasurer's checks drawn on his clients' accounts. These checks averaged over $20,000 each and were issued at a rate of twenty to forty a year from 1976 to 1983. Whenever the account balances fell to uncomfortably low levels (on several occasions to zero), he arranged new short-term loans by the bank to replenish the funds. The loans were renewed forty-six times with approval of other Morgan officers. When one client became suspicious, Gebauer saw to it that more than twenty false bank statements were prepared.

How was he caught? At times a client would ask, on the basis of a false balance provided by Gebauer, for a transfer that exceeded the sum actually available. There would then be a mad scramble to cover the shortfall by other transfers or loans, a task that became far more difficult after Gebauer left Morgan. In the fall of 1985 the inevitable happened: Gebauer was unable to fill the vacuum quickly enough. The client had to be told that the balance he thought was $3 million was in fact just under $2,900. The game was up. The classic principal-agent problem in the presence of secrecy had run its full course.

At first Gebauer's attorney argued that the accusations against him revealed a complete lack of understanding of the way business was done in Latin America. The attorney also noted the importance of discretionary management in dealing with flight capital. This effort to protect his client only served to broaden the scandal, with the Central Bank of Brazil requesting details on the six accounts involved in order to investigate any illegalities. The bank was especially interested because of the country's debt problems and its vulnerability to capital flight. The incident was also highly embarrassing for Morgan, a bank known for its solidity and sobriety. Not only had one of its senior officials managed to misappropriate more than $4 million of clients' funds, but he had taken the funds from offshore accounts, the very existence of which was a delicate matter. It was also embarrassing for Morgan and other banks to be perceived as helping Brazil's elite invest its wealth abroad at the same time that they were so heavily involved in the country's external financial affairs as creditors. That banks were simultaneously performing both functions was common knowledge in the industry, but no bank wanted this dual role to be publicized.

Even if one accepted that Gebauer had discretionary investment authority, the case did not look good for him. He owned a $5.5 million Manhattan cooperative, an apartment in Paris, an East Hampton estate, and one third of a coffee plantation in Brazil. For several years he had lived a lavish lifestyle, been a regular customer of New York antique shops, rare-book agents, and art dealers, and sent his children to the best private schools. Family connections and a senior position in the bank were simply not enough to explain that sort of wealth.

In October 1986 Tony Gebauer pleaded guilty to four felony counts involving bank fraud and tax evasion. He had diverted a total of $8.2 million: $4.3 million from customer accounts, another $1.7 million from other sources, and $2.2 million of interest on the misappropriated funds. In February 1987 he was sentenced (with the words, "You are indeed a Lucifer, a fallen angel of the banking world") to three and a half years in prison and fined $100,000. He also had to make good his debts to the clients and to Morgan, and to meet payments of $6.94 million owed the IRS in unpaid taxes.[27]

Money Laundering

Money laundering can be defined as the process of converting the proceeds of illegal activities—the disclosure of which would trigger financial losses or criminal prosecution—into real or financial assets whose origins are hidden from law-enforcement officials and from society in general. As with secret accounts, the overall objective is to avoid the damage associated with disclosure. Money laundering is, in effect, nothing more than a special global financial-secrecy industry. Although otherwise honest individuals sometimes resort to money laundering in order to evade taxes, exchange controls, and various governmental policies, money laundering has traditionally been associated with organized crime and its proceeds from rackets, protection, prostitution, extortion, gambling, and other illegal activities. But the real growth in the volume of money laundering and its institutionalization at a high level of sophistication has more recently come to be associated with drug trafficking. The laundered proceeds from illegal drug sales alone reportedly amount to some $300 billion, close to the average volume of capital raised per year in the international bond market in the early 1990s.[28] According to a study by the U.S. Customs Service, "We see narcotics organizations now being set up like major corporations, with an operational arm to move the drugs and a financial arm to handle the money."[29] A recent World Bank study "guesstimated" the global total of money laundering at some $500 billion annually, or 2 percent of global GDP, with the total stock of laundered assets exceeding the GDPs of many countries.[30] And a 1997 estimate of global "gross criminal product" went as high as $1 trillion, half of it generated in the United States.

Broadly speaking, then, the goal of money laundering is to permanently conceal the illicit origins of various forms of criminal money, which enables that money to become available in untainted form to the ultimate owners, their families, and associates.

The Laundering Process

Since money laundering converts financial assets from a form whose discovery would lead to confiscation and arrest to a form in which it is safe from discovery, it adds value and must therefore be profitable. During the course of 1985 congressional hearings, one government witness explained that money laundering was

> an extremely lucrative criminal enterprise in its own right. The U.S. Treasury's investigations uncovered members of an emerging criminal class—professional money launderers who aid and abet other criminals through financial activities. These individuals hardly fit the stereotype of an underworld criminal. They are accountants, attorneys, money brokers, and members of other legitimate professions. They need not become involved with the underlying criminal activity themselves except to conceal and transfer the proceeds that result from it. They are drawn to their illicit activity for the same reason that drug trafficking attracts new criminals to replace those who are convicted and imprisoned—greed. Money laundering, for them, is an easy route to almost limitless wealth.[31]

The need to convert currency. The bulk of the illicit funds that are the raw material for money laundering originates as paper currency; the proceeds of illegal activities, including most types of tax evasion (such as "skimming" taxable revenues) are least likely to leave a paper trail if they are in that form. But how does one convert enormous amounts of cash into untraceable and untainted assets?

To understand this problem from the perspective of drug dealers, for example, consider that drugs are almost invariably sold at the retail level for payment in the form of "street money," billions of small-denomination bills from street-level sales in various drug-consuming countries. Currency in small bills is, of course, far bulkier and heavier than money in large bills, and some seizures have involved literally tons of bills. As of 1996, one kilo of cocaine (2.2 pounds) had a street value of roughly $20,000. It might be sold for 666 $10 bills plus 667 $20 bills, which together weigh almost exactly 3 pounds. One million dollars in $20 bills weighs 110 pounds, in $100 bills just 22 pounds. So the drug runner is faced with an initial, very practical problem: how to reduce the volume and weight of narcotics profits for easier manipulation or transportation. Even then, because there are far fewer large-denomination bills in circulation than small-denomination bills, a compact cache of large-denomination bills is much more traceable than the original, bulky cache of small-denomination bills. And there is always the problem of loss or theft. So drug runners place a high premium on converting currency of any denomination into clean money as quickly as possible, whether through domestic or foreign conduits.

Converting currency domestically. Currency conversions undertaken domestically require either large cash deposits with banks that ask no questions or access to cash businesses such as supermarkets, restaurants, and casinos. Law-enforcement authorities see domestic cash conversions as a major focus of their battle against both money laundering and the underlying criminal transactions. The United States, for example, requires banks to complete currency transaction reports (CTRs) for cash deposits in excess of $10,000. This has given rise to the so-called smurf, couriers (often little old ladies) who spend their time visiting banks throughout the country engaging in transactions small enough to avoid the CTR requirement. Smurfs often purchase cashier's checks that do not name the payee. These checks may then, for example, be exchanged a number of times domestically or abroad, most likely as payment for drugs or weapons. Alternatively, the cashier's checks may be transported abroad for cashing or for deposit in a secrecy haven. The banks issuing the cashier's checks also benefit from these dealings; because cashier's checks earn no interest, banks can use the committed funds free of interest until the checks are finally cashed.

Unfortunately for money launderers, the small-scale transactions involved in domestic currency conversions are not well suited to handle large volumes of cash—literally tons in the case of the drug business. Domestic conversions also leave the assets exposed to loss or disclosure unless the domestic banks themselves are crooked or bankers can be bribed to evade reporting requirements and other banking regulations.

Bulk shipments. An alternative to domestic conversions is the physical transportation of banknotes to a foreign jurisdiction, where they can be converted to bankable funds either because no reporting requirements exist or because foreign banks are willing to overlook them. In the absence of exchange controls (so that confidentiality is the only motive for cash as opposed to bank transfers), the rate of exchange legally obtained abroad may be acceptable and (even taking the chance of loss or theft into account) the transactions and information costs involved may also be quite acceptable to the money launderer.

The logistics of bulk shipments from the United States are relatively straightforward. For example, in March 1995 authorities filmed the unloading of 2.5 tons of cocaine from an old Caravelle jet on a makeshift sand runway outside Hermosillo, Mexico, as well as the reloading of some $20 million in small bills destined for the return trip to Colombia. In another example, a Chevrolet Suburban was used to transport a load of small bills to Brownsville, Texas, with a different driver making the trip across the International Bridge into Matamoros, Mexico. Two months later, a similar trip was made in a Tioga camper.[32] And at Benito Juárez Airport in Mexico City, $6.2 million was found hidden inside air conditioners being shipped from the United States to Bogota, Colombia.

Multiple operations. The routes of the more manageable, partially laundered cash vary substantially from one case to the next. Sometimes the criminals will want the money to remain in domestic currency. Alternatively, they may want to transfer the money to an offshore haven. Or they may want a portion of the currency converted into the local currency of the country out of which they operate. According to a statement submitted during congressional hearings in the mid-1980s,

> these launderers carry on a number of activities at one time. They arrange for the deposit of illicit cash into domestic financial institutions; arrange for the transportation or delivery of currency into or out of the U.S.; they may buy U.S. dollars in exchange for Colombian pesos; buy pesos in exchange for dollars; buy and sell both Colombian banking instruments as well as U.S. cashier's checks, personal checks or corporate checks; manipulate U.S. domestic narcotics profits from one U.S. bank

account to another; arrange for disguised wire transfers of funds from the U.S. to relatively secure havens such as Panama, the Cayman Islands and Switzerland; set up sham foreign corporations. . . . Sometimes all these things are happening at the same time.[33]

The U.S. dollar is the predominant currency—whether as paper currency, traveler's checks, cashier's checks, or other monetary instruments—into which funds are converted through laundering. Not surprisingly, there continue to be recurrent anecdotes of airplanes full of cash crossing the Caribbean, and suitcases of cash crossing European borders.[34] The conversion of illicit funds into bearer bonds and registered securities that can be endorsed over to the buyer is also relatively common, as is conversion into gold, silver, other precious metals, gems, jewelry, objets d'art, and similar assets. These assets tend to hold their value and are easy both to move internationally and to sell for foreign currency. But they generally involve greater information and transactions costs.

Laundromats

Both during and after the conversion of illicit funds into bankable assets, various types of financial and nonfinancial organizations come into play. Domestic and foreign financial institutions, lawyers, accountants, airline employees, investment advisers, and even government officials provide information and occasionally act as couriers. They also make money laundering easier by bending the rules, looking the other way, or violating the law in return for a payment.

Bank and securities services help with the laundering process by allowing unidentified clients to make deposits; allowing clients whose funds are not of foreign origin to make investments limited to foreigners; allowing clients, acting without power of attorney, to manage investments or to transmit funds on behalf of foreign-registered companies or local companies acting as conduits; participating in sequential transactions that fall just under national financial-reporting thresholds; allowing telephone transfers without written authorization or without keeping records; and entering false foreign account numbers as the destinations of wire transfers. Any of these practices could result in serious costs to the financial institutions involved. But given the diversity of bank policies and practices, and the relatively small proportion of truly questionable transactions, it is unrealistic to expect banks to devote the substantial resources required to identify such transactions.

A trust agreement (for example, in the form of a normal, discretionary, alternative, or disguised trust) is another common method of hiding the true ownership of assets. Yet another is to set up an investment company in a secrecy or tax haven that is both nonresident and tax-exempt, free of exchange controls and financial reporting requirements, and possibly subject only to an annual flat tax. Such an arrangement may involve beneficial ownership that appears in a fiduciary agreement but nowhere in the records of an official body. The principal's death is an obvious problem with respect to such agreements, however. Heirs or executors may first have to prove their own standing *and* the death of the principal in order to obtain any information about, or access to, the assets involved.

Shells and captives. Owners of laundered assets may also employ shell companies or captive banks. Shares in such entities are normally issued in bearer form, and no guarantees are required from the administrators. The name of the asset holder does not appear anywhere in writing. Even local attorneys who form the company—possibly under instructions from foreign lawyers—may not know his or her identity or how the assets are to be used. Panamanian administrators, for example, used to give executive powers over a shell company to an unnamed individual without knowing how or to what ends those powers would be exercised.

A captive bank is an institution that exists purely for the benefit of one physical or legal person or group of people. It may also take the form of a shell entity. Captive banks allow the owners to take advantage of substantial leverage in financing their activities. These banks are typically formed in tax and banking havens with narrow disclosure laws, low reserve ratios, no withholding tax on interest, and no exchange controls. The owner of the captive bank will be able to remain anonymous, if necessary. Captive banks are often set up as offshore entities and located in countries with no meaningful banking regulations and in which all kinds of financial activity are permitted. Shell companies are also used as conduits for depositing money in overseas banks. The money is then recycled into the system through trading in currency or commodities.

False documents. A technique that can be used in conjunction with various kinds of business fronts and shell companies involves the issuance of false invoices covering international trade transactions. On the import side, the foreign supplier issues an invoice in excess of the agreed price of a product, and on the export side the domestic seller issues an invoice for an amount in foreign currency less than the agreed price. The foreign counterparty deposits the difference (less any commission) in an account belonging to the seller and remits the invoice amount. In both cases, false invoicing can succeed in moving laundered funds invisibly from one country to another.

In one unusual case the Bausch & Lomb office in Miami was taking payment in cash, cash equivalents, and third-party checks for Ray-Ban sunglasses being exported to Colombia and other South American countries, where they could be sold for cash. The amount of money involved was substantial—23 percent of the office's total sales. According to one source, B&L was an unwitting party to a money laundering operation and was not in compliance with U.S. currency-reporting requirements. "If a company was accepting third-party checks not payable to itself, either they were doing so with a blind eye, or they were doing it with knowledge of what they were doing."[35] Overall, officials estimated that $3 billion in money laundering was accomplished through trade schemes that included refrigerators, washing machines, fax machines, building materials, and even brown paper bags, all purchased in the United States with drug money and exported to Latin America.[36]

The Raúl Salinas Affair

In one of the most celebrated cases of money laundering, Swiss police arrested the wife of Raúl Salinas de Gortari (brother of former Mexican president Carlos Salinas de Gortari), who walked into a trap set by the Swiss Central Narcotics Division. In November 1995 she used false documentation in an attempt to withdraw $84 million from Banque Pictet, a Swiss private bank in Geneva. She and her brother Antonio were arrested on suspicion of drug trafficking and money laundering, but were later released without being charged. Her husband, however, who was already in a Mexican jail facing murder and conspiracy charges, was further charged there with illegal enrichment and lying to the government.

Although Salinas had been reporting an income of less than $200,000 per year, he had been transmitting tens of millions of dollars through Citibank accounts to various accounts in Switzerland.[37] The origins of the funds, estimated to exceed $200 million overall, remain uncertain. According to the Swiss federal prosecutor, Salinas had amassed his assets as part of a major drug money laundering operation. Salinas denied that drug money was involved. And in view of Salinas's reputation as a somewhat shady character widely known as "Mr. Ten Percent," many people believe that the money was mostly proceeds from government corruption and influence peddling. Supporting this view is the fact that a large portion of the funds were transferred during the last year that Salinas's brother was in office as president. Under the Mexican political system, presidents serve six-year terms and cannot serve again; any misdeeds committed during a president's term of office need to get cleaned up in the last year of the presidency (popularly referred to in Mexico as *el año hidalgo,* the year of the nobleman). Otherwise, the new president and his team will take political advantage of the opportunity presented and come down hard on the people who have abused positions of power and privilege in the previous administration. No evidence has been found to link the former president to the misdeeds of his brother, but "the probe into Raúl Salinas' activities could be the vehicle for exposing a vast system of business-to- government payoffs that has long been suspected in Mexico. . . . Even if Mexico's own investigations get bogged down, Swiss and U.S. investigators may present [President Ernesto] Zedillo with impossible-to-ignore evidence of high-level corruption."[38]

After the investigation was made public, Salinas's private-banking relationships became the subject of intense media attention, much to the consternation of Citibank and its highly successful private-banking group. Investigative reporters discovered that every couple of weeks during 1993, a cashier's check for between $3 million and $5 million in pesos was made out to a Citibank subsidiary, which converted it to dollars and wired the money via New York to accounts in Switzerland. In total, over $80 million was transferred out of Mexico in this way, with no questions asked as to the source of the funds. Salinas told Swiss investigators that, in view of his brother's position as president, he used false names in the transfers to avoid political scandal and that his private bankers at Citibank "came up with a whole strategy" for getting the funds transferred with the greatest possible anonymity.[39] Once in Europe, the funds were deposited in various banks under the names of shell companies registered in the Cayman Islands. Even after Salinas was indicted for murder in Mexico, Citibankers maintained the anonymity of the accounts and continued to actively manage the assets in order to obtain the best returns.

As the only U.S. bank with a general-banking license in Mexico (grand-fathered in the bank nationalizations of 1982), Citibank was a natural conduit for capital flight on the part of wealthy Mexicans. Salinas's private banker was Amy G. Elliot, a Cuban-American who had started in the bank's human resources department, worked her way into private banking, and very successfully led the New York unit of Citibank dealing with Mexican clients. She was apparently the ideal private banker for Salinas, providing all the services he needed with complete discretion, from the opening and management of accounts and trusts to the chartering of new shell corporations when needed. Ironically, Salinas suspected Elliot had a role in the arrests of his wife and her brother Antonio. "I suppose Mrs. Amy Elliot was looking to clear Citibank of this problem. Or she had information of the charges involving drug trafficking, or perhaps she even played a role in my wife getting caught in this trap."[40]

An internal Citibank investigation of the Salinas affair found that there was "no evidence of violation of the law by the bank or any of its employees" and that "corporate management had no involvement in the opening or management of this account in any way." Nonetheless, it was later discovered that the investigation did not include within its scope one of the bank's most highly regarded compliance officers, whose responsibilities included the detection of money laundering; she subsequently resigned in order to take a job with GE Capital. In addition, Citibank made major personnel changes in its private-banking unit, including its head and its general counsel, after audits discovered poor internal controls and enforcement of know-your-customer rules.[41]

The Salinas affair and the investigation of Citibank also raised once again the widespread use of secret transfers of funds out of Mexico by that country's elite. The element of greed is apparent in Raúl Salinas's remark, "For rich men, money works for them, while people who are not rich think they have to work for money. Rich men believe only two things: That they deserve all the money they can get, and that money should work for them."[42]

BCCI—Avoiding the Regulators

Probably the most sensational case involving financial secrecy and shady practices by a financial firm was that of the Bank of Credit and Commerce International (BCCI). It was probably the largest bank fraud in history, leaving behind some $9.5 billion in depositor and creditor losses, besmirching the reputations of regulators, and leaving a lasting mark on the history of global money laundering. Based in Luxembourg, BCCI was founded in 1966 by a Pakistani, Agha Hasan Abedi. It grew rapidly in the early 1970s, with help from the Bank of America and heavy investments by Middle Eastern interests, most notably Sheikh Zayed of Abu Dhabi. At one point in the 1980s it was the fastest-growing bank in the world. A rarely discussed issue at the time was that BCCI grew to operate in a murky, underground market that thrived on bribery, corruption, and financial secrecy. The bank's collapse in the late 1980s was symptomatic of a much deeper set of issues than normally supposed.

In October 1988 the U.S. government charged BCCI and nine of its officers with laundering more than $32 million in drug money. It was first criminal indictment in U.S. history against a financial institution for money laundering. Federal prosecutors alleged that officers at the Tampa, New York, and Houston branches of BCCI took funds they knew to be from U.S. cocaine sales, invested them in certificates of deposit issued by BCCI branches in France, Britain, Luxembourg, the Bahamas, Panama, and South America, and made loans to drug dealers to be repaid later with proceeds from the maturing certificates of deposit.[43] The loan proceeds were eventually wired back to the BCCI branch in Florida. On the return trip and thereafter, the funds involved were not subject to the U.S. $10,000 CTR requirement and could therefore be transferred to members of the Medellin drug cartel in Colombia without detection. Because at each stage in the chain bank fees and interest spreads were deducted, the circuitous routing of funds was both highly profitable for BCCI and quite costly for the beneficiaries of the laundering operation.

In a two-year investigation involving U.S., British, and French authorities, U.S. federal investigators posed as professional money launderers and approached BCCI in Tampa with a number of transactions. Although the undercover investigators themselves proposed methods for laundering the funds, the investigators alleged that BCCI officers suggested, in response, a number of innovations. In a coordinated effort in financial centers in Europe and the United States, eighty people were arrested in October 1988. BCCI's Florida banking license was revoked. And it soon became clear that the Florida case was only the beginning. Almost two years of subsequent revelations uncovered a systematic pattern of money laundering, fraud, and skullduggery around the world.

Like many other banks, BCCI set out in search of inefficient financial markets. But it was also a bank with a difference. As a self-styled "Third World bank," it created a special niche for itself. The bank ostensibly set out to do well by doing good. And it gained legitimacy and opened the right doors through the manipulation of well-meaning personalities such as Jimmy Carter and through its own, well-placed charitable contributions.[44] At the same time, however, perhaps because of the bank's Third World origins, it was accustomed to questionable business practices and a tolerance for these practices was very much a part of its corporate culture. It was only a small step for the bank to expand these practices into major financial centers, especially since, as we have seen, criminal activities, corruption, and money laundering can provide an assured source of sustained profitability for banks willing and able to take advantage of them. And BCCI certainly was.

As the BCCI scandal developed, almost daily disclosures revealed the bank's transactions with drug traffickers, government officials, arms dealers, and international terrorists. What emerged were portraits of the international market for secrecy and of BCCI's operations in that market. BCCI never had the financial, technical, and human resources required to compete effectively and on a level playing field against other powerful banks. So BCCI quickly gravitated to the most imperfect of financial markets— that for international secrecy—a market that could be both highly profitable and virtually immune from competitive erosion. To exploit this global niche, BCCI had to acquire appropriate resources, the most important of which was people willing and able to evade and suborn law and regulation worldwide, and to engage in a broad array of illicit economic, financial, and social conduct. Most of these people worked inside the bank, but some clearly had to be on the outside as knowing or unknowing accomplices. These lawyers, accountants, and politicians were handsomely compensated by a bank that could easily afford the best available and that recognized the value of the services being rendered.

In order to engage in these activities without being detected, BCCI had to create elaborate camouflage in the form of Byzantine internal and external accounting and reporting arrangements—including a separate bank within the bank—and to generate a large volume of legitimate business. Most of BCCI's balance-sheet liabilities were ordinary customer deposits and funds bought in the financial markets, and many of its assets no doubt reflected ordinary investments, loans, and advances to customers, each bearing ordinary returns. But the bank's extraordinary growth and profitability were impossible to explain in terms of ordinary business. And the solvency problems that gradually became apparent went well beyond the usual "banana peels" (such as real estate) that bedeviled ordinary banks in the 1980s. The bank's competitive advantage came, instead, from deception and from the opacity, when desired, of the bank's activities and transactions. These elements of secrecy made possible the outright looting of the bank's assets and carried the seeds of the bank's eventual destruction.

The BCCI case did, of course, leave its mark on the regulatory system of the United States and of other countries as well. In the United States BCCI had gained control of the American National Bank of Washington, D.C., allegedly with the help of former secretary of defense Clark Clifford and an associate of his law firm, Robert Altman, who was later brought to trial in New York and acquitted for lack of evidence. The legislative response was the passage of the Foreign Bank Supervision Enhancement Act of 1991, which was included within the FDIC Improvement Act (FDICIA). As expected, this legislation imposed an additional layer of federal regulation on foreign banks operating in the United States. The act specifically regulated the establishment, closure, examination, deposits, and other powers of foreign banks in the United States. Although Agha Hasan Abedi was wanted for bank fraud in the United States and sentenced in absentia to eight years in prison by a United Arab Emirates court, he continued to be protected by Pakistan's refusal to extradite him. He died in August 1995.

In 1995 a court in Luxembourg, where BCCI was chartered, issued a worldwide settlement on claims of $10 billion against BCCI's assets (after liquidation costs) of $3.3 billion. In addition, the liquidators were continuing their efforts against the Bank of England for failure to supervise and against Price Waterhouse and Ernst & Young for failures in auditing.[45]

Electronic and Other Transfers

The electronic transfer of funds is a growing conduit for money laundering. It is quick, efficient, and capable of handling massive amounts of funds. And it is almost too easy. As one Scotland Yard official has noted, "Electronic funds transfer has done for money laundering what the washing machine did for clothes washing."[46] Otherwise innocent and reasonably savvy professionals have regularly gotten in over their heads. For example, over $100 million in profits from street sales of cocaine were laundered through a New York law firm. The funds were deposited in lawyers' bank accounts, wired to accounts in Switzerland, and wired again to the Cali drug ring in Colombia. A Swiss couple, a Bulgarian diplomat, a stockbroker, and two rabbis were also accused of being part of the operation.[47] Similarly, as a result of its involvement in an electronic money-laundering scheme, the American Express Bank, an American Express subsidiary, settled civil charges for $36 million, the largest such penalty ever imposed on an American financial institution.

The sophistication and complexity of electronic money laundering can be staggering. In December 1994 the FBI crippled an operation used by the Cali cartel and organized crime groups in Italy. The bureau traced the laundered money by examining wire transfers, cashier's checks, and loans. The enforcement effort itself took years and involved not only the use of a fake bank in the Caribbean, but the creation of corporate shells to serve as conduits for laundered funds. By the end of the operation, federal agents and the fake bank had created forty-one corporate accounts for drug traffickers and handled cash transactions totaling $48 million.[48]

The fall of the Soviet Union has generated a burst of money-laundering activity. According to one report, "Five nights a week, at least $100 million in crisp new $100 bills is flown from JFK nonstop to Moscow, where it is used to finance the Russian Mob's vast and growing international crime syndicate. State and federal officials believe it is part of a multi-billion-dollar money-laundering operation. The Republic National Bank of New York and the United States Federal Reserve prefer not to think so."[49] The alleged scheme involves five steps. First, the mob steals Siberian crude oil, which is sold on the spot market in Rotterdam. Second, the proceeds, say $40 million, are wired to a Eurodollar bank account in London after passing through a number of front companies to disguise their origin. Third, a mob-owned Russian bank orders $40 million in $100 bills from Republic National Bank of New York, which Republic buys from the Federal Reserve Bank of New York. Fourth, the London bank wires the $40 million (plus a commission) to Republic to pay for the banknotes. And fifth, Republic ships the bills from JFK to Moscow, where they are delivered to the mob-controlled bank.

Most criminal money being laundered merges all but invisibly into the stream of global money flows arising from normal commercial transactions. With wire transfers, other interbank transactions, and an unregulated $1 trillion Eurodollar market available to all comers, good and bad money soon mingle. Tainted funds quickly lose their identity. Probably the best chance the authorities have to impede money laundering is at the currency-conversion point. Once that point has been passed, effective action is difficult.

That said, the U.S. Office of Technology Assessment has estimated that one-tenth of a percent of all electronic transfers of money are illegal, and has explored the possibility of using special software to identify suspicious electronic money flows. Law-enforcement officials have suggested developing a computer program that would screen the records of the 700,000 daily U.S. electronic money transfers and flag suspicious ones for investigation. One major obstacle to its implementation is federal privacy law, which prevents the sharing of information regarding electronic money transfers without search warrants. Another is that banks are not at present required to report electronic transfers. Still another is the difficulty of knowing exactly what to look for and what constitutes suspicious activity. Financial institutions have also expressed concern that such a surveillance system would be expensive and would inevitably target the legitimate business of innocent companies and individuals.[50]

An experiment in Australia highlights the limitations of using computer software to catch money launderers. Millions of dollars were being wired from China to dozens of accounts in Australia and then on to accounts in California. An import-export trader from Beijing nearly succeeded in mis-routing $157 million from the Bank of China and keeping $42 million for himself. And because money moves so very quickly in these cases, the launderer had already transferred some of the money to several other banks by the time officials tracked him down.[51]

Easy Money or Playing with Fire?

Private-banking services can generate both substantial profits and substantial risks. The risks are threefold. The first is that firms need to hire people not only because they possess technical competence and professional integrity, but also because they can work effectively in countries where success depends upon whom one knows and upon access to the economic and political elite. If these people prove to be bent or bendable (like Tony Gebauer), the firm is potentially in serious jeopardy. For example, if money is stolen or otherwise misappropriated, the firm will almost certainly find itself compensating the victims. The firm's reputation would undoubtedly suffer, too, causing customers to look elsewhere for private-banking services.

The second risk is associated with the money-transfer process; dirty money may pass through the accounts at the firm, even if only briefly. The firm may be an innocent participant, such as when a money launderer deceives the firm's employees. Or the firm may not be so innocent, as when a corrupt employee colludes with a money launderer. Either way, the firm could be investigated and perhaps held liable for some of the civil or criminal offenses involved. Citicorp was struggling with just such accusations in the case of Raúl Salinas, who had used his private-banking relationship with the bank for his nefarious purposes.

The third risk comes from dealing in good faith with a client who later proves to have assets of questionable origin, such as when a firm faces potential liability for fraud or negligence because it has executed an underwriting or other transaction using the client's tainted assets. As long as the firm is soliciting the private-banking business of wealthy people, it is going to be tested from time to time. Dishonest people will try to become respected clients. They will try every day, and some will get in, no matter how careful the screening.

The legal consequences of exposure to these risks is not yet entirely clear. The law is still evolving—and evolving simultaneously in many different countries. No system for avoiding and managing risks should be built on the assumption that either the probability or the financial consequences of getting into trouble are likely to be low.

To avoid such risks, firms need to recognize that the development of new business in private banking, as in any other area, requires appropriate internal controls and rigorous regulatory compliance. These controls may be different from those in other areas of the firm—and also expensive—but to proceed without them could be fatal. Some other steps, unique to dealing with secret money and money laundering, might include the following:

- Vet new hires and new accounts as thoroughly and carefully as possible. Access to reliable information from an individual's or a company's home country is essential.

- Monitor and supervise the activities of private-banking representatives as closely as those from other sensitive areas, such as mergers or arbitrage trading.

- Restrict private-banking executives to representing clients' interests. Executives should be advocates and advisors for their clients, but the delivery of services should be made the responsibility of the relevant functional departments, which must be responsible, in turn, for exercising due diligence with regard to both clients and transactions.

- Remain fully abreast of regulatory, legal, and law-enforcement developments concerning international money flows.

And finally, there is the public interest. According to federal prosecutor John Moscow:

> Bank secrecy statutes in international finance are used by crooks, tax evaders, securities fraudsters and capital flight fellows. They are used by narcotics dealers. But they are not needed by honest folks engaged in honest transactions. . . . There is no reason why bankers who do what they are told for a fee should consider themselves any better than prostitutes who do the same. If you think the size of the fees makes the conduct better or appropriate, think again, for the penalties are far greater.[52]

10

Whistleblowing

■

In 1965, three years after graduating from Lehigh University, Mark Jorgensen embarked on a career in the financial-services industry.[1] After working in mergers and acquisitions at Donaldson, Lufkin & Jenrette, he moved into the field of real-estate investments. In 1973 Jorgensen went to the Prudential Insurance Company of America's Phoenix office as a senior appraiser. After a few promotions, he was put in charge of Prudential's Southern real-estate investments for several years, followed by a decade as an independent real-estate consultant. In 1992 Jorgensen accepted an invitation to return to Prudential to manage funds that were part of the Prudential Property Investment Separate Account, or Prisa, which invested in real estate for pension funds.

As Jorgensen began visiting the 160 Prisa properties, he discovered that the appraisal values of some of the properties were wildly inflated. Since appraisals are used to determine the net asset values of the funds holding shares in the properties, such inflation would raise the cost of investing in the funds beyond their actual worth. At Prudential, fees for managing funds were proportional to their value, so these fees were equally inflated.

In November 1992 Jorgensen told his superior about his discovery. He speculated that the inflated appraisals would push property values in the funds too high and ultimately prevent the funds from performing well even in a rising real-estate market. His boss replied, according to Jorgensen, that the appraisers should not be blamed; he himself had inflated the property values due to the poor performance of the funds in the late 1980s, which had caused investors to start pulling out their money. Inflating the values gave an impression of superior fund performance and attracted new investors.

Jorgensen felt that carrying the properties at improper values was a violation of his own fiduciary duty to Prisa, and he began a campaign to lower the value of certain properties. His persistence frayed his relationship with his superior, who began threatening to remove him from the management of Prisa. At a meeting with Robert Winters, chairman of Prudential Insurance Company of America, Jorgensen asked whether Winters was concerned that the firm's real-estate units may have been overestimating property values in order to show higher profits. Winters replied that anyone responsible for such a practice would be dismissed. Accordingly, Jorgensen made a report to Prudential's legal department documenting his findings. He assumed that this report would lead to a quick remedy, but he nevertheless retained his own lawyer, who advised him to keep detailed records from then on.

Prudential responded by denying the allegations, claiming that no one person was actually responsible for the overvaluations—they were part of a plan for Prisa to "maximize its opportunities." Prudential's legal department, together with outside counsel hired to investigate the overvaluation, began pursuing accusations of wrongdoing against Jorgensen. They questioned why he had signed Prisa's 1992 financial report if he thought the properties were overvalued, and investigated whether he had warned clients about the problem, thus violating the company's disclosure rules. The legal department offered no advice on whether he should sign the 1993 first-quarter financials, which he refused to do. Eventually the legal department considered reporting Jorgensen to the SEC for disclosure violations, and one of Prudential's lawyers indirectly suggested that he start looking for a new job.

Jorgensen's work environment at Prudential deteriorated rapidly; his career was unraveling. He was advised to take a paid leave while the investigation continued. After it was completed in August 1993, Jorgensen was invited to return to Prudential, but, because of a "divisional reorganization," no longer as a manager of Prisa funds. In his new position, no one reported to him. He was assigned to conduct a feasibility study of real-estate projects but without permission to contact anyone outside Prudential for information. For months, few colleagues spoke to him, and none would sit next to him at meetings. No one wanted to be seen with him, either socially or at work.

In November 1993 Jorgensen filed a lawsuit against Prudential, contending that the company had retaliated against him for whistleblowing. Prudential contended that its investigations had found no evidence of overvaluation of properties and that Jorgensen was simply a bitter employee upset about a reorganization. Judge Dickinson R. Debevoise of the federal district court in Newark agreed and was himself upset that Jorgensen had made the company's confidential records public as evidence in the suit. "I think this is grounds for firing him on the spot," Debevoise said. Prudential agreed, and Jorgensen was fired in February 1994 for unethical conduct in disclosing confidential records as part of his lawsuit against Prudential.

That would have been the end of the story, were it not for the extensive publicity the case had received. Angry investors wanted to know whether there was any truth to the allegations. Prudential was forced to initiate yet another investigation, using external lawyers and accountants. Federal prosecutors subpoenaed Prudential records relevant to the case and to Jorgensen's testimony, apparently intent on initiating criminal proceedings.

Two months after being fired, Jorgensen was asked to meet with chairman Winters in his office. Winters told him that the second investigation had disclosed that many Prisa properties were overvalued. Jorgensen's former boss and another subordinate had been asked to resign. After praising Jorgensen for his "courage" and "persisten[ce]," Winters asked him to return to Prudential. "With that, the emotions built [up] over the past year poured out . . . as he recounted his trials. When no one believed him. When he was threatened. When he was avoided. When his wife cried." Mr. Winters then apologized, and the lawsuit was settled that afternoon. "It was over," he told his family and the people who had stood by him throughout the ordeal. "Prudential realized I was right." In an instant, Jorgensen had changed from pariah to hero.

Once he became aware of the Prisa overvaluations, Mark Jorgensen confronted a no-win situation. By surfacing his suspicions, he faced both financial damage and personal stress: frayed relationships and ostracism at work as well as eventual corporate action, bordering on a vendetta, mounted by Prudential's aggressive and exceptionally protective legal department. On the other hand, had Jorgensen not raised the issue of overvalued real estate, he could later have been accused of breaching his fiduciary duties or, even worse, dragged into a conspiracy to hide the overvaluations. He was damned if he did and damned if he didn't.

Jorgensen's actions were obviously compatible with top management's perspective on appropriate business practices, but top management was itself completely out of touch with what was going on in the company. Rogue behavior seems to have been rampant within the Prudential group during Winters's tenure as chairman, and it is very doubtful that he ever knew it. Not only was Prisa engaging in illegal activities related to property valuations, but misconduct by the life-insurance sales force eventually led to $1.5 billion in settlements against the company and the major scandal at Prudential Securities had cost the company more than $2 billion.

What Is Whistleblowing?

Whistleblowing is the act of calling attention to actions that are seriously wrong—behavior that could damage the firm, its shareholders and employees, its suppliers and customers, even society at large. History is replete with examples of such behavior. Secret dumping of toxic waste into nearby streams that kills marine life and contaminates water supplies. Covering up design flaws in aviation equipment that make it unsafe. Falsifying performance tests in order to meet delivery deadlines. Taking kickbacks from suppliers. Fudging accounts. Mismarking securities positions.

In most businesses, employees aware of such behavior are expected to report the matter to appropriate company officials. In the great majority of such cases, the matter is reported and appropriately addressed by the company. In some cases, however, the senior officials of the company fail (often repeatedly) to correct the misbehavior, and conspire to cover it up. In so doing they are acting contrary to the long-term interests of shareholders and putting their own apparent interests ahead of those who employ them. These interests usually relate to money, advancement, or the need to hide things that might endanger personal goals. Failing to correct the situation may nonetheless put senior officials in the position of breaking the law and of becoming liable for civil damages.

Whistleblowing occurs when an employee familiar with wrongdoing reports it to authorities capable of intervening to correct it and of disciplining the wrongdoers. But whistleblowers themselves are frequently subjected to retaliation and harassment, and they may be fired, too. The examples are endless, but they all have one thing in common: somebody who knows about wrongdoing "blows the whistle" (as a referee in a game would do to stop an errant play) despite the potential personal and professional costs. Ultimately, the whistleblower may report what he or she knows to a higher authority in the company or to outside authorities such as the IRS, the SEC, or the FBI.

Conflicts of Obligation

Whistleblowers face three distinct types of obligations when uncovering information about misconduct:

1. *Obligations to oneself:* first, to survive and prosper in one's profession, and second, to uphold one's own personal standards and values. These obligations raise issues about whether or not to blow

the whistle and, if not, how to dissociate oneself from any practices that may have adverse consequences if discovered.

2. *Obligations to the employer:* first, to serve as a loyal, dutiful, and productive employee, and second, to safeguard the employer against other employees who engage in behavior harmful to the firm.

3. *Obligations to society:* first, to obey the law, and second, to report any behavior that may endanger others.

This tripartite complex of obligations can create serious dilemmas for the whistleblower because each may require quite different behavior.

Assuming that the goal of the company's shareholders is to maximize the organization's long-term value, the interests of the shareholders—and thus of their appointed managers—is to encourage whistleblowers to report actions that could diminish the firm's value as a result of losses, the cost of legal actions, and erosion of reputation. Indeed, whistleblowers inside the organization may be instrumental in maintaining the long-term viability of the enterprise. The interests of shareholders, managers, and whistleblowers are congruent.

This congruence hardly means that the whistleblower faces no personal risks, even if top management appears to be quite supportive. Top management may be out of touch with what middle managers are doing. Priorities may have been shifted because of the fear of lawsuits, in which case voluntary disclosures of wrongdoing would re-open the past. The facts or their interpretation may be in dispute. The credibility or motives of the whistleblower may be unclear. In any case, loyalties and power alliances may take over and distort realities. The net result is that truth telling is risky business from the whistleblower's perspective, no matter what anyone says.

The Whistleblower's Dilemma

The whistleblower's dilemma is all the worse in that there is always pressure—to act and not to act. Should one tell and face the consequences, or not tell and accept responsibility for the harm and dangers that result from allowing the miscreant behavior to continue?

The consequences of whistleblowing are not symmetrical between the whistleblower and management. The company may stand to gain from an inside whistleblower who raises an issue and thus prevents the continuation of a questionable practice. Yet those guilty of the misbehavior, or of covering it up, often have considerable resources at their disposal to protect themselves. And whistleblowers usually have very limited resources and are frequently unaware of the risks they run in stepping forward. The personal and professional costs of whistleblowing are nearly impossible to predict. The immediate consequences may include an undesirable reassignment; loss of rank, responsibility, and promotion potential; and termination in a future "downsizing." Working relationships are likely to deteriorate because of suspicion and erosion of trust between colleagues, and the workplace may become exceedingly uncomfortable. If the whistleblower is unable to overcome these in-house problems, then resignation and the burden of finding new employment under adverse conditions is virtually inevitable.

Incremental Descent into Poor Judgment

The whistleblower's situation is even more complicated when management is itself engaged in questionable business practices or is out of control from the perspective of shareholders' interests. In a recent book discussing the fatal decision to launch the *Challenger* space shuttle despite warnings from engineers, Diane Vaughan, a sociologist at Boston College, went beyond the traditional explanation of "amorally calculating mangers [at NASA] intentionally violating the rules." Looking for a deeper explanation of the disaster, she examined the culture of NASA and found much fault with the organization itself. The result was "an incremental descent into poor judgment," such that the NASA story became "the sociology of mistakes, imbedded in the banality of organizational life."[2]

Such cultures exist not only in government institutions such as NASA, but also in business organizations such as Drexel Burnham and Prudential Securities. There have been, and continue to be, many rogue organizations in business. The whistleblower has no one to turn to inside such firms; the questionable practices are embedded within the organization as acceptable routine. Indeed, management may quarantine the information and, in order to mask and protect ongoing practices, coerce a potential whistleblower to remain silent. The whistleblower may choose to go outside, either to the authorities or the media, in which case he or she may be ostracized, fired, or charged with serious offenses by the company's lawyers. In such instances the goals of the whistleblower and management are incongruent.

The past few years have seen a spate of whistleblowing cases in business and finance. The following illustrate both the process and results of whistleblowing.

The mole at ADM. One of the most dramatic whistleblowing cases in recent years involved Archer-Daniels-Midland Corporation (ADM), a major U.S. agribusiness company long known as one of the most heavily subsidized and politically well-connected firms in the country. ADM had been under investigation since 1992 by the Justice Department for price fixing in its corn-processing business. Much of the information for the investigation came from Mark Whitacre, a senior ADM executive who had supplied the FBI with taped records for over three years. He amassed hundreds of videotapes and audiotapes allegedly showing company officials discussing pricing, production volumes, and market-share objectives with executives of competing companies.

In order to avoid his being suspected as the whistleblower, Whitacre himself was included in the scope of an FBI sweep of ADM's Decatur, Illinois, headquarters. During his conversation with the lawyer to whom ADM had sent him for counsel, Whitacre revealed that he was the Justice Department mole responsible for the investigation. The lawyer, whose firm was closely associated with ADM, immediately informed Dwayne Andreas, the company's then seventy-eight-year-old chairman who had built ADM into a global agribusiness powerhouse.

The lawyer's disclosure triggered a massive retaliation against Whitacre. He was accused of embezzling $2.5 million (later raised to $9 million) of company funds, and then fired. He admitted to taking the money but claimed that it was part of ADM's own scheme to make various senior officers indebted to the company in order to assure their loyalty. The firm, Whitacre said, made covert payments to key employees as an insurance policy against whistleblowing. The money, illegally transferred from elsewhere in ADM, was paid into a Swiss bank account in his name. "They give it to you, then use it against you when you are their enemy," he said. He was subsequently forced to plead guilty to several felony charges related to the payments. Following his plea agreement, a distraught Whitacre attempted suicide.[3]

ADM was subsequently named in at least two dozen shareholder suits, and serious concerns about management and corporate governance were voiced by large institutional shareholders including Alan Hevesi, New York City Controller and manager of employee pension funds that hold some 2.7 million ADM shares. Hevesi wrote to Dwayne Andreas, "I find it particularly disturbing that the board has been virtually silent, despite reports that the investigations have targeted top company officials."[4] ADM had already been graded F on corporate governance policy in 1994 by the California Public Employees' Retirement System (CalPers), one of the country's most active institutional investors.[5]

In September 1995, three executives who agreed to cooperate with federal prosecutors were dismissed for allegedly receiving improper payments abroad. A month later, the head of the company's Mexican operations became the fourth executive to be fired during this period (he had earlier been placed on administrative leave). He insisted that ADM's president had approved a $190,000 signing bonus, which was paid in Switzerland through phony invoices.[6]

ADM continued to be under fire from its institutional shareholders, who complained that the company was slow in making the changes to its board that were needed to make it more responsive to shareholders. In April 1996 the board of ADM made an unusual appearance before members of a council of more than one hundred pension-fund investors. They presented information about the company and its products, but Dwayne Andreas, who was originally scheduled to appear, was not present. One pension representative observed, "I don't see one word here about what most threatens the company," by which he meant the government investigations, more than seventy shareholder lawsuits, and unresolved allegations that Whitacre had stolen millions from the company.[7]

The criminal price-fixing case against the company cast a long shadow over its financial affairs as well, since a conviction would increase the chances of a massive civil award and punitive damages. Civil charges were soon settled, however. ADM agreed to pay $25 million for having conspired with competitors to manipulate the market for the animal-feed additive lysine. Its competitors paid a total settlement of over $45 million. This settlement, in turn, made it more likely that ADM could reach a plea bargain on the criminal charges even though several other civil suits involving citric acid and high-fructose corn syrup were still pending.[8] The plea bargain, pushed by some of ADM's outside directors, concerned culpability only of the corporation, and not that of any of the executives involved.[9] ADM chairman Andreas remained sanguine. "When you get 50 lawyers suing you and you can get rid of them for $25 million, you'd be an utter fool not to do it." He was not bothered by the adverse publicity for his company. "We're not in the publicity business. We don't make any consumer goods. We don't sell anything to the public. Naturally, we don't like bad publicity, but what does it do? As long as we didn't do anything wrong—and we didn't—it can't be a very big problem for me."[10]

In August 1996 ADM's Japanese and Korean co-conspirators pleaded guilty to the government's criminal price-fixing charges and were fined $20 million, followed two months later by ADM's guilty plea to criminal charges covering both lysine and citric acid and its agreeing to pay a $100 million fine. In return, the government agreed to drop its price-fixing investigation related to high-fructose corn syrup.[11] According to one institutional investor, "The $100 million fine represents shareholder assets that are being squandered to pay for criminal activity that never should have occurred. Where was the board of directors?"[12] In all, civil and criminal fines had cost ADM some $190 million.

In addition, Michael D. Andreas (the chairman's son), Terrance S. Wilson (ADM executive vice president), and Mark Whitacre were indicted on criminal price-fixing charges in October 1996. All pleaded not guilty. Whitacre had already been fired, and the other two stepped down. The ADM board named three executives (including Dwayne Andreas's nephew) to "assist the chairman" and presumably play a role in succession. The chairman apologized to shareholders, saying, "I consider this a serious matter which I, of course, deeply regret. The buck stops with me. You have my commitment that things are arranged so that this will never happen again."[13]

Whitacre became the CEO of a start-up medical-technology company. He continued to defend himself against ADM embezzlement charges. In response he filed suit against the company in November 1996, contending wrongful dismissal, defamation, and harassment and that "ADM's claim that Whitacre was fired for embezzlement is merely a pretext. Whitacre was in fact fired for assisting the FBI with its investigation into ADM."[14] Dwayne Andreas in an interview with the *Washington Post* called Whitacre a "dedicated criminal."[15]

Overcharging at CSX. When A. David Nelson told his bosses at CSX about overcharging on government-financed railroad crossings in at least ten states in 1991, he was told to shut up or be fired. "My director told me to back off and said I was beating a dead horse."[16] Instead he resigned, intending to use his exit interview to make his point about the false billings. However, he was denied an exit interview by the company. So in 1992 he reported his concerns to state and federal officials and began what he called "a steady descent into poverty," nearly losing his home in the process. His future employment was blocked by the lack of a favorable reference from CSX.

Among Nelson's allegations was that third-party vendors purchased CSX parts, which CSX then repurchased and billed, with two additional mark-ups, to the government. Nelson claimed that he told at least twenty CSX employees, including a number of vice presidents, about the overcharging problems but that they failed to act. CSX responded by asserting its innocence and arguing that any overcharges—mainly attributed to the use of twenty-year-old data on the time it took to complete the jobs in question—had been repaid as soon as the problems were discovered.

Two years after Nelson blew the whistle, CSX agreed to pay refunds totaling $3.5 million to eighteen states. In addition, CSX paid Nelson $1.18 million as part of the settlement. A company spokesman stated that CSX had settled only to avoid future litigation costs. Nelson said that he had been vindicated and that it was time to move on.

The CSX case introduces a different aspect of whistleblowing, the possibility that the whistleblower may receive a substantial, legally mandated financial benefit from blowing the whistle. These benefits accrue when the federal or state government has been cheated by a supplier under the terms of the Federal False Claims Act. This law, originally enacted to combat fraud in procurement during the Civil War, was amended in 1986 to enable private citizens to bring suit *qui tam* (on behalf of the state and themselves at the same time) and to share in any recoveries obtained by the government. Shares can range from 15 to 30 percent, depending upon the circumstances of the case.[17]

Substandard parts at Lucas Industries. In October 1995 Lucas Industries of Great Britain, after more than two years of investigation and marathon negotiations, agreed to an $88 million civil settlement with the U.S. government for selling substandard parts to the Pentagon. At issue was inadequate testing and bogus quality-assurance reports on critical flight-safety equipment for roughly fifteen hundred F/A18 Navy fighter aircraft. Lucas was the sole supplier. The substandard parts had "caused engine fires, aborted missions, and were factors in the loss of aircraft."[18] The defective parts had put the lives of pilots at risk. In addition to the cash settlement, Lucas had to supply the Navy with $9 million worth of parts free of charge in order to be allowed once again to bid on federal business, a privilege that had been suspended during the period of the investigations and the subsequent settlement negotiations. Several employees admitted guilt and were indicted, or remained under criminal investigation at the time of the settlement.

The Lucas case began when an employee filed suit as a whistleblower under the Federal False Claims Act and charged the company with testing irregularities. Earlier, after becoming aware of the falsification of the test results, the employee had attempted to resolve the matter internally by bringing it to the attention of his superiors. The superiors did not act, so after lengthy deliberation the employee consulted a lawyer and went to court. In this case, the employee was entitled to compensation of up to $17 million for having blown the whistle on Lucas. Such inducements can be expected to encourage whistleblowing in government-procurement cases.

The Federal False Claims Act has had the effect of separating whistle-blowing cases into two categories: those that involve the government and those that don't. Those that don't are by far the more numerous, especially in the financial-services area. In such cases, the employee has little protection from the potentially harsh consequences of blowing the whistle.

Misvaluing bonds at Smith Barney. Michael Lissack had been working at Smith Barney for fourteen years and was one of the firm's top municipal-bond number crunchers.[19] In April 1993 he informed his superiors that he could no longer remain silent about practices taking place both at Smith Barney and within the municipal-bond industry in general.

These practices involved charging artificially high prices for U.S. Treasury bonds sold to state and local governments in complex deals (see Chapter 8). Municipal issuers are prohibited from using proceeds from the refinancing of tax-exempt bonds to invest in U.S. government securities, the interest on which is likewise tax-free to the municipalities. But they can invest in government securities if the bonds are used to "defease" issues that are put into escrow until they can be called for redemption. By defeasing the bonds, the issuer can remove them from its books. The investor is paid in interest and principal from the Treasury bonds that have been placed in escrow with the municipal bonds.

By overcharging the clients for the Treasury bonds, Lissack said, many Wall Street firms were, in effect, skimming off part of the interest differential for themselves. Lissack claimed that securities firms justified the inflated prices by opinions solicited from outside advisers—usually other securities firms active in the municipal-bond business—confirming that the valuation estimates were reasonable. He further claimed that securities firms wrote what amounted to false valuation opinions for each other, often keeping track of who owed such favors to whom. Lissack called Justice Department officials at the end of 1993 to alert them to some of these practices.

Lissack maintained that if state and local officials had been stringently monitoring the valuation opinions, the practice would have been uncovered early in the game. These officials would have noticed that keeping securities in escrow accounts maintained by the securities firms was more profitable than actually underwriting and distributing new bonds. The reason for this differential was simple. Whereas underwriting fees had to be split among the various firms in a syndicate, firms could mark up the prices of escrow securities and keep the entire fee for themselves. In response to Lissack's charges, the municipal-bond firms argued that the markups were fair. The securities were often hard to get, and the municipalities were required to compensate the firms for holding the securities on their books for a period of time.

Smith Barney itself was alleged to have failed to disclose $4 million in fees on debt swaps it arranged between AIG Financial Products and the cities of Los Angeles and Miami. In 1995, the Los Angeles County Metropolitan Transportation Authority indicated that it would try to recover $8 million in overcharges from Lazard Frères and Goldman Sachs. Each firm denied the allegations. Smith Barney stated that Lissack himself had arranged the AIG swaps and billed the clients. Lissack claimed, however, that he was acting on orders from his superiors at the firm.[20]

After Lissack raised these issues with Justice Department officials, Smith Barney reduced his 1994 bonus from $465,000 to $60,000 and cut back his responsibilities. He also was subjected to colleagues' accusations that he suffered from "personal problems" and "disappointment associated with a reduction in pay and responsibilities." The firm announced that it had paid for Lissack's psychiatric care after he was accused of "harassment of subordinates and service personnel."[21] In April 1994 Lissack was forced to take a leave of absence from Smith Barney. And in early 1995, when he told management he would testify in a pending grand jury investigation of the questionable muni practices, the firm fired him. During this period, his marriage ended in divorce, he was diagnosed as suffering from severe depression, and he attempted suicide.

Lissack sought $75 million from his former employer in an arbitration proceeding, alleging psychological damage and impairment of his ability to make a living. Smith Barney successfully subpoenaed his home telephone records as part of the arbitration, and argued that he was pursuing a vendetta motivated by greed and a desire to get even with former colleagues.

The Smith Barney case arose while the SEC was investigating Wall Street firms' alleged undisclosed fees and improper payments to government officials in order to gain preference in issuing municipal bonds. That firm and others were being accused of exploiting federal tax laws aimed at preventing local governments from earning excessive interest on the proceeds of tax-exempt bonds they sold—excess earnings that were the basis for gains for the securities firms that would otherwise have gone to the Treasury.[22] Regulators ramped up scrutiny of the way in which municipal and state escrow accounts were invested, and the SEC requested the staff at the Municipal Securities Rulemaking Board to formulate proposals that would require public disclosure of who is handling escrow accounts and how much they are being paid. An industry group, the Government Finance Officers Association, recommended that municipalities solicit competitive bids from securities dealers for escrow purchases rather than negotiating prices with a single firm. Hoping for a large payoff under the Federal False Claims Act, Lissack subsequently immersed himself in an effort to identify instances of overcharging in escrow transactions with state and local governments.

Here we see the whistleblower's role expanding to include not only a single firm's questionable practices, but also those of an entire industry. To keep industry practices under some semblance of control, it is important to have whistleblowers come forward. In the Smith Barney case, according to one observer, the impact on the industry may prove greater than usual because of the professional standing of the whistleblower: "Never had someone at this level defected before."[23]

Since those who tell are destined to lose within the context of their own firms, reshaping the incentive system (for example, through the Federal False Claims Act) may help balance the gains and losses. The personal costs to whistleblowers may also be mitigated through procedural protections such as allowing evidence to be accumulated before the participants are informed, providing legal counsel, and establishing special investigative commissions immediately upon the presentation of credible allegations.

Phony accounting at Aetna. The 238,000 professional accountants in the United States are subject to a code of ethics promulgated by the American Institute of Certified Public Accountants (AICPA), to which a whistleblowing section was added in 1993: If a corporate accountant discovers that the company's financial statement contains serious misstatements he or she should report this discovery to a superior and, if the superior fails to act, should then report it to the firm's external auditors or to regulatory agencies such as the SEC. Failure to blow the whistle could cost accountants their state certification to practice, and they may also be held personally liable in any subsequent shareholder suit. Prior to 1993 these provisions applied only to accountants working for CPA firms. But now corporate accountants, who by the mid-1990s outnumbered public accountants for the first time in over a century, are covered as well.

The amended code puts the corporate accountant in the position of being a mandatory whistleblower, possibly at great cost to the accountant. Robert C. Reeves Jr., an accountant with Aetna Life & Casualty, blew the whistle in 1993 and 1994 on the overstatement of Aetna's mortgage-portfolio reserves. Reeves duly reported the problem to his superiors, who did nothing. Reeves claims he was then offered an additional seventeen weeks of severance pay if he signed an agreement not to sue Aetna or to speak about the matter to outside regulators or other parties. He refused and was fired. Reeves charged in a lawsuit against Aetna that the company had forced him to violate the AICPA code of ethics, which is designed to protect shareholders from undisclosed losses. Aetna denied the charge as "baseless," and an internal investigation found it to be "totally without merit." The firm argued that shortfalls were never covered up and that Reeves was suing to get a better severance package after his job was eliminated "as part of a reduction in staff in the mortgage-portfolio management area."[24]

Although professional societies have potentially placed their members in serious jeopardy by requiring them to blow the whistle, these societies have, according to one observer, "generally failed to come to the aid or defense of members who have attempted to live up to their codes of professional ethics by blowing the whistle on corrupt practices."[25]

Why Do People Blow the Whistle?

The above examples show that whistleblowing can be risky business. One could argue, however, that in companies that are well managed and culturally sound, whistleblowing is encouraged and results in no punishment for the whistleblower. Small items are dealt with as a matter of routine, and because employees know that their own misbehavior is likely to be reported, they tend to avoid such misbehavior anyway. Perhaps most companies meet this description, but some do not. Indeed, the record indicates that when companies are exceedingly authoritarian, aggressive, bureaucratic, or under extreme pressure to perform, errant behavior is tolerated if it is considered to be in the company's interest. In these situations, a strong institutional resistance to whistleblowing can be anticipated.

Large and Important Issues

By the time a potential whistleblower reaches the point at which a decision must be made whether to act or not, the underlying issue invariably has become large and important. A smaller, easily corrected issue would have already been discovered and addressed in a well-managed organization with a supportive environment. The potential whistleblower generally has no incentive to act until matters reach a stage at which his or her moral conscience becomes involved. At this point the company is likely to face accusations for which the possibility of legal damages or settlement costs looms large. Company lawyers immediately intervene, seeking to minimize the damage, but they often make matters worse by stonewalling and by attacking the credibility and reputation of the whistleblower. After all, if the company is innocent, the whistleblower must be not only wrong but venal and corrupt as well. So the employee gets fired for cause and may also be subject to harassing lawsuits and other forms of intimidation.

Federal False Claims Act

Several federal statutes contain provisions intended to protect whistleblowers. Sometimes the Federal False Claims Act applies and provides the whistleblower with some financial protection against the career damage that the company may inflict. But even if whistleblowers share in the recovery (which is not assured in cases that do not involve the government), the money they receive may not be sufficient to compensate them for a lifetime of rejection by the industry in which they have been trained for a career. For example, a whistleblower who, in 1988, forced General Electric into a $7 million settlement in an overcharging case shared in the recovery, but he was nevertheless branded by the industry as an overzealous troublemaker and was unable to find new employment. Even the two Morton-Thiokol engineers who warned of the problems with the O-rings before the *Challenger* disaster found their careers nearly wrecked. Indeed, they were forced into early retirement despite praise from the federal Rogers Commission inquiry into the disaster.

In short, whistleblowers can expect to be abused by their employers (and often, too, by their fellow workers, who tend to side with the employer) for taking the actions they do. So why do they do it?

Moral Imperatives

In an important article entitled "Whistleblowing: Its Moral Justification," Gene James, a professor of philosophy at Memphis State University, argues that the only reason why whistleblowers come forward, in view of the predictably harsh and unfair treatment that will result, is because of the moral imperative to prevent or uncover illegal or reprehensible behavior that causes or could cause harm to others. Preventing such harm is a higher duty than protecting the confidentiality of information belonging to an employer. Indeed, "the amount of moral responsibility that one has to report actions depends upon the extent to which the consequences of the action are foreseeable, and the extent to which one's own action, or failure to act, becomes a cause of those consequences." In other words, if someone will be seriously hurt unless you disclose the offending actions, you share blame for being the cause of the harm if you do not come forward and reveal what you know. James also argues that focusing on any particular motives of the whistleblower in disclosing what he or she knows "is irrelevant to the real issue of whether what he has to say about the organization doing harm is true or not."[26] It doesn't matter whether whistleblowers are trying to get even for an old slight or to advance themselves at someone else's expense. What matters is only whether whistleblowers' allegations are true.

If the potential allegations *are* true, then disclosure is either permissible or obligatory, according to Richard DeGeorge, another prominent moral philosopher. It is *permissible* when an employee has discovered that the firm, through a product or policy, will do serious and considerable harm to the public, and the employee then makes bona fide efforts to reveal the information to responsible superiors in accordance with the chain of command. If the firm makes no attempt to address the problem, the employee is morally permitted to set aside his or her duties to preserve the company's confidences, and to blow the whistle. Disclosure is *obligatory* if a serious danger to the public is present, the whistleblower has indisputable evidence to prove it, and there is reason to believe that disclosure would eliminate the danger to the public.[27]

In such situations, whistleblowers must be very careful. If companies reject their efforts to repair the damage internally, then they must recognize the danger in disclosing what the companies are attempting to conceal or avoid. Whistleblowers can expect some form of retribution by their employers, which may land them, as it did Mark Whitacre, in serious trouble. Whistleblowers must be sure of the facts and must have documented the information. It also helps if they are completely pure (unlike Whitacre). Because previous efforts to resolve matters internally have failed, whistleblowers must think carefully about how to report the information. And it is crucially important to obtain legal advice and legal representation in handling events subsequent to blowing the whistle.

Economic Welfare of Firms

James and DeGeorge help to clarify the circumstances under which whistleblowing is appropriate. But what about cases in which the potential harm to society is not so extreme? What about people who discover something more local and mundane, like the mismarking of a trading position? In such cases the harm is to the economic welfare of the firm and indirectly to its shareholders and its employees. As a consequence, the residual obligation of employees to protect the firm's and their own economic interests has some force. Nonetheless, the wrongdoers have disregarded this obligation and placed others at risk in order to benefit themselves. Employees acting in such a way are a menace to the firm and its employees. Most superiors and other employees therefore accept that whistleblowing is appropriate under such circumstances.

Despite this, companies have shown themselves to be very weak indeed in dealing with cases of wrongdoing by employees, which often make the plight of a potential whistleblower much more difficult. For example, many top managers have shown a propensity to waffle when confronted by a charge of wrongdoing by a particularly strong producer who is responsible for a significant amount of the firm's earnings. Because managers don't want to lose the services of such key employees, they try to work things out with the wrongdoers instead of punishing or restraining them. There is not much evidence to suggest that such efforts are ever successful. Usually the wrongdoer proceeds as before, believing that senior managers will neither attempt to stop the offenses nor disclose them for fear (among other things) of implicating themselves. In such situations the potential whistleblower's position is untenable.

Even in cases in which wrongdoers are stopped or discharged, whistleblowers may be blamed for ratting on a colleague and causing the dismissal. Unless the offense is made clear to the other employees by the firm, which entails going public with the account of the offense, the benefit of the whistleblowing may be greatly curtailed. Not only will whistleblowers find their situations awkward and without reward, but the message of punishment to wrongdoers will not have been communicated across the firm. Too often superiors are determined to conceal the offense, once it has been detected and acted upon. "Why tell others of our problems?" they may ask. "Why invite lack of confidence in our controls or our management by disclosing bad news when we don't have to? Why open ourselves up to a lawsuit from someone who feels harmed by the actions we are now intent on preventing? If they don't know enough to bring a suit, they won't."

When managers attempt to contain information about misconduct and disciplinary action, employees have few incentives to whistleblow, even if doing so would prevent a major loss or other significant threat to the firm. In other words, absent *qui tam* provisions, if a firm makes limited efforts to prevent wrongdoing or it fails to encourage whistleblowers to report matters that harm the firm's welfare, it should not expect employees to feel duty-bound to report anything. If the employer doesn't care enough about its own welfare to maintain high standards and to encourage employees to identify and report wrongdoing, why should the employee?

To whistleblow in situations that are not obligatory, as defined earlier, is thus entirely a voluntary action. Employees cannot be compelled to do so. If an employer fails to take steps that encourage whistleblowing, which would enable the firm to deal with offenses before they become more serious and more costly, the firm will send the wrong message to knowing employees and also put itself into a position of losing control over subsequent events. And if the original problem becomes bad enough, someone is sure to step forward as a whistleblower in a manner that will maximize the firm's difficulties. Once the cat is out of the bag, stonewalling and aggressive reprisals seem only to make matters worse; an informed whistleblower has a number of alternative courses of action to provide effective protection against corporate retaliation, including appeals to directors, investors, analysts, the media, law enforcement authorities, and the courts.

Alternative Ways to Blow Whistles

In considering whether to whistleblow, the most important thing a person needs to do is to *think through the entire process carefully before any action*

Exhibit 10-1   Whistleblower's Checklist

- What are my personal motives for whistleblowing?

- Am I sure the situation warrants whistleblowing?

  — Do I have solid knowledge of the facts?

  — What harm will be done? To whom?

  — Can I verify my conclusions?

  — Can my information be documented?

  — How much time is there before harm is done?

- What type of wrongdoing is involved and to whom should it be reported?

  — What is the appropriate chain of command for reporting such things in this company? How many of them should I try to go to?

  — What are the company's procedures for whistleblowing?

- Can I prepare a concise and factual statement of my allegations?

- Should I consult a lawyer? If not, why not?

- Am I ready to face consequences of retaliation? Can I document any such retaliation?

Source: Adapted from Gene G. James, "Whistleblowing: Its Moral Justification," in *Business Ethics*, 3d ed., ed. Michael Hoffman and Robert Federici (New York: McGraw-Hill, 1995).

is taken. Professor James's thoughts have contributed to a checklist for whistleblowers (Exhibit 10-1).

There are various degrees of anonymity in whistleblowing. Individuals can stand up and be counted right from the start, thus subjecting themselves to the full benefits and costs of the action. Alternatively, they can disclose the issues confidentially to a superior, though the requested anonymity may or may not be honored. Or the whistleblower can act anonymously, using legal counsel or other representatives to press the case. The following are the main alternatives available to whistleblowers:

- *Inside, through the direct supervisor.* An individual's immediate supervisor is informed. If whistleblowing can be justified, this option should be the first.

- *Inside, through appeal to middle managers.* Second-level or higher supervisors are sequentially informed after lower-level supervisors fail to act. The issue remains within the ranks of middle management.

- *Inside, going to the top.* The issue is brought to the attention of senior management after stonewalling by middle management and perhaps by legal and compliance staff as well.

- *Inside, through an exit interview.* The whistleblower resigns from the company, perhaps because of the misconduct involved, and uses the exit interview as the vehicle for making the issues known.

- *Inside, through outside directors.* An appeal is made to one or more members of the board of directors, with or without first seeking the attention of management. The assumption is that the duty-of-care requirement for board members will trigger a meaningful investigation. The director may take the side of top management, however, to which he or she can be expected to be loyal.

- *Inside, through alumni status.* After having left the company, the whistleblower informs senior management, the board, or an employee.

- *Outside, through regulatory or law-enforcement authorities.* Having failed to get an appropriate response in one or more attempts inside the company (or believing that such attempts would be fruitless or counterproductive), the whistleblower takes the issue to regulatory or law enforcement authorities. They, in turn, may request cooperation in verifying the suspect practices, in which case the whistleblower turns into a mole. The whistleblower has an obligation to exhaust all internal procedures and possibilities before making the issues known outside the firm.

- *Outside, through the media.* In this alternative to informing public officials, the whistleblower discusses his concerns with a journalist. If the story is newsworthy and credible, the journalist will make public the allegations. And if high standards of professional journalism are maintained, the journalist will conduct an independent investigation and protect the source of the original information.

What the Law Says

In deciding whether and how to blow the whistle, it is a good idea to learn what the law has to say on the subject. In the case of U.S. government employees, the United States Code of Ethics for Government Servants requires them to "expose corruption wherever uncovered" and to "put loyalty to the highest moral principles and to country above loyalty to persons, party, or government." There are also federal statutes designed to protect whistleblowers in the areas of labor relations, occupational health and safety, and civil rights, although their effectiveness is open to debate. The Federal False Claims Act appears to be the most effective in encouraging whistleblowing, largely because of incentives built into the *qui tam* provisions discussed earlier.

In cases in which the federal or state government has no stake or legal interest in the problem identified by the whistleblower, there are few statutes relating to whistleblowing. Indeed, the law provides, in general, little support for whistleblowers. It is a basic principle of agency law that employees owe to their employers a duty of loyalty, which requires employees not to disclose to outside parties information that is discovered in the course of their employment and that could be detrimental to the company. Both proprietary information and information about questionable business practices are included within this prohibition. Not included is information that the company has committed or is about to commit a felony, in which case the employee has a separate and overriding legal responsibility to report that conduct.[28]

Once the whistleblower goes public, the allegations have to be proved, usually in court, with the standard of proof being mandated by the nature of the proceedings, whether criminal or civil. If a possible crime is involved, however, how can the very high standard of proof be met through information available to the whistleblower or the prosecutor? What if the charge is not sustained by the evidence? What happens to the whistleblower in such circumstances? Before proceeding with charges outside the company, the whistleblower should know the answer to these questions, and to get them he or she must consult a lawyer competent in handling such cases. After all, if a criminal case is brought but leads to no conviction, the whistleblower may be exposed to countersuits and charges of malicious behavior. Few whistleblowers have the financial means to engage powerful corporations in litigation. Moreover, in virtually all states, firms can still fire whistleblowing employees at will. Retaliation by management is therefore both legal and likely, even if the firm itself had previously acted illegally and as charged by the whistleblower.

Retaliation

According to one observer, "When an employee steps forward and legitimately accuses an organization of wrongdoing, it can bring out the worst in everyone. . . . The company may instigate a cover-up. It can make the *whistleblower himself* the issue by trying to discredit him. Or, perhaps the most insidious of all, the company could pretend to listen, appoint the whistleblower to solve the problem, deny access to needed information, and either accuse him later of "crying-wolf," or make him the scapegoat when the wrongdoing persists."[29]

Retaliation may include firing, withholding of pension benefits, orders to undergo a psychiatric examination, demotion, adverse performance reviews, relocation, reassignment, limiting access to information, assignment of unsympathetic co-workers or supervisors, harassment of family and friends, and investigation of private financial affairs and personal life.[30]

One recent and extensive study of whistleblowing cases suggests that retaliation against whistleblowers is hardly as inevitable or as fierce as frequently supposed. "Retaliation is not a frequent outcome for whistleblowers, although it can be argued that any retaliation is too much. The myth of inevitable retaliation likely continues because the cases reported in the media are likely to be the most dramatic and unfortunate." Retaliation was found to be most common, however, when

- the wrongdoing was likely to harm the general public

- the identity of a previously anonymous whistleblower became known

- initial attempts to convince immediate superiors to right the wrong ended in failure

- the values of the whistleblowers were at odds with those of the organization

- discontinuing the questionable activity would harm the organization

- the wrongdoing itself was perceived to harm the organization's culture or morale, thus diminishing management's self-image

No linkage was found between the likelihood of retaliation and whether or not co-workers felt that the issue concerned warranted whistleblowing.[31]

In the United Kingdom, help for whistleblowers faced with potential retaliation is available from Public Concern at Work, a charitable organization that offers legal advice and support. Much of its caseload turns out to involve relatively junior employees who are afraid they will be ignored or punished if they raise their concerns within corporate hierarchies bent on keeping bad news from superiors.[32] Similar support on the part of private organizations and public interest groups is available in the United States.

Creating a Benign Whistleblowing Culture

Senior management should welcome early warnings of corporate misconduct so that they can be addressed and corrected as quickly as possible. Once aware of wrongdoing, management has a moral obligation—and often a legal one—to take prompt and effective corrective action. In some cases, senior-management response systems are quite effective, especially in companies that have suffered a major scandal in the not too distant past. Where such a system exists, employees may find it comparatively easy to make their concerns known about questionable activities within the firm. Other companies take the opposite and ultimately dysfunctional approach. Senior managers give lip service to issues of corporate conduct but then crack down on whistleblowers, intimidating all but the most conscience-stricken. As one observer notes, "In such companies, deficiencies of management and corporate governance are in any case likely to have deep roots."[33]

If a firm's goal is to encourage behavior that upholds and enforces legal and ethical principles, then it must ensure that whistleblowers suffer no adverse personal and professional consequences from their behavior. In many firms, however, existing reward systems reinforce behavior and attitudes that militate against whistleblowing, even though a nominal consensus encourages it. In view of this ambivalence, and with complex institutional forces at work, protecting the whistleblowers is a difficult task. But unless management is committed to protecting them and makes this commitment known to employees, few whistles will sound. The fear of retaliation may loom too large for prospective whistleblowers to put their professional and personal welfare at risk for what they perceive as a potentially hostile and defensive organization.

Sir John Harvey-Jones, former chairman of Imperial Chemical Industries of Great Britain, has maintained that employees usually stay silent far too long for fear of retribution by their employers, with the result that the ultimate damage to shareholders is far greater than need be. He has suggested that whistleblowers be generously compensated if their information proves correct and they lose their jobs.[34] The bottom line is that if whistleblowers are to be encouraged, the outcomes for them must be consistent with the benefits they bestow on the enterprise.

One authority has the following advice for management uncomfortable in dealing with whistleblowing but intent on identifying problems that may damage the firm's franchise:[35]

- Don't play favorites, above or below you.

- Keep an open-door policy so that your staff knows you are available and accessible.

- Maintain confidentiality on unimportant matters; when important matters come along, your employees know they can trust you.

- Appreciate that, for most employees, it takes courage to come to a supervisor with a problem.

- Investigate all allegations and, if appropriate, act on them.

- Document what you do, and communicate your action to the employee.

- Show by example that you believe ethics are paramount.

The problem is that it's not at all easy to implement such advice. Often employees don't believe or trust the program. In a 1994 article in *Management Review,* Barbara Ettore noted that "the past few years have seen a meteoric rise in [corporate] ethics programs and all the trappings of compliance systems that go into them, including confidential hotlines and employee surveys, ombudspersons and neutral-party inspectors general."[36] Unfortunately, she added, these programs often seem to fall far short of their goals. In this context she summarizes a 1992 study of whistleblowing policies of U.S. corporations that elucidates the continuing prevalence of misconduct.[37]

Companies need a careful and sustained effort to apprise employees of their rights and responsibilities as members of the firm and what they should do when they encounter misconduct. This effort can easily misfire. All too often, notices to employees are written in dense prose provided by the firm's lawyers, or are not recirculated periodically for the benefit of new employees. Exhibit 10-2 is a typical internal notice about "firmwide employee communication channels" that is periodically circulated by a major U.S. securities firm (names are disguised).

The central purpose of such memos is usually to help the firm defend itself against potential lawsuits. The memo supposedly demonstrates that the firm did everything possible to discourage employee misbehavior and that the firm is therefore not responsible for the rogue actions of an errant individual or group. Just how effective these memorandums are depends upon the firm's track record. Employees eventually come to learn whether to take seriously or to ignore the exhortations that come across their desks. Senior executives generally believe that they know how the employees feel about such things, but these beliefs are rarely tested or subjected to critical examination.

This particular memo does affirm the firm's standard policies to pursue wrongdoing and to protect whistleblowers. It also sternly reminds employees of their duties to report offenses and tells them how this might be done, either through a variety of internal channels (mainly lawyers, although none are named) or through an outside source (another lawyer). The notice, however, suffers from a hard-edged and formal style that may be intimidating to a potential whistleblower. It may also convey the impression that the firm's lawyers want to be in control of all matters relating to a reported incident and that they may manipulate the case and the whistleblower in accordance with their own perceptions of corporate interests. Rather oddly, the memo is directed only to U.S. personnel in a truly global firm and—being signed by a faceless body called the "Executive Committee"—conveys no sense that the individual members of that committee have any vital interest or concern in the subject matter of the memo.

An alternative way for corporations to deal with whistleblowing is to take a much less formal, more sincere, and user-friendly approach. Alan C. ("Ace") Greenberg, longtime chairman of Bear Stearns, had a unique style for communicating with employees. Exhibit 10-3 is an example. The memo,

Exhibit 10-2   A Typical Memo about Reporting Legal and Ethical Problems

---

February 5, 1995

Memorandum to: All U.S.-based Personnel

Re: Firmwide Employee Communication Channels

Our Business Principles strongly emphasize that "integrity and honesty are at the heart of our business." The firm employees have the responsibility not only to conduct the firm's business in accordance with applicable laws, regulations and firm policies, but to report promptly legal and ethical problems and concerns whenever they arise. The channels for reporting these matters are set forth below.

General Channels. Any troubling legal or ethical issue or any violation of firm policies should be brought to the attention of your immediate supervisor, or anyone else in or outside the chain of command at the firm, any person with divisional compliance responsibilities or in the Compliance Department, any member of the Legal Department, or any member of the Executive Committee.

Alternate Channels. Any employee who wishes to report a possible violation of law, ethics, or firm policies, but does not feel comfortable using the firm's internal communication channels, may contact one of the firm's outside counsel, William George, a senior partner at George, Lewis and Sheldon. Mr. George is a trial and appellate lawyer who has practiced for over 30 years, and has been active as a teacher and lecturer in the field of professional ethics. His telephone number is 1-212-800-8000.

The firm strictly prohibits retaliation against any employee who reports a possible violation of law, ethics or firm policies by others, no matter who the report involves. You should feel comfortable reporting any behavior that you suspect is contrary to the law, firm policy, or our ethical standards through the communication channels described above. Regardless of the way you choose to report a possible legal or ethical violation, the important thing is that you report your concerns promptly to someone.

The Executive Committee

Exhibit 10-3   An Effective Memo about Reporting Legal and Ethical Problems

---

Bear Stearns

M E M O

DATE: February 5, 1993

TO: Senior Managing Directors
         Managing Directors
         Associate Directors

FROM: Alan C. Greenberg

We need your help. Please help us get a message out to every associate. It is essential that *once again* we stress that we welcome every suspicion or feeling that our co-workers might have about something they see or hear that is going on at Bear Stearns that might not measure up to our standards of honesty and integrity. This should be a H.M.A.* crisis-control yellow warning.

We want people at Bear Stearns to cry wolf. If the doubt is justified, the reporter will be handsomely rewarded. If the suspicion proves unfounded, the person who brought it to our attention will be *thanked* for his or her vigilance and told to keep it up.

Forget the chain of **command!** That is not the way Bear Stearns was built. If you think somebody is doing something off the wall or his/her decision-making stinks, go around the person,** and that includes me.

Haimchinkel Malintz Anaynikal once said that a successful transaction has many fathers but a dumb decision is an orphan. We want our people to tell us of the boneheads or potential improprieties quickly! *Get these messages out loud and clear.*

Source: Copyright © 1996 by Alan C. Greenberg. Used by permission of Workman Publishing Company, Inc.

* Abbreviation for Haimchinkel Malintz Anaynikal [a mythical character who often turns up in Greenberg's memos].

** We have had some senior people who resented "end runs." They quickly became associated with more conventional firms—you can draw your own conclusions about whether their career change worked out for the best.

one of a great many that Greenberg has circulated over the years, clearly comes from the top man himself. It is brief, readable, humorous, and clear. It is believable. And it is *very* different. It is one of many published in his 1996 bestseller, *Memos from the Chairman.*

Old Ace is saying it's okay to spy on your colleagues and bosses. His memo encourages everyone to resist temptation and to be as honest as possible because everyone is being watched! He says those who report misconduct will be "handsomely rewarded" and that honest false alarms will be met with thanks, not punishment. He also says to forget the chain of command altogether. Go around anyone you want, including himself— but go. It's important! So get the word out.

In other memos on the same subject, Greenberg tells his employees to call him personally. What makes such suggestions credible is that the firm actually does what he says it will do. Some of the memos cite specific cases where people have been fired for wrongdoing. Others report about employees who were publicly rewarded on the spot with checks in the amount of 5 percent of the damage prevented. Greenberg has also gone out of his way to hire whistleblowers fired by other firms. "We need that sort here." Greenberg says the system works. But it's not just the firm's policies that are important. It's the character of the communication with employees that is the heart of the system's success.

One thing most whistleblowing cases have in common is that the whistleblowing occurs very late in the game, after much damage has already been done. The problem festers, sometimes for months and even years, and then surfaces with a vengeance, causing serious damage to people, institutions, and reputations. Just imagine the kind of damage that could have been prevented at Salomon or Barings or Drexel or Prudential or Daiwa or Bankers Trust if someone, somewhere had blown the whistle early in the game. Imagine if top management had followed up the complaint personally, quickly, and decisively, cutting out the rot and setting the firm on the right course so that the problem didn't recur.

At most firms, management does its best to address the source of such problems by adopting appropriate policies and procedures and by providing channels for identifying any misbehavior that slips through the cracks. Too often, though, management takes these matters too lightly. Few firms audit their internal communications (using a neutral outside source) to determine how employees perceive them. Few firms know whether or not employees really believe that the firm is determined to carry out its announced policies no matter what the cost. And when misconduct does occur, firms are too often reluctant to take forceful action. They don't want to stir things up too much, to upset employees, or to put too much pressure on aggressive, highly productive executives. This ambivalence undercuts the firm's own policies and goals. And the ultimate cost can be staggering if, as a result, serious misconduct goes undetected. By contrast, it is relatively cheap for a firm to ensure to communicate and enforce its policies effectively, and to create an environment in which misconduct is identified early before it does any substantial damage.

11

Zookeeping

■

The management characteristics of securities firms have long been a mystery to outsiders. To them, the industry appears to be one that is in constant self-actuated turmoil; an industry that has prospered mainly by allowing itself to become increasingly aggressive and risky. Driving it are the opportunities for talented and highly motivated young people to make lots of money in a short time by competing forcefully, pursuing new opportunities effectively, and adapting constantly and ruthlessly to market changes. Complicating the industry is the commoditization of much of the basic investment banking business of old, as well as the dramatic swing toward trading activities that now dominate most of the major firms. Trading—now fully global in scope—requires much more capital than it did twenty years ago, a large and diverse group of employees located all over the world, and sophisticated control systems to go with them. The result appears to be an organizational environment of constant change, a kind of permanent, continuing chaos to which all must adapt or perish. Such conditions bring out all of the animal spirits of those involved, making the directing of securities firms more like "zookeeping" than managing a more conventional business.

Senior executives of firms in the industry, however, are more relaxed about these issues. It may seem strange to outsiders, they say, but this is our industry and we are used to it. Some add that for an industry undergoing enormous technical, regulatory, and competitive change, the securities industry is holding its own. Its great strength is its ability to react to things quickly, to stay with the markets in good times or bad, and to expand or contract its activities accordingly. Compared with commercial banking or insurance, two sectors of financial services that have also been forced through severe restructuring and reengineering during the past twenty years, the securities industry may actually claim some managerial success.

Maybe so, but being better managed than the banks during this period of financial history is not claiming much.

A Matter of Values

No matter how you look at it today, the securities industry's businesses are tough ones to manage. But not tough just because of the trading exposures and market risks. The industry has learned to handle these reasonably well. There has also been increasing pressure from regulators and law enforcement officials to abide by thousands of changing securities regulations that govern markets all over the world. And the serious consequences associated with mistakes and misbehavior have made the business more dangerous than ever before—for its employees, certainly, but also for those who own or invest in the firms. So securities firms are tough to value, or to put a *high* value on, because so much of the wealth created by the firms' efforts can easily be destroyed by fines, penalties, adverse judgments in litigation, and reputation losses.

Two sets of values are present, and sometimes in conflict—*market values* that reflect economic results, and *professional values* that reflect the positive (or negative) intangibles associated with each firm's business franchise. The two are clearly related. Maximizing market value requires maintaining high professional standards that help minimize the damages that can be sustained by mishaps, rogue behavior, and serious compliance failures.

Market Values

For example, at midyear 1996, a time when the price-earnings ratio (based on expected earnings for the full year 1996) for the S&P 500 stocks averaged 16.2, the PE ratios of the top eight publicly owned U.S. investment banks (including J.P. Morgan) averaged only 7.9, and this was in their all-time best year. The PE ratios of the top ten commercial banks at the time averaged 10.3, and those of the top life and casualty insurance companies and various specialty finance and asset management companies averaged about 12. The share price-to-book value ratio for the top ten commercial banks in 1996 was 1.83. For the top ten securities firms it was 1.27.

These ratios, which are computed after payouts for management and staff compensation, have not varied greatly over the past decade or so. An investment bank was considered very fully valued if it traded at twice its book value, even though this may reflect a PE ratio of only 10. That is, the earnings were not capitalized at a high market value for the firm producing them. This was because the market feared low prospective earnings or some other interruption in future cash flows. The market substantially discounted the future cash flows of the industry because of the residual risks, mainly associated with trading positions and regulatory and legal hazards. This discount, arguably, was a large one. Some might think it was too large. After all, the market volatility was no greater than that of many other industries characterized by substantial revenue growth and rapid market developments in which high PEs were typical, such as computer technology, entertainment, and communications. Sometimes the earnings of such companies were disappointing, but the share prices stayed high.

Modern investment banking has been a growth industry, with vast amounts of transactions taking place and new markets and technologies constantly creating new opportunities. The top firms have had high market shares and are expected to keep, if not expand, them both at home and abroad. And the firms have shown repeatedly that they can survive market fluctuations handily. Several endured the crash of 1987 and the bear market of 1994 and still made money. Still, the risk-related discount to which their shares have been subject remains large. One reason appears to be that shareholder value is extremely vulnerable to the consequences of employee and management misconduct, real as well as perceived. The market seems to be applying a discount big enough to cover not only prospective market losses, but also possible losses from fines, settlements, judgments, legal expenses, and erosion of business franchise resulting from professional misconduct. And when such misconduct has actually occurred, the market has punished the stocks very severely indeed.[1]

If this is so, maybe something can be done. If companies can conduct themselves so as to minimize the risk of misconduct and its consequences, then perhaps the market will discount their shares less, with the stock price increasing accordingly. Indeed, this strategy may be the single most effective way of boosting the shareholder value of securities firms. Increasing Salomon's PE from 7 to that of J.P. Morgan's 11, for example, would increase the market capitalization of the firm by $2.5 billion, nearly 60 percent. Morgan is a big, global trading firm, just like Salomon, but the market thinks it is better managed and has a more responsible corporate culture. Deryck Maughan, Salomon's CEO, once noted that the market's valuation of management in the financial-services industry was reflected in the premium over book (liquidation) value at which the stock trades. J.P. Morgan's price-to-book value ratio in mid-1996 was 1.6, and Salomon's was 1.2. Consequently, the market must be saying—despite rather similar businesses operating quite profitably at the time—that Morgan's management has succeeded in making its business more stable, more controlled, and less exposed to risk, including the risk of misconduct, than Salomon's. Therefore Morgan is worth more.

Professional Values

Reducing risks due to instability and misconduct is mainly a matter of raising standards, of increasing the respect for professional values. Strong professional values can increase shareholder values. In the 1970s and 1980s, young investment bankers would learn the firm's standards and values through on-the-job training. They usually stayed with the firm that hired them until they became principals—partners or managing directors. Some left for other opportunities in the industry, but most stayed with their original firms and became part of the culture. They were trained to be risk-averse, service-oriented, team-playing professionals.

Bankers who joined firms in the 1990s, however, have been encouraged to be innovative risk takers, with more focus on profitable trading opportunities than on bidding for client business against other firms. These young bankers also know that their firms now hire aggressively from other firms to get better talent, and cut back ruthlessly when markets are soft. The star system has been in full bloom, regardless of what the firms say about teamwork. Highly talented bankers move around the industry like free agents in sports, and often jump at huge offers from new teams being fielded by aggressive newcomers. Few employees, if any, believe they will spend their entire careers with the firm that initially hired them. Many wonder whether their Wall Street careers will last more than a few years. They know they may be subject to layoffs, burnout, and crises of various sorts at the firms that employ them. What makes it worthwhile is the money and the thrill of it all—while it lasts.

These perceptions reflect a shift in the values of the firms during the past decade or so. Market dynamics and the industry environment have led firms to take more risks to increase or shore up economic performance. Greater incentives were offered to achieve this, and little expense was spared in chasing opportunities in bull markets. When the markets turned and became difficult, no time was lost in slashing overheads and laying off less immediately valuable employees. This cycle was repeated not just once, but two or three times in ten years, producing a dizzying and frightening effect on employees. The basic career message that is continually communicated from the top of the firms to those below, therefore, has changed. It is today a message of insecurity for all but those few whose performance in generating profits is exceptional and continuing.

The pendulum may now have swung too far. Excessive concern for profits may have weakened the firms by eroding employee loyalty and devotion, and by exposing them to inevitable risks that exceptional profit performers encounter in stretching themselves too far. The combination of diffident employees unwilling to blow the whistle on improper activities when they are discovered and the moral hazard associated with extreme incentive compensation for risking the firm's capital has to be a dangerous one. Indeed, it may be time for senior managers to rethink the way their firms set and maintain professional values and communicate them to their employees. Too much has happened since the last time these values and standards were seriously questioned. A review of what a firm regards as its core professional values ought to be a useful and healthy exercise, one very likely to alter the way some things are done within most firms.

Raising Standards

For some years now, in board rooms and universities around the country, people have been asking for more education of students and new employees in standards of professional conduct. "Look at all the rogues in the financial business," they say. "If they had proper ethical training they wouldn't be like that. Business schools should do a better job of teaching ethics to these people." Universities, however, hesitate to do so without a common context in which to anchor it. "Ethics is moral philosophy, dealing with right and wrong," some professors say, "not something we can put into standardized, freeze-dried packages for young business people." Others simply assume the young people they deal with are not criminals who deliberately set out to break the law, so they leave them to pick up professional standards from their firms, standards that come out in the context of doing what they do at the firm every day. "We can't teach that," the business school professors say.

We agree. But what we can do is highlight the many enculturation and leadership issues that are involved in effective management of a diverse group of high-performance employees, and of an equally diverse and complex array of competitive and regulatory issues—"zookeeping," as we call it. Senior managers may find these highlights useful as benchmarks against which to calibrate their own systems and programs. Newcomers to the industry can do the same and perhaps compare their firms, or firms they are considering joining, with each other. Those disappointed with what they discover can then decide whether to change what they do or where they work. And close attention to professional values may very well increase financial values, too.

Management

Management in an investment bank, as anywhere else, demands the assumption of responsibility for the profit-making activities of the firm, such as generating revenues and minimizing the associated costs. In investment banking, the revenues involve fees and trading income after all exposures are closed out. Costs include not only processing expenses, but also the cost of capital, talented personnel, and managing the risks of the business. These costs are all complex and unevenly weighted, but they are an integral part of fielding a team that can distinguish itself in competition with others.

The conventional wisdom of Wall Street (and the modern financial-services industry generally) is to take the *offense* in revenues and the *defense* in cost control and compliance. The underlying assumption is that the two have little to do with each other. A small group of senior "producer-managers," usually called the management committee or executive committee, directs and integrates the offensive and defensive functions from the top of the organization.

Traditionally, most of the emphasis has been on "front-office" revenues, and most of the top managers of the firm are selected because of their ability to generate revenues. The others, the defensive players, are known as *nonrevenue producers,* a sort of core overhead group that has to be tolerated in order for transactions to be processed and administrative functions completed. The "back office" is considered important, and even appreciated as indispensable, but its people are rarely placed among those in the firm considered to be the most uniquely talented and to have star quality. The relative weighting between the two is not equal, protestations to the contrary notwithstanding. The offense team is invariably seen as the more colorful, personable, creative, and productive. These players usually supply the external "face" of the firm, so they are paid more and attract most of whatever glory and fame the firm generates. The defense players are usually seen as just the opposite—lawyers, accountants, and systems people who are there only to support the rest. In short, the revenue producers are the prima donnas and the nonrevenue types are the spear carriers in the great operatic productions of the Street.

The revenue side of the firm is focused on clients and on risk. The clients are there to trade with, or perform services for. But the market is highly competitive, and the same clients usually do business with competitors as well. Firms find themselves exposed to lower spreads and greater trading risks than ever before. The risks are mainly position risks in which, for example, a firm accommodates a client by buying securities for subsequent resale. If the market changes, the firm may well lose money on the transaction. Indeed, revenue producers find that being awarded the trade usually means that the firm's price quotation was the most aggressive and therefore the riskiest. Other things being equal, the profitability of this traditional, client-driven business, especially on a risk-adjusted basis, has been in decline for many years, despite a huge increase in the volume of transactions.

To counter this trend, firms active in capital markets have been forced to seek new revenue opportunities. One way of doing so is to invent new products and services for which higher spreads can be charged, at least for a while. Another is to push into new areas, such as foreign and emerging markets. Yet another is to enter into transactions in which the firm takes trading risks on its own books, which is usually called *proprietary trading* and may involve special strategies or arbitrages devised by the firm. Because such strategies often involve predictions of when particular investments will rise in value, however, proprietary trading is usually relatively speculative and subject to substantial risk. Firms may also engage in merchant banking; their own capital is allocated to bridge loans or minority interests in private placements of debt or equity, usually in small or midsized companies. All of these efforts to develop new business opportunities have required firms to take on increased risks.

Risks and Hazards

The revenue producers, of course, are the ones taking the risks. Or, more accurately, they are the ones who create the risks that the firm takes on. The firm bears these risks with its own capital, which is owned by the firm's shareholders or partners. Although risk creators may also be shareholders, they are usually small shareholders. Usually, too, risk creators are compensated on the basis of performance, that is, in proportion to the revenues of an individual or a unit. If no risk is taken, revenue generation will be negligible. Certainly any individual wanting to be a successful trader needs to take substantial risks all the time. Risks, that is, with the shareholders' capital. The risk creator has a strong incentive to maximize the risks to be taken, but has minimal exposure to the losses, which rest on the shareholders.

Risk comes in various forms. There is open-position risk, a bet that something will or will not happen. There is hedged risk, a position that is offset by another, opposite position that neutralizes all or some of the open-position exposure. There is basis risk, involving a hedge that is not exactly the same as the risk that has been booked, but is something similar to it. There is counterparty risk, the chance that the party on the other side of the trade will not pay or perform as required. And though there are many other kinds of risk, the last we will mention is perhaps the most difficult, involving malfeasance or deception on the part of revenue producers or other employees.

The ultimate risk associated with malfeasance is that the firm's internal integrity will be mortally wounded or seriously compromised because of the conduct of its people. This risk is the most dangerous of all. Actions by employees can get the firm in far deeper trouble than simple trading losses. The list of firms experiencing such problems in recent years is very long indeed. In the majority of these cases, the losses were the result of highly valued, lavishly compensated, star revenue producers who went overboard. Only the lowly back-office people could have stopped them, which they did not. By the time the damage was done, the shareholders had lost fortunes.

Living with Prima Donnas

Controlling the prima donnas of the banking world can be difficult, mainly because they do not like to be controlled or restrained. They see themselves as highly talented people who must be allowed to do their own thing. They hate bureaucracy, regimentation, rules, and strict accountability. Having succeeded in open competition against the best professionals in the world, they view themselves as similar to champion athletes or star entertainers. They expect to be paid for what they contribute, to have a share in the profits they make. They care what other people in their business earn and are upset if they discover that they earn less than a rival elsewhere. They

are always aware of their value in the market and are often in contact with
headhunters representing other firms. They are highly self-confident individuals, usually with large egos. They are prepared to test themselves in
the market every day. And like stars anywhere, they can be difficult to
manage and to discipline.

In 1968, a well-known brokerage firm, F.I. DuPont-Glore Forgan, was
in deep trouble and about to fail. The New York Stock Exchange, hoping
to prevent the firm's collapse, tried to find someone to rescue it. The
exchange found Ross Perot, then head of Electronic Data Systems (EDS).
The firm had recently taken EDS public, and Perot was worth several
hundred million dollars. At the time, he believed that Wall Street represented a fertile new market for EDS, which managed large, on-site computer systems for clients. To demonstrate how useful EDS know-how could
be, he decided to be DuPont-Glore Forgan's white knight. Perot injected
a large amount of capital and soon afterwards rolled up his sleeves and got
down to work. He introduced several new ideas almost at once. The firm
would be open on Saturdays. The perks of executives and top producers
would be slashed. The employees would have to contribute to the rescue
effort by forgoing bonuses and salary increases. Accounting and other
controls would be introduced to tighten management's grip on the risks to
which the firm was exposed. All of these were good ideas for turning around
a troubled firm. The result? None of them were accepted by the high-performance employees and top managers. All rebelled. Most sought jobs
elsewhere. Those who could not get new jobs decided to retire and live on
their savings. These valued and senior employees would rather let the firm
die than conform to Perot's humiliating regime. He was astonished. A year
or so later, he sold the firm and left Wall Street forever. Ironically, some
years later Perot sold EDS to General Motors and himself became a
difficult-to-manage prima donna as a member of GM's board.

Perot's Wall Street experience was duplicated years later by General
Electric, when it acquired Kidder Peabody in 1986, and by American
Express, when it acquired Lehman Brothers in 1984. Both corporate owners later sold the firms, thus ridding themselves of the problems—and the
risks—of managing prima donnas. The Prudential Group still struggles with
Prudential Securities (formerly Bache Halsey Stuart, acquired in 1981).
Sears Roebuck, after several years of effort, seemed finally to have reached
a workable accommodation with Dean Witter Reynolds, a retail-oriented
firm it acquired in 1981, only to spin off all of its financial-services activities
in 1993.

Wall Street insiders commonly observe that outsiders just don't know what it takes to run a successful securities firm. The insiders are right, of course, but that is not to say that Wall Streeters themselves have a much better idea of how to manage their own firms. After all, since 1990 seven of the top ten American securities firms and three of the top six British merchant banks have failed, nearly failed, been rescued by deep-pocketed parents, or been forced into an unwelcome merger.[2] Not an enviable record.

Valuing Results

In the old days, securities firms had only two basic departments: buying and selling. The buying department was the underwriting and corporate-finance unit, and the sales department included mostly fixed-commission brokers. When the firm did an underwriting or advisory transaction, the fees would be allocated to the buying department, and the commissions and other brokerage earnings to the selling department. Within each department, individuals serviced clients they had developed or had been assigned. It was not difficult to determine who did what, and how compensation should be allocated. Once one became a partner (or a shareholder) of the firm, one received a percentage of the annual profits, with the allocation changing every year or two. Even the measurement of the firm's annual performance was much more straightforward than it is today. Because firms did not take many risks, profits were profits and did not have to be discounted for some indeterminate future risk or to be put away to protect the firm against some future uncertainty.

Measuring performance is very different now. Fixed commissions are gone. Block trading and bought deals (ones in which the firm takes often large market positions as a service to its clients) are the norm. An investment banker may maintain an excellent relationship with a tough client, fight through the competition, and win a mandate for a bond issue because of a clever new idea, and in the end actually lose money on the deal because a fixed-income trader he hardly knows misjudged the market. So a mighty, highly professional effort goes for naught, and our hero chalks up a loss. The next time, the solicitation effort may be less successful. Someone else takes the mandate and perhaps loses money. But our man gets no credit for avoiding the loss. At the end of the year his scorecard may look pretty forlorn, despite his having worked hard and displayed great ability.

Or take a salesman who nurtures his clients like a mother hen. Nonetheless, just about every time he asks the equity-block trader, or the government-securities trader, or the corporate-debt trader for a quote to pass on to his client, the client refuses it. Someone else has bid better. And then his biggest client gets burned on a recommendation put out by the firm's research department. The annoyed client boycotts the salesman for six weeks. What will his scorecard look like at the end of the year?

Or what about the trader who works hard and makes a killing in a bull market? Was he scoring points just because he chose to bet more of the firm's capital during a time when interest rates were falling? Could he in fact have been careless with the firm's risk exposure while making all this money? How should he be compared to his neighbor, someone more nervous about the market who, having taken less risk with the firm's capital, made less in return. Or to the proprietary trader who has a deal with the firm to be paid 15 percent of the gross profits from applying the black-box trading program he developed to identify market anomalies? Where does the 15 percent figure come from? Does his neighbor have a 15 percent deal, too, even if that means paying out $30 million or so to a single employee, as Salomon Brothers and other firms have done from time to time? If the same program makes losses next year, are 15 percent of the losses clawed back? How does the compensation formula itself compensate for risk?

Last, but certainly not least, how does a department manager get evaluated? To what extent is he or she to be credited with the success of the group? Has this potential reward for success already been dissipated in individual bonuses and other compensation to the individual members of the department? And what about support staff? Does a research analyst get paid more or less than a credit analyst, a fixed-income salesman more or less than a computer specialist?

Differentials in Compensation

Most firms believe they have to discriminate sharply among their employees in terms of compensation. Firms believe they have to do so to attract and retain the very best talent possible in a business where human skills are the critical difference between winners and losers. But also, in a time of eroding profit margins and constant battles with overheads, firms want to avoid overpaying average performers who are the nominal peers of the extraordinary ones. This problem is far more pervasive than one might think; despite massive recruiting and training efforts, securities firms in fact regard most of their employees as average. And because the compensation differentials between stars and any other employees are so dramatic, many excellent but less than stellar employees feel unappreciated and leave to take jobs at other firms.

This was demonstrated in the early 1990s at Smith Barney, which, having brought in former Morgan Stanley vice chairman and experienced rain-maker Robert Greenhill as CEO, proceeded to build up its investment-banking department by hiring from the outside. The new hires were heralded as stars who would propel Smith Barney to the top of the rankings. And they were promised large guaranteed bonuses for several years as an inducement to leave their old firms. At the end of the first year, however, the firm had not done all that well. Because the bonus pool was limited, there was virtually nothing left for the old employees once the new ones had been paid their guarantees. A year or so later, Greenhill left the firm, having failed to produce the expected results, and his new recruits soon did, too.

So the question becomes, how do you know which employees are ex-traordinary and therefore should be compensated at extraordinary levels, and which are just ordinary or flashes in the pan, therefore deserving much lower compensation? How accurate and reliable is the firm's score keeping? Or are the numbers merely incidental, and the thing that counts most is the standing the employee holds in the eyes of superiors? If so, how is that standing achieved? One might also ask how well and on what basis the firm has selected its managing directors or partners in the past. Has it always succeeded in getting the best of the batch? Have the ones selected moved up to greater responsibilities in the firm, or did they fall by the wayside? One eminent executive compensation consultant told Goldman Sachs some years ago that the best success rate he knew of was 85 percent (that is, 85 percent of persons deserving promotions received them) but that the rate at most firms was well below that.

When one considers the extraordinary compensation levels in the secu-rities industry, one concludes that there are a lot of geniuses working there. Indeed, based on the number of paychecks in seven digits, one can also conclude that a very high percentage of the world's supply of geniuses is concentrated in a handful of securities firms. But are they really geniuses, or just ordinary people who have been more lucky, or more aggressive, or more political at times when the money is there to be paid out? And if they are extraordinarily smart, creative, and productive, are they also honest men and women of good character whom (to use an old test) one would trust to hold the family money over the years? Are the people who succeed in this environment really the ones that one wants to promote and have a good shot at running the whole firm in the future?

Performance Evaluation

Systems that measure individual performance and thus determine compensation are central to the functioning of firms in the investment-banking industry. The most important thing that Wall Street managers do, many of them say, is to attract the most talented individuals to pursue careers at their firms and then to develop them and select the best for advancement. Evaluating performance can be difficult, whether it is based mainly on quantitative data (such as revenues generated) or qualitative considerations (such as the quality of relations with clients). If it is true, as behavioral scientists say, that you get what you measure, then you'd better be sure that the measures are what you want them to be.

Issues of measurement notwithstanding, most Wall Streeters believe that you get what you pay for and that if you pay enough, you will get good results. But did Prudential get the results it wanted from acquiring Bache? Did Smith Barney really benefit from bringing in a new team of investment bankers? Will a hotshot bond trader who was lured to Tokai Bank be able to produce the results expected of him without any of the support systems he had become used to at Salomon?

Firms often overlook a fundamental question about their compensation and promotion policies and practices: what does each firm communicate to its employees through these policies and practices? Whatever the message is, it may be the most important one that a firm sends, and it is certainly the one that employees listen to the most carefully. This message has a pervasive influence on what employees do and on how and for whom they do it. Ultimately, the message communicates the deepest values of the firm—its real agenda—no matter what anyone says to the contrary.

In an effort to inspire and motivate their employees, top managers may talk to them now and again about teamwork, cooperation, mutual support, franchise building, strategic vision, and even the firm's proud history and culture. All too often, however, such remarks by management are met with skepticism. At many firms, employees look around and see that nothing but current production is rewarded. No matter what top managers may say, employees recognize that the only thing that counts is the bottom line and who gets credit for what. They behave accordingly, looking out for themselves first and the firm later. At other firms, however, employees know by observing promotions of colleagues that teamwork, loyalty to the firm, and high integrity are also valued in recognizing individual performance.

Loyalty and Anxiety

Major firms have their pick of the best and brightest among those seeking financial careers; there are about ten qualified applicants for every job. Firms do their utmost to select the best of the best, using multiple interviews and intensive efforts to determine those who fit in better than others. Over the next five to ten years firms endeavor to evaluate and select a small percentage, about 10 to 15 percent, for promotion to their top ranks. But that represents a lot more people than are selected at most companies. For example, of Salomon Brothers' 6,000 employees, maybe 200 are managing directors and another 400 are vice presidents. Altogether, about 10 percent of Salomon's entire staff are so designated in an organization that is otherwise very nonhierarchical. Imagine General Motors with 6,000 vice presidents and managing directors. And most of the people Salomon recruited, trained, and nurtured at great cost in time and money have ultimately been put to use beyond the intermediate ranks. Providing employees with such opportunities for advancement and for using their talents can create a strong sense of commitment and loyalty to the firm.

Although employees of the major firms are paid better than those in most industries, they are also subject to greater employment risk. When they join their firms, employees know that they are submitting to a regime of pay-for-performance, not of seniority. They know that profits can and do vary widely from one year to the next and that there will be times when little is available for bonuses. They know that their firm may possibly go bankrupt or be sold or merged. And they know that firms engage in continuous pruning; 3 to 5 percent of the staff is released each year, to be replaced by better or cheaper employees later. Such pruning may also be supplemented by radical surgery every few years, when far more employees, including senior executives and partners, are let go to get costs in line. Such radical restructuring in the industry has occurred twice since 1990, with layoffs at some firms reaching 15 percent, often over one thousand employees.

Firms no longer stand ready to provide permanent careers to the supremely capable young people they bring in; firms merely rent talent, holding an option to buy. A young MBA joining a Wall Street firm as a broker or an investment banker can expect, based on current patterns, to change jobs three or four times during a career. And these people know that whatever success they may or may not have had at a previous firm, they may very well turn out to be the leaders or even stars at another firm of equal standing. The emphasis is on finding a firm where they are appreciated, well paid, and provided with continuing opportunities to develop their professional skills and talents.

As a consequence of the changing patterns in the behavior of both firms and their employees, the demands of loyalty are less compelling. But does it matter in a business that is so dominated by money and not by professional values? It does. The loyalty of employees can make a difference to a firm. If employees feel themselves to be a part of a first-rate franchise, they will perform better and more faithfully. They will work for less pay than they are worth when the firm needs them to do so. They will turn down marginal job offers and, most important, they will see themselves as defenders of the firm's values and standards and be proud that their firm puts clients' long-term interests first. Employees who feel loyal to the firm can be counted on to carry on its culture and values. They can also help to instill loyalty in others, and make the firm a better place to work.

But to be part of such a franchise employees have to have some sort of equity interest in it that will be worth a lot at the end of a career. They have to feel good about the place, too, and be supporters. And at the same time, they have to feel that their loyalty and service is valued. They have to feel that they retain the respect of their colleagues, and that the firm is not actually a game of musical chairs in which someone is displaced every day and without much regret. They should be able to look forward to a proud and glorious exit—no matter how far off it may seem—the day they give the retiring employee a big dinner, tell a lot of stories about the old days, and send him off on a cruise courtesy of his lifelong partners and colleagues. That's got to be far more satisfying than being pushed out the door, or encouraged to quit, after twenty-some years, to make room for someone "better."

Loyalty is a two-way street. If firms want their employees to be loyal, they have to consider how to be loyal to them in return.

Test Case at Salomon

In 1994, after an unusually difficult year, Salomon Brothers introduced a new compensation system, one that had been worked out over the preceding months to reflect some important concepts suggested by principal-shareholder Warren Buffett and Salomon's CEO, Deryck Maughan. Buffett was not happy with the existing compensation system, under which more than half of the firm's operating profits were paid out to Salomon employees, leaving shareholders (who bore most of the risk) with comparatively little. The shareholders, Buffett argued, should receive at least a minimum return before the employees were paid the millions in bonuses typical of Wall Street compensation, even in years in which the firm as a whole lost money. He wanted the bonus pool limited to what the firm actually earned, and more of the profits allocated to investors and less to employees. He also wanted the profits from proprietary trading to be reserved for the shareholders, who footed the risk, and not used to bolster weak results in the firm's client-driven activities. He thought that bonuses should be paid mainly in Salomon stock in order to strengthen the vested interest that employees had in the firm itself.

The goal of these proposals was to turn Salomon back into the partnership it had been before it was acquired by publicly owned Phibro in 1981. As a partnership, there were no cash bonuses for the partners. They were compensated, instead, by a percentage interest in the firm's profits, which were retained by the firm until a partner retired. What was not earned could not be paid to anyone. Losses, too, were shared by the partners. Limited partners and creditors advancing capital to the firm had to be paid before any income accrued to general partners. Earnings from the firm's own investments (such as proprietary trading) were distributed among the general partners. These earnings were not used to pay bonuses in the fixed-income or investment banking or other departments in which annual earnings had fallen short.

These old rules were fairly strict, but the profits per partner were high, which gave nonpartners a strong incentive to become partners. The firm had a reputation for being very paternalistic toward its employees, who in turn were very loyal. Bad years occurred from time to time, but the partners underwrote them rather than engage in large-scale layoffs. This style of partnership, in which the firm retained most of its income for reinvestment in the business, was also followed by such firms as Goldman Sachs and Bear Stearns.

The Buffett-Maughan proposals were very well conceived. They were intended to increase the firm's internal discipline, loyalty, and cooperation. Salomon would emerge as a stronger and more cohesive firm, it was thought, as a result of policy changes that would emphasize the firm's long-term interests over rapidly changing, short-term considerations.

The proposals were nonetheless a total failure. In addition to being soundly rejected by key Salomon employees, they triggered many departures and substantial internal discord. In the end, they could not be implemented. The basic problem was that Salomon happened to be suffering a year of unusually bad earnings—it would report a loss of about $1 billion for 1994—and employees (including managing directors) did not see how they could continue to earn what they had under the old system in a bad year. This meant a big pay cut for most employees whose work was centered around client-driven activities. Some employees saw their compensation decreasing by 60 to 70 percent relative to what it would have been had no changes been made in the compensation formula. Over thirty senior officers left while the proposals were being aired. Employees leapt at job offers, even from far less prestigious firms, that preserved the level of compensation that they had previously been receiving at Salomon.

Buffett and Maughan had misjudged the situation; the firm's employees perceived the proposals as unfair, exploitative, and especially harsh in a bad year. Both those employees who left and those who fought the proposals from the inside failed to see the potential benefits in recasting the firm's compensation system. Many were not even prepared to listen, and they felt no particular loyalty to the firm. Their attitude was that the firm had to conform to "market conditions" and continue to pay them as before—that the firm had little claim on their loyalty. They failed to see that return to a type of partnership structure might indeed have been highly beneficial in the long run, and that the employees themselves might have prospered accordingly. But this was not evident or widely believed at the time.

Goldman Sachs, a firm much admired for its management and for the loyalty of its employees, was a partnership during that period of turmoil at Salomon, as it still is. Many Goldman employees believed that its form of organization was a competitive advantage in attracting and retaining good people, and that the Salomon compensation proposals were an effort to move the firm in Goldman's direction. But then, in 1994, Goldman Sachs had an extraordinarily bad year—just like Salomon. Nearly 50 of its approximately 200 general partners chose to retire, which enabled them to withdraw some of their capital from the firm and to convert what remained into safer limited-partnership interests. So in bad years, not even an effective partnership structure may be sufficient to retain the loyalty of senior employees.

Principles of Compensation

Taking into account the various dimensions of compensation in securities firms, it appears that some principles are worth fighting for and worth persuading both owners and employees to accept. Each firm needs to find ways to increase employee participation as owner-managers having a long-term vested interest in its health and survival. Such involvement creates internal cohesion, teamwork, and loyalty, all of which are needed to build a stable, vibrant, and resilient enterprise. Different firms have tried different ways of achieving these objectives. Some basic principles of compensation tied to performance evaluation and loyalty are the following:

- *Know what you are paying for.* Pay for the best overall long-term performance, and figure out ways to measure it. Some firms measure production using orthodox methods (for example, revenues or gross profits from completed deals) and then adjust for qualitative factors. Managers' assessments and peer ratings are useful, as are assessments of "potential" by senior officers (at least insofar as such assessments reflect comparisons with employees who have equivalent training and experience).

- *Recognize the weaknesses in the system.* Resist classifying individuals as indispensable stars, of which there are few. Recognize that it takes several years to know someone well enough to accurately assess ability and upward potential. People change and improve (or worsen) from year to year, so performance reviews should be fresh every year, not biased by performance in previous years. Don't rely only on the same people's evaluations. Obtain evaluations from others, too.

- *Communicate "opportunities for improvement" clearly to employees when reviewing them.* Ambitious people seek to correct their own faults. Indicating where employees' faults are, without dashing their hopes for a bright future, can be the best way to improve employees' performance. Too often performance reviews are superficial, overly flattering, and misleading. Make sure that serious flaws, including inappropriate treatment of colleagues or minorities, are put on the table with the understanding that they must be corrected if the individual is to have a future at the firm. Managers ought to be evaluated, in part, on how well their own employees develop under such self-corrective methods.

- *Pay people sensibly.* Think like an owner. Conserve cash and maximize employee-company bonding. Pay a salary based on time-in-grade in the industry, and a bonus based on *this* year's performance against the employee's own predefined goals. Award profit-sharing points, stock options, or deferred compensation in increasing proportions as the employee becomes more senior and more valuable. Involve as many managers as possible in share ownership programs.

- *Recognize the responsibilities of the employer for training and developing people, as well as for paying them.* People are worth more to an organization if they have been trained and shaped for particular activities of interest to them. This approach is a lot cheaper and more reliable than hiring strangers or teams of strangers found through headhunters or scavenged from other firms.

- *Be loyal to employees.* If someone was good enough to get through the hiring process, has not been eliminated subsequently for cause, moral turpitude, or incompetence, and has benefited from training and mentoring, there is likely to be an important job somewhere within the firm that the person can accomplish as well as anyone else. Don't discard employees without a very good reason. Avoid tree pruning and mass layoffs. Fight hard to keep the people you've got, and let the employees see you do so. The loyalty payoff alone should be worth it.

- *Reward good character, integrity, and leadership potential.* Think about the future and who the firm's future leaders will be. Let it be known that the firm is always looking for individuals of good character, high integrity, and strong leadership potential. Reward those who are identified within the firm by peers and superiors to have these qualities. These employees are the last people the firm wants to lose to competitors for lack of appreciation.

Enculturation

The culture of a firm has a lot to do with its success. In a strong, stable investment banking culture, managers and employees will boast of the firm's teamwork and of the cooperation between departments. In a weaker culture, employees may complain about a lack of cohesiveness, about competition between employees for credit and visibility, and about the difficulty they experience in getting some transactions accomplished. In a disintegrating culture, employees emphasize short-term profits above all else (including the clients' interests), describe repeated unfairness practiced by managers, and are cynical about most things related to promotion and compensation.

The corporate culture of a securities firm may embrace many characteristics, values, and practices—some ordinary, others unique to the firm. But it's the drumbeat to which all march, the principles and business regularities that the firm follows year in and year out, regardless of market conditions and competitive pressures. The secret of an effective culture is consistency, homogeneity, and exclusiveness. To establish one, all you have to do is get a bunch of talented people together when they're young; train them well in getting business done; discipline and reward them the same way for years; and inculcate these ways to the new people coming along. Moreover, don't hire anyone from anywhere else if it can be avoided; by sticking only with the ones you've trained, you won't have employees who know and prefer some other way of doing things. Relax any of these constraints to any significant degree and you risk diluting the culture. Ignore them and the culture turns to mush, and soon washes away.

Goldman Sachs, respected by many in the industry for its culture, has an explicit set of business principles that were devised by the firm's partners more than twenty years ago (Exhibit 11-1). These fourteen principles were put forward then as being the most important factors affecting the business life of the firm. They were introduced at a time when the firm was rapidly expanding its role in U.S. and international financial markets but had not yet attained its current position of prominence. The principles were intended not only to guide the firm through its expansionary period, but also to define a stable and continuing culture. They were to provide a base for the firm's business practices and strategies. Ever since they were first commissioned, the principles have been reprinted in the firm's annual review, its pocket diaries, and its telephone listings. They are frequently referred to by the firm's employees and partners at training sessions and policy meetings.

Effective Business Principles

Though perhaps no less obvious than statements of allegiance to motherhood and apple pie, the Goldman Sachs principles collectively define a

Exhibit 11-1   Goldman Sachs Basic Business Principles

1. Our clients' interests always come first. Our experience shows that if we serve our clients well, our own success will follow.

2. Our assets are our people, capital and reputation. If any of these is ever diminished, the last is the most difficult to restore. We are dedicated to complying fully with the letter and spirit of the laws, rules and ethical principles that govern us. Our continued success depends upon unswerving adherence to this standard.

3. We take great pride in the professional quality of our work. We have an uncompromising determination to achieve excellence in everything we undertake. Though we may be involved in a wide variety and heavy volume of activity, we would, if it came to a choice, rather be best than biggest.

4. We stress creativity and imagination in everything we do. While recognizing that the old way may still be the best way, we constantly strive to find a better solution to a client's problems. We pride ourselves on having pioneered many of the practices and techniques that have become standard in the industry.

5. We make an unusual effort to identify and recruit the very best person for every job. Although our activities are measured in billions of dollars, we select our people one by one. In a service business, we know that without the best people, we cannot be the best firm.

6. We offer our people the opportunity to move ahead more rapidly than is possible at most other places. We have yet to find the limits to the responsibility that our best people are able to assume. Advancement depends solely on ability, performance and contribution to the firm's success, without regard to race, color, religion, sex, age, national origin, disability, sexual orientation or any other impermissible criterion or circumstance.

7. We stress teamwork in everything we do. While individual creativity is always encouraged, we have found that team effort often produces the best results. We have no room for those people who put their personal interests ahead of the interests of the firm and its clients.

8. The dedication of our people to the firm and the intense effort they give their jobs are greater than one finds in most other organizations. We think that this is an important part of our success.

9. Our profits are a key to our success. They replenish our capital and attract and keep the best people. It is our practice to share our profits generously with all who helped create them. Profitability is crucial to our future.

10. We consider our size an asset that we try hard to preserve. We want to be big enough to undertake the largest project that any of our clients could contemplate, yet small enough to maintain the loyalty, the in-

timacy and the esprit de corps that we all treasure and that contribute greatly to our success.

11. We constantly strive to anticipate the rapidly changing needs of our clients and to develop new services to meet those needs. We know that the world of finance will not stand still and that complacency can lead to extinction.

12. We regularly receive confidential information as part of our normal client relationships. To breach a confidence or to use confidential infor-

mation improperly or carelessly would be unthinkable.

13. Our business is highly competitive, and we aggressively seek to expand our client relationships. However, we must always be fair to competitors and must never denigrate other firms.

14. Integrity and honesty are at the heart of our business. We expect our people to maintain high ethical standards in everything they do, both in their work for the firm and in their personal lives.

Source: Goldman Sachs, *Annual Report,* 1995.

coherent culture with specific goals and values. The first three, which concern general matters of integrity, reputation, and excellence, may seem a bit saccharine, but that doesn't make them wrong or lacking in universality or usefulness. Publilius Syrus, a Roman orator of the first century B.C., may have been the first to note that "a good reputation is more valuable than money." Goldman says it agrees. The fourth and eleventh principles describe the firm's commitment to creativity and innovation in the service of the clients, a reminder that growth and change are not only healthy, but mandatory if the needs of clients are to be satisfied. And because Wall Street activities are intensely dependent on the quality of the people employed, nearly a third of the fourteen principles (numbers five through nine) address the firm's attitudes toward, and dealings with, its employees. These principles state that "without the best people, we cannot be the best firm" and, as a fundamental matter of business philosophy,

- the firm will make unusual efforts to recruit the best people

- it will offer them the opportunity to move ahead faster than at other firms

- it will dedicate itself to purely meritocratic standards for promotion

- it expressly rejects any kind of discrimination, whether based on race, religion, gender, sexual orientation, age, nationality, disability, or anything else that might diminish the talent pool

- it places paramount importance on the virtue of teamwork

- it expects its employees to be more dedicated to the firm itself and to their jobs than they might be at other organizations.

Here is the Wall Street work ethic formalized into a set of business principles that affirms one organization's belief that the most outstanding people, those who want to be advanced strictly on the basis of their achievements, need to be intensely focused on their work. And if they are, that will be best for all.

Next, Goldman Sachs extols the unique importance of profits and its willingness to share them, together with its wish to be large enough to be great, but no bigger. Indeed, Goldman Sachs should be "small enough to maintain the loyalty, the intimacy and the *esprit de corps* that we all treasure and that contribute greatly to our success." The principles close off with three matters of ethics. In addition to protecting confidential information and competing aggressively but fairly, the firm expects its people "to maintain high ethical standards in everything they do, both in their work for the firm and in their personal lives."

Like all firms, Goldman Sachs has had its ups and downs. Its employee morale has too. But people who know the firm well continue to say that its explicit business principles are routinely honored and practiced, and that they have generated a special Goldman Sachs culture that has contributed substantially to the firm's success over the years. When the firm's partners formulated these principles two decades ago, maybe they were on to something.

Another great firm, Merrill Lynch, articulates its operating principles (Exhibit 11-2) in a rather different way from Goldman Sachs. The contrast is instructive. Merrill's principles reflect the firm's retail business and the thousands of employees involved with it, whereas Goldman's provide a more detailed characterization of the values and goals of a much smaller and close-knit group.

No firm, of course, can expect all of its partners, key executives, or employees to live up to such principles all of the time. Backsliding does occur. But to be a great firm, there must be such principles, and they must be adhered to by a great majority of the people, a great majority of the time. Goldman's and Merrill's principles include basic rules for promoting

Exhibit 11-2   The Merrill Lynch Client Commitment

CLIENT DEDICATION

Our clients' interests come first. By serving them well, we will also succeed.

PERSONAL SERVICE

Our clients are entitled to the personal advice and counsel of professional Financial Consultants whose philosophy and style of doing business are compatible with their own.

A FINANCIAL PLAN

Our clients have the benefit of a personal financial plan to identify their long-term financial goals, and a strategy for implementing their plan.

SUITABLE RECOMMENDATIONS

Our financial recommendations are consistent with our clients' long-term goals, financial circumstances and risk tolerance.

FULL DISCLOSURE

We inform our clients of the costs and benefits of doing business with Merrill Lynch.

THE INTEGRITY OF MERRILL LYNCH

Our principles, financial strength, service quality and market leadership provide comfort and security to our clients through good times and bad.

Source: Merrill Lynch, *Annual Report*, 1995.

both high performance and high standards. The two sets of principles are different yet similar, just as the firms themselves must be if they are going to maintain both their enviable client regard and standards of profitability.

Communicating from the Top

Having principles, of course, is not enough. They must be taken seriously. And they must be communicated frequently and repeatedly so as to enculturate newcomers and remind old-timers of the firm's commitments and guidelines to its future. Ambitious youngsters should be encouraged to study and apply the principles as if they were a blueprint for the firm's whole culture, and to gain insight into what it takes to get ahead. But no principle will be believed by anyone, even for five minutes, unless everyone thinks that the top people in the firm, from the CEO on down, believe it too—and practice it. A crucial element in creating a strong culture that reinforces both professional standards and performance is credibility at the top.

Such credibility doesn't spring forth all by itself. Employees know everything there is to know about their leaders, especially their faults. Employees are fascinated by them, want to be like them, and know how to figure them out or get around them. What leaders do, rather than what they say, gets especially close attention. Of key importance is how leaders handle crises, emergencies, and general difficulties. How effective are their business ideas and principles? How often do they cave in to, or get manipulated by, others? How often do they take the initiative and set a new course? These things determine whether top managers exercise strong and effective leadership, have the power to set the directions for the future, and can expect others to follow.

Honesty and Trust

It is worth returning to Ace Greenberg, until recently the chairman of Bear Stearns, and his highly effective memoranda to the firm, which we discussed in the previous chapter. Through his innumerable, humorous notices to employees about the firm and its business principles, he communicated directly and forcefully the importance he placed on honest and effective dealing with both clients and other members of the firm (Exhibit 11-3). Though light and informal in tone, the memos left no doubt that Ace meant what he said.

It must be recognized, however, that Greenberg's honesty and directness run against the grain for many Wall Streeters. Much of the day-to-day work in the securities industry involves negotiating with clients and with other parties and firms. In such dealings, it is often important to withhold information and even to bluff, that is, to misrepresent what you may or may not be willing to do. Indeed, in most business negotiations, as in diplomacy, bluffing is a necessary part of many transactions if the best competitive results are to be reached. No effective negotiator would tell the truth, the whole truth, and nothing but the truth.

The pervasiveness of bluffing and various forms of deception in business has led some commentators, such as Alfred Carr in a much-cited 1968 article in the *Harvard Business Review,* to claim that "the ethics of business are game ethics, different from the ethics of religion."[3] And since everyone supposedly knows the rules of the game, no harm is done. Indeed, Carr is completely unconcerned that "most executives from time to time are almost compelled . . . to practice some form of deception when negotiating with customers, dealers, labor unions, government officials, or even other departments of their own firms."

Without going to the opposite extreme taken by moral philosophers such as Norman Bowie in a fierce rebuttal of Carr's article[4] or Sissela Bok in her book *Lying: Moral Choice in Public and Private Life,*[5] Carr's position is troubling. To be sure, in business negotiations with sophisticated professionals some liberty with the truth is both acceptable and, indeed, expected. But these cases must be treated as exceptions and not as defining the rule. Colleagues and clients alike, no matter what their level of business sophistication and no matter what their connection with you, generally want and expect you to be honest in your dealings with them. If you are not, you will lose their trust. And in the case of clients, you will probably lose their business as well.

Ace Greenberg would surely argue—and, we think, with good reason—that honest dealings are crucially important within the firm itself. A corporate culture of honesty and trust is one that best promotes effective communication and enables all the firm's work to proceed most efficiently. But Ace would surely argue, too, that honesty and trust are only two of the many virtues that must be insisted upon, supported, and nurtured within the firm. Likewise, a reputation for fairness helps a firm in all of its dealings—with employees, clients, and other firms. It is no surprise that the last of Goldman Sachs's business principles mandates its people "to maintain high ethical standards in everything they do." Both the business conduct and the professional conduct of a firm's employees reflect directly upon the firm itself, for better or worse. No one wants to do business with a firm or an investment banker whose moral standards are questionable. Nor does anyone want to work with colleagues whom one does not trust and respect. As a matter of both good business judgment and effective management, a firm's leaders therefore need to communicate to all employees by word and deed the crucial importance of maintaining high standards of honesty and trust.

Exhibit 11-3   Bear Stearns & Company

M E M O

Date: November 9, 1989

To: Senior Managing Directors
        Managing Directors
        Associate Directors

From: Alan C. Greenberg

Here we go again. Business is tough. The Dow Jones index dropped almost 200 points a month ago. Firms are announcing major layoffs.

What is our posture at this time? Your executive committee feels we should be *hiring, not firing.* This is the time to pick up great people. This position may amaze some newer associates, but those of you who have been exposed to our culture will not be surprised by this move. Being a contrarian has worked for us in the past and it will work again.

Spread the word—*we are hiring, not firing.* The flip side is that our associates should be relieved and maybe the people who work here will even appreciate what a great place this is to build a career.

Nookie points out that we have been remiss in not blowing our horn a little louder.* It amazes him that we have lost people to firms that expand and then contract like accordions. Being bashful was cute in Snow White; Nookie sees nothing wrong in exposing our people to the hiring and firing records of our competitors.

One of the biggest payers of up-front money to registered representatives went out of the retail business after causing us three years of grief. This was not an isolated incident. We have to help our people look beyond their noses.

---

* Authors' notes: November 9, 1989, Memo: Nookie is a mythical character who appears from time to time in Greenberg's memos. April 10, 1990, Memo: Bear Stearns has no corporate aircraft pilots, chauffeured limousines, or television-advertising budget.

M E M O

Date: April 10, 1990

To: Senior Managing Directors
         Managing Directors
         Associate Directors
         Department Heads

From: Alan C. Greenberg

We have built our business on certain principles and there are two axioms that must be repeated constantly to our associates.

We will not employ people who hide or bury trades, even if the delay is twenty-four hours. During the past year, we have had to terminate several people for this infraction. One person had worked as a trader at Bear Stearns for over ten years.

We will not employ people who ever disclose our or our clients' trading activity with *anybody* who is not authorized to have such information. Disclosing this to unauthorized people, who work either inside or outside Bear Stearns, will lead to immediate dismissal.

We have a very liberal policy of rewarding with cash and promotions, personnel that help us improve this firm. If you want to become a lot richer, just give us information that will aid us in discovering employees who violate either of the two rules of behavior that I have just mentioned. Call your supervisor or me with any of your suspicions. You will never be criticized if your information proves to be inaccurate. The fable about the boy who cried "wolf" doesn't fit with the Bear Stearns philosophy. Cry "wolf" at every opportunity. If your doubts prove to be false, you will still be thanked.

Nookie asked me to comment about a particularly vicious rumor. It is *not* true that we are firing any of our jet pilots or company-employed chauffeurs. Any pilot or chauffeur who is *currently* employed by Bear Stearns has a job that is safer than mine. These rumors are getting so ridiculous that it would not surprise me if I heard that we are cutting our TV advertising budget.*

Being Predictable

Senior management's commitment to high standards will strengthen one of the most important characteristics of well-managed firms: the predictability of their business policies and practices. Although employees should always feel they can come in and talk to the boss, they should not be encouraged to believe that the boss is always prepared to make exceptions for them. Senior managers represent the firm. They are responsible for ensuring that its professional standards and business policies are observed. And if the firm maintains high standards, managers should not have an open mind about discussing deviations from them. Managers need to be tough enforcers of these standards. When a high-powered producer screws up, he or she is dismissed from the firm, not invited to work things out. Exceptions are not made for top producers. Firing a couple of uncooperative stars may be the best thing a firm can do to get everybody's attention. There should be a clear expectation that when certain offenses occur, the axe is wielded.

Disaster Analysis

Predictability is also important in some other areas. After something goes seriously wrong (especially in one's own firm, but also at another), there should be a debriefing during which all the relevant facts are examined. And any problem that has led the firm into litigation should be explained to senior managers as soon as possible, insofar as the situation permits. It is essential for them to discuss what went wrong and how to avoid a recurrence. More generally, when a disaster in the industry occurs, everyone in the firm should know about it and be well informed on the issues involved. A close look at the major pitfalls encountered by securities firms and banks, many of which have been discussed in this book, indicates that the trouble almost never began with an individual's explicit intention to commit a violation. In almost all cases something happened inadvertently and then got worse. Subsequent efforts to either cover up the problem or to "trade out" of the situation failed. In several cases supervisors were induced to cooperate with the effort to repair the damage rather than reporting it to regulators or to more senior members of the firm. Soon, these reluctant collaborators themselves became part of the problem and felt the need to conceal their own involvement.

But would the situation ever have arisen if the employees knew better how to avoid the inadvertent event that started the whole thing, or realized the seriousness of covering up, or had a good understanding of what they were supposed to do when such conditions occurred? Would it all have gotten out of hand if a watchful colleague had noticed something amiss and reported it? Failures of the firm's controls are often portrayed after the fact as resulting from minor technical problems. But in reality these failures are almost always ones of human judgment and of management systems.

Persistent Training

Managers need periodic training. They need to know exactly what the firm's profit goals, business plan, and professional standards are, and how the firm expects employees to act if there is rogue behavior on the part of other employees or senior executives. The training should acquaint employees with the current laws, regulations, and internal rules, as well as the penalties associated with violating them, and also make clear that the potential monetary penalties for transgressions are far greater than anything the firm can afford. In addition to getting the word out to their subordinates, managers also need, of course, to set good examples themselves.

Firms do well when they formalize training in "standards setting," preferably as part of firmwide leadership development. In such programs, the firm's own business principles are discussed and perhaps even compared to those of other firms. Case studies of recent disasters or near disasters, both inside and outside the firm, are analyzed in a "what would you have done" context. Then senior officers or outside experts conduct discussions of the industry's latest developments, ones that may make compliance with rules and principles difficult because of the shifting, fluid environment. These developments lie along three different axes: competitive, technological, and legal/regulatory.

Most firms provide some amount of ongoing training for their professional employees. Many managers complain, however, that the time available is never enough. The training time has to be allocated among competing demands—skills training, motivational training, the introduction of new products and services. This training often comes in the form of two or three-day off-site meetings, once or twice a year for major departments. But also it occurs, or could occur, at morning meetings, through firmwide memos or pamphlets, and through electronic means, including e-mail and its intranet, and videotapes. Periodically, firms should send out to all relevant employees videotapes of discussions, much like those on *The News Hour with Jim Lehrer.* A short documentary report on, say, the incident at

Daiwa Bank or Baring Brothers is followed by a panel discussion of key executives. In addition to becoming informed about what happened, employees learn what to do if they suspect irregularities in their own areas. Surely it is not too much to ask employees to watch a ten-minute tape every month or so as a part of their training.

Accountability, Watchfulness, and Alarm Ringing

Finally, there is no substitute for good controls and alert supervision. Such controls would, for example, enable the firm to monitor every action of every trader and every salesman. But because control systems are so expensive, they are often not put in place. Still, no firm can protect itself against all the risks of the business. Inescapably, the firm has to rely on its employees to do the right thing. And as the various scandals demonstrate, they don't always succeed.

Ace Greenberg likes to talk about the "spies" in his trading room. They wander about looking for things that are not right, and have the authority to look at anybody's books at any time. Most firms have similar people, whether from the compliance, internal-audit, or controller's department. They sit in the trading room, where the action is, and are well known to the people involved. In some firms, these risk-control people can be overcome, however, by the authority of a major producer who has the support of many of the firm's top people. In others, they cannot. It's vital that these risk-control employees have all the power they need to confront the most important producers and, when they are right, to win. Firms must also periodically review their risk-control procedures for any deficiencies, including ones that may arise from human failures, and either fix them promptly or drop the employee, product, or customer at their source.

In the end, of course, some senior executive at or near the top of the firm needs to be accountable for risk control and management. Accountability should not be diluted, however, as the responsibilities drift down to operating levels. And accountability should be tied to compensation and promotion. Accountable people are watchful, and watchful people are the ones who ring alarms when they are needed. A basic objective should be to make all of the firm's employees into accountable people—that is, to minimize the need for controls by improving the quality of the people being controlled, thereby reducing the probability of an accident that may grow into a major crisis later on. Developing such awareness among employees may actually save money on control expenses.

Some firms have let their investments in control systems and in the training of employees fluctuate up or down with their profits. Such fluctuations make no sense. The need for such controls is always present. And if anything, employees whose income is tied to performance may have a greater incentive to cut corners—and thereby create risks for the firm—when the market or the firm is performing poorly.

Leadership

For a firm to achieve the best results, everything has to balance: business principles, the desire to be the best, and the shared goal of maximizing the long-term, risk-adjusted value of its business franchise. Through sound business principles one arrives at sound standards and effective communication. To meet these standards, everyone has to pitch in. And everyone has to be educated in what those standards are and what policies and practices are acceptable and necessary to achieve them.

The objective is to build a highly motivated team of people who believe they are the best they can be because of the organization they belong to, feel a part of, and want to nurture and protect. But such things don't happen by themselves or because a committee or a group of consultants says they should. They happen because effective leaders spark employees to do things they haven't done before and to maintain the integrity and stability of the firm's culture and standards even as the world of finance changes.

There are many kinds of leaders, starting with the chief executive but ranging all the way down through the organization to the team leader handling the latest initial public offering. If the many employees who have leadership responsibilities, whether regular or occasional, do not exercise them effectively, the chief executive is lost. If these employees are good leaders, however, they will serve as role models as well as effective on-the-scene executives who can straighten out problems and recognize new opportunities as they occur. The firm must depend heavily on the quality of these intermediate-level leaders to carry out its mission and to achieve its objectives.

So, what can be done to develop better leaders in this difficult, leadership-resistant industry?

- *Understand what you mean by leadership.* Develop a consensus on what your firm means by leadership. Develop this conception of leadership from discussions with senior colleagues and with others at random.

- *Put your money where your mouth is.* Find ways to get leadership quality and potential to be recognized more explicitly in the firm's compensation and promotion systems.

- *Create a "school for leaders" and send the best people to it.* Once or twice a year, select a dozen or so midlevel employees from different parts of the firm for leadership school. Let it be known that it's an elite selection process, covering all parts of the firm, front office and back. Make them attend meetings, and assign homework. Make the work challenging, interesting, and inspiring. Bring in outside speakers on motivating others, living with prima donnas in complex organizations, getting things done under adverse conditions, and managing people in stressful situations. Use successful people— managers from professional sports, entertainment, or the armed services. Get the students to start thinking about what good leadership means in their firm. After a while, the better ones can come back and talk to the next generation.

- *Put the leaders to work.* When people finish leadership school, assign them to a committee or task force studying something important, but somewhat unusual, for the executive committee or the CEO. Appoint them to committees to review and make recommendations for changes in the firm's compensation practices; for instituting professional standards on a firmwide basis; for dealing with diversity in the firm and minimizing problems associated with minorities, women, foreign nationals, and others; and for increasing the loyalty between the firm and employees. There are many tasks for which this specially selected and trained group can provide enlightened assistance to the firm's executive committee. When the recommendations come in, act on them promptly and tell everyone why.

- *Make it permanent.* In order for this process to work and to be credible with employees, the selection and schooling of leaders has to be ongoing. After a few years, the firm will enjoy the contributions of many such leaders, some of whom will be promoted to the most senior positions in the firm.

The leaders of tomorrow's major financial-service organizations will not be just producers. Indeed, as difficult as being a good producer may be, there are thousands of them. The leaders will of necessity be a lot like old-fashioned general managers who are familiar with the basic business of banking and securities, of course, but also economics, technology, law, regulation, and controls, and who are capable of inspiring others to outstanding efforts and achievement. Organizations lacking such leaders may be lucky to be in business for very long, given the escalating risk of destruction by regulatory or litigious land mines that seem ever more prevalent. The more difficult the business, the more important the leaders.

The problem is that most firms believe that leadership is both earned and learned from the ground up. The true leaders of the firm are those who have been brilliant producers and thereby gained the respect of colleagues. Leadership, in this view, is not learned in meetings. Maybe not. But most leadership positions in banking and financial services go to those with little prior experience in that role, and most of these individuals do not in the end distinguish themselves as leaders. If a firm wants extraordinary leaders—and how can it fail to want them when the finance industry is growing larger and more complex every day—then it should endeavor to provide some form of leadership development for them. A firm with hundreds of well trained, properly motivated "junior officers," ones who have a good nose for what's right, is a firm that will prove to be much less accident prone and more valuable to its shareholders than firms with no leadership training or management development effort at all.

Zookeeping, when all is said and done, boils down to shared values, high standards based on them, good management practices, and effective mid- and senior-level leadership. Successful firms recognize these challenges and do their best to invest time and money to meet them as well as they can. They can always do better, and further investments, wisely made and followed up, can provide not just a marginal improvement, but a significant return on investment. Most firms, however, respond to these challenges less aggressively than they should. Too often these firms are either struggling to stay competitive or fiercely attempting to increase their market positions. Under such circumstances, all eyes are on other things. But without effective zookeeping, the likelihood of a firm's achieving long-term success and commensurate shareholder value is low. The odds are definitively against sloppy outfits.

Employees in the securities business are as smart, aggressive, and dedicated to their business as the employees in any other industry. And they are as honest, honorable, and devoted to their careers. A few, of course, are unruly, dishonest, unprincipled, and overly greedy, but there is no evidence to suggest that these people are more numerous in the securities business than in any other that operates in a truly competitive marketplace. The business is not so much plagued by rogue employees as it is endangered by management failures at various levels. These failures are threatening to become a more serious problem, potentially affecting many more firms, as the industry becomes increasingly global in scope and as the number of employees increases. What our work suggests is that for real (that is, monetary) value to result from the efforts of firms and of individuals in the securities business, more attention must be paid to the principles of zookeeping that we have discussed. Weaknesses need to be fixed while they are fixable. The rewards are there, so many firms will see the value in getting on with the fixing. Others, alas, will not, being unwilling or unable to change the way they do things.

Notes

■

CHAPTER 1

1. Anita Raghavan and Stephen Lipin, "Restructuring Angers Clients of Goldman," *Wall Street Journal*, 1 February 1995.

2. James A. Stewart, *Den of Thieves* (New York: Simon & Schuster, 1991), 445.

3. *Report of the Bank of England and the Board of Banking Supervision Inquiry into the Circumstances of the Collapse of Barings* (London, July 1995), 54–77, 232–249.

4. Paul Bluestein, "From Trader's Loss to Daiwa's Scandal," *Washington Post*, 4 November 1995.

5. John Gapper, "Deutsche Bank Learns a Lesson in Discipline," *Financial Times*, 6 September 1996.

6. Kurt Eichenwald, "Scandal's Cost for Prudential Tops $1.4 Billion," *New York Times*, 22 April 1995.

7. Kurt Eichenwald, *Serpent on the Rock* (New York: HarperCollins, 1995).

8. Anita Raghavan, "Paine Webber to Pay $250 Million Relating to Partnerships," *Wall Street Journal*, 19 January 1996.

9. "The Bankers Trust Tapes," *Business Week*, 16 October 1995.

10. "What CFOs Really Think About Investment Bankers," *Investment Dealer's Digest*, 6 February 1995.

11. Laurie Hayes, "Bankers Trust Settles Dispute with P&G," *Wall Street Journal*, 10 May 1996.

12. "Maxwell Pension Funds in Pact on Missing Assets," *Wall Street Journal*, 13 February 1995.

13. Anita Raghavan, "Morgan Stanley Wins Reversal in Suit over West Virginia's Investment Losses," *Wall Street Journal*, 6 June 1995.

14. Michael Siconolfi, "Brokerage Firms Pay Big Damages in 'Dramshop' Cases," *Wall Street Journal*, 17 May 1995

15. Tom Herman, "Wall Street's Image Isn't Very Flattering, Harris Survey Finds," *Wall Street Journal*, 18 October 1996.

16. Rebecca S. Demsetz, Marc R. Saidenberg, and Philip E. Strahan, "Banks with Something to Lose: The Disciplinary Role of Franchise Value," Federal Reserve Bank of New York, *Economic Policy Review*, October 1996.

CHAPTER 2

1. See Samuel Brittan and Alan Hamlin, eds., *Market Capitalism and Moral Values* (London: Edward Elgar, 1995).

2. Elaine Sternberg, "Business in the Moral Haze," *Financial Times*, 1 June 1995. See also her *Just Business: Ethics in Action* (Boston: Little, Brown, 1994).

3. In a broader sense, Smith's invisible hand says nothing about motivation, except that economic conduct should be *as if it were* in enlightened self-interest. By adding a laudatory motivation, bad acts can be made to seem good. In the so-called Robin Hood syndrome, "Stealing from the rich to give to the poor is still stealing, and therefore immoral. However worthy the causes they support may be, when business managers fund them by taking other people's money (i.e., shareholders' assets), their actions are more properly condemned as theft than praised as 'social responsibility'." Sternberg, "Moral Haze."

4. "The Problem of Social Cost," *Journal of Law and Economics* 3 (1960): 144–171.

5. For a good set of applications of the theory of social costs, see Robert H. Frank, *Microeconomics and Behavior*, 2d ed. (New York: McGraw-Hill, 1994).

6. Laurie Hays and John R. Wilke, "Banks Bump Against Cap on Dealing," *Wall Street Journal*, 29 March 1996.

7. "Heat Turned on Self-Regulation," *Financial Times*, 28 July 1995. See also Securities and Investments Board, *Regulation of the United Kingdom Equity Markets* (London: Securities and Investments Board, 1995).

8. See, for example, Fred Barbash, "In London's City, Fraud Thrives on Easygoing Ways," *International Herald Tribune*, 20 June 1996; and Joe Rogaly, "Dodgy Dealers and Morality," *Financial Times*, 22 June 1996.

9. Sara Callan, "One Regulator's Push for Investor Rights Upsets City of London," *Wall Street Journal*, 23 December 1996.

10. "Top Business Court Under Fire," *New York Times*, 23 May 1995.

11. "The Prospectus Tries Plain Speaking," *Business Week*, 14 August 1995.

12. Derivatives Policy Group, *Framework for Voluntary Oversight* (New York: Derivatives Policy Group, 1995).

13. Nicholas Denton, "Supervision of Investment Banks Tightened," *Financial Times*, 27 September 1995.

14. Gary Weiss, "The Mob on Wall Street," *Business Week*, 16 December 1996.

15. See Edward J. Kane, "Competitive Financial Reregulation: An International Perspective," in Richard Portes and Alexander K. Swoboda, eds., *Threats to International Financial Stability* (London: Cambridge University Press, 1987).

16. See Richard Levich and Ingo Walter, "Tax-Driven Regulatory Drag: European Financial Centres in the 1990s," in Horst Siebert, ed., *Reforming Capital Income Taxation* (Tübingen: J.C.B. Mohr, 1990).

17. Edward Kane in "Competitive Financial Reregulation," argues that regulation itself may be thought of in a "market" context, with regulatory bodies established along geographic, product, or functional lines and competing to extend their regulatory domains. Financial firms understand this regulatory competition and try to exploit it to enhance their market share or profitability. Domestic regulators may respond with reregulation in an effort to recover part of their regulatory domain.

18. Rebecca S. Demsetz, Marc R. Saidenberg, and Philip E. Strahan, "Banks with

Something to Lose: The Disciplinary Role of Franchise Value," Federal Reserve Bank of New York, *Economic Policy Review,* October 1996. See also Ingo Walter, "Universal Banking: A Shareholder Value Perspective" (paper presented at the Financial Management Association meetings, Zurich, Switzerland, 28–30 May 1997).

CHAPTER 3

1. Leah Nathans Spiro and Michael Schroeder, "Can You Trust Your Broker?" *Business Week,* 20 February 1995.

2. Marcia Vickers, "Brokers in Hawaii. Clients at the Cleaners?" *New York Times,* 15 January 1996.

3. Bridget O'Brien, "Merrill Lynch Considers Paying Salaries to New Brokers to Cut Interest Conflicts," *Wall Street Journal,* 20 November 1995.

4. Spiro and Schroeder, "Can You Trust Your Broker?"

5. Michael Siconolfi, "Merrill Lures Brokers of Small Town Rival with Signing Bonuses," *Wall Street Journal,* 11 April 1996.

6. "Kick the Tire, Not the Salesman," *Business Week,* 25 December 1995.

7. Patrick McGeehan, "Stockbrokers Face New Rules on Cold Calls," *Wall Street Journal,* 6 May 1996.

8. Charles Gasparino, "Stockbrokers' Sales Practices Are Faulted in New Study," *Wall Street Journal,* 8 July 1996.

9. Floyd Norris, "Licensing-Test Cheaters Face NASD Ban," *New York Times,* 10 July 1996.

10. Kurt Eichenwald, "Prudential Fraud Accord Has Phones Ringing," *New York Times,* 23 October 1993. See also Kurt Eichenwald, "New Case Filed In Prudential Inquiry," *New York Times,* 26 July 1994; and "Prudential Pact Focus of Inquiry," *New York Times,* 26 July 1994.

11. Kurt Eichenwald, *Serpent on the Rock* (New York: HarperBusiness, 1995).

12. Leah Nathans Spiro, "How Greed Poisoned Pru-Bache," *Business Week,* 14 August 1995, 17–18.

13. Ibid.

14. Kurt Eichenwald, "Scandal's Cost for Prudential Tops $1.4 Billion," *New York Times,* 22 April 1995.

15. Kurt Eichenwald, "Prudential Adds to Reserves to Pay for Scandal," *New York Times,* 13 July 1994.

16. Kurt Eichenwald, "Prudential Case May Bring Suits," *New York Times,* 19 January 1995; and Rachel Gabarine, "Claims Deadline Is Near for Prudential Investors," *New York Times,* 31 December 1994.

17. Kurt Eichenwald, "Class-Action Suit Deadline Expired, Prudential Argues," *New York Times,* 18 July 1994.

18. Laurence Zuckerman, "Prudential Unit Getting More Cash from Parent," *New York Times,* 20 December 1995.

19. Michael Siconolfi, "Prudential Executive Said to Face Civil Charges," *New York Times,* 25 January 1995.

20. Leslie Scism, "Prudential Management Knew of Abuses by Its Agents, Regulators' Report Says," *Wall Street Journal,* 9 July 1996.

21. Anita Raghavan, "Paine Webber Posts a Loss Tied to Claims," *Wall Street Journal,* 28 July 1995.

22. Richard Lambert, "Lessons from a Fraud Casebook," *Financial Times,* 15 September 1995.

23. Reed Abelson, "Wide Range of Commissions Found at Brokerage Firms," *Wall Street Journal,* 11 March 1996.

24. William Power, "Order Flow Fees Continue at Schwab," *Wall Street Journal,* 15 December 1995.

25. Jeffrey Taylor, "A Fairer NASDAQ? SEC Approves Its New Rules," *Wall Street Journal,* 29 August 1996.

26. Spiro and Schroeder, "Can You Trust Your Broker?"

27. Andy Pasztor and John R. Emshwiller, "How Jay Goldinger Won Great Publicity and Lost $100 Million," *Wall Street Journal,* 22 January 1996.

28. Andy Pasztor and Fred Vogelstein, "Refco Said to be Target of Investigation by U.S. over Dealings with Goldinger," *Wall Street Journal,* 25 March 1996.

29. Greg Burns, "What's a Small Wall Street Investor Like You . . ." *Business Week,* 17 April 1995.

30. Floyd Norris, "46 Charged in Stock Fraud by F.B.I.," *New York Times,* 11 October 1996.

31. Floyd Norris, "F.B.I. Trap Snares a Wall Street Recidivist," *New York Times,* 13 October 1996.

32. Gary Weiss, "The $700 Million Mystery," *Business Week,* 18 December 1995.

33. Claire Poole, "Hello, Sucker," *Forbes,* 30 March 1992.

34. John Accola, "Chatfield Dean Faces $750,000 in Fines," *Rocky Mountain News,* 5 February 1994; Donald Bauder, "Chatfield Dean Settles with SEC on Compliance," Reuters, 9 December 1993; and "Chatfield Dean Agrees to Pay $2.47 Million," *San Diego Union Tribune,* 4 February 1994.

35. Leslie Eaton, "Radio Host's Pitches Draw Inquiry," *New York Times,* 26 January 1995.

36. "Sonny" Bloch Sentenced to 21 Months in Tax Case," *Wall Street Journal,* 4 October 1996.

37. David J. Morrow, "New York Brokerage Is Accused of Fraud," *New York Times,* 24 May 1996.

38. Floyd Norris, "Stock Watchdogs Can't End Abuses," *New York Times,* 28 July 1996.

39. "Caveat Entrepreneur," *Business Week,* 14 October 1996, and Frances A. McMorris, "Ex-SEC Lawyer, 5 Others Are Indicted for Fraud, Following Dorfman Probe," *Wall Street Journal,* 7 October 1996.

40. Leslie Eaton, "Stiff Penalties Could Drive L.I. Broker out of Business," *New York Times,* 26 April 1996.

41. Linda Grant, "Fidelity's Billionaire Wallflower," *Fortune,* 4 March 1996.

42. Robert McGough and Judith Burns, "Levitt Advises Fund Managers to Fix the Roof," *Wall Street Journal,* 23 May 1996; and Robert McGough, "Few Mutual Funds Ban Personal Shorting," *Wall Street Journal,* 24 June 1996.

43. Jeffrey Taylor, "SEC Limits Money-Market Funds' Risk," *Wall Street Journal,* 22 March 1996.

44. Martin J. Gruber, "Another Puzzle: The Growth of Actively Managed Mutual Funds" (presidential address presented at the American Finance Association, San Francisco, January 1996).

45. Arguably, investors get a better shake in the commodities markets. The Commodities Futures Trading Commission bars commodities firms from requiring mandatory arbitration, and allows investors to go to court if they disagree with a ruling on compensation by an administrative law judge.

46. Margaret A. Jacobs and Michael Siconolfi, "Investors Do Poorly Fighting Wall Street—and May Do Worse," *Wall Street Journal,* 8 February 1995.

47. Ibid.

48. Michael Siconolfi, "Firms That Don't Pay Settlements Face Penalties," *Wall Street Journal,* 13 June 1995.

49. Margaret A. Jacobs, "SEC Faces Criticism for Role in the Oversight of Arbitration," *Wall Street Journal,* 28 February 1996.

50. Floyd Norris, "Broker Loses Arbitration? Keep It Quiet," *New York Times,* 23 February 1996.

51. Michael Siconolfi, "New Arbitration Rules: Mixed Bag for Investors," *Wall Street Journal,* 23 January 1996.

52. Michael Siconolfi, "Revised Rules Are Mapped for Securities Arbitration," *Wall Street Journal,* 23 February 1996.

53. Michael Siconolfi, "NASD Plans High-Tech Overhaul to Track Broker-Discipline History," *Wall Street Journal,* 13 June 1995.

54. Norris, "Broker Loses Arbitration?"

55. Diana B. Henriques, "Making It Harder for Investors to Sue," *New York Times,* 10 September 1995.

56. Neil A. Lewis, "Securities Bill Becomes Law as the Senate Overrides Veto," *New York Times,* 23 December 1995.

57. Shawn Tully, "Merrill Lynch: Bulls Ahead," *Fortune,* 19 February 1996, 97–99.

58. Bridget O'Brien, "Merrill Starting Client-Reward Program," *Wall Street Journal,* 30 September 1996.

59. Ibid.

60. Michael Siconolfi, "Dean Witter Levels Pay Field for Brokers," *Wall Street Journal,* 29 September 1995.

61. Bridget O'Brien, "Merrill Lynch Considers Paying Salaries to New Brokers to Cut Interest Conflicts," *Wall Street Journal,* 20 November 1995.

62. Michael Siconolfi, "Brokerage Firms Fire Potential Problems," *Wall Street Journal,* 1 February 1996.

63. Charles Gasparino, "In-house Funds Still Get Preference at Dean Witter," *Wall Street Journal,* 21 November 1996.

64. Robert McGough, "NASD May Toughen a Broker-Fee Rule," *Wall Street Journal,* 29 December 1995.

65. Deborah Lohse, "New Top Cop at the NASD Talks Tough," *Wall Street Journal,* 25 March 1996.

66. Ellen E. Schultz, "Mutual Funds Skirt 'Contest' Crackdown with Rewards for Independent Advisers," *Wall Street Journal,* 2 October 1996.

67. Robert D. Hershey, Jr., "U.S. Indicts 11 Brokers on Investor Fraud," *New York Times*, 1 December 1995.

68. Securities and Exchange Commission, *Report of the Committee on Compensation Practices* (Washington, D.C.: Securities and Exchange Commission, 1995).

69. "Taking the Mystery out of the Marketplace: The SEC's Consumer Education Campaign," (speech to the National Press Club, Washington, D.C., 13 October 1994).

CHAPTER 4

1. Clifford W. Smith, Jr., "Economics and Ethics: The Case of Salomon Brothers," *Journal of Applied Corporate Finance* 5, no. 2 (1992): 23–29.

2. Institute for Financial Research, Working Paper 1096 (26 August 1995).

3. Discussion with the authors, October 1996.

CHAPTER 5

1. Walter Werner and Steven Smith, *Wall Street* (New York: Columbia University Press, 1991).

2. Ibid.

3. "The Big Squeeze," *Wall Street Journal*, 12 August 1991.

4. Michael Siconolfi and Laurie Cohen, "How Salomon's Hubris and U.S. Trap Led to Leader's Downfall," *Wall Street Journal*, 19 August 1991.

5. Michael Siconolfi, "Salomon Unit Posts a Huge Increase in Quarterly Profit," *Wall Street Journal*, 24 July 1992.

6. Siconolfi and Cohen, "How Salomon's Hubris and U.S. Trap Led to Leader's Downfall."

7. Ibid.

8. "Salomon, Inc. Bond Trader Heads to Jail," *Newsday*, 15 December 1993.

9. Siconolfi and Cohen, "How Salomon's Hubris and U.S. Trap Led to Leader's Downfall."

10. Clifford W. Smith, Jr., "Economics and Ethics: The Case of Salomon Brothers," *Journal of Applied Corporate Finance* 5, no. 2 (1992): 23–29.

11. Roy C. Smith, *The Global Bankers* (New York: E.P. Dutton, 1989), 214.

12. Securities and Exchange Commission, *Report Pursuant to Section 21(a) of the Securities Exchange Act of 1934 Regarding the NASD and the NASDAQ Market* (Washington, D.C.: Securities and Exchange Commission, 1996).

13. William G. Christie and Paul H. Schultz, "Why Do NASDAQ Market Makers Avoid Odd-Eighths Quotes?" *Journal of Finance* 49, no. 5 (December 1994): 1813–1840.

14. "A Crackdown on NASDAQ," *New York Times*, 12 August 1996.

15. Floyd Norris, "At NASDAQ, Time to Repent and Grow Up," *New York Times*, 11 August 1996.

16. Ibid.

17. Anita Raghavan and Jeffrey Taylor, "Will NASD Accord Transform NASDAQ Market?" *Wall Street Journal*, 8 August 1996.

18. *Webster's New Collegiate Dictionary* (Springfield, Mass.: G. & C. Merriam, 1980).

19. Michael Siconolfi and Deborah Lohse, "Inside a Dubious IPO: Sponsor, It Appears, Held All the Cards," *Wall Street Journal,* 5 November 1996.

20. Jeffrey Taylor, "SEC Action Is Unlikely Against Vinik," *Wall Street Journal,* 9 May 1996.

21. Stephanie Strom, "A Market Ripe for Manipulation," *New York Times,* 12 July 1996.

22. Gail Appleson, "SEC Charges Brokers with Cornering Market in a Stock," *Reuters Business Report,* 8 September 1989.

23. Floyd Norris, "Cost for the Shorts in Chase Medical," *New York Times,* 8 September 1989.

24. Floyd Norris, "Brokers' Big Role in Chase Medical," *New York Times,* 16 January 1989.

25. Floyd Norris, "SEC Sues Two over Corner," *New York Times,* 10 August 1989.

26. Floyd Norris, "Chase Medical Is Delisted," *New York Times,* 10 August 1989.

27. Floyd Norris, "Chase Medical Trading Is Suspended by SEC," *New York Times,* 17 January 1989.

28. Julie Waresh, "Clearing Broker's Inaction Did Not Constitute Aiding and Abetting," *Securities Regulation and Law Report,* 23 March 1989, 16–18.

29. Leslie Eaton, "S.E.C. Acts on Stock Promotion on the Net," *New York Times,* 8 November 1996.

30. See Roy C. Smith, *Comeback* (Boston: Harvard Business School Press, 1993).

31. Ibid.

32. James Sterngold, "Bills Coming Due for Japan, Inc.," *New York Times,* 11 November 1991.

33. James Sterngold, "Testimony on Brokers in Tokyo," *New York Times,* 30 August 1991.

34. Clay Chandler, "Nomura's Two Top Officers Will Resign," *Wall Street Journal,* 23 July 1991.

35. James Sterngold, "Japan's Rigged Casino," *New York Times Magazine,* 26 April 1992.

36. Steven Weisman, "Series of Scandals Have Japanese Debating if Country Has Grown Corrupt," *New York Times,* 19 August 1991.

37. Ibid.

38. Robert Steiner, "Two Obscure Firms Struggle for Control of the Largest Piece of the Chinese Pie," *Asian Wall Street Journal,* 5 February 1994.

39. Seth Faison, "Scandal Besets Chinese Markets," *New York Times,* 6 March 1995.

40. Seth Faison, "President of Shanghai Firm Quits After Trading Scandal," *New York Times,* 27 April 1995.

41. Yan Yunlong of China Guotai Securities, quoted in Seth Faison, "Shanghai Stock Market Cited for Scandal," *New York Times,* 22 September 1995.

42. "Troubled Shanghai Broker Merging," *International Herald Tribune,* 16 February 1996.

43. Faison, "Scandal Besets Chinese Markets."

44. Nicholas D. Kristof, "Don't Joke About This Stock Market," *New York Times,* 9 May 1993.

45. John Schmid, "Daimler's Puritan Problem," *International Herald Tribune,* 13 June 1996.

CHAPTER 6

1. Leo Herzel and Richard Shepro, *Bidders and Targets: M&A in the United States* (Cambridge: Basil Blackwell, 1990), 112–115.

2. *SEC v. Texas Gulf Sulphur Co.*, 402 F.2d 833, 849 (2d Cir.) (en banc), *cert denied*, 394 U.S. 976 (1969).

3. Henry G. Manne, *Insider Trading and the Stock Market* (New York: Free Press, 1966), 61.

4. "Disputes Arise over the Value of Insider Trading," *Wall Street Journal*, 17 November 1986.

5. Jennifer Moore, "What Is Really Unethical About Insider Trading," *Journal of Business Ethics* 9 (1990).

6. *Chiarella v. United States*, 445 U.S. 222 (1980). See also Ralph C. Ferrara (former SEC General Counsel) and Herbert Thomas, "Ferrara on Insider Trading and The Wall," in *Corporate Securities Series* (New York: Law Journal Seminars-Press, 1995) for a wide-ranging discussion of the development of insider-trading law in the United States.

7. *Dirks v. SEC*, 463 U.S. 646, 655 n. 14, 103 S.Ct. 3255, 77 L.Ed.2d 911 (1983).

8. *U.S. v. Carpenter*, 791 F.2d 1024 (2d Cir., 1986), *affirmed by an evenly divided court*, 484 U.S. 19 (1987).

9. Chris Welles, "Is Someone Sneaking a Peek at Business Week?" *Business Week*, 3 February 1996.

10. Floyd Norris, "Insider Muddle Seems Headed for the High Court," *New York Times*, 19 September 1996.

11. *SEC v. Siegel*, SEC Litigation Release No. 11354 (13 February 1987).

12. Michael Schroeder and Amy Barrett, "A Bigger Stick Against Insider Traders," *Business Week*, 26 May 1996.

13. Ted C. Tishman, "The Tip," *Worth*, July/August 1994.

14. Jeffrey Taylor, "SEC Hunts Down 'Mystery' Defendants in Praxair Bid for CBI," *Wall Street Journal*, 20 November 1995.

15. *U.S. v. Chestman*, 704 F. Supp. 451, 459 (S.D.N.Y. 1989), *rev'd* 903 F.2d 75 (2d Cir. 1990), *aff'd in part, revised in part* 947 F.2d 551 (2d Cir. 1991) *(rehearing en banc), cert. denied* 112 S.Ct. 1759 (1992).

16. Larry A. Bear and Rita Maldonado-Bear, *Free Markets, Finance, Ethics and Law*, (New York: Prentice Hall, 1994), 340–342.

17. Dominic Hobson, *The Pride of Lucifer* (London: Hamish Hamilton, 1990), 302–305.

18. James Stewart, *Den of Thieves* (New York: Simon & Schuster, 1991), 465.

19. Jenny Ireland, "A Little Knowledge Is a Dangerous Thing," *Eurobusiness*, May 1994; John Gapper, "Exchange Steps Up Fight Against Insider Trading," *Financial Times*, 21 May 1996.

20. Paul Webster, "France May Launch Inquiry into Corruption," *Manchester Guardian Weekly*, 25 September 1994.

21. Richard S. Biegen et al., "Countries Strengthen Insider Trading Laws," *National Law Journal*, 13 November 1995.

CHAPTER 7

1. "More Dust Than Dirt," *Financial Times,* 21 March 1996.

2. In 1995 nearly $1 billion in disgorgement of illicit profits occurred, $34 million of civil penalties were assessed, and 98 criminal convictions resulted due to actions initiated by the SEC. In that same year, 1,523 NASD public-customer cases were decided by arbitration.

3. Bill Richards, "Xylan's Financial Officer Resigns; Investment Bank Blamed for Leak," *Wall Street Journal,* 1 August 1996.

4. A.A. Berle, Jr. and G.C. Means, *The Modern Corporation and Private Property,* (New York: MacMillan, 1932).

5. Bryan Burroughs and John Helyar, *Barbarians at the Gate* (New York: Harper & Row, 1990), 75–180.

6. Kurt Eichenwald, *Serpent on the Rock* (New York: HarperCollins, 1995).

7. John A. Byrne, "What, Me Overpaid? CEOs Fight Back," *Business Week,* 4 May 1992.

8. "FASB Drops Plan Regarding Stock Options," *Washington Post,* 21 December 1994.

9. Allan Sloan, "The Greed Factor Hits a New Level with Turner Broadcasting–Time Warner," *Washington Post,* 3 October 1995.

10. Leslie Scism and Greg Steinmetz, "Conseco Fires Merrill Lynch as Underwriter," *Wall Street Journal,* 15 March 1995.

11. As quoted from the *Wall Street Journal* in Roni Michaeli and Kent L. Womack, "Conflicts of Interest and the Credibility of Underwriters' Analysts' Recommendations," Cornell University Working Paper, March 1996.

12. Scism and Steinmetz, "Conesco Fires Merrill Lynch as Underwriter."

13. Michaeli and Womack, "Conflicts of Interest and the Credibility of Underwriters' Analysts' Recommendations."

CHAPTER 8

1. *Financial Times,* 30 December 1994.

2. As quoted in Robert Chote, "Corruption Undermines Aid Effort," *Financial Times,* 16 May 1996.

3. Raymond Bonner, "The Worldly Business Is Joined: Quiet Battle Is Joined," *New York Times,* 7 July 1996.

4. World Bank, *World Development Report, 1996* (Washington, D.C.: World Bank, 1996).

5. "Surveys Rank Nigeria as Most Corrupt Nation," *New York Times,* 3 June 1996.

6. See Thomas N. Gladwin and Ingo Walter, "The Shadowy Underside of International Trade," *Saturday Review,* July 1977.

7. James Sterngold, "Canadian Bribe Inquiry Said to Focus on Boeing," *New York Times,* 13 February 1996.

8. *New York Times,* 3 May 1995.

9. *Financial Times,* 15 August 1995.

10. "Opel Unit Confirms Official Is Facing Bribery Charges," *Wall Street Journal,* 1

March 1996. See also Peter Norman, "A Hidden Hand of Corruption," *Financial Times,* 5 June 1996; and Gabriella Stern and Joanne S. Lubin, "GM Rules Curb Wining and Dining by Suppliers and Vendors," *Wall Street Journal,* 5 June 1996.

11. Robert S. Greenberger, "Foreigners Use Bribes to Beat U.S. Rivals in Many Deals, New Report Concludes," *Wall Street Journal,* 13 October 1995.

12. James Hines, "Forbidden Payment: Foreign Bribery and American Business After 1977," *National Bureau of Economic Research Working Paper* No. 5266, 1996.

13. "Is Corruption an Asian Value?" *Wall Street Journal,* 7 May 1996.

14. "The New Adventures of Tom Jones," *New York Times,* 19 September 1976.

15. "Exxon's Italian Payments Tied to Specific Benefits," *New York Times,* 17 July 1995.

16. "Securities Firms Make Large Gifts to Congressmen," *Wall Street Journal,* 22 August 1995.

17. Andrew Adonis, "Politics, Money and Crime: A World on the Take," *Financial Times,* 30 December 1994, 4.

18. "The Big Sleaze in Muni Bonds," *Fortune,* 7 August 1995.

19. "Trouble with Munis," *Business Week,* 6 September 1993; and "The Politics of Money," *U.S. News & World Report,* 15 June 1994.

20. Graham Button, "Good Ol' Girl," *Forbes,* 11 September 1995, 60.

21. "Textbook Case in New Jersey: Political Art of Bond Deals," *New York Times,* 24 February 1995. See also "Ex-Florio Aide Pleads Guilty to Kickback Scheme," *New York Times,* 25 February 1995.

22. "A Push to Revamp Municipal Bonds," *New York Times,* 25 October 1993.

23. Karen Donovan, "Limits on Contributions Sought," *National Law Journal,* 15 November 1993; "Bond Firms Disclose Guides for Banning Political Gifts," *New York Times,* 9 December 1993.

24. "Curb on Political Gifts by Bond Underwriters Has Lots of Loopholes," *Wall Street Journal,* 8 May 1995; "Backlash Grows Against Gift Ban," *Bond Buyer,* 14 December 1993.

25. Charles Gasparino, "Merrill Executive's Political Donation in Indiana Curbs Firm's Business There," *Wall Street Journal,* 24 May 1996.

26. Leah Nathans Spiro and Geoffrey Smith, "Lazard Gets Clobbered by Its Own Clout," *Business Week,* 20 November 1995.

27. Leslie Wayne, "Former Partner at Lazard Gets 33-Month Prison Term," *New York Times,* 20 December 1996.

28. Leslie Wayne, "Former Partner at Lazard Frères Is Guilty in Municipal Bond Case," *New York Times,* 10 August 1996.

29. Peter G. Gosselin, "Bond Traders Sobered by Trial," *Boston Globe,* 10 August 1996.

30. Wayne, "Former Partner at Lazard Frères Is Guilty."

31. Spiro and Smith, "Lazard Gets Clobbered by Its Own Clout."

32. "The Politics of Money," *U.S. News & World Report,* 15 June 1994.

33. "IRS Begins Program to Recoup $2 Billion from Muni Issuers," *Wall Street Journal,* 27 July 1996.

34. Charles Gasparino, "U.S. Probe of Muni Bond Market Starts to Have Impact on Funds," *Wall Street Journal,* 17 October 1996.

35. Charles Gasparino, "Rubin Excuses Himself on Muni Ruling That Could Cost Wall Street Millions," *Wall Street Journal,* 1 August 1996.

36. John O'Connor, "Cities' Group Calls for SEC to Moderate Crackdown on Municipal Bond Issuers," *Wall Street Journal,* 11 March 1996.

37. Edward T. Hall, *Beyond Culture* (Garden City, N.Y.: Anchor Books, 1977).

38. See Thomas N. Gladwin and Ingo Walter, *Multinationals Under Fire* (New York: John Wiley & Sons, 1980), Chapter 9, for an analysis of variation by industry of political contributions during the 1970s.

39. Ibid.

40. As quoted in Edward D. Herlihy and Theodore A. Levine, "Corporate Crises: The Overseas Payments Problem," *Law and Policy in International Business* 8, no. 3 (1976): 568.

41. Anthony Sampson, "Lockheed's Foreign Policy: Who, in the End, Corrupted Whom?" *New York Magazine,* 15 March 1976, 86–90.

42. "Wall Street Winks at Bribery Cases," *New York Times,* 12 November 1976.

43. Gunnar Myrdal, *Asian Drama* (New York: Twentieth Century Fund, 1968), 475.

44. "Greasing Wheels: How U.S. Companies Win Friends Abroad," *Wall Street Journal,* 29 September 1995.

45. Ibid.

46. Tracy Corrigan and Robert Graham, "U.S. Regulator Files Fraud Suit Against Montedison," *Financial Times,* 22 November 1996.

47. As quoted in Gladwin and Walter, *Multinationals Under Fire,* 323.

48. "Honesty School for Bureaucrats," *Financial Times,* 29 September 1995.

49. Steven Brull, "Why Korea's Cleanup Won't Catch On," *Business Week,* 18 December 1995.

50. "Ending Trade Corruption," *Financial Times,* 8 March 1996.

51. Nancy Dunne, "Kantor Declares War on Bribes," *Financial Times,* 7 March 1996.

52. "Official of SEC Urges Corporate Post on Ethics," *Wall Street Journal,* 17 March 1977.

53. Gladwin and Walter, *Multinationals Under Fire,* 341. See also Douglas P. Lobel, "Let the Sellers Beware: The Perils of the Foreign Corrupt Practices Act," *Metropolitan Corporate Counsel* 3, no. 3 (March 1995).

54. Paul Lewis, "A World Fed Up with Bribes," *New York Times,* 28 November 1996.

55. Seymour M. Hersh, "Hughes Aircraft Faces Allegations That It Used Bribery in Indonesia," *New York Times,* 25 January 1977.

CHAPTER 9

1. Ingo Walter, *The Secret Money Market* (New York: Harper & Row, 1990).

2. Richard A. Gordon, *Tax Havens and Their Use by US Taxpayers—An Overview* ("The Gordon Report") (Washington, D.C.: Internal Revenue Service, 1981). See also Somchai Richpuran, "Measuring Tax Evasion," *Finance and Development,* December 1984.

3. J.N. Bhagwati, A. Krueger, and C. Wibulswasdi, *Capital Flight from LDC's: A Statistical Analysis* (Amsterdam: North Holland Publishing Company, 1974). See also M.S. Khan and N. Ul Haque, "Capital Flight from Developing Countries," *Finance and Development,* March 1987.

4. Subcommittee on Crime, Committee of the Judiciary, U.S. House of Representatives, 99th Congress, *Current Problems of Money Laundering* (Washington, D.C.: U.S. Government Printing Office, 1985).

5. "Papering Over the Euro-Cracks," *The Banker,* November 1988. See also Stephen Fidler, "Swiss Gain Most from Securities Euro-Tax," *Financial Times,* 4 February 1989.

6. Wolfgang Münchau, "Dresdner Client Jailed for Tax Evasion," *Financial Times,* 13 February 1996.

7. Under German law an individual can file a civil suit for tax evasion against himself, which precludes criminal prosecution if it is filed before the launch of an official criminal investigation. This procedure provides, in effect, a legal way to confess to past tax sins.

8. Greg Steinmetz, "German Tax Collectors Rile Country's Banks with a Series of Raids," *Wall Street Journal Europe,* 4 December 1996.

9. "German Savers Going Swiss," *Financial Times,* 25 September 1995.

10. "Inflows Have Intensified," *Financial Times,* 26 October 1995.

11. Ian Rodger, "Mafia Hunter Targets 'Dirty' Money," *Financial Times,* 26 October 1995.

12. Greg Steinmetz, "Swiss Banks Remain Prime Haven of Those with Money to Hide," *Wall Street Journal,* 9 July 1996.

13. "Swiss Banks' Tax Cheat Warning," *Financial Times,* 20 September 1995; "Swiss Official Calls Banks Lax on Illicit Funds," *International Herald Tribune,* 20 September 1995.

14. John Tagliabue, "Breaking the Swiss Banking Silence," *New York Times,* 4 June 1996.

15. "Banks Challenge Ruling on Marcos Accounts," *Financial Times,* 29 August 1995.

16. Eduard Chambost, *Bank Accounts: A World Guide to Confidentiality* (London: John Wiley, 1983). See also Walter H. Diamond and Dorothy B. Diamond, *Tax Havens of the World* (New York: Matthew Bender, 1984).

17. "A \$15 Trillion Piggy Bank," *Business Week,* 24 June 1996.

18. William H. Davidson, *The Amazing Race* (New York: John Wiley & Sons, 1983).

19. Richard H. Blum, *Offshore Haven Banks, Trusts and Companies* (New York: Praeger Publishers, 1984). See also Benito Legarda, "Small Island Economies," *Finance and Development,* June 1984; and Donald Lessard and John Williamson, *Capital Flight* (Washington, D.C.: Institute for International Economics, 1987).

20. David M. O'Neil, *Growth of the Underground Economy, 1950–1981.* Joint Economic Committee, U.S. Congress (Washington, D.C.: U.S. Government Printing Office, 1983). See also Peter M. Gutmann, "The Subterranean Economy," *Financial Analysts Journal,* November/December 1977; and Vito Tanzi, *The Underground Economy* (Lexington, Mass.: D.C. Heath, 1982).

21. Clay Harris and Norma Cohen, "Currency Trader Played China Card to Entice Ethnic Investors," *Financial Times,* 6 December 1996.

22. Alan Friedman, "Milan Bank Executives Charged Over 10 Million Secret Fund," *Financial Times,* 15 May 1988.

23. Stanley Penn, "Blemished Picture," *Wall Street Journal,* 26 May 1988. See also Carol Vogel, "Financier's Absence Deepens \$130 Million Mystery," *New York Times,* 27 May 1988.

24. James B. Steward and S. Karene Witcher, "US Attorney Launches an Investigation of Former Banker at Morgan Guaranty," *Wall Street Journal,* 22 May 1986.

25. Daniel Hertzberg and S. Karene Witcher, "Banker Quits Drexel Amid Investigation by Former Employer, Morgan Guaranty," *Wall Street Journal,* 21 May 1986. See also 'O Tombo de Tony,' *Veja,* 28 May 1986.

26. S. Karene Witcher, "Brazil is Seeking Morgan Guaranty Account Names," *Wall Street Journal*, 23 May 1986. See also Eric N. Berg, "Brazil Banking Customs Cited in Morgan Case," *International Herald Tribune*, 24 May 1986. See also "Capital Scandal," *Fortune*, 23 June 1986.

27. See Peter Truell and William Power, "Morgan Guaranty Ex-Official Gets 3½ Years in Jail, Fine," *Wall Street Journal*, 3 March 1987. See also James S. Henry, "Fallen Angel," *Manhattan, Inc.*, April 1987.

28. In this context, it is not surprising that Federal Reserve data and the size of reported interbank international currency transactions indicate that a significant proportion of U.S. currency in circulation is held outside the United States.

29. Permanent Subcommittee on Investigations, Committee on Governmental Affairs, U.S. Senate, *Crime and Secrecy: The Use of Offshore Banks and Companies* (Washington, D.C.: U.S. Government Printing Office, 1983), 141.

30. Vito Tanzi, "Money Laundering and the International Financial System," IMF Working Paper No. 96/55, Washington, D.C., 1996, and Peter J. Quirk, "Macroeconomic Implications of Money Laundering," IMF Working Paper No. 96/66, Washington, D.C., 1996.

31. Subcommittee on Crime, Committee of the Judiciary, U.S. House of Representatives, 99th Congress, *Current Problems of Money Laundering* (Washington, D.C.: U.S. Government Printing Office, 1985), 135.

32. Anthony DePalma, "Drug Traffickers Smuggling Tons of Cash from the U.S. Through Mexico," *New York Times*, 25 January 1996.

33. Subcommittee on Crime, Committee on the Judiciary, U.S. House of Representatives, *Current Problems of Money Laundering*, 127.

34. Davidson, *The Amazing Race.*

35. Mark Maremont and Gail DeGeorge, "Money-Laundering in Miami?" *Business Week*, 23 October 1995, 92.

36. Clifford Krauss and Douglas Frantz, "Cali Drug Cartel Using U.S. Business to Launder Cash," *New York Times*, 30 October 1995.

37. Peter Truell, "Citibank Records Examined as Part of Mexican Inquiry," *New York Times*, 30 March 1996.

38. Geri Smith, "Can Zedillo Penetrate Mexico's Heart of Darkness?" *Business Week*, 18 December 1995, 61.

39. Anthony DePalma and Peter Truell, "A Mexican Mover and Shaker Got the Red Carpet at Citibank," *New York Times*, 5 June 1996.

40. Ibid.

41. Laurie Hays, "Citibank Excluded Executive in Salinas Probe," *Wall Street Journal*, 12 June 1996.

42. Julia Preston, "Mexico's Elite Caught in Scandal's Harsh Glare," *New York Times*, 13 July 1996. See also "Cleaning up Latin America," *Economist*, 6 April 1996; Steve Stecklow and Craig Torres, "Mexico's 'Dirty Money' Finds a Handy Laundry Next Door in Texas," *Wall Street Journal*, 8 June 1996; and Laurie Hays, "Private Banker Wooed, Then Sought to Drop Mexico's Raul Salinas," *Wall Street Journal*, 1 November 1996.

43. Ingo Walter, *The Secret Money Market* (New York: Harper & Row, 1990).

44. "Agha Abedi," *Economist*, 19 August 1995.

45. Jim Kelly, "Court Clears the Way for Final BCCI Settlement," *Financial Times*, 21 December 1995.

46. Jeff Gerth, "Vast Flow of Cash Threatens Currency, Banks and Economies," *New York Times*, 11 April 1988.

47. "Law Firm's Downfall Exposes New Forms of Money Laundering," *Wall Street Journal*, 26 May 1995.

48. "Fake Bank Set Up by U.S. Agents Snares Drug-Money Launderers," *New York Times*, 17 December 1994.

49. Robert I. Friedman, "The Money Plane," *New York Times*, 22 January 1996.

50. "Software May Dry Up Money Laundering," *Wall Street Journal*, 13 September 1995.

51. "Computers Keep Tabs on Dirty Money," *Wall Street Journal*, 8 May 1995.

52. Clay Harris, "U.S. Prosecutor Attacks Bank Secrecy Laws," *Financial Times*, 24 April 1996, 14.

CHAPTER 10

1. Kurt Eichenwald, "He Told. He Suffered. Now He's a Hero," *New York Times*, 29 May 1994. Our account, including the quotations, is drawn from this article.

2. Diane Vaughan, *The Challenger Launch Decision* (Chicago: University of Chicago Press, 1996).

3. Kurt Eichenwald, "Archer-Daniels Whistle-Blower Is Said to Agree to Plea Deal," *New York Times*, 27 September 1995.

4. Ibid.

5. Ronald Henkoff and Richard Behar, "Andreas's Mole Problem Is Becoming a Mountain," *Fortune*, 21 August 1995.

6. Kurt Eichenwald, "Archer-Daniels Ousts Executive in Mexico," *New York Times*, 7 October 1995.

7. Sharon Walsh, "Big Pension Funds Quiz ADM on Board Changes," *Washington Post*, 2 April 1996.

8. "Archer-Daniels Cuts Surprisingly Good Deal in Price-Fixing Suit," *Wall Street Journal*, 12 April 1996.

9. Kurt Eichenwald, "Archer Said to Be in Talks to Head Off Criminal Case," *New York Times*, 13 April 1996.

10. Peter Carlson, "Agri-Giant on the Defensive," *International Herald Tribune*, 18 July 1996. See also Ronald Henkoff, "The ADM Tale Gets Even Stranger," *Fortune*, 13 May 1996.

11. Scott Kilman and Thomas M. Burton, "ADM's Guilty Plea Could Doom Andreas Reign," *Wall Street Journal*, 15 October 1996.

12. Kurt Eichenwald, "Archer Daniels to Pay $100 Million Fine in Price Fixing Case," *New York Times*, 15 October 1996.

13. Scott Kilman, "Two ADM Officials Targeted in Probe, Including Andreas's Son, Leaving Posts," *Wall Street Journal*, 17 October 1996.

14. "Archer-Daniels-Midland Sued by a Former Executive," *New York Times*, 23 November 1996.

15. Ibid.

16. Barry Meier, "CSX Will Pay Whistleblower $1.18 Million," *New York Times*, 30 September 1995.

17. Larry Bear and Rita Maldonaldo-Bear, *Free Markets, Finance, Ethics and Law* (New York: Prentice Hall, 1994), 404–406.

18. "Lucas Industries Settles Suit," *Financial Times,* 2 October 1995.

19. Michael Quint, "Accuser in the Municipal Bond Industry," *New York Times,* 3 March 1995. See also Aaron Pressman, "Arbitration Scheduled on Smith Barney," *Reuters,* 23 May 1995, and Joan Pryde, "IRS Seeks to Give Advice on Escrow Pricing Fairness," *Bond Buyer,* 30 May 1995.

20. Brad Altman, "New Light is Shed on Interest Swap Under SEC Probe in L.A. County," *Bond Buyer,* 25 May 1995.

21. Randall Smith, "Whistle-Blower Rattles the Muni Industry," *Wall Street Journal,* 17 July 1995.

22. Joan Pryde, "NABL, IRS Seek to Give Advice on Escrow Pricing Fairness," *Bond Buyer,* 30 May 1995.

23. Joe Mysak, editor of Grant's *Municipal Bond Observer,* as quoted in Smith, "Whistle-Blower Rattles the Muni Industry."

24. Lee Berton, "Code May Force CPAs to Inform on Employers," *Wall Street Journal,* 4 August 1995.

25. Gene G. James, "Whistleblowing: Its Moral Justification," in *Business Ethics,* 3d. ed., eds. Michael Hoffman and Robert Federici (New York: McGraw Hill, 1995), 290–301.

26. Ibid.

27. Richard T. DeGeorge, "Ethical Responsibilities of Engineers in Large Organizations," *Business and Professional Ethics Journal,* Fall 1981.

28. Ibid.

29. Barbara Ettore, "Whistleblowers: Who's the Real Bad Guy?" *Management Review,* May 1994.

30. See Marcia P. Miceli and Janet P. Near, *Blowing the Whistle* (Lexington, Mass.: Lexington Books, 1992).

31. Marcia P. Miceli and Janet P. Near, "Relationships Among Value Congruence, Perceived Victimization and Retaliation Against Whistleblowers," *Journal of Management,* December 1994.

32. "Blowing the Whistle," *Financial Times,* 15 August 1995.

33. Ibid.

34. Ibid.

35. Ettore, "Whistleblowers: Who's the Real Bad Guy?"

36. Ibid. For a thorough discussion of this issue, see Janet P. Near and Marcia P. Miceli, "Effective Whistle Blowing," *Academy of Management Review,* July 1995.

37. John P. Keenan and Charles A. Krueger, "Whistleblowing and the Professional: The Common Response to Whistleblowing is Retaliation," *Management Accounting,* August 1992. The authors also found that 65 percent of the managers surveyed claimed to have been personally involved in a whistleblowing incident within the previous twelve months. Waste caused by a badly managed department, the purchase of unnecessary goods and services, and theft of company property were the most common problems that led employees to blow the whistle.

CHAPTER 11

1. A recent study by Spuma Rao and Brooke Hamilton adds to an extensive body of academic literature on the relationship between ethical behavior of firms and their financial success by linking reports of misconduct at fifty-seven major publicy traded firms with declines in their stock prices. Spuma M. Rao and J. Brooke Hamilton III, "The Effect of Published Reports of Unethical Conduct on Stock Prices," *Journal of Business Ethics* 15 (1996): 1321–1330.

2. The American firms are Drexel Burnham Lambert, Salomon Brothers, Shearson Lehman Brothers, First Boston, Smith Barney, Kidder Peabody, and Prudential Securities. The British firms are Morgan Grenfell, Baring Brothers, and S.G. Warburg.

3. Alfred Z. Carr, "Is Business Bluffing Ethical?" *Harvard Business Review,* January/February 1968, 143–153.

4. Norman E. Bowie, "Does It Pay to Bluff in Business?" in *Ethical Theory and Business,* eds. Tom L. Beauchamp and Norman E. Bowie (New York: Prentice Hall, 1993).

5. Sissela Bok, *Lying: Moral Choice in Public and Private Life* (New York: Pantheon Books, 1978), 19–31.

Index

■

A&P, 163
Abedi, Agha Hasan, 247, 250
ABN-AMRO
 and Louis de Bièvre, 168
 and MMMF bailout, 84
Accor, 162
Account stuffing, 187–188
Accountability, 314–315
Adam Opel AG, 199
Advanced Voice Technologies, 136–137
Advice, bad, 184
AEG, 166
Aetna Life & Casualty, phony accounting at,
 267–268
Agencies
 conflicts, 171
 and secrecy, 234–239
Agents
 fees, 200–201
 secretive relationships with, 237
AICPA code of ethics, 268
AIG Financial Products, 24, 266
Airship International, 77
Alarm ringing, 314–315
Alcatel-Alsthom, 166
Alcoa, 210
All Nippon Airways, 198
Alliance Capital Management, 24
Alter Sales, 79
Altman, Robert, 250
American Depository Receipts (ADRs),
 216
American Express, 190, 292
American Express Bank, 250
American Institute of Certified Public
 Accountants (AICPA), 267–268
American National Bank of Washington, 250
American Stock Exchange, 91, 139, 121, 155
Analyst ratings, 184

Andersen Consulting, 183
Andreas, Dwayne, 261–263
Andreas, Michael D., 263
A.R. Baron and Company, 79
Arbitrage, 7–8, 167
Arbitrage traders, 6
Arbitrageurs, 5–6
Arbitration
 mandatory, 89–92
 process run by NASD, 89–92
Archer-Daniels-Midland Corporation (ADM),
 the mole at, 261–263
Ashland Oil, 200
Asian Drama, 213
Askin, David J., 76
AT&T, 105

Bache Halsey Stuart, 292, 296
"Back office," 289
Bageot, Walter, 29
BahamasAir, 199
Baksheesh, 198
Ball, George L., 17, 68, 69
Bank for International Settlements, 44
Bank Leu, 157
Bank of America, 18, 247
Bank of China, 252
Bank of Credit and Commerce International
 (BCCI), 14, 26, 114, 247–250
 scandal in, 247–250
Bank of England, 12, 13, 44, 49, 250
Bank secrecy statutes, 254
BankAmerica, and MMMF bailout, 84
Bankers Trust, 2, 27, 114–115, 118, 282
 and broker rogues, 17–19
Banking
 control of, 41–42
 international regulations of, 44–45
 questionable payments in, 220–221

Banking Act of 1933, 41, 42
  Glass-Steagall provisions of, 41, 42
Banks, relationships with clients, 103, 116
Banque Pictet, 245
Barbarians at the Gate, 53
Baring Brothers, 2, 26, 44, 114, 118, 282, 314
  and trader rogues, 12–13, 15
Barnett Banks, and MMMF bailout, 84
Baruch, Bernard, 149
Barzini, Luigi, 208
BAT Industries, 181
Bausch & Lomb, 245
BCCI. *See* Bank of Credit and Commerce
  International
Bear Stearns, 5, 22, 76, 145, 114, 118, 279,
  299
  memoranda of, 281, 308, 310, 311
Beazer PLC, 190
Becker, Boris, 226
Bent advisers, 204–206
Berkshire Hathaway, 123, 127
Berle-Means work of 1930s, 173
Bernhard, Prince, 197
Betas, 24
Beyond Culture, 209
Bièvre, Louis de, 168
"Big Bang" (British Financial Services Act),
  110, 164, 165
  reforms of, 61
Big Four securities firms (Japan), 142–143
Bloch, Irwin "Sonny," 78
Bloomberg, 183
Blue Arrow
  scandal, 26, 114
  and stock parking, 140–141
Boeing, 199, 215
Boesky, Ivan, 4, 5, 6, 7, 53, 114, 157–158,
  164, 205
Boiler rooms, 76–79
Bok, Sissela, 309
Bond and stock markets in 1990, 3
Bonds, trading in, 109
Bonfire of the Vanities, 53
Bonsal, Dudley J., 151–152
"Booster shots" for new issues, 185
Booz Allen and Hamilton, 216
Borg Warner Corporation, 189
Bowen, Charles, 216
Bowie, Norman, 309
Brandeis, Louis D., 218
Brazil, Central Bank of, 238
Brazilian-American Chamber of Commerce,
  237

Bretton Woods system of fixed exchange
  rates, 103
Breuer, Rolf-Ernst, 15
Bribery and corruption, proceeds from,
  224–225
Bribes, kickbacks, and payoffs, 194–222
British Petroleum, 210
British Treasury, 13
Broker misconduct
  anthology of, 71–81
  potential for, 62
Broker rogues, 16–19, 65, 66, 101, 122
Broker-client relationship, 59–66, 169–170,
  179–181
Brokerage commissions, 112
  differences in, 71
Brokers
  and client loyalty, 62
  and commissions, 61–62
  and conflict with clients, 89–94, 171–179
  how to obtain information on, 92–93
  industry control of, 97
  and licensing exams, 66
  long-term interests of, 64
  regulation of, 94–101
  regulatory control of, 97–101
  sales contests and trips for, 62
  and self-control, 95–97
Bucket shops, 76–79
Buffett, Warren, 10, 99, 123, 127, 131,
  299–300
Burger, Warren, 154, 155
Burlington Industries, 189
Bush administration, 159
Business financial secrecy, 224, 225
Business principles
  effective, 303–307
  of Goldman Sachs, 304–306
Business Week, 73, 81, 123, 155, 156
Bustarella, 198, 208
Buyers, sellers, market equilibrium, 232–234

Cadillac Fairview, 120
Cady Roberts case, 150
Cali cartel, 250, 251
California Public Employees' Retirement Sys-
  tem (CalPers), 262
Capital adequacy rules, 47
Capital flight, 224, 225
Capital Insight, 73
Capital markets, integrity of, 60
Careers in finance today, 25
Carr, Alfred, 309

Carson, Rachel, 38
Carter, Jimmy, 248
Cash flow, managing, 55
Caveat investor, 147–148
Central Registration Depository (CRD), 92
CFTC. *See* Commodities Futures Trading Commission
Challenger disaster, 260
Charles Schwab, 24, 66, 71, 72
Chase Manhattan, 69, 103, 174, 192
Chase Medical Group, rigging, 138–139
Chatfield Dean, 77
Check-kiting scandals, 26
Chemical Bank, 103, 174
Chestman, Robert, 163
Chiarella v. United States, 153–154, 155
China Economic Trust and Investment Development Corporation, 146
Chinese insurance market, 215
Chinese walls, 48, 182, 185
Choices firm can make in accepting new client, 186
Christie, William, 134
Chubb, 215
Churning, 73–74
CitiBank, 103, 229, 245–247
Citicorp, 24, 252
Citron, Robert, 21
Civil Aeronautics Board (CAB), 40
Class actions, 93–94
Client-broker relationship, 59–66, 169–170, 179–181
Clients
  commitment to, of Merrill Lynch, 307
  and conflict with brokers, 89–94, 171–179
  interests of, establishing, 171
  legal action by, 23
  loyalty of, and brokers, 62
  relationships with banks, 103, 116
  respect for privacy of, 169–170
  rogue, 19–21
Clifford, Clark, 250
Clinton administration, 159
Coase, Ronald, 34
Coase theorem, 34
Coates, Francis, 151–152
Cold calling, 76, 77
Collective bargaining, 40
Collective self-regulation, 219
Collier, Geoffrey, 164
Collins, Martha, 203
Colón, Ramona, 236
Commercial banks, franchised value of, 24–25

Commercial lenders, 5–6
Commerzbank, 226–227
Commission conflicts, 172–173
Commissions, broker, 61–62
Commodities Futures Trading Commission (CFTC), 48, 50, 74, 75, 135, 138
Commonwealth Financial Group, 75
Compensation
  blue-ribbon committee on, 98–99
  and budget structure, 185
  differentials in, 294–296
  most important message regarding, 296
  principles of, 301–302
  test case at Solomon, 298–301
Competition, 29–58, 102
  policy for, 36
Competitive performance
  depending upon information asymmetries, 183
  depending upon interpretation advantages, 184
  depending upon transaction costs, 183
Competitive strength, and questionable payments, 210–211
Compliance
  and detection systems, 160
  taking the defense on, 289
  and treasury securities, 130–131
Comprehensive Environmental Systems, 79
Comprehensive international reform, 217–220
Comptroller of the Currency, 41, 42, 50
Confidentiality, cost of, 233
Conflict-of-interest rules, 120
Conflicts
  involving information, 181–186
  managing, 193
  as principal, 186–193
Conflicts of interest, 169–193
  factors favoring firms, 185–186
  factors favoring firms, "booster shots" for new issues, 185
  factors favoring firms, compensation, and budget structure, 185
  factors favoring firms, punishment, threats of, 185–186
  marketplace influences and, 184–185
Conoco, 197
Conseco, 185
Consolidated Financial Management, 203
Consumer Product Safety Commission, 39
Consumers Union, 39
Container Corporation of America, 189
Contestable markets, 35–36

Continental bonds, and insider trading, 121
Cook, Rodney, 90
Copper trading, and Sumitomo, 137–138
Cornering a market, example of, 136
Corporate gorillas, 106–108
Corporate governance, standards of, 173, 175, 262
Corporate self-regulation, 219
Corrupt payments as market failures, 207–212
Corruption abroad, 195
Corruption, in Germany, 199
Corruption Index, 196
County NatWest, 20, 114, 140–141
"Coupon washing," 226
Cox, James, 156
Crash of 1929, 54
Crédit Suisse, 192, 228, 236
Crédit Suisse-First Boston (CSFB), 21, 105, 192–193
Crédit Suisse-White Weld, 192
Creditability at the top, 308
Criminal funds laundering, 225
CSX, overcharging at, 263–264
"Cultural bridges," 209
Cultural complexity, and questionable payments, 209
Cumshaw, 198
Currency
  bulk shipments of, 242
  converting domestically, 241
  the need to convert, 240–241
  physical weight of, 241
Currency transaction reports (CTRs), 241
Customer gouging, 71–73
Cutthroat competition, 129

Daimler-Benz A.G., 166
  and market rigging, 148
Daiwa Bank, 27, 114, 314
  and trading rogues, 13–15
Daiwa Securities, 13, 142, 144–145, 282
Daiwoo, 217
Damage function, and secrecy, 225
Darr, James J., 67, 68
Dean Witter, 74, 90, 96
Dean Witter Reynolds, 292
DeAngelis brothers, 78
Debevoise, Dickinson R., 256
"Debt decade" of the 1980s, 104
Defense, taking in cost control and compliance, 289
DeGeorge, Richard, 270
del Ponte, Carla, 227

Delaware Court of Chancery, 175
Delors, Jacques, 226
Demsetz, Saidenberg, and Strahan, 24
Den Danske Bank, 170
Den of Thieves, 7, 53, 159
Department of Justice, 126, 133, 215
Deregulation, 40, 102
Derivatives Policy Group, 48
Deutsche Bank, 15, 26, 165, 166
Deutsche Morgan Grenfell, 2, 26
Differential risk, 233
Dirks v. SEC, 154–155
Dirks, Raymond, 154–155
Disaster analysis, and enculturation, 312–313
Discount brokers, 66
Disney, 35
Disney World, 215
Distillers PLC, 164
Doctrine of "parity of information," 154
Domestic questionable payments, 202–207
Donaldson Lufkin, 76
Donaldson, Lufkin & Jenrette, 203, 255
Dow Chemicals, 211
Dow Jones, 155
Dozen, Masahiro, 144–145
Dramshop claims, 23
Dramshop liabilities, 22
Dresdner Bank A.G., 226
Drew, Daniel, 122
Drexel Burnham Lambert, 5, 6, 7, 9, 10, 16, 26, 54, 68, 108, 114, 126, 156–157, 159, 237, 260, 282
Drug trafficking and money laundering, 240–242

Earth Day demonstrations of late 1960s, 38
Eastman Kodak, 180
Economic welfare of firms, and whistle-blowing, 271–272
Economics and the law of speculation, 132–133
Edward D. Jones, 63
E.F. Hutton, 17, 26, 114, 126, 153
Eichenwald, Kurt, 66
Eigen, Peter, 196
Electronic Date Systems (EDS), 292
Electronic transfers, and money laundering, 250–252
Elliot, Amy G., 246–247
Emerging financial markets, and manipulation, 121
Employee misbehavior, 173
Employee misconduct, 24

Employees Retirement Income and Security
  Act (ERISA), 108
Enculturation, 302–315
  and accountability, watchfulness, and alarm
    ringing, 314–315
  and being predictable, 312
  and communicating from the top, 307–308
  and disaster analysis, 312–313
  and effective business principles, 303–307
  and honesty and trust, 308–311
  and persistent training, 313–314
Environmental Protection Agency, 38–39
Equitable, 44
Equity Funding Corporation of America, 154
Equity researchers, four roles of, 184
Ernst & Young, 200, 250
Esso Italiana, 200
E-Trade, 71
Ettore, Barbara, 278
EU. *See* European Union
EU currency, 227
Euro-DM issues, 225
Eurobond market, 44, 112, 103, 104, 105,
  106, 192
Eurobonds, 111, 230
  issues of, 187
Eurocurrency, 192
Eurocurrency market, 44, 51, 113
Eurodollar deposits, 111
Eurodollar market, 251
European monetary union, 227
European Union (EU), 44
  Council of Ministers of, 165
  Second Banking Directive of, 44
Everen Securities, 71
Exit interview, and whistleblowing, 274
External interference, 34
Extortion, 198–200
Exxon, 201, 210

Fair Packaging and Labeling Act of 1969, 39
Fair Trade Commission, 216
Fairbank, 235
False documents, 244–245
Farmers Group, 181
Farrant, Richard, 49
FBI, 75–76, 251, 258, 261, 263
  and Refco, 74
Federal Aviation Administration, 40
Federal Communications Commission, 78–79
Federal Deposit Insurance Corporation, 41
Federal False Claims Act, 264, 265, 267,
  269–270, 275

Federal Reserve Bank, 14, 15, 42
Federal Reserve Bank of New York, 117,
  128, 130, 251
Federal Reserve Board, 50, 124, 126–128, 199
Federal Trade Commission, 39
Ferber, Mark, 204–206
Feuerstein, Donald, 126
Fidelity Investments, 66
Fidelity, Magellan Fund of, 82
  frontrunning at, 137
Fiduciary capacity, ambiguities therein, 170
Fiduciary duties, 171, 174, 175, 255
  breach of, 153, 154, 159, 235, 257
Fiduciary roles, 169–171
F.I. DuPont-Glore Forgan, 292
Finance, rules for appropriate conduct in, 57
Financial community, and Swiss authorities,
  battle between, 227–228
Financial markets, role of speculators in,
  132–133
Financial secrecy, 223–254
  and agencies, 234–239
  demand for, 224–229
  market distortions and, 231–234
  as a product, 223–224
  services available, 224–225
  supply of, 229–231
Financial Services Act (Britain), 164
Financial services, control of, 41–45
Financial services sector, special problems of,
  220
Financial Times, 111, 195, 202, 217
Firms
  as investor, 186–187
  keeping bad ones down, 79–81
  long-term interests of, 56–57, 58
  and relationships with clients, 179–181
  self-control, effectiveness of, 46
  and study of professional integrity, 65–66
  that are payoff-prone, 210
  that have suffered shareholder damage due
    to misconduct, 26–27
  three fundamental components of value of,
    55–56
First Boston, 189, 192–193, 202, 203–204
First Chicago, 199
First Commonwealth Securities, 204
Fitness and properness criteria, 46, 47, 88,
  220
Fleet, and MMMF bailout, 85
Fleming, Jardine, 47
Flight capital, 238, 246
Florio, Jim, 202

Flying stock (*see Tobashi*) in Tokyo, 141–145
Food and Drug Administration, 39
Foreign Bank Supervision Enhancement Act of 1991, 250
Foreign Corrupt Practices Act (FCPA), 214–215
Foreign exchange market, 113
Foreign investors, 109
Fortune, 81
Fox-Pitt, Kelton, 160
Franchise value, managing, 55, 57
Franchised value of commercial banks, 24–25
Frankfurt Stock Exchange, 166
Fraud, 159
Free markets, 29, 30, 31
Freedom House Comparative Survey, 209
Freeman, Robert, 4, 6, 7, 26, 114, 158
Friedman, Milton, 29
Frontrunning
  example of, 135
  at Magellan, 137
Frost, Tom, 141
Fruehauf Corporation, 189
Fujita, Akira, 13

Gebauer, Antonio, 237–239, 252
GE Capital Services, 191–192, 247
General Accounting Office, 98
General Electric Company, 11–12, 114, 191–192, 269, 292
General Motors, 199, 292, 297
Gentz, Manfred, and market rigging, 148
Getty Oil, 158
Gibson Greetings, 113, 115
Giuliani, Rudolf, 6–8, 158–160
Glass-Steagall provisions of the Banking Act of 1933, 41, 42
Goals, incongruence of, 63–64
  and broker misconduct, 64
Going private, 176–177
Golden parachutes, 174
Goldinger, Jay, 73–74
Goldman Sachs, 2, 3, 5, 6, 20, 103, 114, 117, 120, 145, 158, 181, 190–192, 207, 266, 295, 299, 300, 303
  anti-raid policy of, 181
  basic business principles of, 304–306, 309
Goodyear Tire & Rubber, 137, 215
Gould, Jay, 122
Government Finance Officers Association, 267
Government intervention, 30
Graf, Steffi, 226
Grand Metropolitan P.L.C., 156

Grease, 198
Great Depression of the 1930s, 3, 122
Greenberg, Alan C. ("Ace"), 118, 279, 281, 282, 309, 314
  memoranda of, 281, 310, 311
Greenhill, Robert, 295
Growth-and-value funds, performance of, 88
Gruber, Martin, 86–88
Guiness PLC, 164
  and scandal, 26, 114
Gulf Oil, 197, 210
Gutfreund, John, 123, 125, 126, 128

Hafnia Insurance Group, 170
Hall, Edward T., 209
Hamanaka, Yasuo, 137–138
Harvard Business Review, 309
Harvey-Jones, John, 278
Hashimoto, Ryutaro, 143–144
Haughton, Daniel, 212
Hayden Stone, 98
Hayek, Friedrich, 29
Hevesi, Alan, 261
Hills, Roderick, 210
H.J. Myers, 79
Hoffer, Eric, 210
Hoffmann La Roche, 180
Home-country oversight, 218
Home-country sunshine, 218
Honesty, reputation for, 65–66
Hosokawa, Morihiro, 198
Hostile takeover efforts, 5
Hughes Aircraft, 221
Hunt Brothers, and the silver market, 136
Hypo-Bank, 226

IBM, 183, 211, 215
IG Metall trade union, 166
Iguchi, Toshihide, 13–14
Imperial Chemical Industries of Great Britain, 278
IMRO. *See* Investment Management Regulatory Organization
Inadequate internal control, and questionable payments, 211
Industrial and Commercial Bank of China, 145
Industrial organization, economics of, 36
Industries that are payoff-prone, 209–210
Industry control of brokers, 97
Industry self-regulation, 46
Information
  asymmetries, 183

conflicts, 181–186
costs of, 36–38
ING. *See* Internationale Nederlanden Groep
Initial public offerings (IPOs), and organized crime, 49
Inside information, 181–182
Insider trading, 7–8, 9, 149–168
  before 1934, 149–150
  detection facilitated through suspects implicating others, 161
  and effective management, 167
  and European countries outlawing, 164
  through foreign banks, 161
  increased penalties for, 162
  legal issues involved in, 153
  limitations, 152
  and Texas Gulf Sulfur, 151–152
  and tippees, 154–155
  and world opinion, 163–167
Insider trading scandals of the 1980s, 1, 9, 26
Institutional gorillas, 108–110
Insurance, 44
Integrity of firms, study of, 65–66
Interdealer trading, 111
International Chamber of Commerce, 219
International corporate payoffs, 221
International Monetary Fund, 219
International reform proposals, 217–219
  collective self-regulation, 219
  corporate self-regulation, 219
  home-country oversight, 218
  home-country sunshine, 218
  multilateral regulation, 218–219
International regulations of banking and securities, 44
Internationale Nederlanden Groep (ING), 12, 13, 27
Internet, rigging via the, 139–140
Interpretation advantages, 184
Interstate Commerce Commission, 40
Intervention in markets, reasons for, 31–38
Invesco Funds, 82
Investment Act of 1940, 60
Investment advisor, 71
Investment bankers, 5–6
  disappearance of from corporate boards, 107
  political contributions of, 108
Investment banks, 24, 25, 105–107
Investment Management Regulatory Organization (IMRO), 46–47
Investments, information regarding asymmetry of, 65

"Invisible hand," 29–30
IRS, 206, 207, 258
Ishii, Susumu, 143

Jack Eckerd Corporation, 189
James, Gene G., 270, 273
Janney Montgomery Scott, 185
Japan, and anticorruption measures, 216
Japanese equities market, 12
Jett, Joseph, 11, 12
Jinshen, Guan, 146, 147
Johnson, Ross, 176–177
Jones, Thomas V., 200
Jorgensen, Mark, 255–257
Journalistic commentary, and conflict of interest, 185
J.P. Morgan, 24, 103, 114–115, 151, 180, 285, 286, 287
J.T. Moran Financial Corporation, 139
Junk bonds, 5, 190
  experts in, 5–6
  market in, 189
Justice Department, 98, 261, 266

Kaiser, 210
Kantor, Mickey, 217
Kemper fund-management group, 185
Kennedy, Joseph, 149
Kickbacks, payoffs, and bribes, 194–222
Kidder Peabody, 5, 6, 26, 76, 114, 118, 157–158, 189, 292
  and MMMF bailout, 85
  and trader rogues, 11–12, 15
Kim, Young Sam, 217
"King of Wall Street," 123
Kobe earthquake, 12
Kohlberg, Jerry, 189–190
Kohlberg, Kravis & Roberts (KKR), 175–177, 189–190
Koppers Corporation, 190
Korea, and anticorruption measures, 217

Lamont, Thomas, 151–152
Landrieu, Mary, 203
Laundering process, aided by banks and securities services, 243
Laundromats, 243–245
Laval, Pierre, 128
Lazard Frères, 108, 203–206, 266
LBOs, 9
Leaders
  importance of, 56
  steps to develop better, 315–316

Leadership, 315–318
Leeson, Nicholas, 12, 14
Legacies of the 1980s, 4–9
Legacies of the *Den of Thieves* era, 160–162
Legal and ethical problems
  effective memo about reporting, 280
  typical memo about reporting, 280
Lehman Brothers, 20, 24, 157, 292
Lessons of the 1990s, 22–25
Leveraged buyout transactions, 5
Levine, Dennis B., 4, 6, 7, 156–157, 158
Levitt, Arthur, 48, 63, 82, 98–100, 134
Lewis, Michael, 123, 125
Liar's Poker, 123, 125
Li Ka-shing, 145
Limited partnerships, 16–17, 91
  Pru-Bache's, 66–70
Lipper, 81
Lissack, Michael, 265–267
Little, Jacob, the first financial rogue,
  121–122
Lockheed, 197, 198, 212, 215
Lombardi, Enzo, 75
London Interbank Bid Rate (LIBID), 111
London Interbank Offered Rate (LIBOR),
  111, 112
London Metal Exchange, 137–138
London Stock Exchange, 61, 110, 164
  IMAS (Integrated Monitoring and Surveil-
  lance) system of, 165
London, City of, 46
Long-Term Credit Bank of Japan, 15
Los Angeles County Metropolitan Transporta-
  tion Authority, 266
"Low-fat" prospectuses, 48
Loyalty
  and agency law, 275
  and anxiety, 297–298
  conflicts, 179–181
  as a two-way street, 298
Lucas Industries, substandard parts at,
  264–265
Luxembourg bond market, 225
*Lying: Moral Choice in Public and Private
  Life,* 309
Lyonnaise des Eaux, 166

M&A jungle of opportunity, 5–9
  and its "den of thieves," 6–9
Macmillan, 175–176
MAI, 140–141
Mail fraud, 156
Malone, John, 179

Management
  advice for dealing with whistleblowing, 278
  and differentials in compensation, 294–296
  and disaster analysis, 312–313
  excessive payments to, 177–179
  failures as business plague, 318
  high-wire act of, 54–58
  importance of duties, 23–24
  and an incremental descent into poor judgment, 260–268
  indifference, and questionable payments
  212
  in an investment bank, 289–302
  and living with prima donnas, 291–293
  and loyalty and anxiety, 297–298
  and performance evaluation, 296–297
  and persistent training, 313–314
  and predictability, 312
  and principles of compensation, 301–302
  response to whistleblowing, 271–272
  and risks and hazards, 290–291
  and valuing results, 293–294
Management Review, 278
Managing conflicts, 193
Mandatory arbitration, 89–92
Manipulatee, definition of, 136
Manipulation, 7–8, 159
  abroad, 140–148
  before the 1930s, 132
  definition of, 135
  forms of, 121
  undercutting investor confidence, 133
Manipulator, definition of, 136
Manufacturers Hanover Trust, 103, 199
Marcos, Ferdinand, 228
Marcos, Imelda, 228
Market conduct, 29–58
  and basic values, 53
Market distortions for financial security,
  231–234
Market failures, 31–38
  and questionable payments, 207–208
Market for analyst talent, 184–185
Market-imposed discipline, 38
Market manipulation. *See* Manipulation
Market rigging, 121–148. *See also* Rigging
Market sanctions, 113–115
Market values, 285–287
Markets, emerging in 1990s, 194–195
Marmon Group, 175
Marsh Block, 71
Marshall, Alfred, 29
Marubeni Trading Company, 197

Marxism-Leninism, and the "invisible hand," 30
Maughan, Deryck C., 127, 131, 286, 299–300
"Maxwell Affair," 26
Maxwell pension funds, 19–20, 46
Maxwell, Robert, 19–20, 176
May Day, and the NYSE, 108
McDonald's, 64
McLucas, William, 135, 207
Measuring performance, 293–294
Medellin drug cartel, 248
Media, and whistleblowing, 274–275
Meiji Milk Products, 143
Memos from the Chairman, 282
Merchant banking, 2, 290
Merger activity, 5
Merger Mania, 157–158
Meriwether, John, 125, 126, 128, 131
Merrill-Conseco case, 185
Merrill Lynch, 21, 24, 27, 63, 70, 74, 91, 95, 96, 98, 108, 114, 145, 157, 185, 189, 204–206, 226
  client commitment of, 306
Metallgesellschaft, and market manipulation, 148
MetLife Securities, 98
Michelin Red Guide, 116
Micron Technology, 137
Microsoft, 35
Militano, Vincent, 138–139
Milken, Michael, 4, 5, 6, 7, 9, 53, 158, 159, 179, 205
Ministry of Finance (Japan), 142–145, 167
Misconduct at Prudential Bache Securities, 66–70
Mispricing, 206–207
Mitsubishi Bank, 192
Mitterrand and the Forty Thieves, 166
Mitterrand, François, 166
Mobil, 210
Money laundering, 26, 239–254
  and electronic transfers, 250–252
  process, 240–243
Money-market mutual funds (MMMFs), 82–85
  bailouts by managers, list, 84–85
Montaldo, Jean, 166
Montedison, 216
Moore & Schley, Cameron & Co., 138–139
Moral expectations, 53
Moral hazard, 23, 172–173, 288

Moral imperatives for whistleblowing, 270–271
Mordida, 198
Morgan Grenfell, 15, 26, 114, 164, 165
Morgan Grenfell Asset Management (MGAM), and trading rogues, 15, 47
Morgan Guaranty Trust Company, 103, 151, 180, 237, 238
Morgan Stanley, 5, 20, 24, 103, 185, 189, 295
Morningstar, 81, 86
Morrison Knudsen, 174
Morton-Thiokol, 269
Moscow, John, 254
Mozer, Paul, 10, 125, 128–131
"Mr. Ten Percent," 245–246
Multilateral regulation, 218–219
Munger, Charlie, 127
Municipal bonds, and lack of disclosure, 202
Municipal Securities Rulemaking Board (MSRB), 204, 206, 267
Mutual funds, 81–83, 109
  comparative performance of, 87
  incentives for salespersons of, 86
  proposals on how to overhaul, 100
Mutual Series Fund, 174
Myrdal, Gunnar, 213

NASA, 260
NASD (National Association of Securities Dealers), 16, 48, 97, 98, 60, 65, 80, 93, 134, 135, 136, 160
  and arbitration process, 89–92
  "Radar" trade-detection system, 137
  and SEC settlement, 133–134
NASDAQ (National Association of Securities Dealers Automated Quotation System), 61, 72, 97, 155, 161, 165
  spread skimming at, 133–135
National Association of Securities Dealers Automated Quotation System. *See* NASDAQ
National Association of Securities Dealers. *See* NASD
National Bureau of Economic Research, 200
National Environmental Quality Act, 38
National Labor Relations Board, 40
National League of Cities, 207
National Westminster Bank, 140–141, 192
Nations, list of most and least corrupt, 196
NBC, 191–192
Neely, Richard, 20–21
Negative externalities, 34, 35
Nelson, A. David, 263–264

Net regulatory burden (NRB), 49–52
and relocation, 50
as "taxes" and "subsidies," 49–50
New York American, 122
New York Stock Exchange (NYSE), 4, 48, 61, 65, 70, 81, 91, 108, 109, 133, 148, 154, 160, 292
auction market of, 134
StockWatch surveillance system of, 157
New York Times, 124
Newell, Gordon, 91
Newman, Frank, 18, 19
Nikkei-index contracts, fraudulent trading of, 27
Nikkei stock market, 12
Nikkei-225 index, 141
Nikko, 142, 143
1990s, lessons of, 22–25
Nippon Telephone and Telegraph, 198
Nishimura, Yoshimasa, 14
Nomura Securities, 27, 142, 143, 145
Nonrevenue producers, 289
Norris, Floyd, 124
Northern Trust, and MMMF bailout, 85
Northrop Corporation, 200
Norwich & Worcester Railroad, 121
NYSE. *See* New York Stock Exchange

Occupational Safety and Health Administration (OSHA), 40
Offense, taking in revenues, 289
Offshore assets, and secrecy, 229–230
Offshore markets, 51
Onshore assets, and secrecy, 229
Orange County, Board of Supervisors of, 21
Orange County, CA, 21, 27, 207
Organization for Economic Cooperation and Development, 219
Organization of American States, 219
Orion Bank, 192
Orrefice, Paul, 211
Outside directors, and whistleblowing, 274
Over-the-counter (OTC) stocks, 61, 65
Overcompensation, 174
Owner-manager conflicts, 173–175

Pacific Brokerage, 71
Pagoda, 235
Paine Webber, 12, 22, 27, 70, 71, 83, 84, 96, 98
and limited partnerships, 17
and MMMF bailout, 84
Short-Term Government Bond Fund of, 83

P&G. *See* Procter & Gamble
Partner, undermining your, 192–193
Passive (indexed) investments, 109
"Pay-to-play," 203–204
Payment for order flow, 72
Payments, which are questionable?, 197–202
Payoff-prone firms, 210
Payoff-prone industries, 209–210
Payoffs, kickbacks, and bribes, 194–222
Pension funds, 109
Pentagon, 264, 265
PepsiCo, 225
Perfect competition, 29, 35
Performance
benchmarks for, 52–54
evaluation of, 296–297
measuring, 293–294
pressures and franchise value, 82–85
Performance-oriented managers, and unacceptable behavior, 55
Performance-rewarded employees, and unacceptable behavior, 55
Perot, Ross, 292
Personal financial secrecy, 224, 225
Personal Investment Authority (PIA), 46
Phillips & Drew, 141
Physical assets, and secrecy, 230–231
Pignatiello, Joseph V., 76
Pillsbury Company, 156
Piper Jaffray, and MMMF bailout, 84
Political contributions, 201–202
Political corruption, 225
Political process, guiding the economic process, 31
Polo, Roberto, 236–237
Ponzi scheme, 78
Pot de vin, 198
Predation, 189–191
Predictability, and senior management, 312
President's Council on Economic Priorities, 209
Price, Michael, 174
Price Waterhouse, 250
Prima donnas, 291–293, 316
Primary Market Dealers, 124, 128, 129, 130
Principles of compensation, 301–302
Prisa, 17, 27, 255–257
Private Asset Management Group, 236
Private banking, 223
appropriate controls for, 253
risks involving, 252–254
Private wealth, three classifications of, 229–231

Procter & Gamble (P&G), 18, 19, 113
Product safety, 39
Professional conduct, standards of, 288–289
Professional values, 287–288
Profit erosion, 3
Profits
  coming from taking risks, 23
  and professional standards, maintaining balance between, 4
Proprietary trading, 290
Prudential-Bache Energy Income Partnerships, 68
Prudential-Bache Securities, 66–70
  misconduct at, 66–70
Prudential Group, The, 27, 69, 292, 296
Prudential Insurance Company of America, 16, 66, 70, 101, 255–257, 282
Prudential Insurance, fraud at, 27
Prudential Property Investment Separate Account (Prisa), 255–257
Prudential Securities, 2, 27, 44, 63, 66, 69, 96, 98, 178, 189, 257, 260, 292
  and broker rogues, 16–17
Public goods, 33–34
  and privatization, 33
Public oversight, 47
Public Securities Association, 206
Punishment, threats of, 185–186
Pure Food Act of 1906, 39
Purposeful trading, 48

Qingxiong, Xu, 146
Questionable payments, 195–197
  abroad, 195–197
  and ambiguous rules, 208
  in banking and finance, 220–221
  and competitive strength, 210–211
  and cultural complexity, 209
  determining, 197–202
  domestic, 202–207
  four basic kinds, 198–202
  and inadequate internal control, 211
  and industries that are payoff-prone, 209–210
  investigations in the late 1970s, 197–198
  is there a solution?, 221–222
  and management indifference, 212
  and market failure, 207–208
  and payoff-prone firms, 210
  and statist regimes, 208–209
  tackling, 212–220
  and transaction size, 211

Racketeer Influenced and Corrupt Organizations Act. *See* RICO antiracketeering laws
Radio City Music Hall, 191–192
Raising standards, 288–289
Ramping
  and cornering, and other stock market manipulations, 135–140
  example of, 135
  at Sterling Foster, 136–137
Rand, Ayn, 29
Random Access, 77
Raúl Salinas Affair, 245–247, 252
Ray-Ban, 245
Reagan, Ronald, 104
Recontracting costs, 37
Reeves, Robert C., Jr., 268
Refco, 74
Reform, comprehensive international, 217–220
Regulation, 29–58
  of brokers, 94–101
  by customers, creditors, and owners, 43
  inadequate, 46
  over-, 46
Regulatory arbitrage, 50
Regulatory competition, 51
Regulatory control of brokers, 97–101
Regulatory dilemmas, 45–49
Regulatory enforcement, and organized crime, 49
Regulatory interventions, most effective, 47–49
Rent seeking, 35–36
Republic National Bank of New York, The, 251
Research, the many roles of, 182–186
Retail investor and *caveat emptor*, 59–101
Retail investor market, 112
Retail preferred stock, 75
Retaliation for whistleblowing, likelihood of, 276–277
Retirement Systems Consultants, and MMMF bailout, 85
Reuter, Edzard, and market rigging, 148
Reuters, 183
Revlon, 175
Revlon v. Mac Andrews & Forbes, 175
Reynolds, 210
Richard Whitney & Co., 4
RICO antiracketeering laws, 8, 159, 160, 162
Rigging and manipulation in the Tokyo Stock Exchange, 141–145
Rigging at Chase Medical, 138–139

Rigging via the Internet, 139–140
Rights of others, infringement of, 57
Risk arbitrage, 22, 157, 160
Risk-arbitrage businesses, 9
Risk, associated with malfeasance, 291
Risk-control systems, 4
Risk management, 55–56
Risk/return dimension, 233
Risk takers, innovative, 287
Risks
  and hazards, 290–291
  profits from taking, 23
RJR-Nabisco LBO, 176–177
Robertson Stephens & Company, 172
Rockefeller Center Properties, 191
Rockefeller, David, 192
Rogers Commission inquiry, 269
Rogue behavior, 28, 257, 285, 313
Rogue clients, 19–21
Rogue employees, 167, 318
Rogue financiers, 9
Rogue traders, being dangerous, 23
Rogues, 11–22, 24, 122, 288
  broker, 16–19, 65, 66, 101
  trading, 11–15
Roh, Tae Woo, 217
Ronson, Gerald, 164
Roosevelt administration, 150
Royal Bank of Canada, 192
Rubber Industry Chamber, 210
Rubin, Howie, 114
Rubin, Robert, 207
Ruder Commission, 92, 93
Ruderman, S.G., 156
Rudman, Warren, 134
Rule 415, 106
Rule G-37, 204
Rules
  for appropriate conduct in finance, 57
  of conduct in markets, 30–31
  opaque or ambiguous, 208
Ryan, Arthur F., 69

Safe harbors, 93–94
Saint-Gobain, 166
Sales contests and trips for brokers, 62
Salinas de Gortari, Carlos, 245
Salinas de Gortari, Raúl, 245–247, 253
Salomon Brothers, 2, 9–10, 15, 20, 24, 26, 114, 123–131, 177, 282, 286, 287, 294, 296, 297
  compensation test case at, 298–301
  and securities market, 123–131

Treasury-bond auction scandal of, 9–10
  U.S. bond index of, 109
Sampson, Anthony, 212
Samsung, 217
Sanford, Charles, 17, 18
Saunders, Ernest, 164
SBC-Warburg, 42
Scandalous 1980s, 156–160
Schapiro, Mary, 97, 134
Schneider Group, 166
"School for leaders," 316
Schultz, Paul, 134
Schumpeter, Joseph, 29
Scotland Yard, 250
Sears Roebuck, 292
SEC. *See* Securities Exchange Commission
Secrecy-seekers' surplus (SSS), 231–232
Securities, 43–44
  international regulations of, 44–45
Securities Acts of 1933–1934, 37, 43, 60, 93, 97, 104, 122, 126, 140, 148, 149–150, 152, 215
Securities and Exchange Law of 1948 (Japan), 167
Securities and Exchange Surveillance Commission, 167
Securities and Futures Authority (SFA), 49
Securities Exchange Commission (SEC), 11, 16, 17, 21, 43, 48, 50, 63, 65, 67, 68, 70, 72, 74, 78, 79, 80, 82, 83, 91, 94, 98, 100, 104, 105, 106, 126, 128, 130, 133–135, 137, 138, 139, 149, 150–164, 168, 172, 179, 202, 204, 205, 206, 207, 208, 209, 210, 212, 216, 218, 256, 258, 267, 268
  and tough investigations, 162–163
Securities Industry Association, 65, 93
Securities industry firms
  management characteristics of, 284–285
  market values for, 285–287
  professional values for, 287–288
  raising standards for, 288–289
  today's operation of, 107–108
Securities Investor Protection Act, 43
Securities-law violations, penalties for, 8
Securities market, 123
Securities underwriting, 111
Seelig, Roger, 165
Self-control, and brokers, 95–97
Self-regulation in the wholesale market, 113
Serpent on the Rock, 66
Serving the client by acting as principal, 188–189
SGA Goldstar, 139

S.G. Warburg, 42
Shad, John, 153
Shanghai International Securities Corp.
  (Sisco), 145–147
Shanghai Securities Exchange, 147
Shanghai Stock Exchange, 145–146
Shanghai University, 215
Shanks, Eugene, 18
Shearson Lehman, 189, 190
Shearson Lehman Brothers, 69, 73
Shearson Lehman Hutton, 177
Shelf-registration, 106
Shell companies, 210, 246
Shells and captives, 244
Shen Yin Securities, 145, 147
Siegel, Martin, 4, 5, 6, 7, 12, 158
Silent Spring, 38
SIMEX. *See* Singapore International Mone-
  tary Exchange
Simmons, Hardwick, 69
Sing-Sing Prison, 4
Singapore Airlines, 35
Singapore International Monetary Exchange
  (SIMEX), 13
"Skimming" taxable revenues, 240
Smith, Adam, 29–30, 31, 35
  approach as viewed by democratic societies,
  32
Smith Barney, 62, 63, 74, 96, 157, 202, 295,
  296
  misvaluing bonds at, 265–267
Smith v. Van Gorkom, 175
Smithsonian Agreement, 103
Smurfs, and money laundering, 241
Social control, layers of, 38–41
Sonneberg, Milton, 138–139
Souza Querioz, Fernanda de, 237
Speculation, law of, and economics, 132–133
"Spies" in the trading room, 314
Sporkin, Stanley, 218
Spread skimming at NASDAQ, 133–135
Standard & Poor Money Center Bank Index,
  114
Standard & Poor's (S&P) 500 Index, 86, 88,
  100, 109, 285
Statist regimes, and questionable payments,
  208–209
"Stealth junior junk bonds," 75
Steinkühler, Franz, 166
Sterling Drug Company, 180
Sterling Foster, ramping at, 136–137
Sternberg, Elaine, 31
Stewart, James, 7, 159

Stock Exchange Automated Quotations
  (SEAQ), 110, 165
Stock parking, 7–8, 144, 156, 159
  and the Blue Arrow affair, 140–141
StockWatch surveillance system, 157
Stratton Oakmont, 80–81
  chronology of, 80
Strauss, Tom, 126, 128
Strike suits, 93
Stuart James, 77
Stuffing, 74–76
Suez Canal, closing of, 201
Sumitomo Bank, 15
Sumitomo Corporation
  and copper trading, 137–138
  and market manipulation, 148
Supermarkets General, 189
Supreme Court, 90, 91, 92
Swedish foreign exchange scam, 235
Swiss authorities and the financial commu-
  nity, battle between, 227–228
Swiss Bank Corporation (SBC), 42, 228
Swiss Bankers Association, 227
Swiss banks
  and Imelda Marcos, 228
  a special case, 227–229
Swiss Central Narcotics Division, 245
Syrus, Publilius, 305
Systems of Excellence, 139

Tabor, Timothy, 158
Tabuchi, Setsuya, 143–144
Tabuchi, Yoshihisa, 143–144
Takeover lawyers, 5–6
Tanaka, Kakuei, 197, 198
Tax evasion, 224, 225
  and Swiss nonbank secrecy vendors, 227
Tax havens, 225–227
Taxes, 32–33
TeleCommunications Inc. (TCI), 179
Telephone recording devices, and trading, 113
10(b)5 insider-trading violation, 150
Texaco, 158
Texas Gulf Sulfur case, 150, 151–152
Thayer, Paul, 153
The Italians, 208
The News Hour with Jim Lehrer, 313
Third World bank loans, 237
35 Percent limit rule, 129
Thomas James, 79
Time, 177
Time Warner, 179
Tippees, in insider-trading cases, 154–155

Tobashi ("flying around"), 144
Tokai Bank, 296
Tokyo Stock Exchange
  First-Section Companies, 141
  rigging and manipulation in the, 141–145
Tokyu Corporation, 143, 144
Tokyu Department Stores, 144
"Toxic waste," 76
Trading
  detecting irregular patterns in, 160–161
  on the inside, 149–168
  and risk management, 22–24
  and telephone recording devices, 113
Trading rogues, 11–15
Training, persistent, 313–314
Trans Union Corporation, 175
Transaction costs, 183
Transaction size, and questionable payments,
  211
Transactions, costs of, 36–38
Translinear, 200
Transparency, 64–65
Transparency International, 196
  Corruption Index of, 196
Travelers Group, 24, 44
Treasury bills, 83
Treasury-bond auction scandal, 26
Treasury Department, 124, 126, 127, 267
  having jurisdiction over auction activities,
  130
Treasury refunding, and investor demand, 129
Treasury securities, 125, 206
  explosive growth in, 128
Trinity Towne Investments, 77–78
Trump, Donald, 25, 185
Trust, between clients and brokers, 59
Tully Report, 63
Tully, Daniel, 63, 98
Turner Broadcasting System, 179
Turner, Ted, 179

Undermining your partner, 192–193
Unilateral national reform, 214–217
Union Bank, and MMMF bailout, 84
Union Bank of Switzerland, 141
United Services, and MMMF bailout, 84
Up-front payments, 62–63
U.S. bond market, 106
U.S. Code of Ethics for Government Ser-
  vants, 275
U.S. Custom Service, 240
U.S. Export-Import Bank, 221
U.S. Federal Reserve, 138, 251

U.S. Financial Accounting Standards Board,
  178
U.S. Foreign Corrupt Practices Act, 198, 200
U.S. government bond auction, 124
U.S. Navy, 264
U.S. Office of Technology Assessment, 251
U.S. savings and loan crisis, 143
U.S. Supreme Court, 154, 155, 156, 163
U.S. Treasury bonds, 105, 265
U.S. Treasury issues, 142
U.S. Treasury securities, 13
U.S. Treasury, 43, 240. *See also* Treasury
  Department
U.S. v. Carpenter, 155, 156

Value added
  creating, 115–117
  protecting, 118–119
Value Line, and MMMF bailout, 84
Values for securities industry firms, 285–289
  market values, 285–287
  professional values, 287–288
  raising standards, 288–289
Valuing results, 293–294
Vanderbilt, Commodore, 122
Vanguard, 66
Vanguard Index, 500 Portfolio, 86, 88
Vaughan, Diane, 260
Villa, James A., 79
Vinik, Jeffrey, 82, 137
Vitusa, 215
"Vulture investing," 190

Wal-Mart, 35
Waldbaum supermarket chain, 163
Waldbaum, Ira, 163
Wall Street, 53
Wall Street Equities, 71
Wall Street Journal, 91, 111, 154, 155, 159,
  218
Walt Disney, 191–192. *See also* Disney
Washington Post, 263
Watchfulness, 314–315
Water Street Corporation Recovery Fund,
  190–191
Wayne Hummer, and MMMF bailout, 85
Wenyuen, Wei, 147
West Virginia CIF (West Virginia Consoli-
  dated Investment Fund), 20–21, 115
Whistleblowers
  and abuse, 270
  checklist for, 273
  and conflicts of obligation, 258–259

dilemma of, 259–260
main alternatives available to, 273–275
Whistleblowing, 168, 255–283
advice for management, 278
alternative ways, 272–275
creating a benign culture for, 277–283
definition, 258
and economic welfare of firms, 271–272
and the law, 275–277
and management response, 271–272
misvaluing bonds at Smith Barney, 265–267
the mole at ADM, 261–263
moral imperatives for, 270–271
overcharging at CSX, 263–264
phony accounting at Aetna, 267–268
reasons for, 268–272
and retaliation, 276–277
as a risky business, 259–268
substandard parts at Lucas Industries, 264–265
Whitacre, Mark, 261–263, 271
White Weld, 192
Whitehall Street Real Estate Fund, 120, 191
Whitney, Richard, 4
Wholesale market price, 112
Wholesale market, self-regulation in, 113
Wholesale market transactions, principles and practices for, 117–118
Wholesale transactions, 102–120
history of 102–106
Wholesaler, definition of, 110–113
Wholesalers, principles for success with, 115–119
being alert, 118
being consistent, 116
being diligent, 118–119

being first, 116
being good, 115–116
being loyal, 116–117
being "prudential," 118
being tough, 119
being trustworthy, 117
being willing, 117
Wholesalers, success with, 115–120
Wigton, Richard, 158
Williams, R. Foster, 155
Wilmington Trust, and MMMF bailout, 85
Wilson, Terrance S., 263
Winters, Robert C., 16, 256, 257
Wolfensohn, James, 195, 219
WOR radio station, 78
World Bank, 130, 195, 196, 219, 240
World Trade Organization, 200, 217
W.R. Grace, 174

Xylan Corporation, 172

Yamaichi Securities, 142
Yakuza (organized-crime syndicate), 143
Yield burning, 206–207
Young, Peter, 15
Young, William G., 205
Yuppie Five, 157
Yves St. Laurent, 166

Zayed, Sheikh of Abu Dhabi, 247
Zedillo, Ernesto, President of Mexico, 246
Zell, Sam, 191–192
Zookeeping, 25, 284–318
basics of, 317
Zweig, and MMMF bailout, 85

About the Authors

■

For the past ten years, **Roy C. Smith** has been a professor of finance and international business at New York University's Stern School of Business, where he teaches courses in investment banking, global banking and capital markets, entrepreneurial finance, and market ethics and law. Prior to joining the faculty, he was a general partner of Goldman, Sachs & Co., where he worked for more than twenty years. His primary areas of research include international banking and finance, mergers and acquisitions, foreign investments, small business finance, and the financial problems and opportunities associated with emerging market countries. Among Professor Smith's numerous publications are six other books, many articles in books and scholarly journals, and cases in investment banking and international finance.

Ingo Walter is the Charles Simon Professor of Applied Financial Economics at New York University's Stern School and the Sydney Homer Director of the university's Salomon Center. He teaches courses in global banking and international trade and finance as well as in markets, ethics, and law. Professor Walter's other academic experience has been at the University of Missouri-St. Louis; at INSEAD, in Fontainebleau, France; and, as visiting professor, at universities in Australia, England, Germany, Scotland, Singapore, Switzerland, and the United States. He has served as a consultant on economic, financial, and strategic issues to various banks, industrial companies, government agencies, and international organizations, including Citicorp, J.P. Morgan, General Electric, the OECD, the Swiss Bank Corporation, and the World Bank. The recipient of many honors, awards, and grants, Professor Walter has served on various editorial review boards and is the author or editor of some twenty-three books as well as of numerous monographs and articles.